SOVIET
FOREIGN POLICY
IN THE 1980s

SOVIET FOREIGN POLICY IN THE 1980s

Edited by
Roger E. Kanet

PRAEGER

PRAEGER SPECIAL STUDIES • PRAEGER SCIENTIFIC

Library of Congress Cataloging in Publication Data

Main entry under title:

Soviet foreign policy in the 1980s.

    Includes bibliographical references and index.
    1. Soviet Union—Foreign relations—1975-
—Addresses, essays, lectures. 2. World politics—1975-
1985—Addresses, essays, lectures. I. Kanet, Roger E.,
1936-
DK274.S6513   327.47   81-22654
ISBN 0-03-059314-X   AACR2
ISBN 0-03-059316-6 (pbk.)

Published in 1982 by Praeger Publishers
CBS Educational and Professional Publishing
a Division of CBS Inc.
521 Fifth Avenue, New York, New York 10175 U.S.A.

© 1982 by Praeger Publishers

23456789   145   987654321

Printed in the United States of America

PREFACE

The decade of the 1970s was a period during which substantial changes occurred in the international environment that had developed in the years immediately following the Second World War. The process of decolonialization was essentially completed and the developing countries began to assert a more forceful voice in international affairs through such means as the creation of OPEC and the calls for a New International Economic Order. In addition, the relative position of the two superpowers within the international political system continued to evolve. At the beginning of the decade the Soviet Union had reached essential parity with the United States in strategic nuclear power and throughout the next ten years continued to assert its claims to a major role in international affairs. The détente in East-West relations that dominated the first half of the decade deteriorated, however, in the wake of expanded Soviet involvement in Africa, Southeast Asia, and Southwest Asia.

As the Soviet Union entered the 1980s its position in international affairs was still not secure. The invasion of Afghanistan in the final week of 1979 stimulated in the West both a revived concern with security issues and a strong condemnation from the majority of Third World states. China and the United States accelerated the process of normalization of relations, while several strategically positioned Third World states offered the United States the use of military facilities to counter the growing Soviet "threat." In addition, in Europe the Soviets have found themselves faced with a number of serious challenges. Most visible has been the peaceful revolution initiated in the summer of 1980 by Polish workers, which has the potential to undermine the entire system of control established by the Soviets in Eastern Europe in the postwar period. Perhaps an even greater challenge is presented by the flagging performance of the Soviet economy and the potential limitation that this may present for Soviet policy.

The present volume is intended to provide an examination of the major developments of Soviet foreign policy during the recent past and an assessment of likely developments in that policy in the near future. The book begins with a general assessment of Soviet foreign policy by Roger E. Kanet, followed by examinations of the impact of domestic factors. In Part Two Roman Kolkowicz discusses the growing role of the military in policy formulation in the USSR; John P. Hardt and Kate S. Tomlinson review the domestic economic environment and its implications for the evolution of future Soviet foreign policy; and Rasma Karklins and Frederick C. Barghoorn assess the relationship of the nationality factor and political dissent to the development of Soviet policy.

The contributions in Part Three of the book focus on Soviet relations with other Communist states and movements. Robin Alison Remington is concerned with the increasing complexities in the Soviet relationship with Eastern Europe, while Rajan Menon focuses on the continuing competition between the USSR and China—with special emphasis on Asia. The Soviet-Cuban relationship and its implications for Africa and Latin America are examined by Merritt Robbins, and Joan Barth Urban assesses the challenges to Soviet policy presented by several of the major West European Communist parties.

The next group of chapters treats Soviet relations with the industrialized countries. Roger Hamburg provides an overview of both the political and military-strategic factors involved in Soviet relations with the United States and Western Europe, while Hiroshi Kimura argues that recent Soviet global policies have stimulated a reassessment of Japanese policy toward the USSR. Finally, Marshall I. Goldman relates Soviet trade with the West to broader questions concerning the Soviet economy and Soviet foreign relations.

The last section of the book focuses on developments in Soviet policy toward the Third World. In a general review of Soviet policy in the developing world Rajan Menon focuses on the strategic interests of the USSR and the Soviet use of military power. The book concludes with three studies of Soviet relations in regions of the Third World where the Soviets have been especially active—the Middle East and Africa, by David E. Albright; West Asia and the Persian Gulf region, by Zalmay Khalilzad; and South Asia and the Indian Ocean area, by Robert H. Donaldson.

The editor wishes to thank the Department of Political Science and the Russian and East European Center of the University of Illinois at Urbana-Champaign for assistance in preparing this volume and Suzanne E. Kanet for preparing the index.

Roger E. Kanet

CONTENTS

Page

PREFACE
Roger E. Kanet   v

LIST OF TABLES   xii

Chapter

PART ONE: INTRODUCTION

1   THE SOVIET UNION AS A GLOBAL POWER
    Roger E. Kanet   3

    Khrushchev and the First Attempts at Soviet Globalism   5
    Brezhnev and the Foundations of the New Soviet Globalism   7
    The New Soviet Globalism in Practice   8
    Continuing Limitations on Soviet Globalism   10
    An Initial Assessment   12
    Notes   13

PART TWO: DOMESTIC-FOREIGN LINKAGES
IN SOVIET FOREIGN POLICY

2   THE MILITARY AND SOVIET FOREIGN POLICY
    Roman Kolkowicz   17

    Dynamics of Soviet Foreign Policy   17
       Foreign Policy Dependence on Military Capabilities   18
       Disparity of Policy Style and Substance   18
       Policy Orchestration, Priorities, Rules of the Game   19
    Internal Roles of the Military in the Soviet Union   20
    The Military and the Communist Party   25
       The Expanding Scope of Soviet Foreign and Defense Policies   25
       Problems of Legitimacy and Authority: the Ossification
          of the Party and the Waning of Revolutionary Elan   27
       Problems of Hegemonic Maintenance: Succession and
          the Military   29
    Conclusions and Projections   33
    Notes   35

Chapter		Page
3	ECONOMIC FACTORS IN SOVIET FOREIGN POLICY	
	John P. Hardt and Kate S. Tomlinson	37
	A Decade of Crisis	37
	Economic Retardation or Continued Growth	39
	New Economic Era: Modernization and Interdependence	40
	Leadership Succession: Continuity or Change	40
	New International Political Environment:	
	Multipolarity and Postcolonialism	40
	Leadership Alternatives	41
	Modernization/Interdependence	41
	Control/Security: A Neo-Stalinist Variant	45
	Foreign Policy Implications of Alternative Economic Scenarios	47
	Soviet Global Outreach	49
	European Interactions	50
	Asian Relations	51
	Relations with the United States	52
	Choices for Brezhnev's Successors: A New Industrialization Debate?	52
	Notes	54
4	THE NATIONALITY FACTOR IN SOVIET FOREIGN POLICY	
	Rasma Karklins	58
	The Foreign Minorities	63
	The Soviet Jews	65
	The Soviet Muslims	68
	Prospects	71
	Notes	73
5	DISSENT IN THE USSR AND SOVIET FOREIGN RELATIONS	
	Frederick C. Barghoorn	77
	Dissent and Foreign Affairs	80
	The Helsinki Groups, the West, and the USSR	87
	Notes	97
	PART THREE: THE SOVIET UNION AND THE COMMUNIST WORLD	
6	POLITICS OF ACCOMMODATION: REDEFINING SOVIET-EAST EUROPEAN RELATIONS	
	Robin Alison Remington	105
	The Soviet Bloc and Love of Comrade Stalin	106
	Collapse of the Stalinist Interstate System	108

The China Card and East European Options   109
The Dynamics of Conflict Resolution: Soviet Strategies   113
Proletarian Revolution, Polish Style   114
Soviet Temptations and Restraints   117
Conclusion at Intermission   119
Postscript   121
Notes   124

7   CHINA AND THE SOVIET UNION IN ASIA: THE DYNAMICS
     OF UNEQUAL COMPETITION
          Rajan Menon   127

The Context of Competition   128
South Asia: The Intervention and Its Aftermath   131
East Asia: Of Actual and Potential Power   137
Conclusion   141
Notes   141

8   THE SOVIET-CUBAN RELATIONSHIP
          Merritt Robbins   144

Background   145
Economic Dependency   149
Institutionalization of the Revolution   150
Military Relationship   152
Tercermundismo   154
Intervention in Africa   157
     Angola   158
     The Horn of Africa   160
Prospects   163
Notes   165

9   THE WEST EUROPEAN COMMUNIST CHALLENGE
     TO SOVIET FOREIGN POLICY
          Joan Barth Urban   171

The Western Communist Tradition of Loyalty to Soviet Foreign
     Policy: Its Origins and Decline   172
The West European Communist Challenge in Global Perspective 177
     Soviet Dominance in Eastern Europe   178
     Soviet Containment of China   180
     The Projection of Soviet Influence in the Third World 181
     East-West Détente, Soviet Style   183

The Soviet Reaction: from Defensiveness to Confrontation   187
Notes   190

PART FOUR: THE SOVIET UNION
AND THE INDUSTRIALIZED WORLD

10   POLITICAL AND STRATEGIC FACTORS IN SOVIET
RELATIONS WITH THE WEST: SOVIET PERCEPTIONS
Roger Hamburg   197

Soviet Policy in Western Europe   198
Soviet-American Relations   214
Conclusion   224
Notes   226

11   THE SOVIET THREAT AND THE SECURITY OF JAPAN
Hiroshi Kimura   231

Sudden Awakening of Concern over the Soviet Threat   231
The Debate on Security   235
Changed Atmosphere or Policies?   240
Notes   245

12   SOVIET EAST-WEST TRADE: CAN THE MEANS
BECOME THE END?
Marshall I. Goldman   247

Détente and the Expansion of Soviet Trade   248
New Limitations on Soviet Trade   254
Petroleum and the Prospects for Soviet Trade   255
Notes   259

PART FIVE: THE SOVIET UNION AND THE
DEVELOPING COUNTRIES

13   MILITARY POWER, INTERVENTION, AND SOVIET POLICY
IN THE THIRD WORLD
Rajan Menon   263

The Third World and Soviet Military Power   265
Interventionism and the Correlation of Forces   273
A Look Ahead: Intervention as a Future Trend   275
Conclusion   279
Notes   280

14   THE MIDDLE EAST AND AFRICA IN RECENT
      SOVIET POLICY
              David E. Albright   285

      Status in Geopolitical Priorities   287
      The Nature of the Objectives   288
              Establishing a Lasting Presence   288
              Gaining a Voice in the Affairs of the Two Regions   290
              Undermining Western Influence   291
              Curbing and Reducing Chinese Influence in the Two Regions   292
              Other Features   293
      Perceived Opportunities   295
      Strategy for Exploiting Opportunities   298
      Means of Implementing the Strategy   301
      Prospects for the 1980s   303
      Notes   305

15   SOVIET POLICIES IN WEST ASIA AND THE PERSIAN GULF
              Zalmay Khalilzad   312

      Opportunities for Soviet Involvement   315
      The USSR and Iran   316
      The USSR and Pakistan   318
      The USSR and Iraq   320
      Soviet Policy toward Saudi Arabia and the Lower Gulf States   322
      Power, Constraints, and Vulnerabilities   324
      Conclusion   326
      Notes   328

16   SOVIET INVOLVEMENT IN SOUTH ASIA AND THE
      INDIAN OCEAN REGION
              Robert H. Donaldson   330

      Soviet-South Asian Relations in Historical Perspective   331
      The Chinese Challenge   335
      The Soviet-Indian Treaty   338
      Soviet-South Asian Relations in the 1970s   340
      Soviet Naval Activity in the Indian Ocean   343
      After Afghanistan: Changing Regional Relationships   346
      Notes   349

INDEX   351

ABOUT THE EDITOR AND CONTRIBUTORS   361

LIST OF TABLES

Table   Page

12.1   Soviet Exports and Imports   249

12.2   Share of Soviet Foreign Trade by Category of Country   250

12.3   Imports and Exports of Selected Countries with the Soviet Union   252

13.1   American and Soviet Military Expenditures, 1969-78   265

13.2   American and Soviet Power Projection Assets   269

SOVIET
FOREIGN POLICY
IN THE 1980s

PART ONE

Introduction

1

THE SOVIET UNION
AS A GLOBAL POWER

Roger E. Kanet

The Soviet Union that emerged in 1953 from more than a quarter-century of Stalinist rule continued to occupy a precarious position and to play a limited role in the international political system. Clearly the defeat of Nazi Germany and Imperial Japan had eliminated the two major immediate threats to Soviet security. In addition, the establishment of a Soviet empire in East Central Europe, the creation of a Communist regime in North Korea, and the successful Communist revolution in China had greatly expanded the area of Soviet influence and represented a major weakening of the "capitalist encirclement" that had so isolated the Soviet Union in the period prior to the Second World War. In spite, however, of the significant changes in the relative position of the Soviet Union in the international political system, the USSR was still exclusively a regional power whose major international competitor, the United States, commanded far superior resources and dominated the international system politically, militarily, and economically. Postwar Soviet expansion had played a major role in the creation of an American-centered system of alliances in Europe and Asia, all of which were oriented toward containing further Soviet expansion. U.S. military forces were stationed around virtually the entire periphery of the Communist world, from Germany in the West, through the Middle East, and as far east as Korea and Japan.

Not only had the United States greatly expanded its political, economic, and military role in international affairs in the period following the war, but its major allies, Great Britain and France, continued to act as global powers with interests and capabilities scattered throughout most of Asia and Africa. With the exception of its political and economic contacts with other Communist states, the Soviet Union continued to be isolated from virtually the entire international community. In the United Nations, for example, votes on East-West issues invariably resulted in resounding defeats for the Soviet Union, with only the few Communist members voting in its support. Relations with newly independent states of Asia and Africa were virtually nonexistent, in large part as a result of Stalin's refusal to view the leaders of these new countries as more than "lackeys" of international imperialism.

Overall, therefore, in spite of the improvement in its relative military position in the postwar period, the USSR remained in a state of political isolation and of military and economic inferiority. Instead of reducing the security concerns of the Soviet leadership, postwar developments had in fact fed the traditional Russian paranoia concerning security. The Soviet Union remained a beleaguered bastion of socialism surrounded by a hostile—and militarily superior—capitalist world. Stalin's major approach to the problem of security had followed the long-standing Russian policy of expansion and consolidation of control over regions adjacent to Soviet territory. But limited capabilities, the eventual resistance of the West, and the internal demands of the Soviet system itself had prevented the Soviet Union from expanding its zone of control much beyond those territories occupied by the Red Army at the conclusion of the Second World War, with the partial exception of China. In the years immediately following the war, Soviet efforts had focused primarily on consolidating its position in Eastern Europe. As developments in that area between 1953 and 1956 indicated, even these efforts had not been completely successful, for popular resistance to the irrationalities of Communist rule presented serious challenges both to the continued control of these countries by local Communist parties and to Soviet domination over the region.

From the perspective of the 1980s, the position of the USSR in the world has changed drastically in the years since the death of Stalin. Not only is the Soviet Union no longer isolated within the confines of its postwar empire; it now also possesses state interests of a truly global character and is capable of projecting effective power—of a military, political, and economic nature—in virtually all regions of the world. In recent years it has proved both its concern for developments in regions far from the boundaries of the postwar Soviet empire and its ability and willingness to use the means necessary to influence those developments—witness Soviet activities in Angola, Ethiopia, Southeast Asia, and Afghanistan.[1] Soviet interests and involvement in events far from Soviet territory, however, extend beyond the purely military. Soviet commentators continually emphasize the crucial role of the USSR in the solution of virtually all the major problems that face the international community.[2] Other indications of the expanded position of the Soviet Union in the world include the major changes in the relative military balance between it and the United States and the substantial political reorientation of much of the so-called nonaligned movement during the past decade.[3]

The purpose of this first chapter will be to examine the evolution of the Soviet Union during a period of little more than 25 years from the position of a strictly regional power—though one with substantial military capabilities and significant untapped potential to expand its role in the world—to a major actor in all areas of the international political, security, and economic systems. The most important factors that explain the ability of the Soviets to expand their role so dramatically include a persistent commitment by the Soviet leadership since the mid-1950s to break out of the circle of U.S. and Western containment and to expand the active role of the Soviet Union in the world; the steady and continuing buildup of Soviet military capabilities; the collapse of the European colonial system and the ability of the Soviets to profit from conflicts in relations between the West and the developing world; and the basic failure of the United States and its major allies to recognize and respond to what the Soviets refer to as the changing international correlation of forces.

KHRUSHCHEV AND THE FIRST ATTEMPTS AT SOVIET GLOBALISM

One of the very first changes introduced by the post-Stalinist leadership in the Soviet Union related to the overall policy of the state toward the outside world. In Europe efforts were made to reestablish relations with Socialist, but maverick, Yugoslavia and, more importantly perhaps, to reduce the tensions in East-West relations. Peaceful coexistence replaced the two-camp thesis as the foundation of Soviet relations with the members of the NATO alliance in part at least, to reduce the isolation of the Soviet Union and as a prelude to an eventual Western recognition of the existing political realities in postwar Europe. In its policies toward the developing world the new Soviet leadership introduced comparable innovations. No longer were countries such as India and Egypt viewed as mere appendages of Western imperialism, but rather as independent states whose interests overlapped in many areas with those of the Soviet Union and the other members of the newly redefined Socialist community.

In the mid-1950s Khrushchev initiated a decade-long effort to expand the role of the USSR in international affairs. In the Middle East, for example, the beginnings of Soviet military and economic support in Afghanistan, Egypt, and later in other "radical" Arab states, effectively reduced the isolation of the USSR in that region of such great strategic significance for Soviet security. The wave of decolonization that swept over Africa in the period after Ghanaian independence in 1957 found the Soviets willing to proffer assistance to a variety of new African states. The attempted placement of missiles in Cuba in the fall of 1962 was probably the high point of Khrushchev's attempts to challenge the dominant position of the United States in international affairs, but it also indicated most clearly the continuing inferiority of the position from which the Soviet Union was attempting to maneuver.

Khrushchev's fantastic predictions about Soviet ability to surpass the United States in the production of most commodities notwithstanding, the Soviet Union lacked the economic, military, and political capabilities in the early 1960s to compete effectively in most regions of the world. The United States still commanded substantial strategic superiority and this superiority forced the Soviets to move especially cautiously—and even to retreat—in direct conflict situations such as the Cuban missile crisis. In addition, the absence of an effective Soviet capability to project conventional military power outside its own region of control meant that the Soviet leaders had great difficulty in supporting clients or allies in areas outside the core area of Soviet power. In 1956, for example, it was primarily U.S. opposition—not Soviet—that brought the Suez War to a conclusion. In 1960 the closing of the airport in Leopoldville by U.N. officials in the Congo effectively cut off Soviet support for the forces of Patrice Lumumba. In the mid-1960s Soviet-oriented political leaders in several African countries were overthrown with virtual impunity. In sum, the Soviet Union was unable in this period to provide the kind of effective support that would permit it to stabilize throughout the Third World regimes that were viewed by it as friendly and generally supportive of Soviet interests.

The Khrushchev era in Soviet politics witnessed a major break from the past in terms of the expansion of Soviet interests and the attempt on the part of the USSR to play a greater role in the international system. The results of this change in orientation, however, from the Soviet point of view were at best mixed. Even though the Soviet Union had created a foundation for the development of relations with a number of Third World countries and was, therefore, no longer isolated in the way it had been prior to Stalin's death, these relations had remained fragile and had provided the Soviets with few concrete returns on their investment of support. In addition, the Soviet empire itself was beset with serious fissures, which in the view of one analyst threatened its very dissolution.[4] Not only had the Albanians and the Chinese withdrawn completely from the Soviet-oriented "community of nations," but even the Romanians had been successful in resisting Soviet pressures to follow a joint line in foreign affairs and various East European countries were experimenting with their domestic political and economic systems. The accession of Cuba to the Soviet network of states and the reduction of the Western monopoly on contacts with the developing states, though clearly beneficial to Soviet interests, did not outweigh these losses.

In 1964, as the Brezhnev team came to power in the Soviet Union, the position of the USSR in the non-Communist international system was clearly stronger than it had been a decade earlier. Still, the Soviet Union remained primarily a regional power. Its interests and, in some cases, its commitments had expanded beyond the confines of Stalin's empire, but its inadequate capabilities severely limited its ability to affect significantly events in other areas of the world.

Even prior to Khrushchev's overthrow, however, there were already several developments that would prove to have a major impact on the growth of the role of the Soviet Union in the international system. Most important was the initiation in the early 1960s—clearly influenced by the debacle of the Cuban missile crisis—of a program of military expansion in areas that until that time were outside the purview of Soviet military capabilities. Most significant was the new commitment to the creation of a blue-ocean navy and long-range air transport and air reconnaissance capabilities, as well as the development of a network of overflight and "basing" rights that would eventually give the Soviet Union access to areas far beyond Soviet territory.[5]

A second development of great importance for the expansion of the Soviet role in international affairs related to the collapse of the European colonial empires and the gradual "radicalization" of many of the newly independent states. Conflicts of interest between the industrial West and the less developed countries began to provide the Soviet Union with possibilities of expanding their involvement in countries or regions that earlier were closed to them. Related to this was the lessening of Western power—and involvement—in much of the Third World, as evidenced by the British withdrawal from the regions east of Suez.

BREZHNEV AND THE FOUNDATIONS OF THE NEW SOVIET GLOBALISM

One of the most important and visible developments in Soviet-American relations that has influenced the expansion of the international role of the USSR has been the growth of Soviet military capabilities and, in particular, the resulting shift in the balance of military capabilities between the two superpowers. First of all, the Soviets focused on the expansion of their nuclear strategic capabilities in order to offset the superiority of the United States that still existed at the beginning of the 1960s. During the early years of the decade efforts were made to secure the survivability of Soviet nuclear forces with the construction of reinforced missile silos, the placing of missiles at sea, and the development of a first-generation missile defense system. By the mid-1960s the Soviets had begun the expansion of their own strike capabilities and by the end of the decade had reached something approximating strategic parity.[6] Throughout most of the 1970s, therefore, the nuclear power of the United States was largely neutralized by countervailing Soviet strategic capabilities. This "balance of terror" has, in effect, provided the Soviet Union with an international strategic environment in which it has been able to employ its newly expanded conventional military—as well as political and economic—capabilities in ways that it views as conducive to the protection and expansion of its own state interests. Far from making conventional military capabilities obsolete, as many Western commentators had argued in the 1960s, the nuclear stalemate between the superpowers has reestablished a milieu in which conventional weapons can be employed—at least in certain circumstances.

In addition to the expansion of Soviet strategic capabilities begun during the Khrushchev era and continued until the present, the Soviets have also built up their conventional military capabilities—both in Europe and throughout Asia and Africa—to the point where they are now capable of projecting power throughout a substantial portion of the world. Among the most important aspects of this development has been construction of both an oceangoing navy and a worldwide merchant fleet that also engages in military-related reconnaissance. Although the development of the Soviet fleet became most visible only after Khrushchev's fall from power, the decision to develop a surface fleet was made in the late 1950s, prior to the Cuban missile crisis.[7] By the 1970s the Soviets had developed a naval capability that permitted them to play an important military role in various international crises such as the 1971 Indo-Pakistani War, the Middle East War of 1973, and other conflicts.[8]

In addition, however, they had also created a network of agreements with a number of developing countries that gave them access to the naval facilities necessary for the maintenance of this new oceangoing fleet. The development of long-range transport aircraft and agreements for overflight rights and the use of landing facilities provided an important complement to the expanded naval power.[9]

Another important aspect of the development of the Soviet Union as a global power has been the continuing commitment of the Soviet leadership to the expansion of the Soviet role in world affairs. In the mid-1970s, for example, the Soviet minister of defense enunciated the broadened view of the role of the Soviet military when he stated that "the historic function of the Soviet armed forces is not restricted merely to their function in defending our Motherland and the other socialist countries." Aggression by the Western imperialist states should be resisted "in whatever distant region of our planet" it occurs.[10] The changed correlation of forces in international affairs, argue the Soviets, permits the USSR to provide support to the just cause of national liberation and to progressive regimes threatened with intervention by the Western imperialists or their reactionary stooges in the developing world. No longer is the capitalist West able to act with impunity in undermining progressive regimes or in suppressing revolutionary movements.

THE NEW SOVIET GLOBALISM IN PRACTICE

The Soviet leadership has continued to view Europe and East Asia as areas of crucial significance to its security and has, therefore, engaged in a campaign to expand the USSR's military capabilities vis-à-vis both NATO and the People's Republic of China. At the same time, however, Soviet policy in Europe has been oriented primarily toward reducing the tensions that had characterized East-West relations during the cold war. The détente policy of the 1970s has generally blended well with the USSR's overall drive to expand its worldwide role, since part of its purpose was to reduce the likelihood of Western—especially American—response to the extension of Soviet involvement throughout the Southern Hemisphere. Soviet détente policy was motivated by at least three sets of goals. First of all, the Soviet Union was concerned with the possibilities of a two-front conflict against NATO in the west and China in the east. An improvement in or "normalization" of relations with the NATO countries would not only reduce the likelihood of conflict in Europe, but would also permit the Soviet Union to concentrate additional military forces along its Chinese border.

A second important motivating factor was the Soviet desire to acquire Western technology in order to deal more effectively with problems facing the economy at the beginning of the 1970s. The Soviet economy had entered into a period when continued growth could come only from technological innovation. Given the persistent lack of convertible currency on the part of the Soviets, the most appropriate method to acquire the desired technology included a significant improvement in political relations—that is, détente—which would then open the way for credits with which to purchase the needed technology. The record of the 1970s is an indication of the relative success of this policy. The Western industrial states have been willing to provide both the credits and most of the types of technology desired by the Soviet leaders.[11]

A third important motive for the Soviet policy of détente appears to be closely related to the goal of expanding the role of the Soviet state to that of a global power. An improvement in East-West relations might well achieve what various earlier Soviet "peace offensives" had not—the reduction of Western perceptions of fear of the Soviet Union to the point where the Western commitment to military defense would lessen and the response to expanded Soviet involvement in developments outside Europe would be based on acceptance of the legitimate interests of the second superpower. In many respects this set of Soviet goals benefited from several series of developments in the Third World, over which the Soviets themselves exercised only minimal influence.

First of all, the continuing drive toward independence in the Third World and the inability of moderate governments in many developing countries to deal effectively with the problems of economic backwardness and political instability have combined to bring to power throughout much of Asia, Africa, and, more recently, the Western Hemisphere a group of governments more strongly anti-Western than their predecessors. This has provided the Soviets and their Cuban allies with the opportunity to gain access to—if not influence in—a substantial number of developing countries. At the same time the position of the United States and its Western allies has deteriorated significantly throughout the Third World.

Associated with the relative change of position of the Soviet Union and the West in developing countries has been the unwillingness or inability of the West, in particular the United States, to pursue a coherent course of action in its policies. The American debacle in Vietnam, the Watergate scandal, and the exposure of various C.I.A. activities all played a role in the mid-1970s that made it virtually impossible for the U.S. government to initiate any type of response to Soviet activities in the Third World. In addition, given the political environment of détente and the apparent conviction of many U.S. leaders that the period of U.S.-Soviet conflict characteristic of the cold war had been concluded, the political atmosphere in the United States was not at all conducive to checking Soviet attempts to expand their international role by taking advantage of conflict situations throughout the Third World. In both Angola in 1975-76 and in Ethiopia two years later the Soviets assumed correctly that they would be able to intervene without the threat of American counteraction, since the United States did not have the will to challenge the expansion of Soviet involvement in regions then considered far from the center of primary U.S. interest.

A major goal of the Soviet Union during the course of the last decade or more has been the neutralization of the West through détente. That is, the Soviets have attempted to convince the West, including the United States, that developments in direct bilateral relations between East and West are far more important for the Western states than developments in other regions of the world. Their hope has been that the leaders of the Western alliance system would be unwilling to risk the benefits of détente—in particular, economic benefits for economies that have been suffering from the effects of "stagflation"—by attempting to counter Soviet activities elsewhere in the world.

In the Third World itself the Soviets have indicated over the course of the past decade that the political and military foundations that they had laid during the course of the 1960s—and through the 1970s as well—did indeed provide them with the capabilities to project power in order to support outcomes that they deemed favorable to their own interests. In Angola, Ethiopia, and Southeast Asia, for example, Soviet (and Cuban) support has been crucial in either bringing to power or consolidating regimes that are friendly toward and dependent on the Soviet Union. By the middle of the 1970s the Soviet Union had indeed become a state with both global interests and global capabilities. In Angola and again in Ethiopia the Soviets showed that they now have the capability of providing allies with significant military assistance and that this assistance can be adequate to change the local balance of power in favor of the recipients of Soviet support. In return, the Soviets have been provided with access to naval and air facilities that are useful to them in potential future conflicts with the West.

CONTINUING LIMITATIONS ON SOVIET GLOBALISM

In spite of the significant expansion of Soviet capabilities and the new role that the USSR is now able to play in international affairs, its power and influence are still limited. First of all, the new Soviet position in Asia and Africa depends heavily on the coincidence of Soviet interests with those of "client" states. The expulsion of the Soviets from both Egypt and Somalia during the past decade indicates the degree to which the Soviets depend on the goodwill of such client states. Second, even with large-scale Soviet support some Third World states have been unable to accomplish the primary goal of creating a stable political system. In Angola, for example, six years of Soviet and Cuban support have not yet resulted in the elimination of major domestic opposition to the Popular Movement for the Liberation of Angola (MPLA), and the government would collapse without the continued support of its Communist allies. Most important, perhaps, was the virtual collapse of the Soviet-supported Communist regime in Afghanistan. The inability of Taraki, and later Amin, to consolidate their rule in Afghanistan during 1978 and 1979 eventually resulted in the Soviet decision to intervene directly. In spite of the introduction of massive military power the Soviets have not succeeded in eliminating widespread opposition to the new puppet regime of Babrack Karmal. Moreover, the Soviet invasion has resulted in widespread condemnation even from developing countries, which in the past have generally supported the Soviet Union.

Elsewhere in the Middle East, the Soviets have in effect been frozen out of the major developments in the Arab-Israeli conflict for most of the period since the October War of 1973. Only by committing themselves to the support of the members of the Rejectionist Front have they managed to continue to play a role in the developments of the region, but that role is played largely on the terms set by the Arab states. Dependence on the Soviets did not prevent Syria from intervening in the Lebanese Civil War of 1975-76—contrary to Soviet wishes; nor did Soviet displeasure prevent Iraq, a major client for Soviet weapons until its recent efforts to diversify its sources, from invading Iran in the fall of 1980.

When we turn to the position of the Soviet Union in the international Communist movement we find the most serious challenges to its expanded role in the international system. Soviet relations with China have not improved over the past decade, in spite of the death of Mao and the rise of a new, more pragmatic, Chinese leadership. The Chinese continue to represent a threat to Soviet interests in Asia and have been among the most vocal critics of détente with the Soviet Union and of Soviet expansion throughout the Third World. Recent evidence of greater Chinese cooperation—even in the military realm—with the United States, Japan, and Western Europe is viewed with great alarm in Moscow.

In Europe the rise of Eurocommunism—especially in Italy and Spain—has challenged the dominance of the Soviet position within the European Communist movement. An even greater threat is the revolutionary convulsion that has seized Socialist Poland. For more than a year the Soviets have stood by, watching the erosion of the Party dictatorship which they view as the essential hallmark of a Communist state. An independent labor movement, democratic elections within the Polish Communist party, a reduction of censorship, and other significant innovations are all seen as major threats—both to the stability of communism in Poland and to Soviet interests throughout Eastern Europe. The recent imposition of martial law in Poland, although it has stopped the overt challenge to the Polish communist system, has yet to deal with the underlying causes of that challenge.

Besides these external factors that have restricted the expansion of the Soviet role in world affairs, the continuing weakness of the Soviet economy has limited the degree to which the USSR can compete effectively with the West in influencing international economic developments. To date, the Soviets have been required to adapt themselves to the existing international economic system as a means of participating in world trade. Soviet economic relations both with the West and with the developing countries occur in an international economic system still dominated by the Western industrial countries. In fact, the growth of East-West economic relations during the 1970s has created a certain degree of interdependence of the two groups of countries. The Soviets and their East European allies have discovered that they are no longer immune to developments in the international economy such as inflation or shortages.

It is not likely that the Soviets will be able in the coming years to solve the basic structural problems of their economy. Moreover, the probability of increasing difficulty in meeting their (and their East European allies') growing energy needs bodes ill for high growth rates. With the greater likelihood of a continued slowdown in economic growth, the Soviets will find it difficult to make additional commitments of the sort they have already made to Cuba, Angola, Afghanistan, and Vietnam.

AN INITIAL ASSESSMENT

The past three decades have witnessed a substantial expansion of the role of the Soviet Union in the international system. No longer is the USSR an isolated Communist state surrounded by a hostile capitalist world. The development of political ties with countries outside the traditional Soviet sphere, the creation of military capabilities that provide the Soviets with an expanded ability to project power, and the retrenchment of the West in much of the Third World have resulted in a new international balance of forces. In this new balance the Soviets are now in a position to match the power potential of the other established states. The USSR now has the capabilities to compete effectively in influencing international developments, as Britain, France, Germany, and the United States have in the past. The primary motivations of the Soviet leadership are those of *Realpolitik*, just as the motives of other great powers in the past have been related primarily to power politics.[12] To what extent the Soviet Union will continue to be able to expand its role in the international system will depend to a large extent on the response of the other actors in the international system— those in the West as well as the developing countries—and on developments within the Soviet Union itself. A persistent Western policy of nonreaction, combined with attitudes in the developing world that continue to view the West as the primary opponent, would permit the Soviets to expand their relative capabilities to influence international developments on a global scale. In spite, however, of disagreements within the Western alliance and between the industrial states and many of the developing countries, the past few years have witnessed a growing concern about Soviet expansionism and the beginning of efforts to counter that expansion.

NOTES

1. Even though Afghanistan is clearly not far from the core area of Soviet power, the Soviet invasion of that country in late December 1979 does represent a major new form of the Soviet willingness to use power in order to serve state interests.

2. See, for example, the argument of B. S. Fomin of the Institute of Economics of the World Socialist System in Moscow that "no stable and viable world economic system is possible without the equal participation of the socialist states, and without a just consideration of their specific interests." B. S. Fomin, "The New International Economic Order as Viewed in the CMEA Countries," in *Eastern Europe and the New International Economic Order: Representative Samples of Socialist Perspectives,* ed. Ervin Laszlo and Joel Kurtzman (New York: Pergamon Press, 1980), p. 7. Similar statements can be found in all Soviet commentaries on the development of a New International Economic Order.

3. For an excellent discussion of recent changes in the political orientation of the nonaligned movement see the article by William M. LeoGrande, "Evolution of the Nonaligned Movement," *Problems of Communism* 29, no. 1 (1980): 35-52.

4. Ghita Ionescu, *The Break-Up of the Soviet Empire in Eastern Europe* (Baltimore, Md.: Penguin Books, 1965).

5. For a brief discussion of the development of Soviet "power projection" capabilities see W. Scott Thompson, *Power Projection: A Net Assessment of U.S. and Soviet Capabilities* (New York: National Strategy Information Center, Agenda Paper no. 7, 1978), pp. 10-19. See also Roger E. Kanet, "L'Union soviétique et les pays en voie de développement: le rôle de l'aide militaire et de transferts d'armes," in *L'U.R.S.S. dans Les Relations Internationales,* ed. Jean-Louis Martres (Paris: Economica, 1982, forthcoming).

6. For a discussion of these points see Carl G. Jacobsen, *Soviet Strategic Initiatives: Challenge and Response* (New York: Praeger Special Studies–Praeger Scientific, 1979), pp. 1-8.

7. See Norman Polmar, *Soviet Naval Power: Challenge for the 1970s,* rev. ed. (New York: Crane, Russak, for National Strategy Information Center, 1974), pp. 40-45.

8. For a number of studies of the use of the Soviet fleet in international conflict situations see Michael MccGwire, Ken Booth, and John McDonnell, eds., *Soviet Naval Policy: Objectives and Constraints* (New York: Praeger, 1975); Michael MccGwire and John McDonnell, eds., *Soviet Naval Influence: Domestic and Foreign Dimensions* (New York: Praeger, 1977); and Bradford Dismukes and James M. McConnell, eds., *Soviet Naval Diplomacy* (New York: Pergamon Press, 1979). For an excellent analysis of the political role of Soviet military power, see Stephen S. Kaplan et al., *Diplomacy of Power: Soviet Armed Forces as a Political Instrument* (Washington, D.C.: The Brookings Institution, 1981).

9. For discussions of the new Soviet capabilities see Thompson, *Power Projections,* and Jacobsen, *Soviet Strategic Initiatives,* esp. pp. 51-72. For a reasoned argument that one must be careful not to exaggerate the facilities that have been made available to the Soviets,

see Richard Remnek's appendix in *Soviet Naval Diplomacy*, ed. Dismukes and McConnell. See also Kanet, "L'Union soviétique."

10. Andrei A. Grechko, "The Leading Role of the CPSU in Building the Army of a Developed Socialist Society," *Problemy istorii KPSS*, (May 1974), translated in *Strategic Review* 3, no. 1 (1975): 88-93.

11. Even though the record of successful introduction of Western technology into the Soviet economy has been mixed, the overall effect has clearly been beneficial to the development of the Soviet economy. See, for example, George D. Holliday, *Technology Transfer to the USSR, 1928-1937 and 1966-1975: The Role of Western Technology in Soviet Economic Development* (Boulder, Col.: Westview Press, 1979), esp. pp. 172-75.

12. For a discussion of Soviet policy within the context of *Realpolitik* see Jacobsen, *Soviet Strategic Initiatives*, esp. pp. 134-39.

PART TWO

Domestic-Foreign
Linkages in Soviet
Foreign Policy

THE MILITARY AND
SOVIET FOREIGN POLICY

Roman Kolkowicz

No question of any importance in the world can be solved without our participation, without taking into account our economic and military might.

Leonid Brezhnev[1]

DYNAMICS OF SOVIET FOREIGN POLICY

The foreign policy of the Soviet Union serves three broad objectives, in a descending order of priority: to promote the security of the Soviet Union and the power of the Communist party; to expand Soviet influence and control outside of Russia; and to support and promote international communism in support of Soviet national interests. These three fundamental objectives are mutually reinforcing: a powerful Soviet state is able to effectively exert its control on Communist parties and governments in the Soviet sphere of influence and to exert its influence in non-Communist areas of the world; a vigorous and successful Soviet foreign policy enhances the party leaders' power and prestige at home and within the bloc.

In the pursuit of these basic objectives, Soviet foreign policy appears to follow certain patterns of behavior. These patterns are discernible throughout the history of the Soviet state and seem to affect the dynamics of Soviet political behavior that shape its foreign policy.

The author wishes to thank Donna Beltz for invaluable research assistance in the preparation of this chapter.

Foreign Policy Dependence on Military Capabilities

A prime characteristic of Soviet foreign policy is its close relationship to, and dependence on, military capabilities. Soviet perceptions of their own military strength, their ability to support political action with requisite military man-power and technology, and their assessments of the adversary's military capabilities *and* its resolve to use them are the key factors in policy decisions. Thus, Soviet foreign policy appears to be a function of military "reach" and scope.

Stalin's military forces and doctrines were narrowly oriented. His foreign policy remained largely continental in scope, reaching only as far as the "Red Army's bayonets." Moreover, Stalin had little interest in the Third World, the former colonial areas, whose actual or potential leaders he viewed with distrust.

Khrushchev abandoned Stalin's military and doctrinal orthodoxy and launched a massive modernizing arms program, while expanding the strategic horizon of the Soviet military. He sought to reduce the burdensome conventional forces, upgrade the strategic-technological military capabilities, and assign his strategic forces an expanded, global role. Khrushchev's foreign policy, in contrast to Stalin's pessimism regarding policy opportunities in the Third World, became marked by an activist, adventurous optimism. Khrushchev's gambles in the Third World failed, however, in part due to a misunderstanding of the nationalist elites in these countries; but more importantly, his policies failed because they were adventurous, because they reached beyond the scope of Soviet military capabilities. Subsequently, Khrushchev sought to cover up this military inferiority with a blustering, militant pose; but when his bluff was called, particularly in the Cuban missile crisis, he drew the necessary conclusions and reverted to the traditional pattern of Soviet foreign policy: the reach of Soviet foreign policy became commensurate with the reach of Soviet military capabilities.

The Brezhnev regime has finally succeeded where previous Soviet leaders have failed: Soviet strategic and conventional military power is now equal to that of the West; Soviet strategic doctrines are now global in scope. Soviet foreign policy is now globally oriented.

Disparity of Policy Style and Substance

Soviet foreign policy style has frequently been aggressive, militant, and seemingly unyielding. People have become familiar with the tough pronunciamentos and slogans that proclaim, "We will bury you," and that forecast "the inevitable collapse of decadent imperialism." This tough policy style has often been reinforced by rude and unyielding behavior by Soviet political leaders and diplomats at international conferences or bilateral meetings. And yet, the substance of Soviet foreign policy is curiously dissonant with this aggressive style. The Soviet Union has never committed its forces formally and massively to an area outside its direct contiguous sphere of influence and control. Soviet leaders have invariably relented under direct pressure or confrontation with the West (Cuba, Berlin) or under strong resistance by indigenous leaders in opposition to Soviet influence or interference in their countries (Indonesia, Egypt). This is not to say that the Soviets are more moderate than leaders of other countries, but rather to suggest that in areas outside their direct control or influence over events, Soviet leaders tend to favor nonconfrontation, rejecting the possibility of massive commitments to uncertain outcomes.

Policy Orchestration, Priorities, Rules of the Game

A final aspect of Soviet foreign policy lies in its orchestration—that is, the balancing of many interests and commitments around the globe so that its various components can be brought to bear on any foreign policy issue of high priority. This principle of orchestration suggests Soviet perceptions of priorities of interests and of the rules of the game of international politics. The assumed order of Soviet policy priorities suggests the following:

The protection and furtherance of Soviet national, state, and party interests
The protection and retention of their political and military gains within their
    sphere of influence
Gradual Soviet expansion into promising areas of the world, by means of probes
    into "soft" areas that are not considered vital to the United States.

The basic rules of the game presumably perceived by the Soviet leaders in pursuit of the above priorities are as follows:

- Avoid direct confrontation with the other superpower
- Avoid the commitment of Soviet forces or presence in an irrevocable, either-or position to areas of limited Soviet control
- Avoid the possibility of two-front confrontation
- At all times, seek to divide your potential adversaries.

To summarize, Soviet foreign policy appears to be essentially expansion oriented, with this outward pressure defined and shaped by the levels of their military capabilities and by the balance between their forces and the forces of their main adversary. It is a policy that pursues expansion in a careful and calculated manner, avoiding frontal assaults on areas of presumed vital interest to their most powerful adversary. Above all, it is a flexible policy, employing tactics not overly encumbered by ideology, tradition, or significant domestic constraint. These propositions regarding Soviet foreign policy are general and should not be construed as a guide to specific Soviet policy problems, but rather are to serve as a loose framework, within which contemporary Soviet political and military policies can be examined.

In order to properly understand the military's role in the foreign policy process of the Soviet Union, it is necessary first to understand the internal role of the military. For as Lenin taught his disciples, foreign policy is a continuation of domestic politics.[2]

INTERNAL ROLES OF THE MILITARY
IN THE SOVIET UNION

The founding fathers of Marxism-Leninism and of the Soviet Union had only a vague notion about the role of the military in a postrevolutionary society. Although Marx, Engels, and Lenin contemplated differing roles for the revolutionary armed forces, they were in agreement on one fundamental axiom: In a Communist society no one will even think about a standing army; why would one need it? After all, to Lenin a standing army was an army that was divorced from the people. The idea of a massive, professional, standing army in a postrevolutionary society was considered an anathema, a heretical concept that violated fundamental aspects of revolutionary ideology.

So much for revolutionary rhetoric and utopian schemas: the erstwhile revolutionary heresy has become the orthodoxy of Soviet politics. Indeed, the Soviet military today is a vast and complex institution whose interests strongly influence and shape much of the country's social, economic, and even political life. The military has become a state within a state: it is a primary consumer of scarce resources, of skilled manpower and scientific-technological talent; it runs a vast educational network that parallels and often excels that of the civilian sector; and it has become a visible and pervasive presence in society through its control of a network of mass voluntary, paramilitary youth organizations, and military preparedness and civil-defense training activities. The military is also strongly represented in the highest decision-making bodies of the Party, the government, and economic planning bodies.

What are the implications of this steady growth of the military's role and influence in the Soviet Union? Does it suggest an eventual militarization of the Communist party and government? Is this evidence of a concerted program for war preparedness and offensive intentions? Are we witnessing the emergence of a garrison state, a nation in arms, a modern Sparta in Marxist tunics? It is important to consider these questions, because Western perceptions of Soviet politics and decision making rarely touch upon the military's internal roles and influence on policy. Western perceptions of Soviet political process were first shaped by cold-war antagonisms, and more recently, by the more benign perceptions and fantasies of détentism. In either case, the West rarely concerned itself with the military's internal role and policy influence. The Red Army was seen essentially as metal eaters, weapon carriers, and trigger pullers for the Party. To be sure, several theories and models of Party-military relations have gained some renown in the West (ranging from conflict models to cooperation models); however, the scholastic debates on this subject do not necessarily enhance understanding.

The Soviet Union is in many ways an ideal country for the fostering of military values, interests, and goals, and for the military to play a vital and important internal and foreign policy role. The histories of Imperial Russia and the Soviet Union alike are tales of conquest, invasion, and war. It is understandable that Russian leaders would place great trust in their military, and rely on it to defend the country from foreign aggression. While, however, the military's role as defender of the country has been well understood, there is much less understanding in the West of the important internal and policy roles of the military. The vast size and the geographic/linguistic/ethnic/racial diversity of the Soviet Union have presented perennial administrative and political problems, and have led to a strong reliance on the military for maintenance of internal stability, law and order, national coherence, and the legitimacy of authority. The military was considered loyal to the central government and able to provide the necessary instrument for bureaucratic and political control. The replacement of the imperial autocracy with Bolshevik authoritarianism or totalitarianism did not significantly affect the military's role. It did, however, change the dynamics of the relationship and the rules of the game. The military's internal and external roles continued to develop and grow in the subterranean and tacit manner suitable to Stalin's regime. Since then, the military has proceeded to assume public, social, and political roles commensurate with its position in the state. What are some of these roles?

The logic and political dynamics of modern mobilizational (totalitarian) political systems like the Soviet Union create overriding preferences for centralization of political, institutional, economic, and military authority; standardization of rules, processes, laws, producer/consumer habits, and distribution patterns; eradication of deviances, diversities, and idiosyncrasies that inhibit and constrain standardization-centralization objectives; and integration of diverse political, economic, and social entities under the ruling party's banner. The military was seen early on by party leaders as an excellent instrument in the systematic and rapid execution of these primary objectives. Stalin and his successors considered the military an institution that could help eradicate some of the pernicious, entrenched remnants of the bourgeois/imperial past, inculcate desirable habits and patterns in generations of young people, and assist in a swift integration of the diverse Russian society. Thus, to the evils of ethnicity, regionalism/parochialism, separatism, and traditionalism, the military, by means of training, education, and discipline, could counterpose the values and policies of Russification, national patriotism, communization, centralization, integration, and modernization. In other words, the army, with its national network of installations, schools, and bases, would serve as a school for communism and would thus in a short time create the New Soviet Man. And it would do this as a by-product of its primary mission—the defense of the country—and would do it economically and systematically.

The Soviet military did indeed perform many of these vital integrative and modernizing functions in the early decades of Soviet history. And in recent years the military has expanded both the scope and the direction of this educational function by taking a leading role in the development and inculcation of patriotic and military values in the Russian masses.

There are several ways in which the Soviet population is exposed to military discipline and war preparedness:

Preinduction military training. The Soviet army combines the advantages of a volunteer army with compulsory military service. The military establishment encompasses over three and one-half million men in direct active duty, to which can be added other military and paramilitary components (such as command staff, training cadres, KGB/MVD militarized units, and so forth) that would bring the total to above five million. About one-third of the manpower in the armed forces consists of career officers and NCOs, and the other two-thirds is made up of conscripts under the universal military service law of 1967. Since only about one-half of the 18-year-olds in the manpower pool are inducted into the army, the military seeks to prepare the noninductees for military/war contingencies through various programs. Actually, the military preparation of the young begins at the age of 10–15 via the Young Pioneers program embracing about 16 million. Members of the next older group, the *Komsomol*, are organized into permanent military detachments of Eaglets (*Orlenok*) constituting a quasi-militia of 16- to 17-year-olds. They receive compulsory military training at their secondary schools and through mass volunteer organizations of DOSAAF. The latter comprises about 40 million people, distributed in about 300,000 primary organizations. The vast majority of instructors in these paramilitary training programs consist of reserve officers who teach on a full- or half-time basis. Some of the training is quite advanced, including piloting jet planes, operating radar, parachuting, sentry duty, and the like. The performance standards are rather uneven and vary from organization to organization.

Civil defense. This program embraces the whole Soviet population. It is directed by a senior general in the Defense Ministry, and has been expanding in scope and intensity in recent years. Through the civil-defense programs, the military fosters and maintains in the populace a war-preparedness attitude, a certain kind of discipline, and paramilitary habits. The programs have recently received more serious attention from the Party and the military and have consequently been expanded and intensified. In 1971 civil-defense training was introduced into the second grade of primary schools, whereas previously it began in the fifth grade; and it became mandatory in technical and higher institutes of learning. The population has been increasingly incorporated into civil-defense formations with specialized functions. These formations increasingly cooperate with regular army units, and thus serve as quasi-military units, providing intensive training and exercises for the most efficient evacuation of the populace and placing increasingly more intensive psychological/indoctrinational pressures on the populace to adapt to a war-preparedness milieu.

Militarization of the economy, science, technology. In addition to the military's role in the militarization of society, the defense establishment enjoys a preferential position in the planning of economic and scientific goals and priorities in the Soviet Union. This special treatment of the military goes back to the early years of the Soviet state, when the expectations of a world revolution failed to materialize and the Soviet Union found itself to be the only Socialist country, encircled and isolated within a hostile capitalist and Fascist environment. Stalin had at the time radically transformed Soviet economy, agriculture, and industry in order rapidly to develop a modern defense industry that was to serve as the basis for a large and powerful military establishment. Economic planning under the Stalinist five-year plans was built around the needs and demands of defense, and was described by Western economic experts as follows:

> First allocate to the military establishment the resources (labor, materials, capital) needed to fulfill strategic requirements. . . . [S]econd, maximize the flow of resources into the heavy industrial sector. Third, distribute residuals of unrequired and unsuitable resources among other sectors, such as agriculture and light industry.[3]

Current economic planning in Russia is not quite so rigidly prodefense, nor does it follow the stilted and arbitrary Stalinist models. The defense establishment, however, remains the favorite institution, whose interests and demands are usually defined by the Politburo as the highest priorities within the state. Among recent Western estimates of the defense sector's share of the Soviet GNP and budgetary slice, there appears to be general agreement that the defense sector continues to absorb a large share of the GNP (11-13 percent versus 6 percent in the United States). Some analysts maintain that Soviet defense expenditures have grown at an annual rate of 10 percent in the period 1958-70, 8-10 percent in the period 1971-75, and that the trend in the share of the Soviet GNP allocated to defense has been 10-12 percent in 1955, 8 percent in 1958, 12 percent in 1970, and 14-15 percent in 1975; further projections see an 18 percent share in 1981. Recent estimates of the defense budget of the Soviet Union show a constant upward movement from $110 billion in 1974 to about $127 billion in 1976, to $140+ billion in 1978-79.[4]

The defense establishment has clearly established its primacy in the economy as well as in the research and development, scientific, and educational sectors of the state. The Soviet defense industry forms a separate sector of the economy. It enjoys first priority in the allocation of materials and engineering-technical personnel, who along with the workers are better paid than those in the civilian economy.[5] The Ministry of Defense enjoys a special position in the economic-technological sectors of the state. It has what David Holloway has called "consumer sovereignty"[6] –the ability to impose its wishes and preferences on the whole production process–and economic privilege no other group has. The military also dominates the planning and priorities of the scientific and research and development sectors of the state.

The military educational system contains 125 military higher schools (13 percent of all higher schools in the country), leading to an observation by Colonel William Odom that one in every seven college-level institutions in the USSR is an officer-commissioning school roughly analogous to West Point, Annapolis, and Colorado Springs.[7] This has created a large military intelligentsia in the most extensive and intensive officer-education system in the world.

The military has jealously guarded this preferential position in the society and the economy, and military spokesmen have at times publicly defended this position by sharply attacking even leading Party members. This was reflected, for example, in the vitriolic attacks of military figures on Khrusnchev, shortly after his ouster, because he had tried to curb the escalating defense budgets and reduce the wasteful practices of defense-industry establishments that were hiding under the veil of secrecy. The military accused him of dangerous and harebrained advocacy of the "primacy of the stomach" and "goulash communism" because in 1964 Khrushchev had maintained that "the tasks of defense industry could be solved more successfully with less expenditures" and that "we are now considering the possibility of a further reduction in the size of our armed forces . . . to reduce military expenditures next year" because "the defense of the country is at suitable levels."[8] Khrushchev's successors were eager to go on record as rejecting these antidefense ideas, and asserted that "the Communist Party continues to believe that it is its sacred duty to strengthen the defense of the USSR."[9] And when Brezhnev gingerly sought to remind the military, after Khrushchev's ouster, that "the national economy must develop harmoniously, it must serve to achieve . . . constant rise in the people's living standards" and therefore "further development of heavy industry must be subordinated to the requirements . . . of the whole economy,"[10] the party leader received a public reminder from Chief of General Staff Marshal Zakharov, who in attacking Khrushchev served notice to other political leaders. Zakharov asserted that "subjectivism [arbitrary interference by political amateurs in matters of defense] is particularly dangerous in military affairs . . . and it is the sacred duty of the military cadres to protect these military sciences from everything that detracts from their authority." And to drive his point home with particular authority, he cited Lenin in support of the primacy of defense interests in economic planning for the country: "The Soviet people have in the past not for a moment failed to carry out V. I. Lenin's legacy: always be on the alert, protect the defense capabilities of the country and our Red Army like the apple of our eye."[11] It may be instructive to recall that a decade before Khrushchev's ouster, party leader and Prime Minister Malenkov suffered the same fate and earned the military's undying hostility because he argued that "our main task is to ensure the further improvement in the material well-being of all Soviet people which makes it necessary to increase significantly investment of resources for the production of consumer goods." The military and its supporters attacked Malenkov, arguing in the secret organ of the General Staff that "heavy industry is the foundation of foundations of our Socialist economy" and that the main priority for the Soviet Union was "the further development of heavy industry."[12]

THE MILITARY AND THE COMMUNIST PARTY

Even this brief account of the internal roles of the military conveys a picture of its pervasive presence, institutional interpenetration, and expanding social, economic, and political weight within the state. How can one account for these developments and what are their implications?

The Expanding Scope of Soviet Foreign and Defense Policies

Starting from a rather vulnerable, defensive, and contained continental position, the Soviet Union has in the past two decades expanded into the global arena on land, sea, and in space, sharply increasing its commitments abroad. The primary motor and vehicle for this expansion has been the military establishment: Soviet arms, technology, military expertise, and advisory missions have become the most effective exports and influence-building commodities of the Kremlin in the Third World, and the Soviet military is its prime beneficiary.

Current Soviet global role and power are the result of steady vision and planning aimed at making the Soviet Union invulnerable and subsequently enabling its expansion abroad. From Lenin onward, party leaders have tried to make the best of their temporary weakness and vulnerability while planning for the day of great military power. As Lenin told his disciples,

> As long as, from the economic and military standpoint, we are weaker than the capitalist world, we must adhere to the rule that we must know how to take advantage of the antagonisms and contradictions existing among the imperialists. . . . [H]owever, as soon as we are strong enough to defeat capitalism as a whole, we shall immediately take it by the scruff of the neck.[13]

By the 1970s, the Soviet leadership no longer talked about weakness or vulnerability; they asserted that "the historical initiative is now firmly in the hands of the socialist community,"[14] and though peaceful coexistence with the West was highly desirable, that was not to interfere with the historical revolutionary mission of the Communist party: to combat capitalism and imperialism by aiding and supporting national revolutionary and liberation movements in the Third World.

Peaceful coexistence has nothing in common with class peace and does not cast even the slightest doubt upon the oppressed peoples' sacred rights to use all means, including armed struggle, in the cause of their liberation.

Ideologists hostile to socialism are attempting to inculcate in gullible people the idea that in pursuing a policy of peaceful coexistence between states in practice, the Soviet Union is allegedly straying from revolutionary and internationalist principles. . . . [They] even go so far as to claim that the Soviet Union is "losing interest" in the peoples' liberation movement and reducing its aid to the movement.[15]

Party leaders and the military vigorously reject the above implication, asserting that "limitation of strategic weapons does not eliminate the danger of war" and that "it would be utopian to assume that peaceful coexistence between countries with different social systems could at once rule out armed clashes. . . . [T]hat is why all this talk about an end to the 'era of wars' and the arrival of an 'era of universal peace' is premature and dangerous."[16]

In rejecting the universal, peaceful, and stabilizing "linkage" implications of détente and peaceful coexistence, the military emphasizes the expansionistic thrust of Soviet foreign and military policies. The evidence, even in the stilted Party jargon of the *agitprop*, is persuasive enough: the vital political, ideological, and defense interests of the Party and the Soviet government depend on the might of the armed forces. Despite détente, despite arms control, the struggle against imperialism will go on and the Soviets are in the vanguard of that struggle. Translated into everyday language, that means searching for targets of opportunity in the Third World, offering military assistance, seeking some kind of foothold in the process, and then trying to expand Soviet presence and influence in these vital regions. Since the strategic deterrence relationship effectively stabilized East-West relationships, and since the Soviets seek to retain good relations with other industrialized countries for the time being, the old East-West confrontation is being transferred into the Third World, crossing and merging with the newer North-South conflicts.

The Soviet military has in recent years become involved in various countries in the strategically important regions of the Middle East and Africa, from Angola to Mozambique, from Ethiopia to Yemen, from Afghanistan to Iraq. Soviet ships roam the oceans of the globe, while their submarines perform deterrence functions and other missions beneath the sea. Soviet generals train the armies and military technicians of these countries and Soviet marshals negotiate with the political leaders in the name of the Politburo.

Soviet party leaders appear to be committed to a policy of military and political penetration and expansion into the Third World, and the most effective instrument for such a new imperial policy is the military. The current party leadership and the marshals and generals are in this together.

Problems of Legitimacy and Authority: the Ossification
of the Party and the Waning of Revolutionary Elan

In explaining the "routinization of charisma" Max Weber asserted:

It is the universal fate of all parties, which almost without exception
originated as charismatic followings, either of legitimate rulers or of
Caesarist pretenders, or of demogogues in the style of Pericles, or
Cleon or LaSalle, when once they slip into everyday routine or a
permanent organization, to remodel themselves into a body led by
notables.[17]

The notables we are presently concerned with are the leaders of the Communist
party of the Soviet Union, who have indeed routinized the revolutionary charisma of their predecessors and have maintained a progressively more tenuous
hold on society and state in Soviet Russia. If the earlier, totalitarian Stalinist
period may be described as one of "charismatic leadership," the present situation in the Soviet state is more closely reflected in the "postcharismatic" (posttotalitarian) reflections of Weber:

The swing of the pendulum between charismatic obedience and submission to "notables" has now been replaced by the struggle between the bureaucratic party organization and the party leadership.
The Party organization has fallen more and more securely into the
hands of the professional party officials and the further the process
of bureaucratization has gone.[18]

Indeed, as he suggests, "it is as a rule easy for the party organization to achieve
this castration of charisma."[19] This evocative phrase does reflect the Soviet situation, the decay of revolutionary dynamism, the erosion of the Party's claims to
legitimacy, and the spectacular growth of bureaucratic institutions within the
state.

In his analysis of the posttotalitarian trends in Soviet politics, Jerry Hough
maintains that the post-Khrushchev leadership of the Communist party has
modified its role in society and state from a dominant to an adjudicating, arbi-
trating type:

Whereas Stalin in his last years ignored the policy suggestions of the
institutional centers of power, and whereas Khrushchev challenged
the basic interests of almost every one of these centers, the present
leadership has not done major battle with any important segment of
the establishment and seems, on the contrary, to have acceded to the
most central desires of each.[20]

The party leadership seems to desire an untroubled status quo, to avoid hard and
risk-prone choices and decisions that might threaten the delicate balance of the

bureaucratic coalition within the Party and the Politburo: "The unwillingness or inability of the present leadership to remove members of the administrative elite has been matched by its abstention from imposing any major policy change that would seriously diminish the status of any important institutional group."[21] The leadership is seen to "assume the role not of the major policy initiator but of a broker mediating competing claims of powerful interests."[22] And the party over which this gerontocracy presides has changed drastically in its makeup, membership, role, and vitality. In its drive to broaden the base of the Party, to make it a party of all the people, the leadership risks the danger "that the legitimacy of the party as instrument of the proletariat will be undermined," since it is "totally impossible for such a party to be some kind of priesthood that stands outside of society" but rather one where "virtually all societal interests have penetrated into the party" and where approximately "30% of all citizens with completed higher education in 1973 were party members, and over 50% of the men with such an education"[23] belonged to it.

The problems of a mass party are compounded, due to the "logic of rule" which affects the party apparatus and the controllers in the center as well as those in the provinces, because they very often come from the agencies being controlled. And finally, the drive to mass party membership creates "a foremost danger that many persons will proclaim total loyalty to the party's cause and will pretend ideological orthodoxy simply to obtain the jobs and material advantages associated with membership."[24] This trend has as its consequence an influx into a party of people with little talent, prescribed administrative positions, and thus a most ineffective administrative system. In general, one may perceive a pattern of erosion of party authority and legitimacy that undermines the authoritarian features of the system. There are several such erosive trends: the rising educational level of the elite, the gradual disappearance of the economic-social force that generates a propensity toward authoritarianism, the erosion of ideological certainty under the impact of events in the outside world, and the tendency for dissenters to come from the upper stratum of society, a situation that makes it difficult for an elite to suppress its own.

Although one need not accept all of these developments as contributing factors to the decline of a party's authority and legitimacy, nevertheless in aggregate they convey the inexorable momentum of decline of its hegemonic power.

Milovan Djilas, whose insights about the ideological decay of Communist parties are both perceptive and authoritative, describes the "castration of charisma" and the dominant new class of the *apparatchiki* thus:

> The heroic era of communism is past. The epoch of its great leaders has ended. The epoch of practical men has set in. The new class has been created. It is at the height of its power and wealth, but it is without new ideas. It has nothing more to tell the people. The only thing that remains is for it to justify itself.[25]

Problems of Hegemonic Maintenance:
Succession and the Military

In his study of civil-military relations in several political systems, Michael Howard observed that "in States where no orderly transition of power and obedience had yet been established . . . military force is the final and sometimes only arbiter in government."[26] In the Soviet case, problems of transition of power in the Party and the state represent a key source of instability and institutional tensions that contribute to the erosion of the Party's legitimacy and authority within the state.

A change of leadership in the Soviet Union is not a process governed either by tradition or established rules. No Soviet party leader has ever voluntarily relinquished his powers, and no provisions exist for the transfer of authority, should the incumbent die or be removed as a result of disability or political coercion. This serves to explain why Lenin's infirmity and death, Trotsky's forced removal, and Stalin's death proved to be such critical events. A grave leadership crisis can also be expected to arise from an intraparty coup resulting from realignments of political relationships and loyalties among representatives of those institutions that carry the main political weight in the state. The former leader then finds himself with a fait accompli engineered by his opponents, to which he has no choice but to submit. This was the case, though to varying degrees, in the ousters of both Malenkov and Khrushchev.

There is, however, a basic difference in the leadership changes since the death of Stalin: several party leaders competed for the top position, thus enabling an institution outside the party apparat to serve as an arbiter and adjudicator of the leadership competition. That institution is the military, or more specifically, the top leadership of the armed forces. This involvement of the military in the heretofore sacrosanct internal affairs of the Party has fundamentally affected the relations between the Party and the military. The mystique and engineered charisma of the party leader were destroyed and rather shabby personalized politicking replaced them. The scramble for the military's support and the subsequent need to reward the military for that support have undoubtedly impressed the marshals and generals in the post-Stalinist state. Although the consequences of that politicized role of the military have not been fully understood, there is little doubt that party leaders will continue to pay careful attention to the military's basic interests and preferences lest they ignore them at their own peril. The Malenkov and Khrushchev episodes are instructive cases in point.[27]

After the death of Stalin the complex political power system, formerly held together by the dictator as if by a linchpin, became factionalized. Several men with diverse sources of political power entered into a tense, unstable coalition that from the start promised to be short-lived. The spokesmen of three politically powerful institutions—the party apparat, the governmental bureaucracies, and the security organs—maneuvered for position in the ensuing power struggles in the party. Since there was no precedent or procedural mechanism for an intraparty resolution of this political crisis, the military assumed, or was invited to assume, the role of arbiter in the resolution of this grave crisis. Since the security organs under Beria represented a threat to all three institutions (party, government, military) the military arranged to have Beria arrested, tried in a military tribunal, and executed.

In the subsequent power struggle between the two remaining claimants to Stalin's power mantle, the military again played a vital role. Having little experience with party politics (since Stalin kept them tightly controlled and subordinated), and since neither Malenkov nor Khrushchev had any special connections with the military, the marshals and generals at first found it difficult to decide which was worthy of their support. That ambivalence was quickly resolved, however, once the military made known their institutional preferences and interests, whereupon one of the contenders, Khrushchev, quickly adjusted his public "platform" and avowed political programs to coincide with those of the military. After that, Malenkov's fate was sealed. Ironically, a decade later Khrushchev was to suffer the same fate that he had inflicted on Malenkov: having alienated the military and other powerful institutions, Khrushchev was easily ousted from power in 1964 without any fuss or resistance.[28]

The Political Demands of the Military

It is instructive to review briefly the political maturation of the Soviet military, their initially tentative and timid steps into the political arena, and the subsequent growth of their institutional strength and mounting demands upon the Party. In offering their support to a challenger or victor in the two recent power struggles in the Party, the military followed a readily perceivable pattern: a direct and indirect declaration of its interests and of demands on the Party, followed by vigorous support of the victorious faction.

The military seeks assurance that their needs of technology, weapons, and associated capabilities will receive the highest priority in the nationally planned economy, assuring a steady flow of such resources into the military establishment. This demand is usually contained in the code words "heavy industry," which was once spelled out by Marshal Zhukov: "Above all, the major achievements of heavy industry have permitted us to rearm our army, air forces and navy with first class military materiel."[29] Thus, both in the post-Stalinist succession crisis and in the post-Khrushchev succession period the military loudly proclaimed its heavy industry priorities: Malenkov rejected them in 1953-54, while Khrushchev loudly proclaimed them. Malenkov stated his views in August 1953, when he stressed the need to assign higher priority to consumer needs and a lower priority to the heavy industrial/defense-oriented sector of the economy. Several weeks later Khrushchev jumped on the military's bandwagon and thundered that "the main thing is the further development of heavy industry,"[30] thus ensuring the marshals' support in the coming confrontation with Malenkov.

The military clearly prefers a set of foreign and defense policies that assign a high role to the defense sector by conveying a sense of threat expectation from outside. This need for international tension is again reflected with predictable results in the post-Stalin power struggles. Malenkov pushed for a relaxation of tensions, for a détente with the West, arguing that nuclear war would be suicidal, since there would be no victors or survivors. Khruschev sharply rejected this at the time, pushing hard for a tough, blustering, and uncompromising strategic and political doctrine that rejected détente and peaceful coexistence proposals and spoke instead of final victory and the destruction of the bloodied capitalists.[31]

Once Khrushchev got rid of Malenkov in February 1955, the military was accorded a number of highly desired and awaited concessions: long-postponed promotions to the highest ranks, rehabilitation of purged military heroes, rewriting of history so as to assign the military a heroic and vital role as defender of the country. A number of military officers were promoted to the Central Committee and other bodies of the Party; the political organs in the military were curtailed and their representation in the party bodies was reduced; and Marshal Zhukov, the most popular military leader and war hero, was freed from his Stalin-consigned obscurity and steadily promoted until he was minister of defense and a full member of the sacrosanct Politburo.

The military was asked by Khrushchev to bail him out on several other occasions: during the antiparty plot episode in 1957, Khrushchev's position was in effect saved by the military's swift actions and full support. The military also gave Khrushchev strong support in the developing Sino-Soviet crisis and in the Berlin crisis. Once Khrushchev was securely in power, however, after removing or outliving his main challengers in the Party, he turned against the military in his efforts to curb their excessive demands for resources and for corporate autonomy. Having frustrated, alienated, and disappointed his erstwhile supporters in his struggles against Malenkov, Khrushchev became, in effect, politically isolated, enabling his enemies and rivals in the Party to arrange for his ouster in 1964.

Between 1959 and the time of his ouster Khrushchev challenged the three main military demands. First, he proposed to reduce the military's manpower by about one-third; second, he actively pursued ways to stabilize relations with the West on the basis of peaceful coexistence and détente, particularly after the Cuban missile crisis fiasco; and third, he constantly harangued the military about their wasteful and excessive uses of resources.[32]

In the Khrushchev succession episode, the military still played their supportive arbiter role, but in a much more muted and less public fashion. Predictably, the military leaders were expected to denigrate and thus effectively destroy the predecessor's political and party record, his prestige and achievements, thus both justifying his ouster and freeing the new leadership from any associations, commitments, or obligations of the ousted Khrushchev. The military was rewarded with a reversal of Khrushchev's reductions in the defense sector and with the launching of a massive arms program that was eventually to match, and in part eclipse, that of the United States. Military leaders were also rewarded with important political roles as heads of important foreign missions, as spokesmen for the party leader in client states, and as dominant members of international negotiating missions involving arms control and related issues.[33]

The major difference in the two succession episodes, as far as the military's role is concerned, is the fact that after Stalin's death there were no precedents, no rules of the game, for the establishment of a viable coalition of bureaucratic hierarchs in a collective leadership mode. Thus, each contender had to press hard against his opponents and seek allies, while doing much of this political linen washing in public. The decade of post-Stalinism, the diminution of the security organs as a potential threat to all, and the semi-institutionalization of collective leadership have negated the need for public histrionics. The deal to oust Khrushchev was made *in camera*; the new coalition was agreed upon and the only thing left was to let the incumbent know that he was through.

What does the party leader obtain as his quid pro quo from his military supporters? Military support in the power struggle during the succession episode; a loyal military elite that he can rely on in the future; the acceptance of institutional "fealty"—that is, the party leader's retention of authority to appoint, promote, and remove military personnel, the right to define the general and military-specific goals, priorities, and directions for state policy; and acceptance within the military establishment of the Party's controlling, educational, and propaganda instruments.

Consequences of Military "Succession Management"

The near three-decades-long period of post-Stalin party-military politics in the Soviet Union suggests that the two institutions have become thoroughly interdependent and that they interpenetrate each other to a remarkable extent. The military has come to the party leader's support on a number of occasions, aiding him in intraparty struggles and in conflicts with other Communist challengers from abroad. The military has also assumed a number of key roles and positions within the system:

As the main vehicle and supporter of the ever-expanding Soviet external military and political commitments to clients and proxies in Africa, the Middle East, and Asia;

As the key stabilizing factor in the restless alliance system in East Europe, where in the final analysis only the military restores order, punishes opponents, and serves as the policeman on the beat;

As the main bulwark against the pressures and demands from the former Chinese ally;

　s the educator, national integrator, and disciplined Spartan model for the restless and diverse young and old from the various geographic, linguistic, national, religious, and class-based sectors of society.

The logic of the posttotalitarian rule and the imperial expansion of the Soviet state have endowed the military with vital, indispensable tasks and roles. As the party leadership becomes more dependent upon the military for purposes of internal, alliance, and external policy, and as the military shows itself to be a loyal, conservative, and stable force within the state, the Party becomes in a sense the captive of the military. The party leadership's insistence on a protracted internal status quo and avoidance of hard choices and risky decisions force them to support, mollify, and rely on the military. There is no alternative institution to perform these varied tasks in a responsible and loyal way. The Party and the military have become mutual captives: they need one another and they cannot let go, for there are no viable alternatives. Only a systemic change or a radical regime change might break that interdependence.

CONCLUSIONS AND PROJECTIONS

The Soviet military is assuming increasing institutional and political roles and influence in the Soviet Union as protector of the CPSU's waning legitimacy in the state, as guardian of the ideological-revolutionary heritage of the Party at home and in the bloc; as integrator of the disparate and diversified sociopolitical forces and movements at home and in the bloc; as quasi-revolutionary agent of Soviet interests in the Third World; and as traditional defender of the homeland. It is postulated here that in the face of eroding hegemonic power and control by the Party within the system, it becomes the military's interest to retain and support the forms of the Party's hegemony within the state, while at the same time seeking change in the content and substance of the Party's roles within the state. In other words, the military is likely to seek continuity of form and change in the content of the Party's traditional roles. This increased military role within the Soviet Union is postulated not within a "conflict model," but as an evolutionary, adaptational process of institutional accommodation between the Party and military leadership. These postulates are also based on existing conditions auspicious for such projections:

A weak center: gerontocracy, bureaucratic fiefdoms, coalition politics, localist pressures;
Erosion of revolutionary elan: waning of ideological dynamism and legitimacy
Vast power of the military, due to growing external involvements and commitments, internal defense needs and claims;
Expansionist foreign policy in Africa, the Middle East, Asia;
Threat perception: concerns with "encirclement" by alliances led by the United

States and including the Chinese, Japanese, West European, and Third World countries; concerns with divisive nationalist threats to cohesion and unity of the USSR.

It is postulated here, therefore, that if these patterns and conditions persist, the party leadership will find itself progressively more dependent upon the military for the efficient maintenance of internal political and economic policies, for the retention of the Party's leading role within the state, for the maintenance of Soviet influence and power within the bloc, and for the efficient conduct of foreign and military policies. It is further assumed here that the military's voice, style, and preferences will become more pervasive in the deliberations and choices of national policy. And finally, that the party and military leaderships will arrive at a modus vivendi for the changed institutional and political relationship within the state under conditions of internal stress and external opportunity.

We ought to ask, therefore, what does the military want, now that it has gained such influence in the Soviet Union? Are we likely to see some significant changes in the military's relationship with the Party? That is, if we describe the military's role and place under Stalin as one of unchallenged dependency, and if we characterize current party-military relations as those of interdependency, are we likely to see a military bid, in the foreseeable future, toward *independence* from party control? It is the assumption here that the military is not likely to embark upon Bonapartist adventures, or banana-republic palace coups. The military and the current party leadership have established a modus vivendi that suits both partners. The Brezhnev policy lines appear to be those of high defense budgets, controlled expansion into the Third World, normalization/détentification in the industrial world, and controlled consumerism at home, and the military is a beneficiary and supporter of these policy lines. Expansion abroad legitimizes the steady growth of the defense establishment; détente does not threaten military interests and gives them access to Western technologies; and controlled consumerism and its attendant threat of embourgeoisement endow the military with the important role of spartan educator and patriotic revolutionary model for the youth at home, and the firm party gendarme in the troubled Communist bloc.

The Soviet military sees its internal role as a conservative, nationalistic, disciplined force, pursuing institutional interests that coincide with and support those of the Party and the country. The Soviet military, however, has also accumulated a vast arsenal of modern weapons, skilled soldiers, and advanced technology based in a war-preparedness indoctrinated society. This vast arsenal is growing and proliferating at a remarkable rate, apparently uninfluenced by the theories, policies, and fantasies of détente, deterrence, and arms control. The military and its vast armory seem to be in search of a purpose, a goal that goes beyond the static balances and inertias of deterrence.

NOTES

1. L. I. Brezhnev, speech in Minsk, March 14, 1970, on the Soviet army's "Dvina" maneuvres, reported in Foy D. Kohler et al., *Soviet Strategy for the Seventies* (Washington, D.C.: Center for Advanced International Studies, University of Miami, 1977), p. 228.

2. Vernon V. Aspaturian, *Process and Power in Soviet Foreign Policy* (Boston: Little, Brown, 1971), p. 491.

3. U.S. Congress, Joint Economic Committee, *Allocation of Resources in the Soviet Union and China–1979, Hearings before the Subcommittee on Priorities and Economy in Government*, 96th Cong., 1st sess., 1979.

4. Ibid.

5. David Holloway, "Soviet Military R&D: Managing the Research-Production Cycle," in *Soviet Science and Technology*, ed. John R. Thomas and Ursula M. Kruse-Vaucienne (Washington, D.C.: National Science Foundation, 1977).

6. Ibid., p. 204.

7. William E. Odom, "The 'Militarization' of Soviet Society," *Problems of Communism* 25 (September–October, 1976): 34–51.

8. *Pravda*, December 15, 1963.

9. *Pravda*, July 12, 1965.

10. *Pravda*, November 7, 1964.

11. *Krasnaia Zvezda*, February 4, 1965.

12. Marshal Zhukov, "Order of the Day," February 23, 1955. See also speeches by top military leaders forcefully reiterating the "heavy industry primacy" theme: About a week before the decisive meeting of the Central Committee and its announcement of the Malenkov "resignation," Marshal I. S. Konev states that "the general line of the Party in the economic sphere that foresees the development of heavy industry by every conceivable means, will be firmly continued." *Pravda*, February 23, 1955.

13. *Kommunist*, no. 9, (June 1972, "Editorial").

14. Milovan Djilas, "The New Class," in *Essential Works of Marxism*, ed. A. P. Mendel (New York: Bantam Books, Matrix Edition, 1965), p. 332.

15. CPSU Central Committee, Theses of December 1969, cited in Kohler, *Soviet Strategy*, p. 72; also V. Korionov, "The Socialist Policy of Peace," in *Pravda*, July 13, 1972.

16. Ibid.

17. Max Weber, *Selections in Translation*, ed. W. G. Runciman (Cambridge: Cambridge University Press, 1978), p. 245.

18. Ibid., p. 246.

19. Ibid., p. 247.

20. Jerry Hough, *The Soviet Union and Social Science Theory* (Cambridge, Mass.: Harvard University Press, 1977), p. 28.

21. Ibid., p. 29.

22. Ibid.

23. Ibid., p. 7; see also the chapter titled "Party Saturation," detailing the statistics of growth of Party membership by age, education, sex, and so forth.

24. Ibid., p. 6; see also the chapter titled "The Bureaucratic Model and the Nature of the Soviet System" for a perceptive analysis of the bureaucratization of the Soviet system, on the evolution of a "government by clerks" (Brzezinski), and on the intractable innovation-resistant system of management of the government and economy.

25. Harriet F. Scott and William F. Scott, *The Armed Forces of the USSR*, Ch. 9, "The Soviet Military-Industrial Complex and Defense Costs" (Boulder, Col.: Westview Press, 1979).

26. Michael Howard, *Soldiers and Governments: Nine Studies in Civil-Military Relations*, "Introduction" (London: Eyre & Spottiswoode, 1957).

27. For descriptions of the politics of the Stalinist succession, see Robert Conquest, *Power and Policy in the USSR* (New York: St. Martin's Press, 1961); Lazar Pistrak, *The Grand Tactician; Khrushchev's Rise to Power* (New York: Praeger, 1961); Myron Rush, *The Rise of Khrushchev* (Washington, D.C.: Public Affairs Press, 1958). The ouster of Khrushchev has been examined by many Western analysts, including P. B. Reddaway, "The Fall of Khrushchev," *Survey*, no. 56, (July 1965): 11-30; the November 1964 (No. 11) issue of *Osteuropa*, containing articles on the theme "Nach Chrushtschow," by Richard Lowenthal, David Burg, and Herman Achminow; also a series of contributions on the theme of "The Coup and After" by Merle Fainsod, Robert Conquest, and Adam Ulam in the January–February and May–June issues of *Problems of Communism*, 1965.

28. The reasons for his "resignation" were given as "advanced age and deterioration in the state of his health." *Pravda*, October 16, 1964.

29. *Pravda*, August 9, 1953.

30. *Pravda*, December 28, 1954.

31. Malenkov maintained in 1954 that "a thermonuclear war would result in a new world slaughter" and "would mean the destruction of world civilization" (*Pravda*, March 13, 1954); also, that the "danger of war was to a great extent lessened," due to the sufficiency of various weapons capable of "checking the aggressors" (*Izvestiia*, March 12, 1954). Soon after Malenkov's ouster, the Party's main theoretical journal formally asserted: "No matter how severe the consequences of atomic war, they cannot be identified with the fall of world civilizations" (*Kommunist*, no. 4, [April 1955]: 16-17).

32. *Pravda*, April 26, 1963.

33. See Scott and Scott, *The Armed Forces of the USSR*, Ch. 4, "The Soviet High Command," for some descriptions of prominent military leaders in the post-Khrushchev period. Some, like Marshals Ogarkov and Zakharov, had been entrusted by the Party with vital and politically sensitive missions on SALT delegations and Soviet-Egyptian joint military and political missions. Note also their discussion of the Council of Defense, the Main Military Council, and the General Staff, which "are not constrained by a division of powers, such as exists among the American executive, legislative, and judicial branches of government. As a group, these bodies, especially the Council of Defense, *have virtually complete control over the military-economic direction of the Soviet Union.*" p. 97, emphasis added.

3

ECONOMIC FACTORS IN
SOVIET FOREIGN POLICY

John P. Hardt
Kate S. Tomlinson

A DECADE OF CRISIS

The 1980s will present the Soviet Union with economic challenges and opportunities in a degree unprecedented since the introduction of central planning in 1928. According to pessimistic U.S. intelligence estimates of energy and agricultural production and changes in the efficiency of labor and capital, the aggregate growth rate may be halved in the next decade to an average of little more than 2 percent or less in specific years, with negative growth potentially occurring in some years.[1] In contrast to what may be called the growth-reduction school, others in the West conclude that a continuation of a 4 percent growth rate is a reasonable expectation, on the basis of similar data and the Soviet plan figures for the Eleventh Five-Year Plan (1981-85).[2]

This decade of economic crisis will almost inevitably coincide with the Brezhnev succession. The immediate successor may well be Kirilenko but sooner or later a new generation of leaders will come into power. This new generation, which will start to move up during the 1980s, is likely to be different from the current leadership class. It is not only too young to have been involved

The views expressed herein are those of the authors, not necessarily those of the Congressional Research Service or the United States Congress. An earlier version of this paper was presented at a seminar at the Institute of Social Sciences, Seoul University, Seoul, Korea, in March 1980 and was published by the Institute as Special Issue I: *On Soviet Foreign Policy*. John P. Hardt prepared the original version of the paper, while Kate S. Tomlinson has made editorial and substantive contributions to the current version.

in the Bolshevik Revolution, but many of its members also lack personal knowledge of the Stalinist system and the Great Patriotic War. Thus, the 1980s may well be a decade of political change unprecedented since the Lenin succession of the 1920s. As in the past—most notably in the "industrialization debate" of the 1920s, but also during the Stalin and Khrushchev successions—economic issues will doubtless be debated. Debate on economic policy is especially likely to become intertwined with the leadership struggle, given the potential for economic crises. While the industrialization debate of the Lenin succession will naturally not be repeated, that succession is likely to prove to be the historical frame of reference for the 1980s. Greater change is possible in the leadership and in economic life than at any time since the late 1920s. The economic course that the Soviet leaders set in the 1980s is likely to be decisive for the nature of leadership in the Soviet Union and for Soviet foreign policy for several decades.

While a policy of muddling through,—that is, keeping economic policy as is—is an option for the Soviet leadership, it is liable to result in a significant slowdown in growth and shortfalls in key sectors. Nor would such a policy be likely to advance Soviet international security goals. Likely alternatives for change in economic policy that are available to the Soviet leaders fall into two divergent groups: policies that foster economic modernization and interdependence with the global economy, and neo-Stalinist policies of extreme centalization, tight control, and isolation from the non-Communist world. The modernization/interdependence and the control/security scenarios or tendencies can be described in terms of the differing policies they would entail for national economic development: the allocation of resources among "guns," "butter," and modernization; planning and management; economic relations with the industrialized West; and relations with the smaller members of the Council for Mutual Economic Assistance (CMEA). Of the two variants, the modernization and interdependence scenario is liable to yield the better economic results and is more likely to be chosen, if economic improvement is the first priority. If considerations of internal and external security are paramount, the control/security option is more likely to be adopted. While it would appear to advance the internal and external security goals of the Soviet leadership, it would probably not be as beneficial economically as the modernization/interdependence option.

These two scenarios have sharply divergent implications for Soviet policy on global outreach, Western Europe, Asia, and the United States. If the modernization/interdependence option is chosen, Soviet policy will be likely to emphasize international cooperation over competition. If the neo-Stalinist control/security option is selected, competition and confrontation with the capitalist countries are liable to be the focus of Soviet policy.

While one of these two tendencies is likely to dominate, some combination of the modernization/interdependence and control/security scenarios is, nonetheless, possible. One feasible combination is a policy of dividing the West and pursuing an economic *Westpolitik* with Western Europe and Japan, but pursuing a neo-Stalinist control/security policy with the United States and domestically in the Soviet Union. Although the two options or tendencies are not mutually exclusive, the component elements of each tend to be mutually reinforcing and to flow from similar policy stimuli.

Economic Retardation or Continued Growth

The winter of 1978-79 was particularly bad for the economy: agricultural production fell, construction slowed, rail transport was chaotic in some regions, and output in key energy, metals, and machine-building branches fell short of planned levels. This slowdown was thought by some to be a forerunner of a decade of slow or even no growth in the 1980s. Reductions in oil output, unfavorable weather for agriculture, increasing labor shortages, rising capital equipment and infrastructure costs all would contribute, it was argued, to lower economic performance in the 1980s. To be sure, all industrialized economies grow at slower rates as they mature. The rate of Soviet growth, by most comparative standards, has been impressive to date and might not be expected to continue. But the possible steep decline in economic growth in the 1980s—from around 4 to 1 or 2 percent a year on average—would be a significant negative change in a short time period. As demand exceeded the supply of new goods and services, while national income grew at an average of 4 percent annually, how would competing demands be satisfied with a 1 or 2 percent growth rate? Specifically, how would priorities be assigned among defense, investment, and consumption? Continued priority for defense, with a possible increase in the growth of allocations to the Soviet military—seemingly another premise of the growth-reduction school—would sharply restrict consumption and investment.[3] Completion of large modernization projects, new housing construction, and increased production of meat and consumer goods would have to be deferred. While one could argue that during the Brezhnev era (1964 to the present) the Soviet Union had guns, butter, and modernization, developments in the 1980s are likely to force a choice of one or two of these alternatives.

Alternatively, there are those who believe that a growth rate close to that of the past is possible, if the Soviet Union has some good fortune with weather and resource availability and if policies favoring modernization and improved economic performance are instituted. Modernization would, however, entail some politicoeconomic costs: a more flexible, efficient, but less politicized managerial system, greater emphasis on economic over security goals, increased and more efficient use of foreign economic ties, including those with East Europe, and a reduction in the role of the Party as an economic intervener at the local level. The last mentioned change might entail or require an increase in the economic role of the Party at the Central Committee level.

New Economic Era: Modernization and Interdependence

Soviet economic planning and management seem to be on the verge of a new stage characterized by an increasing emphasis on modernization, efforts to attain Western-style efficiency, and an openness to global interdependence. This new stage will not, however, derail the Soviet Union from the Leninist and Russian path. Central planning may be blended with market-stimulating mechanisms, but Western methods are not likely to be adopted without modification.[4] Because of its relative backwardness and obsolescence, Soviet plant and infrastructure must be replaced and structural change brought about, if the Soviet Union is to attain competitiveness with the modern Western economies. Soviet writings evidence a desire to benefit from the "economic miracles" of the West through increased interdependence. For instance, in a description of the future of Soviet relations with the capitalist countries, a group of noted Soviet economists discussed large-scale projects with Western companies based on compensation or buy-back arrangements, industrial cooperation, scientific-technical interchanges, and a closer relationship between the USSR and the capitalist world market system.[5]

This new stage in the Soviet Union may coincide with and be reinforced by qualitative changes in the world market economy. In the world economy there is now a need for interdependence to take advantage of advanced technology, cheaper raw materials, and other economies of the international division of labor.

Leadership Succession: Continuity or Change

Because of the age and ill health of Leonid Brezhnev and most of his close associates, wholesale changes in the top leadership may be expected in the 1980s. The new generation of leaders will not be direct products of either Lenin's revolution or Stalin's rule. Some of the new leaders may be more technical than political-professional ("expert" rather than "red"). Others may be reactionary or neo-Stalinist. Old party loyalties and the tradition of control by the Center may be further moderated by institutional and regional ties. Although Brezhnev's immediate successor may be Kirilenko, in not too many years a new generation of leaders will advance, not only to the Central Committee of the Party and in the government bureaucracy, but also to the "commanding heights" of Soviet power in the Politburo and the Council of Ministers.[6]

New International Political Environment:
Multipolarity and Postcolonialism

The United States and the Soviet Union have developed the custom of considering global events as resolvable through bilateral conflict and accommodation. The United States, indeed, still retains the habits and disposition of a globally dominant power and is emulated by the Soviet Union. The USSR and much of the Third and Fourth Worlds still act in the context of a colonial world dominated by the Western powers of the First World.

In strategic arms control discussions, the negotiations over Namibia, and a few other cases, the bipolar, colonial pattern of the past is still relevant. But in many other areas these old patterns are no longer dominant. The New International Economic Order (NIEO) is being formulated, though what full shape and alignments will be is not yet clear. The energy-rich OPEC nations have taken a position of global power and significance and newly industrial countries such as Korea, Taiwan, Singapore, and Brazil are becoming important in regional affairs. Within the Eastern and Western blocs change is continuing as well. The Eastern bloc, no longer a solid, Soviet-led entity, continues to evolve along an uncertain course, as the Polish "renewal" evidences. In the Western bloc, the Federal Republic of Germany and Japan are now global economic superpowers, rivaling the United States, and several of the West European countries are seeking a larger role in the formulation of Western policy.

These elements of international continuity and change are likely to influence the new Soviet economic environment of the 1980s. On issues such as the law of the seas, commodity trade, and the various aspects of the NIEO, the United States and the Soviet Union may find common great-power interest and purposes. While the East-West rivalry will continue, North-South differences may become greater than East-West Europe cleavages. Regardless of whether this occurs, the patterns of world politics are changing.

LEADERSHIP ALTERNATIVES

Modernization/Interdependence

If a new Soviet leadership considers economic performance along Western lines of efficiency to be a paramount goal, a policy of modernization and interdependence could significantly improve performances. Such a policy would include the components outlined below.

Regional Policy: A Nationwide Development Strategy [7]

Traditionally, Russia and the Soviet Union have developed along regional lines with self-sufficiency for each region as a primary goal. In the past, the vast distances involved and the dispersion of resources and population made regionalism a rational and workable Russian and Soviet strategy. Now, however, continued regionalism will tend to retard economic growth.

The very unequal distribution of natural resources, labor, and capital makes a unified national development strategy an economic necessity. The resource potential of Siberia in energy, metals, timber—indeed, all materials—is as yet only partially explored and largely untapped. The labor potential for Soviet economic expansion is largely in the eight republics of the Caucasus, Central Asia, and Kazakhstan. European Russia is deficient in both natural resources and labor, but has most of the Soviet economy's existing plant and infrastructure. With each major regional economy—European USSR, southern republics, Siberia—rich in capital, labor, or resources and critically deficient in the other two factors of production, regional integration is not only attractive but essential for economic progress. National electric-power transmission, oil and gas pipelines, and transport networks provide some of the necessary infrastructure but are not sufficient for the establishment of an integrated national economy.

Military Support Policy: Guns or Modernization[8]

With some exceptions, during the post-Stalin period a growing share of high-quality capital and labor resources has been allocated each year to military pursuits. The incremental burden on civilian machinery output of military procurement and the incremental impact on the civilian labor force of maintaining military manpower will be significantly greater in the 1980s than in previous years. A shift of labor and capital resources from military activities to economic modernization would help improve economic performance—the guns or modernization option.

The fact that potentially competitive programs have been approved in long-term modernization projects and long-term defense programs does not mean that important choices may not be made on the margin, as they have in previous cases.[9] For example, a decision to slow down or defer the expansion of agricultural equipment output was made in 1966, presumably to speed up the production of armored, tracked vehicles, which are often made in the same enterprises. Conversely, the priority of the Baikal-Amur railroad in Siberia appeared to be elevated in 1974 with a step-up in imports and use of military construction crews to facilitate progress on that so-called project of the century. In January 1970 and December 1977, West Siberian petroleum development was elevated to top priority. In the last two cases the development of Siberian resources and infrastructure was accorded top leadership priority. These crash efforts—characteristically referred to as "storming" by the Soviets—were probably made at the expense of deferred civilian and/or military projects. In a 1970 party and government decree according priority to West Siberian petroleum development, the Ministry of the Defense Industries—as well as the relevant civilian ministries—was instructed to support the project.[10]

Overcommitment of resources to meet the economic expansion targets of the Soviet economy is not a new phenomenon; tautness in planning or systematic overcommitment is traditional. More projects have always been authorized than could be funded and the operational priority was established by the choice among projects to be preferred or deferred. The new characteristic of the Brezhnev period appears to be a willingness to choose between civilian and military projects as well as among civilian projects, which may be described as the emergence of a marginal guns or modernization choice in Soviet resource allocation.

While defense allocations have grown more rapidly than national income since the beginning of the Brezhnev era in 1965, real per capita income has risen and a respectable growth of industrial output has been achieved. In effect, the Soviets have been able to have guns, butter, and modernization, but Soviet leaders may now have to choose. Continued modest consumption growth appears to be politically necessary. If defense spending continues to rise as in the past there will be shortfalls in civilian production and industrial manpower. An American econometric study has estimated that if defense spending continues to grow at a rate of 4.5 percent per annum, the share of the incremental output of the machine-building and metal-working industry (MBMW) devoted to military procurement will rise from 35 percent in the Eleventh Five-Year Plan to 54 percent during the Twelfth Five-Year Plan.[11] This sharp increase in the incremental burden of military procurement would stem from the expected slowdown in the rate of growth of the MBMW industry, which implies that stable procurement requirements would take an increasing share of total or marginal output. If increases in defense spending were stepped up beyond the current average rate of 4.5 percent per annum, the burden of defense procurement on the MBMW industry would be even greater. If military manpower is to be maintained at about 4.5 million men with continued educational deferments, the civilian labor force will fall in absolute numbers after 1983.[12] The manpower shortfall is the demographic "second echo" of World War II. These sharp increases in the incremental burden of defense procurement and military manpower may force a guns or modernization choice on the Soviet leadership in the 1980s.

The major large-scale modernization projects may be given alternating priority status. Indeed, it seems that a variety of large-scale projects fluctuate from low priority (deferral) to high-priority (storming). In the latter case, priority is given to the supply of hard-currency imports, domestic intermediate projects, and the attraction of skilled construction crews by such methods as wage differentials and worker housing. From a comparison of reported imports and domestic investment figures it appears that the size of these latter claims on high-quality Soviet domestic resources is two to three times the value of hard-currency imports for such projects as the Kama River Truck Plant.[13]

Consumer incentives are also important in the economy as a whole. The availability of adequate housing, reliable passenger cars, meat, and other quality foods provides important incentives for raising worker productivity and managerial efficiency. Incentives will gain in importance, as future increases in output will have to come primarily from increases in labor productivity rather than increases in the number of workers. In this sense guns or butter is also a choice.

Economic Reform in Planning and Management and
Introduction of New Programs and Methods

With better economic data, improved analysis, modern econometric tools, and appropriate use of computers, planning might become more efficient. With more authority for enterprise managers and improved incentives, managerial efficiency might be improved. How much improvement is possible with more efficient planning and management is hard to estimate, but it appears that it would be substantial.

The preconditions for modernization of the central planning process have developed over the last decade and a half: more and better statistical information has been generated; more rigorous economic analysis has been developed in many research institutions; mathematically oriented techniques of planning and accounting, such as linear programming and input-output tables for the nation and constituent republics for a series of years, have been developed; and a nation-wide computer system for economic reporting has been established.[14] These preconditions for improved central planning, however, have generally not been brought to bear on the central process of plan formulation. Were this operational step taken, some improvement in efficiency of central planning might be expected.

Innovative methods designed to improve the quality of output, raise labor productivity and capital efficiency, and accelerate technological change have been tested in a few cases and approved.[15] Examples of this kind of experimentation include the Lieberman reforms of 1962, which set new success indicators, most notably for several textile factories like Bol'shevichka, and the granting of more power to managers in the Shchekino scheme during 1966–68. They have not however, become the standard mode. In 1965 Kosygin identified the post-Khrushchev government with reform, but the principles of change in planning and management were not carried out in widespread practice. Large-scale adoption of a new planning and managerial system would be possible through the general application of programs and procedures already approved in principle. Local-level party organizations might oppose this kind of reform, as it would mean the reduction of their role in economic affairs, but increased party control and intervention at the Central Committee level might facilitate this new laissez faire policy at the local and regional levels.

Western Technology Transfer: Selective Economic Interdependence

Judicious imports of Western technology and the use of Western management techniques for utilizing the imported technology, coupled with high-quality plant and equipment from domestic sources, might accelerate technological change and improve economic performance. The gains from interdependence might not equal the economic miracles of the Western economies, but technology transfer is liable to have a growth-accelerating effect.

To use imports of Western technology more effectively, Soviet planners must revise traditional resource allocation policies and reform the institutional context in which the new complexes operate.[16] The large Western-assisted complexes place a heavy new demand on high-quality domestic inputs, such as technicians, materials, and machinery. As such inputs are now largely committed to traditional high-priority sectors of the economy, especially the defense industries, Soviet planners will have to make difficult choices if projects tied to Western trade are to receive adequate resources. Moreover, traditional Soviet enterprise management practices do little to assure effective utilization of foreign technology. More effective absorption of Western technology could be facilitated by significantly reforming enterprise management, especially by adopting Western management techniques. One approach might be the creation of foreign technology-related "enclaves" that operate outside the present bureaucratic chain of command. For example, the degree of independence and enhanced authority granted to the managers of the Volga Automobile Plant and the Kama River Truck Plant appears to be a limited step in this direction.[17] Although some Soviet officials will undoubtedly see such changes as threatening the traditional economic role of the Party and the bureaucracy, they may be a necessary condition for effective modernization.[18]

CMEA Policy: Modern Interdependence in East Europe[19]

In the short run, Eastern European requirements for energy and other goods that the USSR can export for hard or convertible currency are a drain on the Soviet economy. When the Soviet Union diverts energy and other material resources from domestic consumption or Western markets and supplies these commodities to East Europe at less than world market prices, it provides an economic subsidy. In the short term the subsidy tends to retard Soviet hard-currency trade and growth.

In the longer term, however, intra-CMEA relations may stimulate growth to the extent that the East European economies modernize and supply products and systems to the Soviet Union in a more absorbable or adaptable technological form. A positive Soviet balance of growth-stimulating benefit and growth-retarding cost in its economic relations with East Europe may provide a major boost to Soviet economic performance in the long run. In order for the Soviet Union to obtain the long-term benefit of intra-CMEA modernization and integration, however, a substantial burden of diverting hard goods to Eastern Europe may be necessary in the short term. In the longer term, more active technology transfer mechanisms with which Soviet officials are experimenting could facilitate more effective intra-CMEA technology transfers.

Control/Security: A Neo-Stalinist Variant[20]

A post-Brezhnev leadership may give priority not to domestic economic performance but to a revived control system justified by perceived foreign or domestic threats or opportunities.[21] A revival of the "encirclement mentality" of the Stalinist era may be fostered by a perceived PRC-Western military alliance, a militarily strong Federal Republic of Germany armed with nuclear weapons, a strong Islamic resurgence on the Soviet Union's southern border, or the spread of Poland's renewal to other countries in Eastern Europe. Such external threats, coupled with an increasingly dissident non-Russian population in the USSR, could further revive Slavic nationalism. Just as the modernization/interdependence scenario would include several policy elements, the control/security variant might have the following different set of possible components.

With a revival of a national siege mentality, rising non-Russian nationalist sentiment within the USSR might make the Russian-dominated Soviet Union seem embattled from within. The likelihood that the next census will find Great Russians in the minority might deepen the sentiment of internal endangerment among the largely Russian or Russified leadership. In this environment economic development policy might revert to the Stalinist tradition of extreme centralization and party domination of decision making and management. In that case, in Siberia, the Baltic republics, the Caucasus, Kazakhstan, and Central Asia control would remain firmly in the hands of Great Russians or those who had been accepted as Russified, but might have to be exercised more severely.[22] The development of the eight southern republics would be closely tied to the interests of the Center.

If the Soviet leadership's perception of the international arena as militarily dangerous deepens, it will probably feel compelled to approve additional military programs. Such a development might follow from a breakdown of the SALT process, an increase in the perceived threat posed by China—particularly if it began to purchase arms from the United States—NATO's decision to base Pershing missiles in Western Europe, a continuation or worsening of the unrest in the Islamic countries to the south, or a Soviet conclusion that the rail and road connections between Poland and the German Democratic Republic could no longer be relied upon. In this context, the development of the Baikal-Amur Railway would be given a more military orientation.

In a more controlled environment, labor availability might be ensured by a revival of the universal labor draft and Stalinist economic criminal code. Mobility between and among regions might be achieved by the revival and expansion of the economic role of the penal camp (GULAG) system. Centralized planning and control might be facilitated by more extensive use of computerized control systems.

With the perception of greater hostility at home and abroad, commercial relations would be restricted. In this case hard-currency exports of petroleum products and gold, the use of Western government and private credit, tourism, merchant marine interchanges, other balance-of-payments-related activities, and foreign managerial involvement in the USSR would be restricted. Reduced exports of goods and services and an unwillingness to obtain credits from the West would sharply reduce Soviet imports from the West. Moreover, the large civilian projects in Siberia would have less domestic priority and the need for imported foreign systems would be reduced.

The attraction of centrifugal forces drawing the smaller East European nations toward closer relations with the West would be more than balanced by the centripetal forces drawing them closer to Moscow. Emphasis, in turn, would revert to control mechanisms rather than consumer incentives and modernization. Political instability—even violence—might result, as in the Berlin riots of 1953, the Hungarian uprising in 1956, and the Polish Baltic port upheavals in 1970. The Warsaw Pact clearly has adequate forces to contain East European instability, if the cost of using military force within the Eastern bloc is deemed acceptable. The West would respond to Eastern trade, travel, and investment restrictions with renewed restrictions of its own.

FOREIGN POLICY IMPLICATIONS
OF ALTERNATIVE ECONOMIC SCENARIOS

It is assumed here that the Soviet leadership's perception of security needs has primacy over all other considerations. If security threats and opportunities appear to be limited, domestic economic considerations may dominate in the 1980s, especially as they intertwine with a leadership succession struggle. The consequences for foreign policy of the modernization and the revived control alternatives are quite different. Modernization at home is likely to foster interdependence and cooperation, while revived control in the USSR would tend to encourage international confrontation and ideological orthodoxy.[23]

The security threats and opportunities perceived may be related to the Soviet state, the Party, or the top leader(s). While developments that threaten to unleash impermissible changes in the Party, such as those tested in the Polish renewal, or threats to the tenure in office of Brezhnev and his successors are relevant, it is the first case—threats to or opportunities for the Soviet state—that is of primary importance for this formulation. Concerns about the international security of the Soviet state may lead to increased priority and even storming for defense projects. In the absence of overriding international security concerns modernization projects may take priority and benefit from storming efforts. In the first case the all-out development of a new strategic system—a new Soviet ICBM—might be the overriding priority. In the second, a storming effort to complete a resource project such as the natural gas pipeline to West Europe could become the chief goal.

One may hypothesize that the factors triggering increases in the priority of defense that might lead to storming are largely international, whereas the factors elevating the place of modernization are largely domestic. For example, factors that would increase the priority of defense efforts might be new concern or opportunity along the Chinese border or with respect to other Asian countries; new concern or opportunity arising from development or shelving of the new, technologically advanced American strategic programs; or new concern about or opportunity with respect to Europe, especially Germany. Deployment of new nuclear weapons systems in this area would be of special concern. Factors that would increase the priority of modernization might include serious macroeconomic crises such as a sharp slowdown in growth or a shortage of labor; shortages of critical goods and services like hydrocarbons, steel, grain, or transport; natural disasters such as crop failures; and dramatic shifts in export prices for domestic output, balance-of-payment opportunities such as increased oil prices, or international payment crises such as nonpayment of debts by East European nations.

If neither a clear threat nor a vital international security opportunity exists, domestic modernization may be assigned priority or dominate resource allocation decisions. Thus, if Soviet leaders are assured that military parity is stable, that their borders are secure, and that opportunities for projecting Soviet military power are limited, they may be less likely to approve storming on defense projects. If, however, the perceived threat or opportunity is persuasive, they may then give defense buildup high priority. The lesson of the Cuban missile crisis is presumably that it demonstrated to the Soviet leaders the USSR's unfavorable strategic position, causing them to launch the strategic buildup of the 1960s and 1970s. As for the future, if the West Germans were to gain access to nuclear weapons and a leadership position in NATO or if the United States were to arm China or conclude a formal security alliance with it, the Soviets would clearly assign a high priority to military projects. The probability of these particular events aside, what is important is the Soviet leadership's perception of the threats and opportunities presented by developments in the international arena. Any power vacuums in strategic areas, such as the Middle East or Africa, would present attractive foreign opportunities and might, therefore, enhance military priorities. It appears probable that the pressures for modernization and interdependence arising from economic problems will mount in the 1980s, but that security threats or opportunities that the leadership perceives as significant could override them.

If, however, the reverse were true—no new security concerns or opportunities—the urgent needs of economic modernization might lead to a high priority for one or more of the major civilian projects. This might not amount to an economic transformation, but it could suffice to arrest the downward trend in economic performance.

International factors can clearly increase the priority of Soviet defense efforts, but their ability to decrease it seems weak. For example, a Soviet perception of an increasing threat from NATO or China is liable to lead directly to an increase in allocations for the Soviet military, while a perception that the threat posed by these countries is decreasing is not likely to lead to a decrease in military allocations. Likewise, the Soviet leadership would view U.S. arms sales to China as increasing the China threat and as a reason for increasing troop strength on the Chinese border, but the absence of such sales would have little influence on Soviet military deployments. Pressures to stretch out military projects and increase the priority of modernization are more likely to come from domestic forces than international developments that the Soviets perceive as favorable to them.

The modernization/interdependence and control/security scenarios or tendencies may not be mutually exclusive. If the European members of NATO and/or Japan were to differ sharply with the United States on economic policy toward the East, the Soviet leaders might perceive an exploitable security opportunity in Europe or Asia. In that case they might choose to build up defense capabilities, while pursuing a policy of active economic cooperation with selected Western nations. Such an economic *Westpolitik* might be security dominated, but include important elements of a modernization/interdependence strategy.

Thus, there is a wide range of strategies between the poles of modernization/interdependence and control/security. Their implications for Soviet global outreach and for Soviet relations with the United States, Western Europe, and Asia will be examined, presenting first in each case the foreign policy implications of the modernization/interdependence scenario.[24]

Soviet Global Outreach

- Membership in international economic organizations such as the GATT, World Bank, and the International Monetary Fund
- Encouraging East European membership in these organizations
- Contributing to the stability of the international economy by policies designed to foster economic growth and dampen inflation

or

- Reversion to a two camp, anti-imperialist, ideological approach designed to control the West's access to materials and to foster unrest and anti-Western sentiment
- Attempts to reap the benefits of disruptions in the evolving process of international change

If domestic modernization were given priority, the USSR might adopt policies more in line with those of the industrial nations of the North and expand East-West economic cooperation. On North and South issues such as terms of trade, commodity agreements, and the law of the sea, the Soviet Union might act as a Northern power or assist in developing consensus between North and South. In international-political terms the Soviet Union might join in efforts to preserve political stability and to foster peaceful change. It might even adhere to some mutually acceptable codes of international conduct. As an economic moderate and participant in the world community of nations and the world economy, the Soviet Union might permit or encourage its Communist allies in East Europe and Asia to join the community of nations and international economic organizations.

If, however, the Stalinist control system were revived, the Soviet Union would very likely turn toward an anti-imperialist, adversarial policy. Lenin's classic, *Imperialism, the Highest Stage of Capitalism*, would provide the underpinnings for a policy of continued strife between the Socialist and capitalist camps. The Soviets would view conflict among the Western capitalist nations as inevitable and would probably try to exacerbate it. A policy of political and economic denial of Western access to developing countries might be focused on energy and strategic minerals—a form of resource war.

East European and client states, such as Vietnam and Cuba, would be encouraged to continue to exacerbate unrest and foster violent change, acting as surrogate military and political forces in regions beyond the effective reach of Soviet power.

European Interactions

- Increased economic interrelations
- "Humanization" of borders and social interchange
- Moderation of military confrontation
- Tolerance of closer ties between Eastern and Western Europe and of East European experimentation in economic policy

or

- Heightening of tensions and potential for political or military confrontation
- An increase in efforts to divide the West
- Return to greater control and orthodoxy in East Europe, insulating the region from interchange with the West

If the modernization/interdependence alternative were chosen, the Soviets' strategy towards Western Europe might conform more closely to the letter and the spirit of the Helsinki Final Act in such areas as arms limitation, commercial relations, and political and social interactions desired by the peoples of Europe. The increased flow of goods, services, and people might reinforce a policy aimed at reducing military buildups and international tensions. With improved Soviet-American relations, Soviet commercial relations and cooperative activity with Western Europe would be likely to increase. Even if Soviet-American relations deteriorated, Soviet-European cooperation in energy, automotive, and other areas would be likely to continue, albeit more modestly than if Soviet-American relations improved.

If the Stalinist control/security system were reinstituted, the Soviet Union would isolate itself and its East European allies from the global economy, North America, West Europe, and Japan. Alternatively, selective development of trade, credit, and technology flows could be used to divide the West and make West European countries susceptible to threats of withholding critical energy and strategic materials. This could be seen as a form of Finlandization.[25]

Asian Relations

- Greater involvement of Asian countries in Siberian development
- Increased interchange with developed and new industrial economies
- Reduction of tensions and military buildup

or

- Enhanced efforts to become the preeminent political-military power in the Pacific region
- Redoubled efforts to isolate the PRC by developing encircling alliances, a Soviet version of containment
- A sharpened division between Communist and non-Communist countries

Normalization in Asia would have a significant effect on Soviet commercial relations with the Asian Pacific countries. Closer economic, social, and political relations with Japan and other Pacific-rim nations might make the Soviet Pacific area a part of the world's most dynamic economic region, which is developing into an economically integrated community.[26] Some economic and political rapprochement with the People's Republic of China might be sought and obtained, further facilitating Soviet participation in a developing Pacific community.

A revival of Great Russian nationalism, withdrawal from the world economy, and enhancement of the control mechanism of the Stalinist era would not stimulate Soviet participation in the emergent Pacific community. In this case the Soviet Union would probably adopt a more contentious policy toward Japan and the other Asian capitalist countries. Such a divisive policy based on political and military imperatives, as seen by the Kremlin, would tend to offset economic factors that would bring about a united Pacific community. The Soviet military buildup in Kamchatka, the Kuriles, and throughout the Soviet Maritime Provinces would probably continue and further retard Asian normalization and Soviet Siberian modernization. The Soviets would no doubt adopt a policy of containing and isolating China. The encirclement of China would be achieved through a militarily aggressive Vietnam in Southeast Asia, a Soviet-controlled

Afghanistan in Southwest Asia, and a revived Soviet-North Korean relationship in Northeast Asia.

Relations with the United States

- Revival of arms control measures
- Normalization of economic, political, and other relations
- Lessening of tensions

or

- Increased emphasis on military buildup
- Greater use of political-military power
- Increased competition on all fronts and heightened tensions

Progress in arms negotiations and normalization of commercial relations are likely to affect Soviet economic performance. American comparative advantage would suggest cooperation in agricultural, energy, and automotive technology. A Soviet modernization policy emphasizing interdependence, increased trade turnover, industrial cooperation, and technology transfer could be of singular importance to the Soviet Union. In such areas as agriculture and energy, large, long-term projects using American technology and management expertise and the possibility of large, long-term credit facilities could provide substantial benefits. Significantly higher levels of production could be attained if U.S. agriculture or energy projects on- and offshore could be replicated in the USSR. Selective economic relations with the United States, including normalized trade but without large-scale, long-term cooperation, would be marginally beneficial to the USSR.

As most of the industrial technology needed by the USSR can be obtained from Western Europe and Japan on favorable credit terms and often in exchange for energy and raw materials, a U.S. policy of restricting industrial exports would not be very damaging to Soviet interests.[27] The United States does, however, have some leverage on agricultural exports, especially in poor crop years in the Soviet Union. If the United States and its Western allies were not able to arrive at a common policy on commercial or political issues in East-West relations, the Soviet Union might receive considerable economic benefits and political-security opportunities from a divided Western policy.

CHOICES FOR BREZHNEV'S SUCCESSORS: A NEW INDUSTRIALIZATION DEBATE?

In assessing Soviet choices between defense and modernization in the short and long terms (through 1990), the nature of Brezhnev's leadership and the implications of succession are important factors. The Brezhnev era has been characterized by consensus and status quo policies. Soviet acceptance of both qualified global economic interdependence and military buildups ought to be assessed against this past resistance to change and penchant for compromise. Brezhnev's immediate successor is liable to be from his generation, but power will eventually pass to a new generation of leaders.

If the Soviets choose to stay on their current course of military development, they must defer or forego the option of joining the Western industrial nations as an economic superpower. But if economic interdependence and economic modernization were to become not only a priority aim but an operational program of the Soviet leaders, their country might in time join the Western industrial nations as an economic superpower. This choice would require a budgetary emphasis upon, and increased priority for, economic modernization rather than military spending. It would also require expanding imports of Western technology, which could affect both the economic and the political systems in the Soviet Union. This, in turn, would require a pattern of accelerating or storming modernization projects and delaying or deferring competitive military programs. This presumably might occur, especially in a succession period, if neither a threat nor an opportunity for effective use of additional military power were evident.

If present trends continue with little change in economic policy or in the stability of the leadership, economic slowdown seems very likely, even inevitable, especially if the natural uncertainties of weather and resource availability turn out badly. In this case, annual growth rates would hover around 2 percent— roughly half that of the recent five-year plan.[28] Under these circumstances the least effective policy for Soviet leaders would be one of equivocation or muddling through. Continuation of current policies would be especially costly in a period in which demands on resources were increasing while economic performance was deteriorating. At the same time, the likely benefits of policy change might appear greater. Even an equivocating, conservative leadership would probably view such an outcome as an unacceptable crisis requiring action. The Brezhnev era tendency to compromise, equivocate, and seek conservative solutions might be overcome, but watershed policy changes in the direction of modernization seem unlikely for Brezhnev's immediate successors. Important incremental changes, influencing resource allocation and the economic management system, are quite possible, however—perhaps likely. Changes in these policy components might well serve as the beachhead for or induce further changes in economic policy, since its components are mutually reinforcing.

If the likely deterioration in economic performance occurs or persists during the period between the elevation of one of Brezhnev's current colleagues on the Politburo and the coming to power of the new generation, it may well have a significant impact on economic policy. In this environment leadership factions vying for power could advocate economic reform or nonequivocal economic solutions in order to advance their political ambitions.

It seems likely that economic issues will be intertwined with the political succession struggle, as in previous succession crises. A major debate on economic policy similar to the industrialization debate, if it occurs, may find its forum in the Central Committee of the Party, in which all the important regional, institutional, governmental interests are represented. Just as names of the successors to Lenin, Stalin, and Khrushchev were difficult to foretell, precise identification of the eventual successors to Brezhnev and other top leaders will have to await the unfolding of events. In this new industrialization debate the new generation of leaders may see and wish to act on a widening gap between perceived economic needs and actual performance. The emerging post-Brezhnev generation may be able to overcome the institutional stagnation and traditionalism of the Brezhnev generation, which is still partly rooted in the Stalinist system, and the habitual attraction to Stalinist control in solving difficult problems. This kind of fundamental change in the objectives, priorities, institutions, and cadre of the Soviet leadership may not prove possible, yet recent economic developments in Hungary, Poland, and the People's Republic of China illustrate the possibility of major change without abandonment of the system.

NOTES

1. Primary sources for this chapter include the two-volume compendium of the Joint Economic Committee of the U.S. Congress, *Soviet Economy in a Time of Change,* vols. 1 and 2 (Washington, D.C.: U.S. Government Printing Office, 1979); Holland Hunter, ed., *Future of the Soviet Economy* (Boulder, Col.: Westview Press, 1979); and Seweryn Bialer, ed., *The Domestic Context of Soviet Foreign Policy,* (Boulder, Col.: Westview Press, 1981). Earlier papers presented by John Hardt at NATO-SHAPE and the U.S. Military Academy are liberally drawn on. See, for example, John P. Hardt, "Soviet Economic Capability and Defense Resources," in *The Soviet Threat: Myths and Realities,* ed. Grayson Kirk and Nils H. Wessell (New York: Academy of Political Science, 1978); "Military and Economic Superpower: A Soviet Choice," in *Integrating National Security and Trade Policy,* Final Report of the Senior Conference of the U.S. Military Academy (West Point, N.Y., June 1978); and "The Military-Economic Implications of Soviet Regional Policies," in *Regional Development in the USSR, Trends and Prospects,* NATO Colloquium held in Brussels, April 25-27, 1979 (Newtonville, Mass: Oriental Research Partners, 1979).

2. "Statement of Adm. Stansfield Turner, Director of Central Intelligence," in U.S. Congress, Joint Economic Committee, Subcommittee on Priorities and Economy in Government, *Allocation of Resources in the Soviet Union and China—1979 (Part 5),* Hearings, 96th Cong., 2d sess., June 26 and July 9, 1979, (Washington, D.C.: U.S. Government Printing Office, 1980), pp. 2-3; and Daniel L. Bond and Herbert S. Levine, "The 11th Five-Year Plan, 1981-1985," paper prepared for the RAND Corporation and Columbia University Conference on the 26th Congress of the CPSU, held April 23-25 in Washington, mimeo, pp. 22-24. Cf. Donald W. Green, "The Soviet Union and the World Economy in the 1980s: A Review of the Alternatives," in *Future of the Soviet Economy,* ed. Hunter, pp. 46-48; Abram Bergson, "Soviet Economic Slowdown and the 1981-85 Plan," *Problems of Communism* 30 (May-June 1981): 24-36; Philip Hanson, "Economic Constraints on Soviet Policies in the 1980s, *International Affairs* (London) 57, no. 1 (Winter 1980-81): 21-42.

3. "Statement of Adm. Turner," pp. 14-15.

4. John P. Hardt, "Stages in Soviet Economic Development: A Sixty Year Record," in *Economic Issues of the Eighties*, ed. Nake M. Kamrany and Richard H. Day (Baltimore, Md.: Johns Hopkins University Press, 1979), pp. 202, 220-22.

5. A. I. Bel'chuk, ed., *Novyi etap ekonomicheskogo sotrudnichestva SSSR v razvitymi kapitalisticheckimi stranami (New Stage of Economic Cooperation of the USSR with the Developed Capitalist Countries)* (Moscow: Nauka, 1978), passim. Several collected works of prominent Soviet economic authors refer to a new stage of economic relations and prescribe new political tactics for dealing with the developed capitalist nations.

6. Jerry F. Hough, "The Generation Gap and the Brezhnev Succession," *Problems of Communism* 27 (July-August, 1979): 3-12.

7. Hardt, "Military-Economic Implications of Soviet Regional Policy," pp. 237-38. See also Martin C. Spechler, "Regional Developments in the USSR 1958-78," Theodore Shabad, "The BAM, Project of the Century," Holland Hunter, "Soviet Economic Problems and Alternative Policy Responses," and Paul K. Cook, "The Political Setting," in *Soviet Economy in a Time of Change*, vol. 1.

8. John P. Hardt, "Strategic Alternatives in Soviet Resource Allocation Policy," in U.S., Congress, Joint Economic Committee, *Dimensions of Soviet Economic Power* (Washington, D.C.: U.S. Government Printing Office, 1962), p. 19.

9. For examples, see John R. Thomas, "Political-Strategic Factors in Soviet Modernization: Continuity and Change," Henry Schaefer, "Soviet Power and Intentions: Military-Economic Choices," and Abraham Becker, "The Meaning and Measure of Soviet Military Expenditure," in *Soviet Economy in a Time of Change*, vol. 1.

10. *Pravda*, January 15, 1970.

11. Bond and Levine, "The 11th Five-Year Plan," pp. 26-28.

12. Murray Feshbach and Stephen Rapawy, "Soviet Population and Manpower Trends and Policies," in U.S. Congress, Joint Economic Committee, *Soviet Economy in a New Perspective* (Washington, D.C.: U.S. Government Printing Office, 1976), p. 150.

13. George D. Holliday, "The Role of Western Technology in the Soviet Economy," in U.S., Congress, Joint Economic Committee, *Issues in East-West Commercial Relations* (Washington, D.C.: U.S. Government Printing Office, 1979), pp. 56-58; and Imogene U. Edwards, "Automotive Trends in the USSR," in U.S., Congress, Joint Economic Committee, *Soviet Economic Prospects for the Seventies* (Washington, D.C.: U.S. Government Printing Office, 1973), p. 296.

14. For background on these methods see John P. Hardt et al., eds., *Mathematics and Computers in Soviet Economic Planning* (New Haven, Conn.: Yale University Press, 1967); and Vladimir G. Treml and John P. Hardt, eds., *Soviet Economic Statistics* (Durham, N.C.: Duke University Press, 1972).

15. For an excellent overview and assessment of recent Soviet economic reforms, see Gertrude E. Schroeder-Greenslade, "Soviet Economy on a Treadmill of 'Reforms'," in *Soviet Economy in a Time of Change*, vol. 1 especially pp. 331-40. For a recent book on reform in the Brezhnev era, see Thane Gustafson, *Reform in Soviet Politics: Lessons of Recent Policies on Land and Water* (New York: Cambridge University Press, 1981).

16. For several useful articles on technology transfer, see Lawrence Brainard, "Foreign Economic Constraints on Soviet Economic Policy in the 1980's," in *Soviet Economy in a Time of Change*, vol. 1; Philip Hanson and Malcolm Hill, "Soviet Assimilation of Western Technology: A Survey of UK Exporters' Experience," and Francis W. Rushing and Catherine P. Ailes, "An Assessment of the USSR-US Scientific and Technical Exchange," in *Soviet Economy in a Time of Change*, vol. 2.

17. John P. Hardt and George D. Holliday, "Technology Transfer and Change in the Soviet System," in *Technology and Communist Culture: The Socio-Cultural Impact of*

Technology under Socialism, ed. Frederic J. Fleron, Jr. (New York: Praeger, 1977), pp. 217-18.

18. John P. Hardt, "Soviet Commercial Relations and Political Change," in *The Inter-action of Economics and Foreign Policy*, ed. Robert A. Bauer (Charlottesville: University Press of Virginia, 1975), p. 73. Reprinted in *Issues in East-West Commercial Relations*; see pages 89-90.

19. For an excellent collection of essays on intra-CMEA trade and integration, see Paul Marer and John Michael Montias, eds., *East European Integration and East-West Trade* (Bloomington: Indiana University Press, 1980). For a view of CMEA integration by a Hungarian CMEA staff economist, see Kalman Pecsi, *The Future of Socialist Economic Integration* (Armonk, N.Y.: M. E. Sharpe, 1981); also published as Vol. 19, no. 2-3 of *East European Economics*. For several recent articles on Soviet-East European trade, see Martin J. Kohn, "Soviet-East European Economic Relations, 1975-78," Raimund Dietz, "Price Changes in Soviet Trade with CMEA and the Rest of the World Since 1975," and Morris Bornstein, "East-West Economic Relations and Soviet-East European Economic Relations," in *Soviet Economy in a Time of Change*, vol. 1.

20. A discussion with Hans Heymann, Jr. about the earlier version of this chapter presented in Seoul led the authors to emphasize the element of control in this set of policy variants.

21. For an authoritative restatement of the Leninist views on imperialism and the struggle between capitalism and socialism, which were stressed during the Stalinist era, see O. T. Bogomolov et al., *Mirovoi revoliutsionnyi protsess i sovremennost' (The World Revolutionary Process and the Contemporary Era)* (Moscow: Nauka, 1980). Bogomolov is the director of economics of the World Socialist System Institute. The main editor of the book was N. N. Inozemtsev, who is the head of the Institute of World Economics and International Relations.

22. Cf. U.S. International Communication Agency, Office of Research, "Conference on Russian Nationalism in the USSR: Summary Report," *Research Memorandum* M-7/16/81, especially pp. 9-11. For related articles, see James Gillula, "The Economic Interdependence of Soviet Republics," Stephen Repawy, "Regional Employment Trends in the USSR, 1950 to 1975," and Murray Feshbach, "Prospects for Outmigration from Central Asia and Kazakhstan in the Next Decade," in *Soviet Economy in a Time of Change*, vol. 1.

23. For a number of views, including Hardt's, on the linkages between economic and political factors, see Robert A. Bauer, ed., *The Interaction of Economics and Foreign Policy*.

24. For an overview of Soviet policy toward the Third World after Afghanistan, see U.S. Library of Congress, Congressional Research Service, *Soviet Policy and United States Response*. A Report Prepared for the Committee on Foreign Affairs, U.S. House of Representatives, 97th Cong., 1st sess., (Washington, D.C.: U.S. Government Printing Office, 1981), especially Ch. 2. For a discussion of Soviet-East European economic relations, see Marer and Montias, *East European Integration*.

25. For a discussion of Soviet-West European relations that focuses on the question of Finlandization, see George Ginsburgs and Alvin Z. Rubinstein, ed., *Soviet Foreign Policy Toward Western Europe* (New York: Praeger, 1978).

26. For a recent report on the emergent community on the Pacific rim, see U.S. Congress, Joint Economic Committee, *Pacific Region Interdependencies*, 97th Cong., 1st sess., (Washington, D.C.: U.S. Government Printing Office, 1981), especially pp. 1-10. For a view of East Siberian development and the role in it of some of the countries of the Pacific rim, see Allen S. Whiting, *Siberian Development and East Asia: Threat or Promise?* (Stanford, Cal.: Stanford University Press, 1981). For a useful discussion of how economic factors influence foreign policy in one of the countries of the region, see Young C. Kim, "The

Interaction of Economics and Japanese Foreign Policy," in *The Interaction of Economics and Foreign Policy*, ed. Robert A. Bauer.

27. For a discussion of the impact of U.S. and Western denial of technology to the Soviet Union, see U.S. Library of Congress, Congressional Research Service, Office of Senior Specialists, *An Assessment of the Afghanistan Sanctions: Implications for Trade and Diplomacy in the 1980s*, A Report Prepared for the Subcommittee on Europe and the Middle East of the Committee on Foreign Affairs, U.S. House of Representatives, 97th Cong., 1st sess., (Washington, D.C.: U.S. Government Printing Office, 1981), especially pp. 7, 73-78.

28. U.S. Central Intelligence Agency, National Foreign Assessment Center, *Simulations of Soviet Growth Options to 1985*, Washington, D.C., ER 79-10131, March 1979, p. 22.

4

THE NATIONALITY FACTOR IN SOVIET FOREIGN POLICY

Rasma Karklins

Studies of Soviet foreign policy motivation and behavior usually pay no attention to the nationality factor, or do so only in passing.[1] This is due, in part, to the past neglect accorded to all domestic sources of Soviet foreign policy making, a neglect that has been remedied only in recent years, and in part, to a widespread insensitivity to the role of ethnicity in domestic and international politics. It is paradoxical that the Soviet Union, which purportedly adheres to an internationalist ideology and practice, has been especially aware of the political implications of ethnicity in general and national movements in particular. The Soviet tendency always to take account of this factor in its policy making has various sources, but the most basic relates to the composition of its population and territory. In spite of a prevailing tendency of Westerners to speak of "Russia" when referring to the Soviet Union, it is both a multinational and a federal state and these characteristics have major consequences, not only for its domestic politics but for international relations as well.

The impact of the nationality factor on Soviet international relations is evident in fundamental geopolitical considerations and in numerous specific foreign policy interactions to be elaborated upon below, but it also has a less tangible side relating to the sphere of political imagery. Soviet propaganda has consistently tried to convey the image of complete harmony among the peoples of the USSR in order to hold it up as a shining model for other multinational entities, as well as for relations among states all over the world. The international significance of their nationality policy has frequently been pointed out by Soviet commentators and is one of the reasons they react very sensitively to criticisms of this policy.[2] In reality the Soviet model of nationality relations is highly ambiguous, and awareness about its problematic side can easily undermine the international image of the USSR. Thus, the nationality factor can constitute both an asset and a liability to Soviet foreign policy making, as the following analysis will point out again and again.

Turning first to the two "given" factors that constitute the source of the impact of nationality on Soviet politics—composition of population and territory—it is important to be aware that the Russians make up only a little over half of the population of the USSR. According to the census held in 1979, Russians constituted 52 percent of the total Soviet population, the others being non-Russians of varying ethnic, religious, and cultural backgrounds.[3] In large part, the non-Russians form historical nations inhabiting their traditional homelands. The contemporary multinationalism of the Soviet Union, in fact, reflects the colonial expansion of Russia into geographically contiguous regions during the past few centuries, and as a result, the 14 non-Russian republics of the USSR— each of which is named after the respective indigenous nation—form a belt around Russia proper. This borderland status of the main Soviet nationalities has various strategic and geopolitical implications, one of the main ones being that nearly all territorial changes affecting the USSR are linked to nationality. It should be noted that this holds true for the past as well as for the present and the future. Thus the treaty of Brest-Litovsk, which was such a shock to Russians of varying political outlook, foresaw the loss of territories that were in the main inhabited by non-Russians, and the addition of territories to the USSR has on its part usually involved predominantly non-Russian populations.[4]

The other major geopolitical consequence of non-Russians inhabiting borderland areas is that there is always a potential for the development of autonomous or separatist movements, especially in crisis situations and in the event of war. There can be little doubt that the Soviet leaders are very aware of it. This awareness was first generated by experiences during World War I and the overthrow of Czarism, and then during the drawn-out formation of the Soviet Union, which reached its consolidation stage only in 1923. The disaffection of the minority nations of the Czarist empire was a crucial factor in its demise, and although the Bolsheviks did much to promote this disaffection in order to use it as a revolutionary tool, they soon discovered that borderland nationalism was directed not only against the Czarist empire but against any union with Russia. After 1917 just about all the non-Russian nations established independent governments and states, and the Bolsheviks encountered significant opposition in their subsequent reconquest by political and military means.[5] The Baltic nations were successful in keeping their independent statehood until 1940, when they were forcibly annexed in the context of the Hitler-Stalin Pact. The historical memories of independent statehood and a resulting consciousness of alternatives to the status quo are especially strong in their case, but are present among other Soviet nations as well. As has been convincingly argued by Andrei Amalrik, a reactivization of separatist tendencies is most likely in the context of war,[6] which implies that in this sense the nationalities are a cautionary influence on Soviet foreign policy making.

The cautious and defensive impulse of the USSR in regard to its border-lands is not only due to the fact that these areas are inhabited by non-Russian peoples with autonomous aspirations, but is also related to irredentist claims by neighboring states. Besides Chinese claims to parts of Soviet Central Asia, Soviet territorial annexations during World War II—from Finland, Poland, Czechoslovakia, and Romania—constitute a latent source of tension. As the example of both China and Romania has demonstrated, there exists a correlation between the revival of irredentist demands against the Soviet Union[7] and the development of an independent foreign policy course, which suggests one of the reasons the USSR has been eager to contain such tendencies.

The dual side of the nationality factor in Soviet foreign policy, however, can be noted in this case just as in others. Thus, the territorial status of the major non-Russian nations is not only a source of latent defensiveness in Soviet international behavior, but has also formed the basis of active policy ventures, such as the involvement of union republics in the United Nations (and other international organizations) and the utilization of local irredentism as a justification for territorial expansion. Stalin was especially adept in making such beneficial use of the non-Russian nations and republics of the USSR. He recognized that the national interests of the individual subunits of his empire enjoyed a credible legitimacy abroad and repeatedly capitalized on it by using them to defend sensitive foreign policy moves. Thus, several territorial acquisitions were made or attempted under the pretext that the territories in question represented the irredenta of a national republic or that "ethnic brethren" needed help. When the Soviets annexed eastern Poland in 1939 with the collusion of Hitler Germany, Molotov tried to justify it in the name of the Ukraine and Belorussia, which had "a sacred duty to extend the hand of assistance to its brother Ukrainians and Belorussians inhabiting Poland."[8] Similar ethnic claims were advanced one year later when Bessarabia and Northern Bukovina were annexed from Romania. In this case the national justification was especially opportunistic, since the territories taken were not made part of the Ukrainian SSR, but of a newly created Moldavian SSR.

As is well known, the fate of eastern Poland emerged as one of the primary issues in the negotiations between the USSR and the Western Allies at the end of World War II. It should be noted in the present context, however, that in these prolonged and very difficult negotiations Stalin consistently exaggerated the independent position of the Ukraine and the impact of an undefined Ukrainian lobby in order to enhance his diplomatic leverage. He was quite successful; and he was equally successful in pushing through the annexation of the Carpatho-Ukraine from Czechoslovakia in 1945 as another Ukrainian irredenta.[9]

Similar but less successful attempts were made in the context of Soviet designs on Turkish and Iranian territories. In 1945 the USSR abrogated its treaty of friendship and neutrality with Turkey and issued—in the name of Armenian and Georgian irredentism—demands for a cession of Kars and Ardahan. This claim was unsuccessful, but was formally retracted only in 1953, after the death of Stalin. Efforts to gain a foothold in northern Iran by sponsoring Azerbaidzhani and Kurdish quests for territorial autonomy in 1945 were frustrated within months by a strong Western stand. In this instance the Soviets had not raised the issue of irredenta, but had played on local Azerbaidzhani and Kurdish attempts to gain autonomy.[10]

In the cases mentioned, especially those of the Ukraine and Armenia, the territorial demands made by the Soviet government without doubt did coincide with the national aspirations of the respective nations. It should be emphasized, however, that Stalin utilized these interests for the general aims of the USSR, and there was little input from the nationalities themselves. Recognizing that any real involvement in these policies could easily develop its own momentum, he tried to use the representatives of the nationalities only as instruments in policy execution without allowing them to become active participants in policy formulation. Nevertheless, experience has shown that once the Soviet leadership has legitimized a national aspiration by supporting it at one time, it is difficult to avoid unwelcome consequences after the policies are changed, and this poses a serious policy dilemma for the Soviet leadership. Thus, even though Moscow has reversed its policies toward Turkey, Armenian irredentist claims for their historical homeland in Turkey persist and the lack of official support by the central government has been a source of Armenian alienation.[11]

Soviet federalism has not only formed the basis for active foreign policy ventures in regard to neighboring territories or national groups but has also been utilized in the enhancement of Soviet international contacts and representation. Among these initiatives, the most important has been the involvement of union republics in the United Nations and other international organizations.

In the course of negotiations about the forming of the United Nations, the USSR proposed in 1944 that each of its constituent republics (at that time 16) be given a seat. When this proposal was rejected by the Western allies, the number of requested seats was scaled down, first to three additional seats, and then to two. This latter proposal was accepted and as a result two union republics, the Ukraine and Belorussia, have been represented in the United Nations since its creation, alongside the USSR. This has been a certain asset to Soviet foreign policy making, not only in providing additional seats but also by enhancing its diplomatic flexibility. Thus, the Ukraine has been especially active in the United Nations in trying to create the image of a true champion of anticolonialism and national self-determination. This pursuit has aimed not only at discrediting any remnant of Western colonialism but also at convincing the international community that the USSR is on the side of all peoples struggling for self-determination.[12] By using the Ukraine in this role, the suggestion that no such problems exist within the Soviet realm was also very much underlined, thus defusing attempts to direct the colonialism debate to the situation in the USSR. Apprehension about the latter possibility was also evident in various attempts by the USSR to obtain de jure recognition of its annexation of the Baltic states in 1940; thus Lithuania was suggested as a U.N. member at the time when the Soviet Union claimed three additional U.N. seats.[13]

As in all the Soviet attempts to use the non-Russian peoples and republics to its advantage, however, there is a potential political risk as well. Thus, when justifying the Soviet claim for U.N. representation for the union republics, Molotov drew parallels between them and the dominions of the British Commonwealth. By stressing that the British dominions had achieved international sovereignty by a step-by-step process, he implied that a similar process was occurring in the case of the constituent parts of the USSR.[14] This parallel clearly does not hold up in retrospect, but it is nevertheless significant that the Soviet government went on record on this occasion to state that it regards the union republics as entirely equal and sovereign entities with the right to international status, as well as with the right to secede from the USSR. In addition, the Soviet constitution of 1936—which had already cited the right to secede—was amended in 1944 by two articles that gave the republics the right to have their own armed forces and diplomatic representation. These two amendments juridically enhanced the status of the union republics, even though the clause concerning national army units was never implemented—and was dropped from the new Constitution of 1977—and the one concerning international representation was implemented only to a very limited degree. The legal constitutional act in itself has a certain weight and can attain new political significance in certain contexts. In the words of Vernon Aspaturian, "the Amendments may unwittingly provide a legal cover for separatists in the Union Republics or furnish a gratuitous fissure into which hostile powers might insert their diplomatic wedges. These hazards would be increased in the event of a serious political crisis."[15] He believes that the Soviet authorities are quite conscious of this danger and that this is why they have cautiously circumscribed the diplomatic activities of the republics.[16]

Turning the focus away from the territorial aspect of the international role of the nationalities to interactions involving specific groups, one finds that here too the Soviets have to balance very carefully in order to keep the interactions from becoming a liability. Their success has varied from case to case, depending on a large number of factors. By necessity, the scope of analysis has to be limited to those factors most closely related to Soviet policy making. Since one also finds that certain Soviet nationalities such as the "foreign minorities," the Jews, and the Muslims have had an especially pronounced foreign policy involvement, their cases are to be analyzed in more detail.

THE FOREIGN MINORITIES

The foreign minorities are ethnic groups such as the Soviet Germans, Koreans, Poles, Uighurs, et al., who, although Soviet citizens and long-time residents of the territory now comprising the USSR, have strong ties of kinship to the bulk of their nations living abroad. These minorities have played four distinct roles in Soviet foreign policy, one of which has hampered the promotion of Soviet foreign policy goals, while the other three have served to enhance it. Since the same multiple roles can be played by other Soviet nationalities as well, it is worthwhile to explicate them one by one.

Among the three beneficial roles the first is that of the bridge builder, in which a minority acts as linkage group facilitating Soviet dealings with a foreign state. Feelings of ethnic solidarity and past contacts are utilized to gain such benefits as diplomatic goodwill, cultural or scientific exchange agreements, and economic advantages such as credits and trade. Among the foreign minorities, this role was played most successfully by the Volga Germans in the 1920s, during the Rapallo era of German-Soviet relations.[17]

The second active role Soviet foreign minorities have played is that of revolutionary vanguards working for the political transformation of their kin-states abroad. Beginning with 1917 and throughout the 1920s the Soviet Germans, Poles, Koreans, and others were actively engaged in propaganda directed toward their kinsmen abroad, and were made part of various political organizations and military detachments. Soviet Koreans and Poles were especially involved in the latter; while Soviet Poles played a major organizational and military role in the war with Poland in 1920-21, the Koreans were engaged as anti-Japanese fighters in the Soviet confrontation with Japan. Both were not merely involved as auxiliary forces, but were depicted as the human nuclei of a future Communist Poland and Korea. While this effort receded into the background during the 1930s, when revolutionary politics consisted mainly of propagandistic messages, it was revived at the end of World War II when members of the Soviet Korean and Polish communities were utilized as cadres in the Communist takeover of their respective kin-states.[18]

The third type of active foreign policy involvement of Soviet minorities focuses on the exploitation of ethnic disaffection abroad. In this instance the message projected is that nationality relations in the USSR have been resolved in an exemplary manner, whereas national oppression reigns in the target state. The purpose of such agitation can vary; it can aim at strengthening the Communist movement, or it can constitute a tool for implementing a specific Soviet foreign policy goal. Thus one finds that in the interwar period the status of the Bulgarian minority in the USSR was projected abroad as a model of successful ethnic accommodation, contrasting sharply to alleged national oppression in Romania, in order to influence the Bessarabian Bulgars to work for Bessarabia's incorporation into the USSR.[19] A very similar rationale appears to form the primary motive for the exceptionally generous treatment of the Soviet Hungarians since 1945; they have been implicitly and explicitly used to promote ethnic dissatisfaction among the Transylvanian Hungarians and thus have formed a tool of Soviet pressures on Romania.[20]

An especially clear illustration of the role of ethnic politics in Soviet international relations is provided by the Uighurs. They form the primary ethnic group in the Sinkiang province of the People's Republic of China, and there are numerous indications that the USSR has actively competed for their allegiance since the outbreak of the Sino-Soviet dispute. Thus one finds that the relatively small Uighur minority living on the Soviet side of the border has come to enjoy disproportionate cultural privileges, which can only be explained by the exigencies of Soviet diplomatic strategy. By posing as the champion of the national and cultural rights of the Uighur people, the USSR has tried to undermine the attractiveness of the "Chinese path to socialism" and has at the same time attempted to strengthen pro-Soviet leanings in the Xinjiang province by enhancing its own image.[21] The interdependence of the exemplarily generous Soviet nationality policy toward the Uighurs with foreign policy considerations is directly evident in Soviet propaganda. Since the open break with China in 1963, the Soviet press has published a great number of reports on the happy life of the Soviet Uighurs, contrasting it to alleged national oppression and persecution of Uighurs in Sinkiang, speaking of concentration camps, armed suppression of minorities, and of Peking's intention of "Sinifying" Xinjiang. The Chinese leaders are being accused of pursuing a traditional great-power chauvinistic policy, of discriminating against the non-Chinese peoples, and of forcibly assimilating them. The contrast to the Soviet Union is always pointed out. One report in 1967 praised the generous Soviet policy of giving the Uighurs in the USSR cultural rights and social opportunities and went on to say, "contrasted to this the fate of our brother Uighurs in the PRC is especially frightful."[22]

While reports on the plight of the minorities in China were highlighted in the Soviet press in 1963 and 1967, a new peak was reached in the summer of 1969, following the most serious border clashes to date. This correlation of Soviet publishing on the Uighurs in Xingjiang and the state of Sino-Soviet relations exemplifies its purpose as a convenient tool of political polemics. At the same time it is an indirect way of exerting political pressure by raising the specter of ethnic unrest and secessionist dangers. In fact, the Chinese have reacted very sensitively to Soviet activities directed toward Sinkiang and have mentioned attempted subversion in a number of accusations since the open split with the USSR in the autumn of 1963.[23]

Soviet propaganda broadcasts, as well as other ways of ethnic incitement of the Uighurs and other minorities of China, are likely to continue as long as the conflict between the USSR and the PRC is unresolved, and the same applies to similar efforts on the part of the Chinese. Interestingly enough, the Chinese have directed their external propaganda not only to the Muslims of Soviet Central Asia but to other non-Russians as well. The Soviets have reacted very sensitively to these attempts, especially to contacts between the Chinese and disaffected Ukrainians,[24] which once again illustrates that they are very aware not only of the potential of exploiting ethnicity in offensive foreign policy ventures but also of their own vulnerability in this sphere.

This leads to the fourth type of foreign policy role of nationalities, namely, the one in which they do not form an active tool of Soviet policies but rather, constitute the object of external pressures or concern. One has to distinguish between instances in which the foreign initiatives are manipulative and intent on primarily benefiting the foreign actor rather than the minority and those in which the concern shown is sincere and aims at truly benefiting the minority. While the Chinese attempts mentioned are of the manipulative kind, there have been a number of occasions on which more sincere efforts have been made on the behalf of individual Soviet nationalities. Most typically, these efforts have centered on general human rights or on emigration rights.

Among the various campaigns to ease the status of Soviet minorities, the one involving Soviet Jews has been the most intensive and will be analyzed separately. One of the less well known other cases concerns the Soviet Germans, descendants of old-time colonists of Russia, who have made extensive emigration demands both in 1929-31 and again in the period since 1955. In both instances one finds an intriguing foreign policy constellation in which both the Soviet and German governments had a stake in good relations and would gladly have ignored the minority demands, but found themselves unable to do so because of intense efforts of the Soviet Germans themselves, as well as the resulting public opinion pressures within Germany. In the end, the Soviets granted a certain number of exit visas during both these periods as a gesture of accommodation to this public opinion. The outcome exemplifies Soviet sensitivity to negative foreign propaganda generated by intransigence toward minority guests, but on the other hand is an example of flexibility in Soviet foreign policy making, since the concession on this one point removed an obstacle for attaining a larger foreign policy goal, generally friendly relations. During the 1970s the Soviets even took the initiative in making their concession "pay," and carefully timed the increases in the number of exit visas granted. Thus a most dramatic increase in the flow of emigrants occurred just prior to German national elections in 1972, when the election success of the Social Democratic government was uncertain.[25]

THE SOVIET JEWS

The controversy over the fate of Soviet Jews, as it developed during the 1970s, is the most vivid example of a minority emerging as an obstacle in the conduct of Soviet foreign relations. Their case also illustrates the close inter-connection between the domestic treatment of specific minorities and international affairs, as well as the consequences of a one-time Soviet policy attaining its own momentum in spite of official attempts to control it.

Until the mid-1950s, and somewhat even until 1967, there was little con-flict between the foreign policy goals of the USSR and those of its Jewish popu-lation. During World War II an anti-Fascist Jewish committee was created in support of the war effort,[26] and Soviet Jews clearly were also very much in harmony with Soviet policies surrounding the creation of the state of Israel. They warmly welcomed the quick recognition of Israel by the USSR, as well as the funneling of military assistance to it through Czechoslovakia. This harmony was disturbed when the Soviets began to adopt a pro-Arab stance in the Israeli-Arab conflict after 1955, and the gap between Soviet foreign policy pursuits and Jewish perceptions and interests opened widely in 1967 at the time of the Six-Day War. In fact, this war became a watershed in Soviet Jewish identification with Israel, and most analysts agree that it was the catalyst of the Jewish emigra-tion movement, which was soon to emerge as a major issue in Soviet interna-tional relations, together with the general question of the treatment of the Jewish minority in the Soviet Union.

Although it frequently is difficult to draw boundaries between domestic and foreign politics, it is impossible in this case. First, there has emerged a close tie between Soviet anti-Israel policies, their campaign against "international Zionism," and an increase in domestic anti-Semitism in the USSR noticeable after 1967. One also finds an escalation effect on the Jewish side in that the alienation over pro-Arab policies has led to increasing disenchantment with the Soviet system in general, and this has reinforced emigration wishes. On the other hand, both emigration and growing Soviet Jewish disaffection were a factor in increasing discrimination.[27] Thus a vicious circle involving domestic and external variables has developed.

During the 1970s growing Soviet Jewish disaffection expressed itself in manifestations of solidarity with Israel and demands for broad emigration rights, as well as demands for general democratic and specific Jewish cultural and religious rights within the USSR. Soviet oppressive measures against all these aspirations were not accepted passively by either the Soviet Jews or Jewish communities abroad. An unprecedented flow of communication developed, which in a sense opened up the borders of the USSR by making public opinion abroad more and more aware about events inside the USSR. This resulted in massive protests throughout the Western world, which have created serious dif-ficulties for the conduct of Soviet foreign policy. The issue of Soviet Jewry has been widely publicized in Western media and has generated all kinds of activity. While Jewish communities, especially in the United States, have organized a broad range of activities in support of Soviet Jews, formal protests have also been lodged by heads of Western governments and at the United Nations, and numerous demonstrations of disapproval of Soviet policies have been made by various groups and prominent individuals.[28]

All these activities had a concrete effect detrimental to Soviet foreign policy interests. Considerable negative propaganda for the USSR resulted, which was not limited to perceptions of Soviet oppressiveness in regards to Soviet Jewry alone, but spread to other areas as well. The Soviet Union was embarrassed by protests such as picketing of Soviet cultural performances in the United States, and various scientific and cultural exchanges were undermined by the disenchantment and pressure politics of numerous Western scientists, artists, and other professionals. Most importantly, however, serious obstacles emerged for Soviet efforts to increase trade with the West and to expedite technological transfer.

Developments over what came to be known as the Jackson amendment began in October 1972, when the Nixon administration signed a trade agreement with the USSR by which the latter pledged to repay its lend-lease debts of World War II, and the U.S. administration promised in return to seek congressional approval for a positive tariff treatment known as the most-favored-nation status. In the course of widely publicized problems encountered by Soviet Jews seeking to emigrate, amendments were offered in both houses of Congress in late 1972 and early 1973, proposing to delay the granting of trade benefits until emigration was liberalized. During the ensuing political struggle in which numerous groups played a role, one could observe unique events, such as Brezhnev in effect lobbying for his case before congressional committees and big business circles during his visit in the United States in June 1973, and U.S. Secretary of State Kissinger subsequently acting as mediator between Soviet officials and the majority of Congress, which supported the Jackson amendment. In the course of the latter attempts, an agreement about the modification of the amendment—which had been passed in December 1973—was agreed upon in the fall of 1974. This modification, in the form of an unofficial understanding, implied that the Soviet government had backed down and had promised the easing of emigration in exchange for trade benefits. When this became publicly known, however, the Soviets denied the existence of such an understanding and in January 1975 revoked the entire original trade agreement.[29]

Soviet decision making in this matter was affected by many complex considerations, a discussion of which goes beyond the scope of this chapter. One should note, however, that the Soviets did—as in the case of Soviet German emigration—show a certain willingness to compromise[30] in order to enhance overall détente with the West. When too many complications developed and the trade agreement with the United States was rescinded in 1975, this was a major blow to détente, of which increased trade forms an important part. This is a clear example of the detrimental influence that a minority issue can exert on Soviet foreign relations, if it becomes the focus of international public opinion and protest activities.

THE SOVIET MUSLIMS

Six of the fourteen non-Russian union republics of the USSR are named after indigenous peoples who are Muslim, and five of these republics border on territories inhabited entirely or in part by close ethnic kin. Thus one finds that the Uzbeks, Turkmen, Kirgiz, Kazakhs, Tadzhiks, and Azeri[31] living in the Soviet Union have special ties to peoples living abroad, not only due to a common Islamic background, but in some cases also through ethnic kinship and geographic proximity. Another dimension of affinity is provided by the experience of having been colonized by "Westerners" and by representing relatively underdeveloped societies. All these varying identities of the Muslim population of the USSR have played a role in their international involvement, but it is intriguing to note that the emphasis on the one or the other has shifted over time.

During the initial revolutionary phase of Soviet foreign policy immediately after the October Revolution, the colonial theme was preeminent. Basing themselves on Lenin's theory about imperialism constituting the weakest link of capitalism, the early Soviet leaders envisioned their own colonial peoples taking on the role of revolutionary and anticolonial beacons abroad, which at that time meant the immediately adjacent areas of British India, Afghanistan, and Persia. Besides a strong rhetoric and a few colorful congresses, however, nothing much materialized, and the revolutionary expectations faded into the background during the 1920s. Nevertheless, this early emphasis on a special foreign policy role of the Soviet Muslims left its mark, not least on the perceptions of the Soviet Muslims themselves who had begun to develop their own interest in this role.[32] It was also kept partially alive by the continued use of anticolonial themes in Soviet foreign propaganda throughout the 1930s and 1940s, which always included references to the model of national and economic liberation presented by Soviet Central Asia.[33]

After Stalin's death in 1953, the Muslims of the USSR again emerged as a significant adjunct of Soviet foreign policy. They attained this role in the context of Soviet policies toward the Third World as well as toward individual Muslim countries. The latter have come to play an especially important role in the light of Soviet interest in the Middle East and their recent intense involvement in Afghanistan, Iran, and Pakistan, Muslim countries adjacent to the USSR. By 1980 it was possible to note an intense Soviet interest and involvement in the politics of practically the entire Muslim world.

The foreign policy role of the Soviet Muslims has had various dimensions. After the activization of Soviet Third World policies in the mid-1950s, attempts were made to use them as diplomatic spearheads in the establishment of Soviet influence in the newly independent states of Asia and Africa. Delegations from numerous countries were invited to Soviet Central Asia, and Soviet Muslims on their part were included in official delegations to various Third World conferences, where the USSR claimed that it was as much as Asian as a European nation and, therefore, qualified to participate. The primary propaganda theme raised on these occasions was the anti-imperialist nature of the USSR and the shining example of the Soviet Central Asian republics as models of social and economic development.[34]

The commonality of ethnic and cultural background has been stressed in the context of Soviet Turkic groups serving as a beneficial linkage group in the course of Soviet attempts to improve relations with Turkey since the late 1960s. Cultural exchanges have been intensified and reciprocal visits between representatives from Turkey and Soviet Turkish nationalities have been organized with increasing frequency. These activities were designed to enhance the overall efforts of the USSR to change Turkey's Western orientation and to detach it from NATO. While it is unclear to what degree this goal has in fact been enhanced by the intensification of cultural contacts, there can be no doubt that they have been greatly appreciated by the people involved and have intensified feelings of kinship on both sides.[35]

While in this case the ties of Soviet Muslims to Muslims abroad were reinforced by special cultural and ethnic ties, and while anti-imperialist themes have continued to play a role in all contacts, it is intriguing to note that in recent years the religious and cultural affinities resulting from a common Islamic background have been increasingly emphasized. The Soviets have recognized the growing impact of Islam in various parts of the world and this has resulted in a small group of Soviet Muslim clerics taking on the role of specialists in international contacts. They have participated in Soviet international broadcasts in various languages and have frequently toured Muslim countries. Numerous delegations of foreign Muslims have visited the areas inhabited by Soviet Muslims, especially Tashkent, which has become the primary location for international conferences and where the spiritual leader of the Soviet Muslims, the mufti Ziautdin Babakhanov, has emerged as the chief organizer of various friendly encounters. A recent article in *Pravda* has characterized all these efforts in the following way:

> [T]he Moslem organizations operating in our country take an active part in the struggle for peace and friendship among peoples. They have contacts with coreligionists in almost 80 countries, invite dozens of foreign Moslem delegations to the USSR every year, pay regular reciprocal visits, and participate in international Islamic forums and also in measures sponsored by the World Peace Council, the Organization of Solidarity of the Peoples of Asia and Africa and other organizations.
>
> In the past few years, the Moslems of the Soviet Union have held six rather large international forums. Just two of them, those held in 1979 in Tashkent and Dushanbe, were attended by eminent religious leaders and executives of Islamic publications from more than 30 countries of Asia, Africa and Europe. Along with purely

religious questions, they discussed problems of the struggle for peace, disarmament and just relations among peoples, the liberation movement of the Arab peoples and solidarity with the victorious revolutions in Afghanistan and Iran.[36]

Clearly, the official Soviet foreign policy line is actively promoted at these forums. In addition, various strongly worded declarations are issued, of which one adopted by a meeting in July 1979 attacking "Israeli, USA, South African, and Chinese imperialism" is typical.[37]

Overall, the Soviets have been quite successful in using Islam as an asset in their foreign policy conduct, but there have been setbacks as well. A number of foreign Muslims participating in official visits have subsequently published reports critical of the position of Islam in the USSR by, for example, citing the small number of truly working mosques. In addition, Soviet efforts to pose as a friend of Islam and as a champion of anti-imperialism were seriously undermined by their occupation of Afghanistan, which has been denounced by virtually all Muslim and Third World countries. Among the many detrimental repercussions was a call by the secretary-general of the World Muslim League to boycott a major international Muslim conference organized in Tashkent in September 1980, a call that apparently was followed by a number of important Islamic states such as Pakistan, Saudi Arabia, Jordan, Algeria, Iran, and others.[38]

Afghanistan has emerged as a catalyst for a confrontation between Islam and Soviet-style communism in other ways as well. The guerrillas fighting the occupation forces in Afghanistan do so mainly in the name of Islam, the impact of which is so strong on the Afghan nation that the Soviet-backed regime of Babrak Karmal has also reverted to presenting its policies as being closely in accord with Islamic teachings. More importantly for the theme discussed here, the Afghan regime also tries to convince its people that the Soviet Union has provided a prime example for the compatibility of Islam and communism. In the course of this effort, various delegations of Afghan religious leaders have been sent to Soviet Azerbaidzhan and Central Asia as the guests of the local ecclesiatical administrations. According to self-confident Soviet press reports, the participants in these tours have become convinced that Muslims in the USSR enjoy not only a high level of cultural and economic development but complete freedom of religion as well.[39]

In another effort many Afghans have been sent for training in the Soviet Union, and although it is not clear exactly where they are sent, it would not be surprising to find that in many cases the pattern used in the past is repeated, when numerous foreign Muslims were sent for an education or specialized training to Central Asia.[40] The Soviet policy makers have also tried to win the allegiance of the Afghan people by sending a considerable number of Soviet Muslims to Afghanistan since 1978, including a new ambassador of Tatar background who arrived in Kabul just a few weeks before the Soviet invasion. This ethnic staffing has not been limited to diplomatic and technical missions, but has played an especially important role in a Soviet attempt to export the Soviet model of nationality policy. Afghanistan has a number of ethnic minorities, and it declared in 1978 that new cultural and educational policies were following the Soviet example. The Soviets have much to gain from this attempt, since the apparent success of these new policies would represent a major propaganda victory and would also create badly needed sympathizing population groups in Afghanistan. It is thus not surprising that they have made a major effort to assist in the implementation of the new nationality policy by helping to produce new school books in the minority languages and similar efforts. This has been facilitated by the fact that some of the minorities in Afghanistan—such as the Uzbek—have ethnic counterparts in the USSR.[41]

The success of these various policies and activities is still uncertain, but some problems are evident even now. Thus, a large number of the Uzbeks and other Turkic-speaking minorities of Afghanistan are unlikely to be very receptive to Soviet policies and sponsorship, since they are descendants of refugees from Soviet Central Asia—including the Basmachi who fought an intense guerrilla war against Soviet rule in the early 1920s.[42] A more fundamental problem relates to the difficulty of reconciling Islam and Soviet ideology and practice. Although the Soviets currently assert that this is entirely possible, this assertion is mostly a rhetorical facade covering numerous deep contradictions. If there were serious attempts to overcome these contradictions, major adjustments would have to be made not only in the interpretation of Islam as it is practiced in Afghanistan but also in Soviet-style Marxism. As past experiences have repeatedly shown, the Soviets find it very hard to make such adjustments.

One of the basic reasons the Soviets find it so hard substantively to adjust their political ideology and program to local conditions abroad is their fear of repercussions at home. It is impossible to isolate the domestic and international spheres. One illustration of this is provided by a controversy that developed over the journal *Muslims of the Soviet East.* This journal is primarily aimed at a foreign audience, but has nevertheless been sharply attacked by other Soviet publications with a domestic focus because its interpretation of Islam diverges too much from the one they present. While they frequently attack Islam as reactionary, unenlightened, and culturally stagnant, *Muslims of the Soviet East* emphasizes its compatibility with Soviet-style modernity.[43] Although this message is very useful in contacts with foreign audiences, it is problematic domestically, and one finds that considerations of domestic ethnic politics set a limit to the flexibility of such politics internationally.

PROSPECTS

In the light of past experiences one can expect that the USSR will continue to try to utilize its Muslims as a foreign policy asset, but that it will proceed with caution in order to minimize detrimental repercussions domestically. In the course of intensified contacts between foreign and Soviet Muslims it is unavoidable that influences are also exerted from the former on the latter, and as a result a clear limit is set to how far such contacts can go. Many principles and ideas that are strongly held in Third World or Muslim countries impose a danger to Soviet rule if transmitted to the USSR. This is especially true in regard to ideas about the benefits of self-determination or about the need to reject nonindigenous modernizing influences and models, as recently expressed in Iran. The turn toward radical and fundamentalist teachings notable both in Iran and in other Islamic countries would have an equally explosive effect if they were to spread to the USSR. In fact, concern about the latter was being openly expressed in the Soviet Azerbaidzhani press by late 1980s, when several reports noted calls by local officials to step up security in the regions bordering on Iran and Afghanistan.[44]

Soviet experiences in Afghanistan have highlighted a further complication arising from multiethnicity, namely, its effect on military efficiency and strength. Many of the Soviet units sent to Afghanistan in December 1979 had a strong Muslim component, and this apparently was the main reason they were pulled out and replaced by predominantly Russian units a few months later; the Western press reported that there had been ethnic tension between Muslim soldiers and European officers, that desertions had occurred, and that the Afghans had begun to exert too much religious and political influence on the Muslims serving in the Soviet forces.[45] The same kind of problem, resulting either from ethnic disunity within the armed forces or from disaffection of a segment of the conscript forces due to ties of kinship to a particular foreign adversary, is likely to have some impact in future situations as well.

In this sense the nationality factor clearly has a cautioning influence on the conduct of Soviet foreign policy, as is also more broadly the case in regard to the effects of the borderland status of the non-Russian nations mentioned earlier. The consideration about a potential lack of loyalty on the part of the Soviet Central Asians who inhabit one of the frontline regions in the Sino-Soviet dispute has most likely defused Soviet adventurism in their confrontation with China[46] and will probably continue to have this influence in the future. A similar constraint on risky foreign policy behavior will also continue to be in force in regard to the other non-Russian borderland areas. This caution, however, can express itself in various ways, one of them being that the Soviet leadership is anxious to eliminate any political influence in its neighboring countries that has a contagious potential in regard to the non-Russian population. Thus one finds that concerns about the Ukraine being affected by the Czechoslovak developments in 1968 constituted one of the reasons for Soviet intervention,[47] and similar fears about the contagiousness of the Polish experiment of 1980/81 could very well affect Soviet decision making in regard to Poland. This anxiety may even be more pronounced in the Polish case, since Poland has for years been a "window to the West" for both the Ukraine and Lithuania, a role that has been very much supported by the Polish minority living in these two republics and in Belorussia.[48]

In the event of serious confrontations of the USSR with neighboring states, speculations are raised that the Soviets might consider the option of territorial annexation. In those instances where this would result in a further increase of the non-Russian population of the USSR, one can assume that the Soviet leadership will hesitate to do so, since this would imply pushing the percentage of Russians in the Soviet population below the psychologically significant 50 percent mark. It is, furthermore, very likely that the addition of a new minority population would add to centrifugal tendencies among the non-Russians. The danger of ethnic overextension thus clearly argues against the likelihood of the USSR annexing Xinjiang, or Afghanistan, or Persian Azerbaidzhan, or parts of Poland.

As has been pointed out before, the nationality factor is closely linked to the general image that the USSR can project of itself abroad, and there can be little doubt that the Soviets will continue to do their utmost to present themselves in the best light. The experience of the 1970s has shown that their success to a large part depends on the strength of minority dissent movements within the USSR and the international response they are able to generate. Even though confronted by innumerable difficulties, protests against the violation of national and cultural rights within the USSR have been continuing and have been addressed to international forums such as the United Nations or the follow-up conferences to the Helsinki Accord of 1975. Jews, Ukrainians, and Balts have been at the forefront of such protests and appeals, and one can expect that the same will be true throughout the 1980s.[49]

One can also expect that the Soviet Union will continue to try to use its nationalities as a policy asset. Although it is difficult to make predictions, Pakistan may very well emerge as a focal point for such attempts. There have been recurrent conflicts between the five million Baluchis and other minorities in Pakistan and the central government, and there are signs that minority separatism has been promoted by the Soviet Union. By early 1981 the Pakistani government began to react to such pressures by showing a more conciliatory attitude to Soviet aims in their region.[50]

In sum, ethnicity clearly plays a role in both offensive and defensive Soviet foreign policy calculations and there is thus every reason to consider the nationality implications of any international development affecting the USSR.

NOTES

1. The most notable exception is that of Vernon V. Aspaturian, *Process and Power in Soviet Foreign Policy* (Boston: Little, Brown, 1971).

2. Soviet publications have repeatedly attacked Western scholars specializing in Soviet nationalities questions as "bourgeois falsifiers" intent on promoting anticommunism. See,

for example, *Pravda*, July 26, 1979, as translated in *Current Digest of the Soviet Press (CDSP)* 31, no. 30 (1979): 12–13. For a Soviet statement about the international role of their nationality policy see I. F. Anushkin, "Mezhdunarodnoe znachenie opyta KPSS v reshenii natsional'nogo voprosa," *Voprosy Istorii KPSS* no. 19 (June 1972), pp. 17–31.

3. For Soviet census data, see *Naselenie SSSR, Po dannym vsesoiuznoi perepisi naseleniia 1979 goda* (Moscow: Politizdat, 1980), pp. 23–24; for a good survey about the nationalities see Teresa Rakowska-Harmstone, "The Nationalities Question," in *The Soviet Union: Looking to the 1980s*, ed. Robert Wesson. (Stanford, Cal.: Hoover Institution Press, 1980), pp. 129–54.

4. For an excellent analysis of the nationality factor in the Brest-Litovsk negotiations, see Adam B. Ulam, *Expansion and Coexistence: Soviet Foreign Policy 1917–73*, 2d. ed. (New York: Praeger, 1974), pp. 51–75.

5. Richard Pipes, *The Formation of the Soviet Union: Communism and Nationalism 1917–1923* (Cambridge, Mass.: Harvard University Press, 1970).

6. Andrei Amalrik, *Will the Soviet Union Survive Until 1984?* (New York: Harper & Row, 1970), p. 63.

7. The Romanians have been careful about raising the "Bessarabian question," but it has obtained more saliency since 1962, when Romania began to break away from the USSR. Compare Robert R. King, *Minorities Under Communism: Nationalities as a Source of Tension among Balkan Communist States* (Cambridge, Mass.: Harvard University Press, 1973); and Robert R. King, "Verscharfter Disput um Bessarabien. Zur Auseinandersetzung zwischen rumänischen und sowjetischen Historikern," *Osteuropa* 26 (December 1976): 1079–87. On Chinese territorial claims see, for example, Thomas W. Robinson "The Sino-Soviet Border Dispute: Background, Development and the March 1969 Clashes," *American Political Science Review* 66 (December 1972): 1175–1201.

8. As cited in Aspaturian, *Process and Power*, p. 442.

9. Ibid., pp. 461–68.

10. Ulam, *Expansion and Coexistence*, pp. 426–28.

11. Vernon V. Aspaturian, in U.S. Congress, House, Committee on Foreign Affairs, *Soviet Involvement in the Middle East and the Western Response, Hearings*, before a subcommittee of the Committee on Foreign Relations, House of Representatives, 92d Cong., 1st sess., 1971, pp. 85–87.

12. Konstantyn Sawczuk, *The Ukraine in the United Nations Organization: A Study in Soviet Foreign Policy 1944–1950* (New York: Columbia University Press, 1975), p. 59.

13. Compare Aspaturian, *Process and Power*, pp. 473–75. The United States has consistently refused to recognize the Soviet incorporation of Lithuania, Latvia, and Estonia.

14. Ibid., pp. 42, 117.

15. Aspaturian, *Power and Process*, p. 669.

16. All the union republics, including the RSFSR, established foreign ministries of their own and engaged in varied—mostly minimal—direct international contact. Ibid., p. 689. It appears that Soviet caution in this regard has increased in recent years, since the new constitution of 1977 omitted repeating that the republics could enter into foreign relations "directly." Compare A. Shtromas, "The Legal Position of Soviet Nationalities and Their Territorial Units according to the 1977 Constitution of the USSR," *Russian Review* 37 (July 1978): 265–72.

17. For a more extensive analysis, see Rasma Silde Karklins, *The Interrelationship of Soviet Foreign and Nationality Policies: The Case of the Foreign Minorities of the USSR.* Ph.D. diss., University of Chicago, August 1975, pp. 205–32.

18. Ibid., pp. 39–112.

19. Ibid., pp. 85–91.

20. Ibid., pp. 146–61; and King, *Minorities under Communism*, pp. 163–69.

21. Rasma Silde Karklins, "The Uighurs between China and the USSR," *Canadian Slavonic Papers* 17 (Autumn 1975): 341–65.

22. *Literaturnaia Gazeta*, June 16, 1967. Among the central newspapers, *Literaturnaia Gazeta* has excelled in publishing numerous similar stories, although *Pravda* and *Izvestiia* have carried them as well.

23. Karklins, "The Uighurs," pp. 363–65; see also June Teufel Dreyer, "Ethnic Minorities in the Sino-Soviet Dispute," in *Soviet Asian Ethnic Frontiers*, ed. William O. McCagg and Brian D. Silver (New York: Pergamon Press, 1979), pp. 175–94.

24. In 1972, various Soviet Ukrainian newspapers published harsh attacks on a group of Ukrainians in Canada and West Germany who had established links to Communist China. It appears that this cooperation began as an exchange of literature, as a result of which Chinese propaganda emphasized the suppression of nationalities in the USSR more and more. Later, the Chinese also apparently began radio broadcasts in Ukrainian for the Ukrainians living in the Soviet border areas. M. Panchuk, "The Chinese Splitters and the Ukrainian Nationalists," *Rabochaya Gazeta*, February 27, 1972, as translated in *CDSP* 24, no. 8 (1972): 13. See also "Kiev Attacks Ukrainian 'Pro-Chinese' Group," *Radio Free Europe Research*, March 10, 1972.

25. For a more extensive treatment compare Karklins, *The Interrelationship of Soviet Foreign and Nationalities Policies*, pp. 233–94.

26. Shimon Redlich, "Soviet Uses of Jewish Nationalism During World War II: The Membership and Dynamics of the Jewish Antifascist Committee in the USSR," *Nationalities Papers* 5 (Fall 1977): 136–66.

27. Compare, for example, Zvi Gitelman, "Moscow and the Soviet Jews: A Parting of the Ways," *Problems of Communism* 39 (January–February 1980), especially pp. 25–34.

28. Compare Lukasz Hirszowicz, "The Soviet-Jewish Problem: Internal and International Developments 1972–1976," in *The Jews in Soviet Russia since 1917*, 3rd ed., ed. Lionel Kochan (Oxford, London, New York: Oxford University Press, 1978), pp. 366–409; and William W. Orbach, *The American Movement to Aid Soviet Jews* (Amherst: University of Massachusetts Press, 1979).

29. On the unofficial understanding, see various documents in the *New York Times*, December 18 and December 19, 1974; on the negotiations over the Jackson amendment, see William Korey, "Soviet Decision-Making and the Problems of Jewish Emigration Policy," *Survey* 22 (Winter 1976): 112–31, and Hirszowicz, "The Soviet-Jewish Problem," pp. 375–77.

30. Besides the original Soviet willingness to compromise on the Jackson amendment, the general increase in exit visas granted in the early 1970s was a concession to Western pressures, as was the rescinding of the "diploma tax" which triggered widespread protests in 1972 and 1973. Korey, "Soviet Decision-Making," p. 125.

31. There are other Muslim nationalities as well, but not all can be mentioned here. For basic data see Zev Katz, Rosemarie Rogers, and Frederic Harned, eds., *Handbook of Major Soviet Nationalities* (New York: Free Press, 1975).

32. Alexandre A. Bennigsen and S. Enders Wimbush, *Muslim National Communism in the Soviet Union: A Revolutionary Strategy for the Colonial World* (Chicago: University of Chicago Press, 1979).

33. Frederick C. Barghoorn, *Soviet Foreign Propaganda* (Princeton, N.J.: Princeton University Press, 1964), pp. 153–56; and Teresa Rakowska Harmsone, *Russia and Nationalism in Central Asia: The Case of Tadzhikistan* (Baltimore, Md.: Johns Hopkins Press, 1970), especially pp. 72–74, where she also mentions that the promotion of the Tadzhik ASSR to the status of union republic in 1929 was designed to increase Soviet influence in neighboring Muslim countries.

34. Aspaturian, *Process and Power*, p. 697; and William C. Fletcher, *Religion and Soviet Foreign Policy 1945–1970* (London: Oxford University Press, 1973), pp. 73–78.

35. Kemal H. Karpat, "The Turkic Nationalities: Turkish-Soviet and Turkish-Chinese Relations," in *Soviet Asian Ethnic Frontiers*, pp. 134–38.

36. *Pravda*, July 14, 1980, as translated in *CDSP* 22, no. 28 (1980): 7. See also Alexandre Bennigsen, "Soviet Muslims and the World of Islam," *Problems of Communism* 29 (March–April 1980): 38–51.

37. Ibid., p. 44.

38. *Radio Liberty Research* bulletins dated August 8 and September 10, 1980.

39. *Izvestiia*, October 5, 1979 and September 7, 1980; see also Zalmay Khalilzad, "Soviet-Occupied Afghanistan," *Problems of Communism* 29 (November–December 1980): 25–27.

40. Eden Naby, "The Ethnic Factor in Soviet-Afghan Relations," *Asian Survey* 20 (March 1980): 250; and Bennisgen and Wimbush, *Muslim National Communism*, p. 104.

41. Naby, "The Ethnic Factor," pp. 250–52.

42. David C. Montgomery, "The Uzbeks in Two States: Soviet and Afghan Policies Toward an Ethnic Minority," in *Soviet Asian Frontiers*, pp. 160–67.

43. Geoffrey Wheeler, "Islam and the Soviet Union," *Asian Affairs* 10 (October 1979): 249; and Karpat, "The Turkic Nationalities," p. 140.

44. *Bakinski rabochii* of December 19 and December 25, 1980, as reported in the *New York Times*, January 8, 1981, p. 4.

45. *Christian Science Monitor*, January 10, 1980; *U.S. News & World Report*, January 25, 1980, p. 20; *The Economist*, February 16, 1980; *Newsweek*, February 25, 1980, p. 19; also Bennigsen, "Soviet Muslims and the World of Islam," p. 48.

46. A Soviet dissident reports: "In our Central Asian cities I and many others have often heard the cry: 'Just wait till the Chinese come, they'll show you what's what!'" Igor Shafarevich, "Separation or Reconciliation? The Nationalities Question in the USSR," in *From Under the Rubble*, ed. Alexander Solzhenitsyn et al. (Boston: Little, Brown, 1974), p. 88.

47. Grey Hodnett and Peter J. Potichny, *The Ukraine and the Czechoslovak Crisis*, Occasional Paper No. 6 (Canberra: Department of Political Science, Research School of Social Sciences, Australian National University, 1970).

48. According to the 1979 census, there were 1,151,000 Poles in the USSR and among these 403,000 lived in Belorussia, 258,000 in the Ukraine, 247,000 in Lithuania, and 67,000 in Latvia. *Po dannym perepisi 1979 goda*, pp. 28–31. For an analysis of the Soviet Polish minority in the past, see Karklins, *Interrelationship of Soviet Foreign and Nationalities Policies*, especially pp. 255–64.

49. On the expression of Western concern for the rights of various non-Russian groups in the USSR during the Madrid follow-up conference to the Helsinki Accord, compare the *New York Times*, November 25, 1980; on the general impact of national protests in the USSR, compare Jeremy R. Azrael, "Emergent Nationality Problems in the USSR," in *Soviet Nationality Policies and Practices*, ed. Jeremy R. Azrael (New York: Praeger, 1978), p. 379.

50. *New York Times*, January 9, 1981; see also Naby, "The Ethnic Factor," p. 240.

5

DISSENT IN THE USSR AND SOVIET FOREIGN RELATIONS

Frederick C. Barghoorn

This chapter examines linkages between dissent in the USSR and problems that dissenters' criticism of Soviet policies, both domestic and foreign, create for the conduct, and especially for the propaganda justification, of Soviet foreign policy. Alexander Dallin's judgment that "overt dissent over foreign policy" in the USSR is "even less permissible than public differences on internal affairs"[1] appears to be essentially correct. The exceptionally harsh repression inflicted by the Soviet authorities on Soviet citizens who sought to persuade their government to fulfill the human rights provisions of the Final Act of the Helsinki Conference on Security and Cooperation in Europe, as well as much of the other evidence to be examined herein, lends credence to Dallin's statement. The evidence indicates, however, that the criterion by which the Soviet leadership decides how dangerous dissent is, does not focus on "foreign" as distinguished from "domestic" Soviet affairs. Rather, the Soviet authorities regard as especially damaging, and hence most severely punishable, transmission abroad of information and opinions about Soviet domestic or foreign policies that they believe may hinder the achievement of Soviet foreign policy goals. It is obvious that statements of dissenters on such matters as official throttling of freedom of expression in the USSR are considered intolerable because of their incompatibility with the glowingly positive image of Soviet reality projected to the outside world by Soviet leaders and disseminated by the controlled Soviet communications network. As dissenters have frequently pointed out, they are punished not for the "crimes" of which they are accused, but for violating implicit prohibitions against making statements annoying to the Soviet authorities.

Pertinent in this connection is the explanation offered by five prominent

Soviet dissidents for the arrest in 1974 of the free-thinking poet Victor Nekipelov. They issued a statement that said, inter alia, "It is hardly necessary to look hard for the real reason behind Nekipelov's arrest: certain worlds cannot bear their own reflections."[2]

An approach to the significance of dissent different from that of Nekipelov's well-wishers was offered by Yuri Andropov, Politburo member and chairman of the KGB (Committee of State Security) in a September 1977 speech. According to Andropov, the "special services of imperialism" were engaging in "ideological diversions" with the purpose of "shaking the communist convictions of Soviet people," and inculcating in them "views foreign to socialism," so as to bring about changes in Soviet society beneficial to "imperialism." A few "renegades," or "so-called dissidents," he stated, were violating Soviet laws, and supplying the West with "slanderous information," and "false reports"; for such activities, he asserted, these people were paid "generously."[3]

Andropov's astonishing but typical outburst reflects official Soviet anger over dissenters' addressing criticism of Soviet policies and practices, domestic or foreign, to foreign audiences. Such unauthorized communication, in the eyes of the Soviet leaders, is intolerable for several reasons. It violates the regime's monopoly control of communication. It undermines the Soviet propaganda myth of enthusiastic, unanimous public support for the regime and its policies. It also reflects, in hyperbolic language, to be sure, the regime's sensitivity to the possibility that "bourgeois" governments might somehow profit from the activities of Soviet dissidents. In addition, statements of this tenor by Andropov and by other Soviet leaders, including Brezhnev himself in a speech in March 1977, are characteristic of a strategy that dates to the earliest period of Soviet power, which, by linking dissent with the hostile machinations of "imperialism," seeks to discredit it both at home and abroad.[4]

Of course, anyone familiar with the thought and character of dissenters like the physicist Yuri Orlov, founder of the Moscow Public Group to Promote the Implementation of the Helsinki Accords, the computer scientist and Jewish emigration activist Anatoli Shcharanski, the Ukrainian writer and head of the Ukrainian Public Group to Promote Implementation of the Helsinki Accords, Mykola Rudenko—all of whom were, as Andropov spoke, undergoing interrogation for exercising their right and duty to monitor fulfillment by the USSR of obligations they considered it had assumed in signing the 1975 Final Act of the Conference on Security and Cooperation in Europe—can hardly fail to regard Andropov's statements as calculated distortion. Such statements, however, help us to understand the fear and anger with which Soviet rulers respond to efforts of Soviet citizens to disseminate what the latter regard as truthful accounts of the conduct of the Soviet authorities toward Soviet citizens who criticize official policy, especially if such criticism becomes known outside the USSR. Such attitudes and the punishment that follows are not surprising in view of the traditional Soviet intolerance of freedom of criticism.

Dissenters are usually described, in the infrequent references to them that appear in the censored Soviet press, as *inakomysliashchie*, or "persons who think differently." Dissenters themselves for years criticized this term, but have gradually come to accept either it or "dissident" as more or less descriptive of their stance. Academician Andrei Sakharov, however, has expressed a preference for the term *volnodumaiushchiesia*, or "free thinkers." When in this chapter terms such as dissidence and dissent are used, they will refer to the open expression by Soviet citizens of independent thought, critical of established institutions, practices, or doctrines, and its dissemination outside the controlled official communications network. As systematic repression of its articulators indicates, independent thought—especially if its articulators attempt to share their thoughts with others, particularly with foreigners—or to form even the tiniest, most informal groups, or to exert pressure on the authorities to change policies that dissenters regard as morally wrong or simply ineffective—can endanger the careers, health, or even the lives of the people whose convictions compel them to speak out against what they regard as intolerable evil.

The Stalin constitution of 1936 and the new Soviet constitution adopted in 1977 promised a wide range of social, economic, political, and personal rights and liberties. Article 50 of the 1977 constitution makes it plain, however, that the crucially important rights of freedom of speech and press, of assembly, and so forth are "guaranteed for the purpose of strengthening and developing the socialist system," thus indicating the intention that in practice, whatever rights become available will be determined by the Soviet authorities who alone are empowered to decide what these words will mean in any given situation.[5] The constitution and the loosely drafted articles of the republics' criminal codes in effect hand over to the administrative officials of the CPSU (Communist Party of the Soviet Union), to the courts, to the procuracy, and in most political cases to the KGB security police the power to interpret and determine the rights of Soviet citizens.

In practice, constitutional and legal texts have been invoked to justify arrests and convictions of many Soviet citizens for "reading, keeping or passing on to friends of *samizdat* [uncensored, self-published] typescripts and books of undesirable content (although usually they are, by Western democratic standards, completely harmless)."[6] Courts often convict persons of having engaged in anti-Soviet propaganda and agitation without requiring the prosecution to prove—as the relevant articles of the law ostensibly require—that the defendant intended to undermine the Soviet system, or knowingly prepared, distributed, or stored materials containing falsehoods slandering the Soviet state. Also, as an impressively documented Amnesty International report points out, "in no case known to Amnesty International has a Soviet court acquitted a defendant brought to trial specifically or in disguised form for his political or religious activity."[7] According to Amnesty, more than 400 people "were tried and sentenced to imprisonment, internal exile or other punishments involving physical restriction or were forcibly confined to psychiatric hospitals for exercising their human rights . . . between June 1975 and May 1979." The report indicates that "the real number of prisoners of conscience in the USSR" is "much larger than the known number."[8] The Commission on Security and Cooperation in Europe of the United States Congress reported in August 1980 that in 1979 the Soviet authorities "began the most massive campaign against human rights activism in the last decade."[9] Of course, figures for arrests and trials account for only part of the total pattern of repression of dissent in the USSR, which includes also numerous cases of forced emigration, expulsion of writers from the official Writers Union, loss of employment, and so on.

Soviet citizens who persist in expressing opinions objectionable to the authorities can expect—and apparently do expect—to be treated harshly. Presumably to minimize unfavorable publicity abroad, however, in the post-Stalin years repression has often been applied cautiously, beginning with small doses and only after years, in some cases, culminating in shockingly severe punishment. Yuri Orlov, for example, was expelled from the CPSU in 1956 and lost his job, after he called, at a meeting of his party organization, for de-Stalinization more thorough than that which had just been advocated by Khrushchev. He was permitted to pursue his career as a physicist in Armenia for several years; again he lost his job when he publicly defended Sakharov. Then, after he organized the Moscow Public Group to Promote Fulfillment of the Helsinki Accords, he was arrested and received, despite his bad health, a sentence of seven years in labor camp, to be followed by five years of internal exile.[10]

Intensification of repression after the formation of the Soviet Helsinki monitoring groups brought increasing numbers of arrests of dissidents. It was also manifested in stiffer sentences, including sending record numbers of women to labor camps for long terms. As Ludmilla Alekseeva, foreign representative of the Moscow Helsinki group, noted in the New York Russian-language daily *Novoe russkoe slovo* for April 7, 1981, the KGB, at least in Moscow, had until 1979 refrained as a rule from arresting women civil rights activists, not out of chivalrous motives, of course, but out of concern over the effect arrests of women always had had on Western public opinion.

DISSENT AND FOREIGN AFFAIRS

Dissenters' views on Soviet foreign policy prior to 1976 have been dealt with elsewhere.[11] It is, however, appropriate to review events before the watershed years 1975–76. Beginning in 1976 the Soviet Helsinki groups were to alarm and anger the Soviet authorities and to gain considerable foreign support by a vigorous, tenacious campaign to pressure their government to fulfill the obligations in the area of human rights that the groups believed the USSR had assumed in adhering to the CSCE Final Act. This effort to mobilize Soviet and foreign public opinion to implement "Basket 3" represented, in effect, the crescendo of efforts begun as early as 1968 by Sakharov, and even earlier by Pavel Litvinov, Vladimir Bukovski, Andrei Amalrik, Natalia Gorbanevskaia, and others. Sakharov had gone farther than most in insisting on the link between domestic reform and international peace.

The core of what Sakharov in 1978 called the "international ideology" of "active international defense of human rights" was his by then well-known argument that true détente and stable peace in the world were ultimately dependent upon "democratization" in the USSR.[12] The formation in May 1976 of the Moscow Public Group to Promote Fulfillment of the Helsinki Accords inaugurated the most acute phase in regime-dissenter and Soviet-Western conflict over human rights. In particular, conflict over interpretations of the human rights provisions of the CSCE Final Act made human rights a major issue of Soviet-Western relations.

As was indicated in the formal announcement of its establishment, the primary goal of the Moscow Helsinki group was to inform heads of governments that had signed the Helsinki Final Act of violation of "human rights and basic freedoms, including freedom of thought, conscience, religion and convictions," by gathering information from Soviet citizens, by requesting foreign governments to form an international commission for on-the-spot verification of complaints received, and so forth. The founding statement of the group also asserted that "problems of humanitarianism and openness of information are directly related to problems of international security."[13] Thus, the new group shared Sakharov's ideological perspectives. There was also a family connection between it and Sakharov. One of its 11 founding members was Sakharov's wife, Elena Bonner, its first press conference was held in Sakharov's apartment, and Sakharov made numerous statements in support of its members.

The group sought to exert influence on the conduct by the Soviet government of important aspects of both domestic and foreign policy—spheres that its members regarded as inextricably linked. As events soon showed, the Soviet rulers regarded this effort to expand citizen political participation as intolerable. Probably official hostility was expected by the veteran civil rights activists who created the Helsinki group and the organizations that cooperated with them, but the dictates of their consciences and hope that their efforts would be supported in the West provided motivation to embark on their unequal struggle against the Soviet authorities.

Of course, years before Sakharov and others articulated systematic criticism of Soviet foreign policy, some of its outcomes, particularly the invasions of Hungary in 1956 and of Czechoslovakia 12 years later, has been targets of widespread protest, expressed in the Hungarian case by the slogan "Hands Off Hungary!"[14] The Hungarian operation did not generate a large body of protest documents, such as were to be produced following the Warsaw Pact invasion of Czechoslovakia. It occurred before dissenters had developed fully the techniques of using samizdat to propagate their views or had even thought of making them available to foreign news media, as they were to do in the 1960s and 1970s. Two dissenters, however, the mathematician Revolt Pimenov and the actor Boris Vail served long terms in camps for condemning intervention in Hungary.[15] Also, widespread indignation resulting from the Kremlin's violence in Hungary is indicated by reported arrests of thousands of Soviet secondary school and university students. Apparently more than 4,000 were expelled from higher educational institutions in Leningrad alone.[16]

The "Prague Spring" of 1968 coincided with the blossoming of the Soviet "democratic movement." Protest had been fanned by a series of arrests and trials beginning late in 1967. It is therefore not surprising that Warsaw Pact steamrollering of Czechoslovakia gave rise to a substantial body of widely disseminated protest documents.[17] On August 25, 1968 seven Soviet citizens "sat on the parapet at Execution Place [in front of St. Basil's Cathedral] and unrolled banners" displaying slogans demanding "Hands Off Czechoslovakia," and proclaiming the principle "For your freedom and ours."[18]

Soviet suppression of the freedom movement in Czechoslovakia intensified defiance among a minority of the most courageous dissidents; this action, however, also gave rise to fear and despair among many. Well before the invasion, Roy Medvedev's samizdat *Political Diary*, the organ of moderate, within-system dissent, had expressed misgivings about the famous "Two Thousand Words" Manifesto of the Czechoslovak writer Ludwik Vaculik.

It is perhaps indicative of his continued adherence to a cautious, moderate position in 1968 that Andrei Sakharov did not publicly criticize the Warsaw Pact invasion of Czechoslovakia until 1972. In 1972 Sakharov wrote that the year 1968 had ended for him, "as for everybody else, with the rumbling of tanks in the streets of unyielding Prague"—an indication that, in retrospect at least, Sakharov traced the change from the optimism generated in his thinking by the Prague Spring to his pessimistic stoicism of the 1970s at least partly to the smashing of Czechoslovak freedom.[19] Thus, both the hopes generated by positive developments in Czechoslovakia and the disillusionment and anger engendered by Moscow's snuffing out of democratization in that country influenced Soviet dissenters' attitudes toward the problems and prospects of their country and of the world. Perhaps even more important was the impact on world opinion of dissenters' protests over Soviet conduct toward Czechoslovakia. The wide reporting in the Western press of the August 25, 1968 demonstration, for example, was probably one of the most embarrassing, from the point of view of the Soviet rulers, of a long series of embarrassing disclosures, resulting from dissent, repression thereof, and reporting thereon in Western news media, and finally, broadcasting back of information on all this to the Soviet Union by Western shortwave radio stations. Without those broadcasts this information would have been available only to a small circle of readers of samizdat and their families and friends. There can be no doubt that Soviet aggression against Czechoslovakia tarnished the image of the USSR abroad, perhaps most of all among some Western liberals, Socialists, and even some Communists.[20] It is difficult to demonstrate explicit links between Soviet dissent and the impact abroad of developments in Czechoslovakia. The brief Prague Spring and its untimely end did, however, play a role in contributing to the militancy of dissenters such as Leonid Plyushch. In turn, the persecution of Plyushch and other dissidents in the USSR led, even in the hard-line Moscow-oriented French Communist party, to criticism that Robert Legvold has termed "an incipient challenge to Soviet communism," and even a threat to the USSR's legitimacy. There is considerable evidence that lends credence to the hypothesis that Soviet dissenters indirectly but significantly contributed to the impact on Western public opinion of the intervention in Czechoslovakia.[21]

In the late 1960s and early 1970s foreign policy matters bulked ever larger in the activity of Soviet dissidents. Analysis of five major "programmatic" dissident works circulated in 1968–70 revealed that all five of them stressed the need for democratization of Soviet society—a demand that had implications for Soviet foreign relations—and that four of them contained criticism of Soviet foreign policy as expansionist or "messianic."[22]

A significant theme was introduced in protest activity by the most important and durable samizdat protest journal, the *Chronicle of Current Events*, by quoting in April 1968—on the front page of its first, and in all subsequent issues—the text of Article 19 of the United Nations' Universal Declaration of Human Rights: "Everyone has the right to freedom of opinion and expression," including the right "to hold opinions without interference," and to "impart information . . . regardless of frontiers." When in May 1969 the newly formed 15-person Initiative Group for the Defense of Civil Rights in the USSR petitioned—fruitlessly—the U.N. Human Rights Commission to investigate arrests and trials of Soviet citizens who sought to avail themselves of "universal" rights, such as freedom of speech, freedom of religion, freedom to emigrate, and so forth, its members and others who joined them in the appeal also cited Article 19. The appeal, incidentally, cited trials of some of the demonstrators against the invasion of Czechoslovakia, the trial of the writers Siniavski and Daniel for "publishing abroad artistic works critical of Soviet reality" and trials of "Jews demanding the right to depart for Israel"—all matters relevant to international relations.[23] This Initiative Group appeal is noteworthy in two respects significant here: first, by citing Article 19 it implicitly affirmed the principle, which was to be central to Sakharov's activity in the 1970s, of the interconnection between Soviet domestic and foreign policies; second, the appeal claimed a right to turn for redress of domestic grievances to foreign audiences and institutions. Of course, appeals to Soviet and foreign Communist officials and organizations and the protest against political trials and repression in the USSR, addressed by Pavel Litvinov, Petr Grigorenko, and ten other Soviet citizens to the 1968 Budapest Consultative Conference of Communist Parties, went unanswered.[24]

Litvinov has pointed out that the dissidents' practice of getting published in the foreign press protests originating in the USSR was a logical application of the principle of openness (*glasnost '*)—which was central to the Soviet democratic movement—in view of the impossibility of having them published at home.[25] Litvinov notes also that when the facts about persecution of Soviet citizens for their convictions became known abroad, Western public figures who shared the same values as the Soviet civil rights advocates came to the assistance of the latter. He pointed out that the Soviet government was sensitive to foreign opinion, and that, in a period of increasing international contacts, it was more and more difficult to prevent embarrassing discussions of cases of political persecution.[26]

Except for Sakharov and perhaps a handful of other Soviet dissidents, Litvinov probably made the greatest contribution to the dissidents' practice of appealing to what Howard Biddulph calls "external publics." According to Biddulph, this strategy failed because it violated the mores of Soviet political culture. According, however, to the prominent former dissident Boris Shragin, one of the signers of the appeal to the 1968 Budapest conference referred to above, "the appeal of the dissidents to Western public opinion was no more a 'tactic' than a drowning man's cry for help."[27] Biddulph on the one hand and Litvinov and Shragin on the other captured parts of the truth about the conflicting perspectives of regime and dissidents. Of course, from the point of view of Soviet ruling circles, accustomed to an elitist, manipulative-coercive style of rule, the dissidents' violations of hitherto sacred tabus against unauthorized, uncensored public communication constituted criminal behavior. But the dissidents considered it their duty to criticize what they regarded as the authorities' unjust, illegal behavior, which they viewed as incompatible with obligations assumed by the Soviet regime in associating itself with the Universal Declaration of Human Rights and other international instruments and covenants. A record kept by Pavel Litvinov of a conversation between himself and KGB official Gostev on September 26, 1967 sheds a vivid light on the conflict that had arisen between the democratic, legalistic, and objectivist outlook of Soviet civil rights activists and the authoritarian-subjectivist, opportunistic perspectives of the regime. Gostev warned Litvinov that his plan to compile and distribute a report on the recent trial of Vladimir Bukovski and other protest demonstrators (against the arrests of Aleksandr Ginzburg and Yuri Galanskov) would cause Litvinov to be charged with a criminal offense. Asked by Litvinov how Gostev could assume in advance that his report would be punishable as a crime, Gostev replied that it would, because it would distort the facts about Bukovski's demonstration— regarding which, he said, all that the Soviet public needed to know had already been published in the Soviet press. Gostev added that a report such as Litvinov was planning to distribute "could be used by our ideological enemies."[28]

Litvinov, of course, ignored Gostev's advice not to go ahead with compilation and distribution of the trial record. He took part in the Red Square demonstration protesting the invasion of Czechoslovakia. And among other activities, he meticulously edited an important document on the trial of Ginzburg, Galanskov, and two other persons involved therein (known as *The Trial of the Four*). In January 1968 Litvinov and Larisa Bogoroz attracted considerable attention abroad with their "appeal to world public opinion," denouncing the Ginzburg-Galanskov trial. They distributed copies of this document to Moscow correspondents of foreign news organizations. As Karel van het Reve noted, "for the first time in Russian history since 1917, two citizens of the USSR not only protested openly against what they considered injustice but appealed openly to their fellow citizens to join in their protest."[29]

After the arrest and sentencing of Amalrik and Bukovski to labor camps and of Litvinov to the lesser rigors of exile, Andrei Sakharov and his wife, Elena Bonner, in effect constituted themselves unofficial representatives to world opinion of the Soviet dissident community. Throughout the 1970s the diverse subgroups of this loose aggregation of tendencies—champions of Jewish rights to emigrate, rights of Russian Orthodox and other Christian believers to genuine freedom of worship, and of Ukrainians, Lithuanians, Armenians, Georgians, Czechs, and other nationalities to rights promised by the Soviet constitution but thwarted in practice, and of a new unofficial labor movement, all tended, increasingly, to coordinate their efforts to bring their case to the forum of world opinion. The major contributors to this effort were the ceaselessly active and constantly harassed Sakharov and, for a time, Solzhenitsyn.

From July 1973, when he forthrightly answered questions on sensitive issues of Soviet domestic and foreign affairs put by Olle Stenholm of Swedish National Television, Andrei Sakharov was launched on his astonishing effort to mobilize world public opinion on behalf of democratization in the USSR, and genuine, as distinguished from what he was frequently to label "false," détente in Soviet-Western relations. In the Stenholm interview Sakharov characterized Soviet socialism as an "extremely monopolized form" of state capitalism. He expressed fear that the foreign world might soon accept Soviet "rules of the game" in foreign policy and offered as a justification for his activity—which he admitted might not achieve anything inside the USSR—its role as a warning that "should hold back the West and the developing countries from committing mistakes on such a scale as we have done."[30]

The Soviet authorities quickly countered what they apparently perceived as behavior threatening their domestic legitimacy and international prestige. In August 1973 Sakharov was called into the office of USSR Deputy Procurator General Mikhail Maliarov, who informed him that his statements "published in the anti-Soviet press abroad" had caused "noticeable harm" to the USSR. He charged that Sakharov was "seeing foreigners and giving them material for anti-Soviet publications." By violating his pledge—in connection with the secret work he had done years earlier—not to meet with foreigners, Sakharov was beginning to be "used by foreign intelligence."[31] Maliarov concluded with a warning to Sakharov, who reiterated his denial that his actions were illegal.

The Sakharov-Maliarov conversation was an encounter between utterly incompatible world outlooks. When, a few days later, the Soviet mass media opened an abusive campaign against Sakharov, and 40 members of the USSR Academy of Sciences signed a letter accusing Sakharov of opposing détente, desiring to wreck the soon-to-begin European Conference on Security and Co-operation, and so on, it appeared to many in the West that he might be prosecuted. That he and Solzhenitsyn, who also was engaged in a verbal battle with the Soviet authorities, were not at this time subjected to administrative action was perhaps due to numerous statements by foreign intellectuals and political leaders supportive of the two men, and in particular to warnings by the president of the American National Academy of Sciences that action against Sakharov, as distinguished from verbal condemnation, would severely damage United States–Soviet scientific cooperation.[32]

The Stenholm interview and the Maliarov warning were early manifestations of a protracted confrontation and struggle to influence world opinion that continued even after Sakharov denounced the Soviet invasion of Afghanistan, even after his exile to the provincial city of Gorki in January 1980. Prior to that first major police action against the man whom many in the West have called the conscience of mankind, the regime apparently regarded as the better part of valor the limitation of anti-Sakharov activity to such measures as cutting off of international telephone communication, constant surveillance, and a host of harassments and severe psychological pressures, including anonymous death threats and arrests of Sakharov's friends and supporters. It should be noted, however, that in January 1977 Sakharov was again officially warned by a deputy USSR procurator not to continue his "slanderous" activities and he was, as the editors of *Alarm and Hope* put it, "haunted" by the unexplained deaths of two men who had come to Moscow to ask him for help—and by other uninvestigated beatings and deaths of dissenters, as well as by lesser but still extremely shocking police actions—these well attested by trustworthy sources—such as planting money or bullets in dissidents' apartments for the purpose of incriminating them.[33] Despite the enormous pressure brought to bear on him, Sakharov again and again succeeded in bringing to the attention of important foreign audiences his message that, as the Nobel Peace Prize Committee said, "the individual rights of man can serve as the only sure foundation for a genuine and long-lasting system of international cooperation."[34] Sakharov's greatest victory, perhaps, in his struggle to gain Western support for the champions of human rights in the USSR, was U.S. President Jimmy Carter's February 5, 1977 letter to Sakharov, replying to one handed by Sakharov to an American visitor in Moscow on January 21. In his letter, presented to Sakharov in the American Embassy in Moscow, President Carter stated that "human rights is a central concern of my administration." Carter also promised to "use our good offices to seek the release of prisoners of conscience," and concluded with the words "I am always glad to hear from you, and I wish you well."[35]

Although the Sakharov-Carter correspondence was perhaps the supreme moment in the trialogue among Soviet "democrats," the West, and the Soviet regime, it was, of course, only one of many important episodes. Others included a series of "international Sakharov hearings," the first of which was held in Copenhagen in October 1975 in the building of the Danish Parliament.[36] The first hearing heard testimony from Soviet emigrants on persecution of dissenters in the USSR and on violation of rights of religious believers and members of national minorities. Its "jury," consisting of prominent European writers, scholars, and religious leaders, concluded that the proceedings had furnished grounds for doubting that the Soviet government was observing the principles of the Helsinki Final Act and other international agreements that it had signed. Sakharov addressed to it an appeal on behalf of prisoners of conscience in the USSR.[37] Later Sakharov hearings took place in Rome in 1977 and in Washington in September 1979. The Rome hearing investigated issues similar to those analyzed in Copenhagen two years before and came to similar conclusions, but its geographic scope was far broader, for it dealt with human rights problems not only in the USSR but also in Eastern Europe. Moreover, it occurred during the Belgrade follow-up meeting on the fulfillment—and nonfulfillment—of the Helsinki Final Act, a circumstance that Sakharov, in a message he sent to the Rome gathering, especially stressed.[38] Mention should also be made of the appeal sent by Sakharov, Turchin, and Yuri Orlov to the Conference of European Communist Parties in East Berlin in June 1976, in which this distinguished trio urged the assembled Communist leaders to ponder the situation in the USSR with respect to "human rights and democratic forms of government."[39] It is interesting in this connection that Sakharov, a few months before the European Communist Conference, had expressed the view that Enrico Berlinguer, the leader of the Italian Communist party, held views very close to his own on subjects such as the lack of democracy in the USSR.[40]

THE HELSINKI GROUPS, THE WEST, AND THE USSR

The Final Act of the Conference on Security and Cooperation in Europe "had profound influence on dissident groups and individuals in the Soviet Union." As Albert Boiter noted in the foreword of the largest one-volume collection of Helsinki samizdat, in the years after *Pravda* published the full text of the Final Act, "new groups of activists" made their appearances and older groups "found in the Helsinki text a new basis and a new framework for the statement of their grievances."[41]

A glance at the table of contents of this massive collection indicates the sharpening of focus and the amplification of the scope of dissent that resulted from Helsinki—and from factors associated with the international atmosphere in the early post-Helsinki years, such as President Carter's publicly expressed interest in human rights. Comprising 15 pages, this list of topics begins with 22 documents of the Moscow, Lithuanian, Georgian, and Armenian Helsinki groups. Then follow documents of other human rights organizations.

Part II covers ten individual human rights issue areas; Part III, problems of religious freedom; Part IV, rights of Soviet ethnic minorities, and the concluding section, Part V, is entitled "Soviet-American Relations and Human Rights." This last section includes the letters exchanged by Sakharov and Carter, as well as an earlier appeal by Sakharov to President Ford and candidate Carter during the U.S. 1976 presidential election campaign. It should be noted that six other documents written by Sakharov alone and one in which he collaborated are included.[42]

Particularly relevant to the relation between dissent in the USSR and relations between the USSR and both governments and public opinion in foreign countries were the general evaluations of the degree of fulfillment by the Soviet government of the Helsinki Final Act human rights provisions made by the Moscow Helsinki group. In its very first public statement, dated May 12, 1976, the Moscow group had signified its intention to inform heads of governments that had signed the Final Act of violations, by Soviet authorities, of the principles listed in Point VII of the Final Act. Significantly, the group asserted that "problems of humanitarianism and disclosure of information" were directly related to international peace.[43]

In July 1976 the group issued two evaluations, the shorter of which, expressly prepared for Western media, is quoted below. Its tenor is indicated by the statement that "analysis of the domestic policy of the Soviet Union in respect to the rights of man convinces one that the Soviet Government does not intend to fulfill the international obligations it assumed in Helsinki." It cited increasingly harsh treatment of political prisoners, failure to relax controls over emigration, "persecution" of all forms of free information, and of any attempt to form associations independent of the Communist Party of the Soviet Union, and so forth, as well as heightened sensitivity of the Soviet authorities to criticism of violations of human rights in the USSR. It mentioned the trials of noted human rights activists, characterizing them as efforts to frighten sympathizers with the human rights movement. The document accused the authorities of crudely violating the Final Act by measures intended to prevent the dissemination of exposés of official lawlessness, such as searches and seizure of manuscripts and documents. It also complained that the Soviet authorities had made it impossible for the Helsinki group to deliver documents regarding violations of the Final Act to the heads of governments that had signed it. In conclusion, the document expressed the opinion that if the Soviet human rights movement could substantially broaden its work of informing the Soviet public and the West, and if the West effectively supported this movement, the Soviet authorities would be constrained to moderate their repressive policy; this in turn would facilitate the realization of democratic rights. The unlikelihood of such a development, it continued, should not lead to a reduction of efforts, since it was precisely "our efforts" that increased this possibility.[44]

Documents similar in tone and content to the one just cited continued to appear. Thus, in February 1977 an interim report entitled "Three Months before Belgrade" noted that in the USSR and in Eastern Europe there was growing activity by individuals and groups basing their struggle for civil rights on the Helsinki Final Act. More and more prisoners of conscience were asserting that their inhumane treatment in places of detention was an outrageous violation of the Helsinki accords. In retaliation, the Soviet authorities were stepping up their offensive against those who openly busied themselves with informing the West about violation of the rights of man in the USSR. Arrests of activists were preceded by searches, during which evidence was planted by police agents and then discovered in the residences that had been searched. Moreover, all this was accompanied by defamation of rights activists in the press.

The Soviet government, the document went on to assert, sought to demonstrate its indifference to Western criticism of its repression of dissent, but this very repression was incompatible with the climate of trust that, presumably, the CSCE participants had sought to create. Concluding, the report saw in the Soviet leaders fears of growing unity of action among people in Eastern Europe and the USSR, interested in fulfillment of obligations assumed by the governments of these countries. It was obvious that the Soviet government was doing all it could to splinter the unity of human rights activists, all the more since their struggle had begun to receive some support from a number of West European Communist parties.

The group announced that Ludmilla Alekseeva, who had just emigrated, would act as representative of the group abroad, and it called on her and other emigrant dissenters to explain the true aims of the group to Western officials and opinion leaders and to combat the Kremlin's massive campaign of slander.[45]

In early May 1977, the Moscow group issued a very long report intended, like the one just referred to, for the attention of the then forthcoming Belgrade review conference on the fulfillment of the Helsinki accords, which after considerable delay opened in October of that year. It accused the Soviet authorities, among other things, of attempting to use the language of the Helsinki Final Act to justify restricting rather than facilitating emigration from the USSR. Condemning the official Soviet practice of combatting "ideas, emanating from the West," not by discussion but by force, the report argued that the essence of Helsinki lay in the connection between human rights and international cooperation. Regardless of the degree of probability of early realization of this idea, it would never disappear from the political scene, and it represented a big step toward individual freedom and collective security for mankind. It was necessary, however, to recognize that the obligations assumed at Helsinki were informal, and there were no generally accepted criteria for their application. Such an agreement as that arrived at in Helsinki required goodwill for its fulfillment.

The document predicted that at Belgrade the Soviet side would claim that, if human rights were being violated anywhere, it was in the West. At Belgrade the West ought to face up to the fact of Soviet violation of its humanitarian obligations and should strive for agreement of formal criteria for observance of human rights. At the least, the West should demand the release of the arrested members of the Soviet Helsinki groups. To this category belonged Yuri Orlov, arrested in February 1977. The report pointed out that in May 1976 Yuri Orlov had publicly stated that, according to the authorities, the Moscow group was an "illegal organization," and that an "enormous number" of KGB agents constantly shadowed him and other group members.[46]

The documents cited above are ethically and intellectually impressive. They pass judgment on the USSR's domestic and foreign policies—with specific reference to the human rights provisions of the CSCE Final Act—logically and cogently. They argue from the position, taken for years by Sakharov and others in the USSR, that international peace and security would be promoted by, and indeed required, the willingness of all governments, including that of the Soviet Union, to grant effective citizen participation in policy making, together with effective popular control over government by its submission to the rule of law. Their authors, particularly Yuri Orlov, the guiding spirit among them, were idealists; but they were keenly aware of the overwhelming power possessed by the Soviet regime. Orlov, who along with Sakharov and others added his voice to the struggle for peace and freedom, had in various writings acknowledged the heavy odds against reformers in the Soviet Union.[47]

If the Soviet Helsinki groups criticized the Soviet authorities in a manner that the latter could interpret only as incompatible with Bolshevik norms, it was because they were convinced that the struggle for justice and peace justified running big risks. Orlov and his colleagues were doubtless also aware that, as Bilinski and Parming point out, "built into the text" of the Final Act's statements on individual and national rights "were implicit and explicit limitations," and presumably, they were aware that in its approach to the Atlantic Charter, the Yalta Declaration, and other broad statements of principles, the USSR government had insisted that their texts be interpreted by taking into account the traditions and customs of each of the signatories.[48]

After mid-1977 or thereabouts, the focus of most of the output of the Helsinki groups and of other, loosely associated, or parallel-acting groups, such as the Christian Committee, shifted from broad concepts and principles to appeals and protests regarding firings, searches, vilification in the press, arrests and sentences to camps, commitments to mental institutions, and other actions taken by the authorities against persons seeking to persuade the regime to abide by what the protesters regarded as moral obligations assumed by the Soviet government in Helsinki.

As is well known, the Kremlin responded to both theoretical polemics and anguished protests with steadily increasing repression.[49] Only such words as "shocking" and "brutal" can begin to convey the nature of the repression visited upon the members of the Helsinki and associated groups. These Soviet actions are the best indicator of the regime's hostility to persons who without authorization demand rights, which, according to the authorities, are available in abundance. Less significant than the KGB's actions, but by no means negligible, were the sometimes ingratiating, sometimes indignant or blustering words or evasive silences of Soviet propagandists such as Georgi Arbatov and Aleksandr Chakovski. Before offering speculative remarks on the reasons for the harsh punishment of Soviet Helsinki monitors and the angry words addressed to their defenders abroad, it will be useful to add somewhat to what has been said about repression of dissidents, and also to present some examples of the official propaganda justification thereof. By the fall of 1978 a majority of the 60-odd participants in the Helsinki monitoring effort had suffered more or less severe repression at home or had been forced to leave the USSR. Jewish activist Anatoli Shcharanski was sentenced July 14, 1978 to three years in prison and ten years in a strict regime camp for "treason" and for "anti-Soviet agitation and propaganda." The treason charge against Shcharanski is believed to have been the first in the post-Stalin era. Yuri Orlov was sentenced May 18, 1978 to seven years in a strict regime camp and five years of internal exile for "anti-Soviet agitation and propaganda." In 1979 and 1980 there were further arrests of Moscow and other Helsinki group members, and in January 1980 Sakharov was, in effect, kidnapped and exiled to Gorki with his wife, whence, however, he has managed to send a large number of messages regarding the plight of fellow dissidents and to provide the world with depressing details of the surveillance-ridden life he and his spouse are forced to lead. As Sakharov said in an autobiographical note received from him by the International Conference in Honor of Andrei Sakharov, held at Rockefeller University May 1–2, 1981, the action taken against him and his wife and the regime imposed upon them "lacks any legal basis."[50]

Obviously the Soviet regime decided that the best way to rid itself of the annoyance of dissidents' supplying the world with information on the seamy side of Soviet life was to put them behind barbed wire or force them to leave the country. It proceeded to do so, regardless and indeed in contempt of the sectors of world opinion that had expressed sympathy and offered moral support to Soviet dissenters. Elsewhere the opinion has been expressed that the regime's terror campaign against the dissidents after Helsinki was inspired by fear.[51] Now, after further study and reflection, it seems more and more probable that it was based on the calculation, which has proven only too correct, that the best defense was a good offense, and that the risks of suppression of dissent were small. Suppressing dissent and portraying the dissenters as agents of Western imperialism was, among other things, a good way to capitalize on the rather primitive antiforeign sentiments widespread in various segments of Soviet society. It was a way of showing the Americans that the Soviet Union was strong and would brook no interference in its internal affairs—a somewhat inconsistent position for a government, the ideological rationale of which, set forth twice a year in November 7 and May Day slogans, is that it is leading "progressive mankind in a sacred struggle against world imperialism." Also, one surmises that the Soviet leaders shrewdly saw in the hints their propagandists dropped in communications addressed to Western audiences—to the effect that support for Soviet dissidents might adversely affect arms control negotiations—an effective instrument for playing on the lingering guilt feelings vis-à-vis the USSR of certain influential Western elite circles.[52]

There is, nevertheless, good reason to believe that the Soviet leaders thought that dissent, especially if vigorously supported by the West, was potentially dangerous to them. There is considerable evidence that the determined campaign of the Helsinki groups to expose abuses and defects in the USSR was beginning to mobilize sectors of Soviet society hitherto untouched by dissenters' influence. Ludmilla Alekseeva, one of the most active members of the Moscow Helsinki group, in an interview on West German television a few days after her enforced emigration in 1977, stressed the response of Soviet people to publication in the Soviet press of the Helsinki Final Act. For the first time in Soviet history, she noted, the Soviet people had heard that their government, in a document signed by the top Soviet leader, had assumed the obligation of safeguarding their civil rights.

The founding of the Helsinki groups had, she observed, been reported on foreign radio broadcasts. Her group had, from the beginning, sensed that its existence was known to the public. In spite of the persecution of the Helsinki groups, the flow of visitors and letters reaching them from the public had kept increasing. These contacts between groups independent of the government and the people had apparently alarmed the government. One reason for the "popularity" of the Helsinki groups was the deteriorating economic situation of the people, especially, but not only, in the provinces.[53]

A point of particular significance in Alekseeva's testimony was its reference to links between the Helsinki movement and workers. There is probably nothing that would alarm and anger the Soviet leaders more than a Polish-style alliance between intellectuals and workers. For such to develop, workers would have to achieve a level of consciousness and organizational independence vastly different from the apathy and conformity that have traditionally characterized their outlook and behavior. Equally important, reformist intellectuals would have to join hands with the workers in defense of the common interests of the two groups. Partial moves were made in the USSR in the 1970s, particularly from November 1977 on, toward creation of a partnership between workers and intellectuals in the struggle for democratic reforms. The former coal miner Vladimir Klebanov and six other workers called an informal press conference for Western correspondents and announced their intention of forming a labor union, independent of the official union organization, which Klebanov and his friends regarded as totally unresponsive to the rights and legitimate aspirations of labor. Prior to this development, of course, there had been numerous worker protests, the most notable of which was the Novocherkansk strike of 1962, bloodily suppressed by armed force.[54] In the fall of 1976 and in February 1978, respectively, Valentin Turchin and Elena Bonner wrote for the Moscow Helsinki group separate studies dealing with workers' problems. Turchin presented data on the economic problems impelling four individual workers to want to emigrate. Bonner and four collaborators hailed the establishment of the Independent Trade Union, headed by Klebanov, on February 1, 1978. They sought to link this development with principles contained in the Universal Declaration of the Rights of Man and the Helsinki Final Act, and expressed the opinion that its formation was in full conformity with Soviet law. This view was obviously not shared by the Soviet authorities, who quickly proceeded to arrange for commitment of Klebanov and other leaders of the new union to mental institutions. Persecution also befell the organizers of the successor to Klebanov's union, the Free Interprofessional Union of Workers, in which a prominent role was played by Vladimir Borisov. Borisov, after years of harassment by Soviet authorities, including several commitments to mental hospitals, was forced to leave the USSR in June 1980.[55]

If the Soviet leaders were concerned by what was still more a potential than actual threat of Polish-style worker-intellectual cooperation, they were probably even more worried by evidence of increasing ferment among such non-Russian nationalities as the Ukrainians, Lithuanians, Estonians, Georgians, Armenians, and of course, the Jews. Doubtless there is a correlation between worry about increasing disaffection among the non-Russians and the exceptionally severe sentences meted out to many members of the Kiev, Vilnius, Tbilisi, and Erevan Helsinki groups.

In February 1977 Leonard Garment, who had served as the U.S. representative to the U.N. Human Rights Commission, told the Congressional Commission on Security and Cooperation in Europe that "something important has happened to the place of human rights in American foreign policy." He noted that "the fate of human rights in the world, and in Eastern Europe—in particular" had become "a matter of practical concern" in American policy. He asserted that the forthcoming Belgrade conference to review the fulfillment of the 1975 Helsinki accords would mark the beginning of a process that could "have momentous human rights consequences." Mr. Garment—like Sakharov and other Soviet civil rights activists—rejected the argument of critics of Jimmy Carter's human rights policy that it could jeopardize the possibility of arms control agreements. American weakness in respect to this issue, he said, would "harm the cause of liberty" throughout the world.[56]

The official American position at the Belgrade conference of October 1977–March 1978 was probably softer than the one urged by Leonard Garment. It was certainly weaker than Soviet dissidents such as the noted Soviet human rights activist, former Soviet Major General Petr Grigorenko, thought it should have been. Grigorenko, in an article setting forth his views and those of like-minded dissidents, asserted that the final communique of the Belgrade meeting was "without content," "gray," and "useful only for concealing the USSR's predatory countenance."[57]

The official American position was apparently one of agreeing to disagree; this involved acceptance of a statement noting that the meeting had taken place and announcing future ones. The White House, however, rebuked the Soviet Union in a statement that said, inter alia, "We regret that the Soviet Union failed to permit the conference to fulfill its commitment to respect human rights."[58]

It would seem that if Carter's stance toward the champions of human rights in the USSR is to be criticized, it is not because it was belligerent or provocative, but rather because, like so many of his policies, it was poorly thought out, hesitant, and intermittent. While Carter's policy probably, for a time, blunted the Politburo's campaign to destroy the Helsinki groups, the evidence that came to Moscow's attention of division in the Carter administration on this issue, and Carter's shifts and hesitations, may have convinced the Soviet leadership that the risks of severely repressing the Soviet human rights fighters were not intolerably high.[59]

Western policy at the Madrid review conference was much better planned and coordinated than had been the case at Belgrade. A major role was played by a number of dissidents, now emigrated. The Western delegations, particularly the American, vigorously and specifically cited violations of human rights in the USSR and East European countries. It was reported that the American delegation alone had cited 60 individual cases of such violations in the USSR and Czechoslovakia.[60] Interestingly enough, the attitude of Soviet representatives at Madrid and the tone of the Soviet media seem to have been somewhat less abusive than at Belgrade. On the other hand, the Soviet authorities expressed their hostility by continuing the campaign to destroy the Soviet Helsinki groups, which had, as Grigorenko pointed out, gotten into high gear in early 1979. As was indicated in the sources cited above, the tasks of the conference could be expected to become more difficult as it completed its review portion and turned to "a general search for new measures which could strengthen the CSCE process."[61] It was clear from Soviet press coverage even during the first months of the conference that Moscow was seeking to divert attention from human rights questions to arms control and generally, what it chose to call "positive" efforts—in contrast to Western, especially American, "negativism." Anticipating the difficulties that might confront the West in the later portion of the conference, Grigorenko expressed pleasure at Western firmness in the opening days at Madrid, including condemnation of Soviet intervention in Afghanistan, but expressed fear that the West, in an effort to achieve unanimous decisions, would settle for partial, temporary, and illusory Soviet "concessions."[62]

In conclusion, a few words are in order regarding the campaign against "forces" and "circles" in the West, especially in the United States, often referred to in the Soviet media as the "enemies of détente." The Soviet media embarked on this campaign in full vigor about the middle of 1977, no doubt in preparation for the forthcoming Belgrade meeting. A long *Izvestiia* article on June 6, 1977 attributed what its author chose to call hostility to the results of Helsinki to an effort in Washington to "complicate" the preparatory phase of the Belgrade conference. Focusing mainly on an official report submitted by President Carter to the CSCE Commission, the article accused its authors of attempting to prove—by references to the "illegal actions" of alleged "fighters for freedom" in the USSR and Eastern Europe—that the USSR was violating the Helsinki Final Act. The article also charged that American officials were pressuring their NATO allies to step up the international arms race, and in conclusion and at length it attacked the domestic American record in the area of human rights.[63] Considerably fiercer were two articles in *Pravda*, which appeared under the signature of "V. Bolshakov," a name that often appears under articles flaying dissenters. Both of these articles charged that the Central Intelligence Agency, in cooperation, to be sure, with other U.S. government agencies and with private American mass media organizations, was the heart of the American domestic and foreign propaganda effort. Both charged that the C.I.A. was using dissenters in the USSR and Eastern Europe to facilitate achievement of its objectives, consisting of the "suppression of individuality, as a result of which man is deprived of the right to think independently," and of "changing the existing political system in and liquidating the revolutionary achievements" of the Socialist countries.[64]

In keeping with the saturation technique characteristic of Soviet political communication, a spate of books and pamphlets was also published on the same subject. Like the newspaper articles, this literature argued that the USSR took a constructive approach toward fulfillment of the Final Act, but that it also "decisively rebuffed the intrigues of the opponents of détente," who sought, among other things, to make use of "malicious renegades, who had betrayed the cause of socialism."[65]

Much Soviet discourse on human rights argues that, because the USSR is a Socialist society, it is *ipso facto* an open, participatory society, while, as the Soviet polemicist Samuil Zivs claims, Western society is "increasingly open to covert government surveillance."[66] Curiously enough, Zivs bases this claim largely on "the public outcry" in the United States and other Western countries on civil rights violations, blithely ignoring the high probability that any such "outcry" in the USSR would lead to the prosecution of those who raised it on charges of "anti-Soviet agitation."[67]

The intellectual and moral level of Zivs's book is perhaps best indicated by his devoting about half of it to what can best be described as character assassination of Sakharov, Orlov, Shcharanski, Solzhenitsyn, Bukovski, and other leading Soviet dissenters. The efforts of dissenters, Zivs asserts, have been "cancelled by history." Echoing the Kremlin's voice, he says that they committed criminal offenses; therefore, there is no point in debating with them. Regarding Orlov,

for example, Zivs says that his "material was used by those who opposed détente . . . which proves that his subjective and deliberate activities were *objectively harmful*" (italics in original).[68] About Sakharov, Zivs says that he "termed
the fraternal assistance" by the Soviet Union "to the Afghan people on their
request . . . arbitrary acts to launch an unjust war." Moreover, Sakharov supplied "deliberately slanderous" information to the Western press, and his appeals
to the United States to build up its armaments amount, says Zivs, "to a betrayal
of national interests."[69] Of course, Zivs says nothing about the failure of the
Soviet authorities to respond to the early, respectful petitions of men like
Sakharov, which was part of a pattern of unresponsive, arrogant regime behavior
toward nonviolent dissent that impelled some courageous, independent Soviet
citizens to run the awesome risks of remaining true to their consciences and
speaking out about what they regarded as morally wrong and politically harmful
Soviet domestic and foreign policies. The pattern of repression and vilification of
dissenters in the USSR and attempts to discredit their foreign supporters and
sympathizers described herein is deplorable but not surprising. Intensification of
repression at home and of attacks on Western governments, the Western press,
and nongovernmental groups and individuals, after the signing of the Helsinki
Final Act, is startling but also understandable. From the beginning détente was
understood differently by East and West. The USSR subordinated it to the
doctrine of "peaceful coexistence of states with different social systems," according to which there could be no diminution of the ideological struggle
between socialism and imperialism. Moreover, the Soviet side expressly excepted
the Third World, where it proclaimed its intention of continuing to support
national liberation struggles, from the détente relationship. Perceived only dimly
at first in the West, especially in a United States slowly emerging from the "Vietnam syndrome," these features of Soviet perspectives eventually had a chilling
effect on public opinion. In the meantime, in important areas of Soviet-Western
relations—such as trade, arms control, and human rights—tensions, instead of
relaxing, multiplied and intensified. Awareness of such factors, it seems, should
help in understanding the Soviet official attitudes and policies examined here. If
today the détente that seemed to many, perhaps even to some on the Soviet
side, to be blossoming in 1972-75 looks like an untypical conjuncture in the
relations between the USSR and the West, particularly the United States, one
can understand why Moscow has considered it necessary to eliminate from
public life all who disagreed with its interpretation of human rights, détente,
and the Helsinki agreement. It is also understandable that all this has generated
indignation and concern in the West.

　　The confrontation between dissenters and the Soviet regime is in many
ways sad and tragic. There is reason to believe, however, that as long as the
causes—censorship, party and police interference in intellectual life, and un-
responsiveness to honest criticism—persist, so will dissent. Inspiration can be

derived from the courageous struggle of Soviet dissidents and a great deal can be learned about the Soviet system by careful study of their writings.

NOTES

1. Alexander Dallin, "Soviet Foreign Policy and Domestic Politics: A Framework for Analysis," in *The Conduct of Soviet Foreign Policy*, ed. Erik P. Hoffman and Frederic J. Fleron, Jr. (New York: Aldine, 1980), pp. 36–49, at p. 40. Dallin's article was first published in 1969.

2. Victor Nekipelov, *Institute of Fools* (New York: Farrar, Straus & Giroux, 1980), Appendix 1, p. 190.

3. "Doklad tovarishcha Iu. V. Andropova," *Izvestiia*, September 10, 1977.

4. See the long quotation from Brezhnev's attack on dissenters and cogent remarks on Soviet efforts to discredit them in Peter Reddaway, "Policy Towards Dissent Since Khrushchev," in *Authority, Power and Policy in the USSR*, ed. T. H. Rigby, Archie Brown, and Peter Reddaway (London: Macmillan, 1980), pp. 158–92, at 159–61.

5. *The New Soviet Constitution of 1917: Analysis and Text*, with analysis by Robert Sharlet (Brunswick, Ohio: Kings Court, 1978), pp. 89, 93.

6. Andrei Sakharov, *My Country and the World* (New York: Knopf, 1975), pp. 33–34.

7. See *Prisoners of Conscience in the USSR: Their Treatment and Conditions* (London: Amnesty International, 1980), pp. 13, 14, 65. This is an updated version of a similar report published by Amnesty International in 1975. See Frederick C. Barghoorn, "The Post-Khrushchev Campaign to Suppress Dissent: Perspectives, Strategies and Techniques of Repression," in *Dissent in the USSR*, ed. Rudolf L. Tökés (Baltimore, Md.: Johns Hopkins University Press, 1975), pp. 35–95; and Peter Reddaway, "Policy Towards Dissent Since Khrushchev."

8. *Prisoners of Conscience*, p. 1.

9. *Implementation of the Final Act of the Conference on Security and Cooperation in Europe: Findings and Recommendations Five Years After Helsinki*, 96th Cong., 2d sess. (Washington, D.C.: U.S. Government Printing Office, 1980), pp. 67, 161, 176.

10. See F. Barghoorn, *Détente and the Democratic Movement in the USSR* (New York: Free Press, 1976), especially pp. 23–118, and parts of the following: F. Barghoorn, "Political Dissent," in *The Soviet Union: Looking to the 1980s*, ed. Robert Wesson (Stanford, Cal.: Hoover Institution Press, 1980), pp, 155–76; Ferdinand J. Feldbrugge, *Samizdat and Political Dissent in the Soviet Union* (Leyden: A. W. Sijthoff, 1975); Reddaway, "Policy Towards Dissent Since Khrushchev"; Joshua Rubenstein, *Soviet Dissidents* (Boston: Beacon Press, 1980). Some of the memoirs of dissenters in emigration, particularly Vladimir Bukovski, *To Build a Castle* (New York: Viking, 1978), and Aleksandr Solzhenitsyn, *The Oak and the Calf* (New York: Harper & Row, 1980) contain pertinent information.

12. See Barghoorn, *Détente and the Democratic Movement*, pp. 50–52, and Barghoorn, "Political Dissent," p. 175.

13. Quotations of the Moscow Helsinki group's aims are from Arkhiv Samizdata, 2542, in *Sobranie Dokumentov Samizdata*, vol. 30, (Munich: Samizdat Archive Association, 1978), pp. 3, 5. This 750-page volume contains Helsinki samizdat covering roughly the first two years of the existence of the activity of the groups that sought to promote observance of the Helsinki agreement; hereafter cited as Helsinki Samizdat. Individual Arkhiv Samizdata items will be referred to by the initials AS and their number.

14. Cornelia Gerstenmaier, *Die Stimme der Stummen*, 3rd ed., (Stuttgart: 1972), p. 62.

15. See Abraham Rothberg, *The Heirs of Stalin* (Ithaca, N.Y.: Cornell University Press, 1972), pp. 337-40; *A Chronicle of Current Events No. 16* (London: Amnesty International, 1970), pp. 6-10.

16. Gerstenmaier, *Die Stimme der Stummen*, pp. 61-62, 196, 375. According to Joshua Rubenstein, friends of Natalia Gorbanevskaia "were expelled from the University for opposing the invasion." See his *Soviet Dissidents*, p. 99.

17. For a description of these documents and their contents, see Barghoorn, *Detente and the Democratic Movement*, pp. 23-26. The number of protesters against the invasion of Czechoslovakia appears to have been smaller than in the case of Hungary, but Wright Miller, in *Who Are the Russians?* (New York: Taplinger, 1973), p. 199, reports that 100 students were expelled from one Siberian University alone for protesting the invasion of Czechoslovakia.

18. Quoted from translation in Peter Reddaway, *Uncensored Russia* (New York: American Heritage Press, 1972), p. 99.

19. *Politicheskii drevnik*, vol. 1 (Amsterdam: Alexander Herzen Foundation, 1972), pp. 397-401; Andrei Sakharov, *Sakharov Speaks* (New York: Vintage Books, 1974), p. 152.

20. Several contributors to Rudolf L. Tökés., ed., *Eurocommunism and Detente* (New York: New York University Press, 1978) point to links between Eurocommunism and Soviet action in Czechoslovakia.

21. Besides the statement by Sakharov cited above, others by him on the same subject could be mentioned. See, for example, Roy A. Medvedev, *On Socialist Democracy* (New York: Knopf, 1975), pp. 79, 217. For Robert Legvold's statements on Soviet dissent and Eurocommunism, see "The Soviet Union and West European Communism," in Tökés, *Eurocommunism*, pp. 314-84, at p. 343.

22. For details, see Frederick C. Barghoorn, "The General Pattern of Soviet Dissent," in *Dissent in the Soviet Union*, ed. Peter J. Potichnyj. Papers and Proceedings of the Fifth Annual Conference, Interdepartmental Committee on Communist and East European Affairs, McMaster University, Hamilton, Ontario (Hamilton, Ontario: Interdepartmental Committee on Communist and East European Affairs, Winter 1972), pp. 16-19.

23. English translation of text and list of signers in *In Quest of Justice*, ed. Abraham Brumberg (New York: Praeger, 1970), pp. 458-61.

24. Text in Reddaway, *Uncensored Russia*, pp. 86-88.

25. Paul Litvinov, "O dvizhenii za prava cheloveka v SSSR," in *Samosoznanie*, ed. P. Litvinov, M. Meerson-Aksenov, and B. Shragin (New York: Khronika Press, 1976), p. 82.

26. Ibid., p. 184.

27. See Howard L. Biddulph, "Protest Strategies of the Soviet Intellectual Opposition," in *Dissent in the USSR*, ed. Rudolf L. Tökés, p. 116; and Boris Shragin, *The Challenge of the Spirit* (New York: Knopf, 1978), p. 203.

28. Karel van het Reve, ed., *Pavel Litvinov and the Voices of Soviet Citizens in Dissent* (New York: Pitman, 1969), pp. 2-15.

29. See Van het Reve's introduction to ibid., p. xv.

30. Text in *Sakharov Speaks*, ed. Harrison E. Salisbury (New York: Vintage, 1974), pp. 165-78.

31. Ibid., pp. 180-92. Quotations on pp. 181, 184.

32. See Peter Dornan, "Andrei Sakharov: The Conscience of a Liberal Scientist," in *Dissent in the USSR*, ed. Tökés, pp. 355-417, at 400-7.

33. See Andrei D. Sakharov, *Alarm and Hope* (New York: Knopf, 1978), pp. 47, 70, 128-30.

34. See "Citation for the 1975 Nobel Peace Prize Award," in *Alarm and Hope*, pp. 4-5 and on pp. 5-18 of Sakharov's Nobel lecture entitled "Peace, Progress and Human Rights."

35. Text of Sakharov's letter to Carter and Carter's reply and background and follow-up material in *Alarm and Hope*, pp. 43–46. Quotations on p. 50.

36. See *Mezhdunarodnoe slushanie sakharova v kopengagene* (Copenhagen: Polyglott, 1977).

37. It is not surprising that the USSR did what it could by threats against the Danes, and by sending an uninvited "anti-hearing delegation," headed by the hard-line editor of the Soviet *Literary Gazette*, Aleksandr Chakovski, and including a bogus rabbi, to prevent the holding of the hearing. See ibid., p. 11.

38. See *Alarm and Hope*, pp. 129–32.

39. Ibid., pp. 28–31.

40. See Wolfgang Leonhard, *Eurocommunism: Challenge for East and West*, tr. Mark Vecchio (New York: Holt, Rinehart and Winston, 1979), p. 138.

41. Albert Boiter, in foreword to *Helsinki Samizdat from the USSR*, p. v. This volume, No. 30 in the series *Sobranie dokumentov samizdata* (see Note 13), contains 140 selected documents written between mid-1975 and mid-1978.

42. A fuller collection of the documents of the five Helsinki groups (Moscow, Kiev, Vilnius, Tbilisi, Erevan) than that in the above-cited volume, but not including those produced by the other human rights, religious, and other organizations represented therein, is in the series *Documents of the Helsinki Watch Group in the USSR*, published by Khronika Press, New York. By early 1981, seven volumes, containing the texts of 124 documents, had been published, almost all in Russian, but a few in English.

43. AS 2605.

44. AS 2651.

45. AS 2652.

46. AS 2904. See also Orlov's comments on the "nervousness" displayed by agent Tikhonov when in January 1977 he searched Orlov's residence, incidentally confiscated as allegedly subversive books officially published in the USSR, in vol. 2, p. 71, and vol. 3, p. 66, of *Documents of the Helsinki Watch Group in the USSR*.

47. See, for example, Orlov's contribution to *Samosoznanie*, pp. 279–304, written in 1975, entitled "Is Socialism of a Non-totalitarian Type Possible," which he begins by noting that for seriously discussing this topic in the USSR one can get seven years of strict regime in a labor camp; or Turchin's pessimistic preface to the Russian edition of *The Inertia of Fear*, written in 1976 before his emigration to the United States, where he asserts that in the USSR there is not even the 1 percent minority willing—and necessary if change is to occur—to risk their lives for changes, even though "long-overdue changes" are "passively favored by broader strata." Quotation on p. xvii.

48. Yaroslav Bilinski and Tonu Parming, "Helsinki Watch Committees in the Soviet Republics: Implications for Soviet Nationality Policy," *Nationalities Papers* 9, no. 1 (Spring 1981): 1–25.

49. For details, see, besides the sources cited already in the discussion of the Helsinki groups, the numerous, fact-crammed documents prepared and distributed by the Commission on Security and Cooperation in Europe, including *CSCE Digest* and the multivolume *Basket III: Implementation of the Helsinki Accords. Hearings before the Commission on Security and Cooperation in Europe* (Washington, D.C.: U.S. Government Printing Office, 1980). The semiannual report series of the Bureau of Public Affairs, U.S. Department of State, is another useful U.S. government source. See also *Freedom Appeal* and *Freedom in the World*, published by Freedom House in New York and, of course, publications of such organizations as Amnesty International, The International Human Rights League, and other similar organizations in Europe and America. On religious rights, there is a substantial body of data distributed by religious organizations in the West. To keep abreast of ongoing developments in all aspects of dissent in the USSR, it is necessary, of course, to read Russian-language sources, such as *Novoe russkoe slovo, Posev, Kontinent*, and so forth.

50. In addition to the above-cited "autobiographical note," Sakharov sent to the International Conference, a "statement for press and radio" reporting new instances of "KGB penetrations" of his residence, and on March 13, 1981, KGB theft of the bag in which he had been keeping his scientific manuscripts, personal diary, and three volumes of his autobiography, as well as other, more personal materials. For important material on his seizure by the police, after he denounced the Soviet invasion of Afghanistan, and his first days in exile, see "Iz materialov Akademika A. D. Sakharova," *Novoe russkoe slovo*, March 27, 1980. See also *New York Times* dispatches and editorial of January 23, 1980.

51. See "Political Dissent," p. 168.

52. See, for example, Georgi Arbatov's play on this theme in an interview he granted to *Atlas World Press Review* of July 1977, entitled "A new U.S.-Soviet Era." In fact, Arbatov turned to the subject of "the so-called dissidents" near the beginning of his remarks and very quickly, though indirectly, yet deftly, suggested that American "interference" could indeed harmfully affect arms control negotiations.

53. See "Lyudi stali menshe boiatsia, chem ranshe," *Posev* 3 (March 1977): 5–6. Also Alekseeva's earlier cited article on Tatiana Osipova, in *Novoe russkoe slovo*, April 7, 1981, quoting Ivan Kovalev, Osipova's husband, on the flood of visitors and letters the couple had to deal with, and also Barghoorn's "Political Dissent," p. 169. The author has heard accounts similar to Alekseeva's and Kovalev's from a number of refugees now in the United States.

54. More information is available on labor unrest in the USSR than is commonly supposed. See, for example, pp. 320, 330, of Julian Birch, "Nature and Sources of Dissidence in Ukraine," in *Ukraine in the Seventies*, ed. Peter J. Potichnyj (Oakville, Ont.: Mosaic Press, 1975).

55. See Valeri Chalidze, *SSSR-rabochee dvizhenie?* (New York; Khronika Press, 1978); Chalidze's article, "A Worker's Movement in Russia?" *The Wall Street Journal*, May 16, 1978; Tulia Wishnevski, "Members of Unofficial Trade Union Harassed," *Radio Liberty Research*, RL 132/80, April 2, 1980.

56. Commission on Security and Cooperation in Europe, News Release, Washington, D.C., February 23, 1977.

57. Petr Grigorenki, "S chem i za chem my edem v Madrid," *Novoe russkoe slovo*, October 16, 1980.

58. Bernard Gevertzman, "U.S. Rebukes Soviet on Belgrade Talks," *New York Times*, March 3, 1978; also James Reston, "Letter from Belgrade," ibid., March 1, 1978, quoting Arthur Goldberg, chief of the U.S. delegation, terming the results "disagreeable," but "not intolerable."

59. The position taken here differs slightly from that set forth on pp. 175–76 of *Détente and the Democratic Movement in the USSR*, where the author was somewhat critical of overt intervention by the executive branch of the U.S. government on behalf of Soviet dissenters. The author would, however, now take the position that if there is to be such intervention, it should be very carefully thought out and be undertaken only as part of a consistent program, in which specific cases and the general thesis of the differences between democracy and dictatorship should be linked. In part, the present position is based on study of statements by people like Bukovski and Grigorenko, and data in Friendly and Yankelevich, eds., *Alarm and Hope*, and also on cogent evidence cited in Peter Reddaway's contribution to *Authority, Power and Policy in the USSR*, especially pp. 178–79.

60. See "The Madrid CSCE Review Meeting: An Interim Report," by Staff of the Commission on Security and Cooperation in Europe, January 6, 1981; and William Korey, "Rattling the Russians in Madrid," *New Leader*, February 9, 1981, pp. 6–7.

61. See "Madrid CSCE Review Meeting," p. 22.

62. P. Grigorenko, "Sovetskaia taktika v Madride," *Novoe russkoe slovo*, December 3, 1980. The title of a typical article on Madrid, "Madridskaia v strecha–vtoroi etap," subtitled "razoruzhenie–velenie vremeni," in *Pravda* for January 27, 1981, suggests the line the Soviets had mapped out for the second stage.

63. V. Matveev, "Slova i dela," *Izvestiia*, June 14, 1977. Matveev is identified at the end of this article as "Political Observer of *Izvestiia*."

64. V. Bolshakov, "Manipuliatory soznaniem," *Pravda*, September 17, 1979, and "Na volne kholodnoi voiny: ideologicheskii front," *Pravda*, September 23, 1980. The 1980 article accused the Chinese Peoples Republic of cooperating with Western radio stations in anti-Soviet propaganda.

65. It is startling that this far from subtle statement occurred in a collective work, *Vneshniaia politika sovetskogo soiuza*, published in Moscow, 1978, by the Publishing House for Political Literature, and with a preface by A. A. Gromyko! Similar in tenor are K. Slavinov, *Moguchii faktor mira i stabilnosti v mezhdunarodnykh otnosheniakh: k 25-letiiu varskoskogo dogovora* (Moscow: Mezhdunarodnye otnoshenia, 1980), and *Varshavski dogovor i NATO: dva kursa, dve politiki* (Moscow: Mezhdunarodnye otnosheniia, 1979).

66. Samuil Zivs, *Human Rights: Continuing the Discussion* (Moscow: Progress Publishers, 1980), p. 149.

67. Ibid., pp. 180, 181.

68. Ibid., p. 102.

69. Ibid., pp. 105, 106.

PART THREE

The Soviet Union and the Communist World

6

POLITICS OF ACCOMMODATION: REDEFINING SOVIET-EAST EUROPEAN RELATIONS

Robin Alison Remington

Eastern Europe is Moscow's backyard. Long before there was a Soviet Union, national security concerns combined with religious-cultural pan-Slavism to put the region high on the list of Czarist Russian foreign policy priorities. Russian conviction that Moscow had become the "third Rome" added a sense of messianic responsibility for the fate of Christian Slavs taken subject by the Ottoman Empire. It was not only that Eastern Europe could become a military highway into the heart of Russia. Even before a Bosnian nationalist's assassination of the Austrian archduke in Sarajevo enflamed passions that convulsed all Europe in World War I, political instability in Eastern Europe had dragged Russia into war—a historical record that did nothing to calm fears about Soviet reaction to the increasingly political demands of Polish workers during 1980 and 1981.

World War II began in Poland. When it ended, Soviet ideology reinforced the historic habit of policy makers in Moscow of considering Eastern Europe a natural sphere of influence to be consolidated. Despite subsequent cold-war demands for liberation of captive East European nations, initially such thinking was not rejected by the West. Witness the concessions of Churchill, Roosevelt, and even Truman. For Truman the key was Soviet troop locations;[1] for the British, it was the larger issue. Caught in a geographic vise between Germany and the USSR, these unfortunate nations were natural victims of power politics, doomed to be dominated by one or the other of their powerful neighbors.[2] In 1941 the British preferred the Soviets, and that opinion had not wavered as the war progressed. It lay at the root of Churchill's often condemned percentages agreement in which the British wartime leader suggested that Great Britain and the USSR come to an understanding about their postwar spheres of influence in the Balkans. Therefore, not surprisingly, the Yalta Agreement spun a web of vague generalizations that in practice amounted to Western acquiescence to Stalin's security demands.

THE SOVIET BLOC AND LOVE OF COMRADE STALIN

In fairness, Soviet postwar objectives in Eastern Europe were not clear or visibly revolutionary. Policy goals for these nations were tangled in Stalin's East-West expectations with hopes for Western reconstruction aid operating as a short-lived restraint. Undoubtedly, there were minimal and maximum contingency plans. Minimally, the emphasis was strategic; Stalin demanded buffer states, a roadblock to future military attacks. Had the wartime alliance continued, had the hope materialized that the United States would rebuild the USSR rather than Germany and Japan, the Soviet leader conceivably might have accepted real rather than token coalition governments. As Brzezinski points out, the speed with which East European "people's democracies" were transformed into dictatorships of the proletariat was not inevitable.[3]

This is not the place to recapitulate the debates on the origin of the cold war so well documented elsewhere.[4] For the present purposes, it is sufficient to recall that the collapse of the postwar international system into total hostility escalated Soviet ambitions in Eastern Europe. East European economies subsidized postwar reconstruction of the Soviet Union.[5] The area served not only as a strategic buffer but as a revolutionary staging ground with at least the potential for offensive action against a war-weary Western Europe. It was no accident, in Marxist jargon, that the Communist Information Bureau (Cominform), set up in 1947, included France and Italy, two nonruling Communist parties with one foot on the ladder to power, as well as the ruling East European Communist parties. Finally, East European imitation of the Soviet model reaffirmed and legitimized the Soviet road to socialism both for Soviet domestic consumption and possibly among those developing countries intent on breaking the shackles of colonialism.

As a consequence, the Stalinist interstate system dominated Communist East Europe from 1948 until Stalin died in 1953. During this period informal control mechanisms provided the infrastructure of Soviet–East European relations. Soviet cadre "advisers" penetrated East European Communist parties, security apparatus, and armed forces. Joint stock companies functioned as conduits for economic exploitation, while the Soviet embassy operated as a headquarters for political commands rather than diplomatic communications. The Soviet ambassador gave orders, and East European leaderships jumped.

The resulting dominant-subordinate relationship directly conflicted with the legal fiction embodied in the bilateral treaties of friendship, cooperation, and mutual assistance that pledged Soviet respect for East European sovereignty, territorial integrity, and the principle of noninterference in internal affairs. In reality there was a substantial level of political, economic, and military integration of these countries into the Soviet system that, it would seem, can be correctly characterized as a Stalinist empire in Eastern Europe, commonly referred to as the Soviet bloc.

The system emerged only partly because of active Soviet policy initiatives and Western strategic disengagement. Rather, it was the logical consequence of the fact that the East European Communists who rode to power on the coattails of the Red Army during World War II had subsisted on a Soviet dole for years. Typically these were prewar Communists dependent on the Soviet Union for financial survival, organizing principles, and legitimizing myth. They accepted the fact that Moscow paid the bills and called the tune; they saw nothing wrong with the idea that proletarian internationalism was synonymous with Soviet national interests and love of Comrade Stalin.

Hence, the East European leaders almost automatically continued to function as docile instruments of Soviet foreign policy. Caught in a web of past political commitments, psychological dependency, and the knowledge that their power over largely hostile populations depended on Soviet occupation forces, theirs was a natural reaction.

On the surface, the rules of the intra-Communist political game remained the same. Yet during World War II the status of some Communist political actors had subtly changed. Yugoslav Communists led an indigenous struggle for national liberation that produced a seasoned revolutionary leadership unwilling to tolerate the Soviet penetration accepted as a matter of course in most East European systems. The Albanians also came to power during a civil war and without the assistance of Soviet troops. The Polish Communist party, rebuilt after being formally dissolved in 1938 during the ravages of Stalin's purges, experienced armed struggle both in resistance to German occupation and in a bloody consolidation of power that verged on an undeclared civil war. Asian Communist regimes took power without benefit of Soviet liberation. Indeed, Mao Zedong picked up the mandate of heaven in 1949 against Stalin's explicit advice.

Once in power, East European Communist leaders became subject to pressures from below in the form of nationalistic, in some cases historically anti-Soviet, political cultures. At first concessions to domesticism appeared permissible in Moscow. But as the cold war grew colder, deteriorating East-West relations interacted with the Soviet-Yugoslav split in 1948 to end Stalin's toleration of detours from the Soviet road to socialism. Much as during the purges of the 1930s, anti-Titoist show trials swept East European Communist parties, eliminating elements regarded as unreliable by the Soviets. Stalin was determined to neutralize the Yugoslav alternative. There would be no proliferation of little Titos on his doorstep.

Thus the Stalinist interstate system came to depend on fear and naked force, justified by the Soviet dictator's increasingly macabre personality cult.

These tactics must be considered as a failure of Soviet foreign policy. They not only prevented any genuine political institutionalization of East European Communist parties, but ultimately undermined Soviet control as well, for Stalin's empire was glued together by the myth of Stalin's personal infallibility. When worship of Comrade Stalin did not survive his death, the control began to crumble.

COLLAPSE OF THE STALINIST INTERSTATE SYSTEM

A tacitly collective leadership within which no one of Stalin's successors was strong enough to eliminate his competitors papered over the subsequent intense struggle for power. The New Course and de-Stalinization were essential components of the factionalism sweeping the Soviet Communist party. Domestic imperatives overshadowed the foreign policy consequences of jettisoning Stalin's demigod like image.

In 1956 Khrushchev attacked Stalin as a tyrant, murderer, and military incompetent with a mania for greatness that had come perilously close to destroying the CPSU itself. This ostensibly "secret" speech dropped like a bomb in the midst of the 20th CPSU Congress,[6] depriving East European Communists of an essential mooring. Their regimes were fragile. Too much had been done in the name of Stalin that could not be undone. A Czechoslovak analysis captured the sense of anguished dismay:

> Much has happened this year. Much that was dear to us has been smashed. . . . Our souls are full of pain because strings have suddenly been touched which we thought were inviolable. . . . [M]any old Communists will feel sadness. They may even feel bitter.[7]

The Polish party leader Bierut returned to Warsaw to die of a heart attack. Other East European leaders were caught in the ebb tide of disillusionment, compounded by the political instability that came from their reluctant rehabilitations of purge victims, at Soviet insistence.

In short, de-Stalinization did not mean abandoning a Stalinist mode of interaction between the new Soviet leadership and their East European counterparts. The Soviet model was still the norm. If the New Course and de-Stalinization was good for the Soviet Union, it must be good for Eastern Europe. Notwithstanding the changing attitude signaled by the declining number of Soviet advisers and dissolution of the joint stock companies, Stalin's successors took the necessity for East European domestic emulation of the new Soviet line as a matter of course. The dominant-subordinate nature of Soviet–East European relations remained essentially the same, only now the fate of individual East European leaders and policies rose and fell with that of more than one Soviet patron. Note the fall of Hungarian reformer Imre Nagy as Malenkov slipped down the hierarchy of power in 1955.[8]

Gripped in their own succession struggle, the Soviets were oblivious to the destabilizing impact of their policies on Eastern Europe. Moreover, Khrushchev's decision to woo Yugoslavia back into the Soviet bloc proved costly. Admission of Soviet mistakes and a formal acceptance of the legitimacy of national roads to socialism opened a political Pandora's box. Within barely a week of the June 1956 Declaration on Relations between the League of Yugoslav Communists and the Communist Party of the Soviet Union a strike in Poznań threatened to become an anti-Soviet uprising. Polish troops fired on the striking workers, setting in motion events that, in retrospect, can be seen as the beginning of mobilized Polish workers' demands for a genuine proletarian revolution. A wave of revolutionary unrest cracked the Stalinist empire beyond repair.

In Poland Moscow settled for the return of Wladyslaw Gomulka and expanded autonomy.[9] When these concessions ignited the abortive Hungarian revolution, the Red Army put its shoulder firmly behind the wheel of history that Molotov had confidently predicted assured the continued construction of socialism in Eastern Europe.[10]

The wheel wobbled, but did not turn back; Soviet military intervention accomplished its objective. The unfortunate British, French, and Israeli attack on the Suez lessened the risk entailed in Moscow's decision to resort to force in 1956. Seen in terms of the basic foreign policy calculations that go on in Communist and non-Communist countries alike—benefit weighed against cost and risk—Soviet troops had stemmed the tide of political disintegration. Moreover, it was now quite clear to East European opposition forces that U.S. rhetoric about liberating their "captive nations" would not materialize as military assistance if the East Europeans should attempt to liberate themselves.

Yet the long-run costs of Soviet decisions in Poland and Hungary were substantial. Poland symbolized the end of mandatory imitation of the Soviet model in Eastern Europe. In the wave of decollectivization that followed, some 85 percent of Polish agriculture went back into private farms, and today more Catholic priests are trained in Communist Poland than in Italy. The "leading role of the Communist party" remained the bottom line. Nonetheless, how that leading role should be interpreted would increasingly be decided in East European capitals and not in Moscow.

THE CHINA CARD AND EAST EUROPEAN OPTIONS

This trend toward genuinely national roads to socialism was reinforced by another unintended consequence of Soviet policy in 1956. Faced with the disastrous results of de-Stalinization, Khrushchev inadvertently opened the door to Chinese influence in Eastern Europe.[11] During the winter of 1956/57 Zhou

Enlai toured East Europe, preaching Soviet leadership and the need to reconstruct a recognizable center in the international Communist movement. Moscow welcomed Chinese support without fully realizing the implicit challenge to Soviet hegemony. By 1960 China had moved from being a junior partner into open opposition to the manner in which Moscow exercised Soviet leadership of world communism. Thus, the power configuration of intra-Communist politics changed, making the East European parties ever more valuable allies and thereby increasing their room for political maneuver.

The Soviet strategy of surrogate polemics, attacking China's Albanian disciples in hopes of getting the situation under control before an open split, backfired. Steeped in traditions of blood feuds and guerrilla warefare, the Albanians struck back. At the November 1960 Moscow Conference of Communist Parties, the Albanian party leader Enver Hoxha accused the Soviets of interfering in the affairs of fraternal parties, mishandling the situation in Hungary in 1956, factionalism, and using economic pressure against Albania.[12] By the 22nd CPSU Congress, Khrushchev escalated the dispute, charging that the Albanian party had purged Soviet sympathizers, refused to consult the Soviets concerning their differences, and practiced a galaxy of Marxist sins including dogmatism, sectarianism, narrow nationalism, and revisionism. In short, when faced with Albanian defiance, the Soviet leader adopted precisely the same tactics he had criticized in Stalin's handling of the Yugoslavs.

Khrushchev's attempt to bring Albania back into line proved equally unsuccessful and costly in terms of long-range Soviet objectives. Tirana publicly split with Moscow, Zhou Enlai not only supported Hoxha at the 22nd CPSU Congress but ostentatiously laid a wreath on Stalin's grave before he left Moscow—an explicit signal that all was not well in Soviet-Chinese relations. This was picked up even in the West, where policy makers had been oblivious to the increasing tension between Moscow and Beijing. Moreover, not only had Albania become a Chinese client in the Balkans, but the Romanians were able to manipulate the Sino-Soviet split to the advantage of their increasingly autonomous foreign policy.[13]

Khrushchev's effort to substitute organizational ties for the declining ideological unity and direct Soviet control upgraded both the Warsaw Pact (1955) and Stalin's essentially moribund Council for Mutual Economic Assistance (CMEA) as instruments of Soviet policy in Eastern Europe. This drive to institutionalize Soviet hegemony meant abandoning the bilateralism characteristic of the Stalinist interstate system for multilateral forums that involved subtle pressures for Soviet concessions to East European national needs. Indeed, lack of such sensitivity vis-à-vis the CMEA led first to Romanian resistance, then to Bucharest's flirtation with Beijing.

By the mid-1960s Soviet leadership of the world Communist movement had been aptly characterized as in a state of disarray that combined with the consequences of de-Stalinization to weaken Soviet influence over East European Communist leaders, themselves ever more subject to the demands of domestic legitimization. Unwittingly, Khrushchev's penchant for East-West summit diplomacy, devoted to selling Soviet-style peaceful coexistence, reinforced the emerging polycentrism, as did normalization of Soviet-Yugoslav relations.

Khrushchev's fall in October 1964 was not because he had presided over the dissolution of Stalin's empire in Eastern Europe. His dismal record in achieving Soviet policy objectives in this vital region was probably fairly low on the list of "harebrained schemes" that convinced the other members of the Politburo to get rid of him. Nonetheless, it must be counted among Moscow's foreign policy failures.

Brezhnev and the other Soviet leaders inherited a deteriorating situation. The Soviet invasion of Czechoslovakia in August 1968 temporarily appeared to stem the tide. Yet the use of Soviet troops to prevent the Dubček regime from sweeping the ashes of Stalinism off the Czechoslovak road to socialism had unintended repercussions. The substance of Czechoslovak socialism with a human face reemerged in the form of Eurocommunist demands for inner-party democracy, Socialist pluralism, and parliamentary politics.[14] Although Eurocommunism has been dealt with in Joan Barth Urban's contribution to this volume, from the Soviet-East European perspective the challenge of what can be more precisely called autonomist parties to Soviet hegemony within the international Communist movement has its own history and special significance.

This analysis assumes that what we call Eurocommunism represents ongoing change in the power configuration of the Communist subsystem of the contemporary international community. As a growing number of Communist parties in Europe and Asia acquired real estate, government bureaucracies, and the need to relate to their own populations, the Soviet Union's ability to maintain Moscow's leading role and the primacy of Soviet interests declined. That challenge has been going on since the late 1940s, variously identified as domesticism, national communism, reform communism, or polycentrism. It is the process by which the egalitarianism of pre-1917 Communist tradition has begun to reassert itself in new circumstances, recreating the old dilemma of class versus national priorities. In the author's judgment, that process began not in Western Europe but in Eastern Europe, where the components of Eurocommunism—nationalism, pluralism, regionalism—are all essential elements of a readily documentable Yugoslav experience.[15] Nonetheless, it is correct that Eurocommunism is returning to Eastern Europe with new forms and new implications.

The Eurocommunist rejection of the former dominant-subordinate relationship between the CPSU and other ruling and nonruling Parties is three-pronged: first, there is an insistence that the nation be rehabilitated and reunited with class in the form of national roads to socialism—a principle accepted by the Soviets in the Belgrade Declaration of 1955 despite subsequent breaches in practice; second, the Soviet model is no longer considered essential either for taking power or building socialism; and third, Soviet-defined proletarian internationalism is considered unacceptable as the basis for relations among states and parties in the Communist world, which should be founded on the principles of sovereignty, equality, noninterference in internal affairs, and mutual advantage. This attempt to democratize intra-Communist decision making so as to reflect the changing correlation of forces emphasizes Soviet responsibility rather than privilege. No longer are Soviet policy and behavior sacrosanct, uncritically defended.[16]

Although the June 1976 Berlin meeting of 29 Communist and workers parties of Europe endorsed the main lines of Soviet foreign policy, on balance the conference solidified the earlier procedural victory of the Eurocommunists. The final document made no mention of preferred Soviet ideological formulas— proletarian internationalism, the general line, the dictatorship of the proletariat. Rather, interparty relations were described as based on "comradely and voluntary cooperation," entailing strict adherence to the principles of equality and sovereign independence of each Party, noninterference in internal affairs, and respect for their "free choice of different roads in the struggle for social change of a progressive nature and socialism."[17] Collaboration between Communist and Socialist or Social Democratic parties was welcomed. The nonaligned movement was characterized as "one of the most important factors in world politics."

The 1976 Berlin Conference must be considered a watershed in European Communist politics. These Eurocommunist successes were to a significant degree the result of the tactical organizational skill of the East European members of the "Southern Axis," Romania and Yugoslavia. The prolonged preparatory process had given the Yugoslavs and Romanians an ideal forum from which to put forward their own views so prominent in the final document. In the end, the oft-postponed Pan-European Communist conference essentially had reaffirmed the autonomy of all Communist parties in running their own affairs.

On the economic side, renewed Soviet efforts to advance East European integration and thereby tie these Communist states closer to the USSR must be seen as more of the same Khrushchevian solution. It worked no better for the Brezhnev team. The ambitious 1971 CMEA Bucharest program for achieving full coordination of economic policies by 1980 was essentially abandoned in 1976 at the thirtieth CMEA session in Berlin.[18]

As for the military aspect, the Romanians publicly rejected Soviet demands to other Warsaw Pact members to increase their defense budgets in 1978. The Poles, who had promised to go along, subsequently quietly abandoned plans for higher defense spending, pleading economic hardship. In sum, institutionalization of Soviet interests in Eastern Europe has fared only marginally better under Brezhnev, although his efforts in that direction have been even more sustained than those of Khrushchev.

THE DYNAMICS OF CONFLICT RESOLUTION:
SOVIET STRATEGIES

As we enter the 1980s, Soviet hegemony in Eastern Europe has been challenged by every member of the Warsaw Pact except Bulgaria. These deviations from Soviet preferences have included both domestic change unacceptable to Moscow and foreign policy initiatives. To counter them the Soviets have utilized over the last 25 years a full range of military, economic, and diplomatic strategies vis-à-vis their East European allies: the invasion of Hungary, 1956, and Czechoslovakia, 1968; high-level negotiation and compromise with the Poles in 1956; severing of relations with the Albanians in the 1960s; patience and conflict containment involving both bilateral interactions and organizational maneuvering in the Warsaw Pact and Council for Mutual Economic Assistance in the case of differences with Romania dating from 1963 and with the East Germans in the 1969–71 period; economic assistance and political pressure on Poland in 1970, 1976, and 1980. In each instance Moscow's response to East European deviation from the Soviet norm appears to have depended on a limited set of variables involving both the internal dynamics of the East European party in question and potential external restraints. Briefly, the key items to consider are as follows:

Political-organizational: Is the East European Communist Party united and in the Soviet judgment can that party maintain control of the situation? To what extent is the "leading role" of the party at stake? What sector of the East European society is involved? (It is obviously easier to move against intellectual dissidents than a mass working-class movement.) How will the outcome impact upon the situation of other East European Communist parties and, indeed, the CPSU itself?

Military: What is the risk, both in terms of resistance to a military solution and of the danger of precipitating a NATO reaction?

Economic: What would be the cost of options ranging from political pressure to use of force in terms of actual expense of action, long-term economic cost, and potential loss in terms of Western reaction.

Circumstantial consideration: Timing—is there a cutoff point after which it will become much more difficult to intervene and potential Soviet losses will be virtually inevitable? What is the domestic and international context within which Soviet policy makers involved must make their decisions?

Now it is obvious that the thrust of Soviet policy toward Eastern Europe in the 1980s will be radically influenced by what Moscow decides to do about the rise of an independent working-class movement in Poland and the resultant crisis of credibility of the Polish Communist party. As of this writing, September 1981, the Polish party's attempt to adjust to the demands of increasingly militant competition from the independent trade union Solidarity appeared strained almost to the breaking point. The Soviet reaction might best be characterized as one of perpetual agonizing reappraisal. The outcome is a matter of intense concern in Washington as well as Moscow. There has been no consensus among Warsaw watchers, although in view of the growing factionalism within Solidarity evident during the union's two-stage congress this month, the seesaw of hopes and fears at least tilted toward growing apprehension even among the most optimistic.

Always at the pessimistic end of the scale there have been those who assumed that Polish communism could not exist with a mobilized working class demanding to speak for itself. This is a new version of the domino theory that predicts the collapse of East European Communist systems and a fundamental weakening of Soviet communism as well.[19] Some analysts have long considered a Soviet invasion inevitable; indeed, according to press reports from "high State Department officials" in February 1981, the question was not whether the Soviets would invade but when.[20] Other observers, moderately more optimistic, pointed to the unanticipated nature of Polish gains.[21]

Of necessity, this chapter deals with a large number of unknowns. Poland is a living political drama. A theater critic normally avoids reviewing the play at intermission, but political analysts do not always have that luxury. Yet this is not the first act. It is possible to analyze the relationship of political actors, to put them in a context that makes their current roles somewhat more understandable. Like any other foreign policy, it is possible to analyze Soviet options in Poland from the perspective of cost, benefit, and risk, taking into consideration the variables that would appear to have been important in earlier Soviet decisions to move troops into Eastern Europe. This assessment is tentative and the reader should remember that the scenes to come will evolve in the crucible of a political struggle in which strengths and weaknesses are constantly changing and no outcome is inevitable.

PROLETARIAN REVOLUTION, POLISH STYLE

This is not the first time that Polish workers have raised anxiety levels in Moscow. Reference was made earlier to the 1956 worker riots in Poznań, which began the process that despite Soviet objections, brought Wladyslaw Gomulka back as head of the Polish Communist party during what is known as the Polish October. At that time Soviet Prime Minister Bulganin attacked the workers involved as hooligans and enemy agents and blamed the Poznań riots on "the mad plans of international reactionary elements."[22] A substantial part of the Soviet Politburo flew uninvited to Warsaw, and reportedly Soviet troops simultaneously began to move toward the Polish capital. After tense negotiations with a visibly united Polish leadership,[23] the Soviets acquiesced in expanded Polish autonomy.

Gomulka came in on a wave of hope. Yet the gains were gradually whittled away, partly due most likely to Soviet pressure and the Polish leader's own fundamental conservatism. The political renaissance faded; the Polish party was gripped in political and economic paralysis. Gomulka fell in December 1970 as a direct result of food riots and striking workers in Gdańsk and other coastal cities. Within three days Edvard Gierek replaced him as head of the Polish Communist party. Soviet congratulations came the next day, December 21. Given the speed with which this transition took place, it is probable that the Soviets were informed rather than consulted.

There would have been no particular reason to object to Gierek. A former miner and party secretary of the Katowice region, he appeared to have been selected on the strength of his record as a successful economic manager. If there were doubts in Moscow, the fact that the new head of the Polish party was paired with Piotr Jaroszewicz as prime minister undoubtedly proved reassuring. In the USSR during World War II Jaroszewicz had served as defense minister in the Moscow-sponsored Government of National Unity in the 1940s.

Gierek personally talked with the workers in Gdańsk and Szczecin. Jaroszewicz went to Lódz, where textile workers continued to threaten a general strike, despite the change in government. A package of political and economic concessions—freezing prices, subsidies to the poorest families, greater freedom of the press, party reform, and expanded autonomy for the Polish Catholic church—defused what Gierek admitted was a crisis of confidence between the Party and the workers. In doing so, he accepted an implicit partnership between the Party and growing worker power.

These resolutions involved months of high tension. Czechoslovak and East German commentaries spoke of Polish socialism as endangered, suggesting that Poland was a candidate for "international aid," a euphemism for a military solution involving the Red Army. Gierek held negotiations in Moscow. Other Polish Politburo members held talks in East European capitals to calm the fears so evident in Czechoslovakia and the GDR. When the Soviets decided that it was the course of wisdom to alleviate the Polish situation by giving the Gierek government hard-currency credits of 100 million U.S. dollars,[24] the Brezhnev Doctrine[25] used to justify sending Soviet troops into Czechoslovakia appeared in a new light. Moscow's responsibility to "save socialism" in other Socialist countries evidently could be fulfilled by economic as well as military means.

The implications of this Soviet decision are central to the options and expectations of both Polish and Soviet leaders responding to the ongoing politicization and institutionalization of worker power in Poland. This is not the place to go into the collapse of the great expectations concerning the Gierek regime. Nor is there space to retell the truly remarkable story behind the Gdańsk charter granting Polish workers free trade unions and the right to strike.[26]

It is, however, essential to make a few points. The retreat from the promises of 1970 came about, in part, because reformers could not agree and the

Party was riddled by corruption and favoritism. The more basic problem was that however sincerely intended, Gierek failed to shake off the middle strata of bureaucratic hard-liners within the Party, whose refusal to cooperate made it virtually impossible to implement genuine reforms in any sector. Economically the Polish government could not take unpopular austerity measures and stay in power; consequently, Gierek attempted to live on borrowed capital, which proved a disastrous strategy as the world economy staggered under recession, inflation, and rising oil prices.

The Polish party's attempts to cope with this situation led to worker riots in 1976 that, in turn, brought into being a loose alliance between the workers and intellectual dissidents,[27] among which the best known is the Committee in Defense of Workers (KOR). At the same time increasing links were established with Catholic intellectuals, and the Polish Catholic church itself gradually became a support base of the workers' movement.

Thus, by September 1981 the Polish workers' movement had moved beyond the Gdańsk Charter to become institutionalized, both in independent trade unions and the trade-union federation Solidarity. Although that organization is most frequently identified with the chairman of its presidium, the charismatic Lech Wałęsa, who rose to prominence during his leadership of the Leningrad shipyards strike, it is an ever more complicated organization with a rapidly expanding constituency. In August 1980 Solidarity had an estimated 190,000 members; by November its membership had swelled to 10 million of Poland's work force. The workers' federation has a largely unknown leadership. Reportedly during the initial organizational phase of Solidarity, the key figures dated back to the Gdańsk strike committee of 1970, as does Wałęsa himself. Tactics have involved a nonviolent resistance backed by threats of general strikes, direct negotiations with high-ranking government delegations, in-system maneuvering involving the Polish courts, and pressure generated by statements to the foreign press.

The impact upon the Polish Communist party has been painful and destabilizing. Gierek resigned officially for reasons of health after the Gdańsk charter, on September 6. He was replaced by Stanislaw Kania, former Central Committee secretary in charge of the army, police, and internal security. Kania openly admitted that the Polish party is divided on how to deal with Solidarity. He conceded that there is disagreement on how best to meet the rising political challenges from Polish workers who recognize the leading role of the Party in principle, but insist on being given a voice in public policy concerned with food subsidies, the distribution system, workers' rights, and economic reform.

Kania himself has demonstrated considerable ambivalence, alternating between describing Solidarity as an "important link in the socialist democracy of Poland" and warning that the federation is becoming prey to anti-Socialist, counterrevolutionary elements. Nonetheless, he traveled across the country, talking to all sections of the Polish population as well as to Solidarity leader

Wałęsa and the former head of the Polish Catholic church, Cardinal Stefan Wyszyński. For the most part, his approach was low-keyed. He promised much less than Gierek had promised and admitted that the only real change would have to be institutional, calling for an extraordinary Polish Party Congress. Kania and General Wojciech Jaruzelski rode out the July 1981 extraordinary Polish Party Congress in which only four members of the former 11-member Politburo were among those elected to the new, enlarged 15-member body. Kania by no stretch of the imagination orchestrated the 1981 restructuring of the Polish Communist party. Despite the increasing polarization between the Party and Solidarity, however, he and the new leadership, for all its internal strains, have kept the dialogue going, not only with a politicized/mobilized, independently organized Polish proletariat, but also with the Soviets and the East German and Czechoslovak regimes, where party leaders are most threatened by developments in Poland.

SOVIET TEMPTATIONS AND RESTRAINTS

It is not surprising that the Soviet press has emphasized that independent trade unions are anti-Leninist or that escalating attacks on anti-Socialist elements within Solidarity have appeared.[28] Former U.S. national security adviser Zbigniew Brzezinski has claimed that Soviet troops were ready to move into Poland in December 1980 and, by implication, that the strength of U.S. and West European warnings held them back.

Moscow's denial[29] notwithstanding, according to the report of the House Intelligence Oversight Committee it appeared that Soviet forces were militarily prepared to intervene, with the most dangerous period being between mid-January and March 1981.[30] Nor were the massive maneuvers conducted by Soviet forces in Poland during the Solidarity congress in September 1981 a particularly subtle signal of the limits of Soviet patience. What is more pertinent from our perspective is the fact that military preparedness is a necessary, but not sufficient, condition when decision makers decide whether or not to resort to attempted military solutions. Soviet military mobilization during the moments of high tension in 1980-81 functioned both as pressure on the Polish Communist party to hold the line against escalating demands from farmers and students, as well as workers, and to support the forces of moderation within the Solidarity leadership. The distinction between the threat of force and marching soldiers is not academic.

If variables that appear to have tipped the scales in earlier cases of Soviet military intervention in Eastern Europe are applied, the Soviet Politburo undoubtedly perceives the Polish Communist party as divided and exceedingly fragile. Kania has little room for maneuver. The outcome of the restructuring required for the Polish party to accommodate to the demands for partnership from a mobilized working class is unclear. The chips are down, but all the cards have not been played and the stakes are high. The best result, for the Polish party to travel side by side with an independent trade-union movement on the Polish road to socialism, would probably raise on expectations in other East European Communist societies, and indeed, within the USSR itself.

If Poland were Czechoslovakia in 1968, it would be an easier decision. The Prague Spring was rooted in the intelligentsia and liberal elements of the Czechoslovak Communist party itself. Dubček's socialism with a human face gained significant support from Czechoslovak workers, but it did not originate on the factory floor or represent a mass workers movement. In Poland the demand for change comes from that sector of society fundamental to the legitimacy of any Communist state. The consequences, if the Polish party is openly rejected by ten million workers, could shatter far more than Polish socialism.

Moreover, the Czechs had not fought on their own territory since the Battle of the White Mountain in 1620. Poles were known to charge tanks with cavalry during World War II, and they have a reputation of fighting fiercely, even in the sure knowledge that they will be defeated. To be hopelessly courageous in the face of overwhelming odds is a Polish national tradition.

Hence, the risk is substantial in terms of the Polish part of the question. The ugly prospect of the Red Army fighting in Polish factories might well have repercussions for the morale of Soviet soldiers as well. At the same time, the U.S. and West European reaction to the flash points, when invasion seemed likely in December 1980 and April 1981, increases the risk of economic, if not military, retaliation.

The economic cost that Soviet policy makers must calculate goes far beyond the expense of any actual invasion and subsequent Western economic sanctions. Once occupied, the Polish economy would become essentially a Soviet problem. That is not a small matter, considering that estimates range from twice the cost of maintaining Cuba in the style that Fidel Castro has been able to convince his Soviet patrons to support to perhaps three times what Vietnam is costing Moscow. The Western support that Kania has been able to generate would be cut off, while demands on other East European societies to foot their share of the bill might prove disastrously destabilizing.

This must also be seen in the context of a declining Soviet growth rate, which, according to Prime Minister Tikhonov's report to the 26th CPSU Congress, will be only 1 percent in 1981.[31] Even without an invasion of Poland, this means that the annual standard-of-living increases Soviet citizens have enjoyed for the past 15 years (roughly 3.5 percent) will be cut in half.[32] Milk production is down, and there are reports that distress slaughtering following the poor grain harvest in 1980 has led to a drop in meat production.[33] Estimates for the 1981 harvest continued to slide to such an extent that Soviet leaders may be faced with importing as much as 40 million tons of grain just to feed their population. Much of this grain would have to come from the

United States, and Soviet ports are predicted to have difficulties with handling imports of that magnitude.

It is not unreasonable to conclude that in a system that evaluates performance in terms of the steady improvement of living conditions of its population and, indeed, views such improvement as an element of domestic stability, domestic economic restraints operate as a brake on Soviet options in Poland and elsewhere in the 1980s. The hard trade-offs may well be that rising consumption, necessary investment, and military expansionism cannot all be maintained.

Cost calculations do not mean that, if Polish socialism were visibly collapsing, the Soviets would not intervene. Moscow is not prepared to concede that the wheel of history can roll away from as well as toward socialism. Quite apart from the ideological repercussions, Soviet decision makers must consider the political-strategic consequences of inaction—a message undoubtedly communicated by CPSU Politburo member Mikhail Suslov during his talks with Polish leaders in Warsaw, April 24-25, 1981[34] and in Brezhnev's conversations with the Polish leadership in August.

Soviet restraint and flexibility in responding to the challenge of a mobilized Polish working class has surprised many observers in the East and West alike. The situation undoubtedly is a foreign policy nightmare for decision makers in the Kremlin, for even if Poland did not collapse into a civil war or mount sustained guerrilla resistance to Soviet occupation, how would the Soviets cope with a general strike in which ten million Polish workers refused to work? Nor would there be any guarantee that Soviet troops would produce a viable alternative within the Polish Communist party; that is, benefits are uncertain.

CONCLUSION AT INTERMISSION

In the author's opinion, the choice of Defense Minister Wojciech Jaruzelski as prime minister is the best of all possible transitional solutions. Even if he considers himself "first of all a soldier," Jaruzelski is no political novice. He has been an alternate member of the Polish Politburo since 1970; a full member since 1976. His reputation is that of a moderate, reluctant to use force against the workers. He has credibility as the commander of Polish armed forces dedicated to maintaining Poland's position in the Warsaw Pact. If anyone can minimize the level of anxiety in Moscow, it is Jaruzelski. Conversely, if the Soviets decided to move over his objection, they could face the prospect of fighting professional Polish soldiers instead of unarmed workers.

As of September 1981, the primary focus is on the sad state of the Polish economy and the growing strains both between Solidarity and the Polish Communist party and within the independent trade union itself, where Wałęsa's leadership is increasingly subject to challenge and criticism. Ground appears to have been lost since Solidarity's tacit cooperation with Jaruzelski's insistence on a two-month parliamentary ban on strikes, following the barely averted general strike in early April, temporarily stabilized the situation internally. Brezhnev's April 7 statement to the 16th Czechoslovak Party Congress that Polish Communists were capable of defending Polish socialism was cautiously balanced by his repeated assurance that the Soviet Union remained ready to come to their aid.[35] Issuing his warning in Prague was a none too subtle reminder of the type of "aid" rendered Czechoslovakia in 1968. Nonetheless, Warsaw Pact maneuvers in Poland ended on April 8, 1981. The tension subsided and on April 25 the Reagan administration announced that it was ending the grain embargo imposed after the Soviet invasion of Afghanistan—a move that President Reagan had personally linked with Soviet restraint vis-a-vis Poland.

Despite the Soviet leader's charge that the pillars of Polish socialism are endangered,[36] Moscow has accepted high levels of Polish instability in the past. As early as February 1981, the Soviet claimed to be assisting Poland with $260 million.[37] By September, Western sources estimated that Moscow was keeping the Polish economy afloat with hard-currency loans of as much as $3 billion, while Kania and Jaruzelski's August 1981 meeting with Brezhnev brought a Soviet promise to defer all Polish debts until 1986 and to provide unspecified emergency supplies of food. As in 1970, it would appear that economic instruments for saving Polish socialism are preferred to the uncertainties of military intervention.

Much hangs on ongoing negotiations of Solidarity with the Polish Communist party, on the as yet tenuous possibility that the restructured Party can form at least a marriage of convenience with the independent trade union—a solution fervently supported by the continued appeals of the Polish Catholic hierarchy for moderation. And policy makers in Moscow and Washington alike must accept the reality that the outcome depends on the skill, discipline, and patience of Polish workers and Polish Communists, rather than on letters exchanged between U.S. Secretary of State Alexander Haig and Soviet Foreign Minister Andrei Gromyko.[38]

If Solidarity comes apart at the seams because of the inability of Wałęsa's moderate leadership to control a genuinely revolutionary workers' movement with an increasingly hungry and harassed constituency, the last act of this drama will be first and foremost a Polish tragedy; second, a tragedy of those struggling to reform East European societies into viable autonomous socialist systems; and unless leaders in Moscow and Washington alike are much more mature than recent history would indicate, a potential catastrophe for us all. It is an irony of Western impotence that the Reagan administration's inability to come up with a coherent economic package to match its verbal support for Polish political freedom may contribute to disaster. At the same time, the stubbornness of Western commercial banks in refusing to reschedule their portion of the Polish $27 billion debt is partially to blame for the current deterioration in Poland. There is the sad possibility that Western bankers may "objectively" collaborate with Soviet opponents of Solidarity to strangle Poland economically, thereby becoming inadvertent allies of a Soviet policy of sustained pressure to protect the leading role of the Communist party against the Polish workers' demand for a political voice. Much will depend on the courage of ordinary Poles standing in endless lines during this inevitable winter of discontent.

To conclude, the Soviet–East European relationship in the 1980s will parallel increasing boundary disintegration between the Communist and non-Communist worlds. Declining Soviet energy resources mean that Moscow is already telling the East Europeans to look elsewhere for oil and pressuring them to contribute to internal Soviet energy industries with hard currency. The economic dimension is further complicated by Soviet demands that these regimes pay at least part of the bill for Vietnamese economic development via CMEA.

In short, the instruments of Soviet policy in Eastern Europe are potentially less and less effective in the context of Soviet global commitments and priorities. The other side of expanding Soviet influence in Asia and Africa is overextension of Soviet resources. Whatever happens in Poland, Brezhnev's successors will inherit an unenviable situation along with the need to consolidate their domestic positions, a time of vulnerability when factional struggles may well be fought out in terms of conflicting foreign policy initiatives. The specific dynamics of the impending Soviet succession can not be predicted. Although the stage is set, there is no script. And still faceless political actors are waiting in the wings.

POSTSCRIPT

During the night of December 13, 1982, General Wojciech Jaruzelski proclaimed martial law and assumed power as chairman of the Military Council of National Salvation. Thus, the curtain fell on the Polish drama that began with the Gdańsk Charter in August 1980. The relationship of political actors in Poland has been radically altered. It is far too soon to second-guess the outcome of Jaruzelski's takeover. However, in terms of the broader Soviet-East European context certain facts should be kept in mind.

To the extent that a Soviet policy goal has been to eliminate the independent trade union movement, Solidarity, as a political challenge to the Polish Communist party, Moscow welcomed the crackdown. It is undoubtedly true that General Jaruzelski was under strong Soviet pressure to neutralize Solidarity; to get Polish workers back to work; to restore the order necessary for minimal stabilization of the Polish economy. When the general replaced Stanislaw Kania as head of the Polish Communist party on October 18, 1981, he was expected to act. Indeed, as head of the party, premier, and defense minister, Jaruzelski already had accumulated whatever power existed in the staggering Polish political system in his own hands.

Despite assumptions by U.S. policy makers to the contrary, there is a genuine question as to whether the actual events of December 13 were orchestrated from Moscow. Given the ideological propositions underlying party-army relations in Communist societies, it is doubtful that the Soviet leadership expected Jaruzelski to take over as head of the army rather than in his capacity as leader of the party. Jaruzelski explicitly spoke to the Polish nation that Sunday morning as head of the Polish government and the Polish army, a fact immediately noted by Yugoslav commentators in Belgrade where this author listened to the justification given for declaring martial law in Poland. There was scant mention of the Polish Communist party. The Military Council of National Salvation is composed of 15 generals and 5 colonels. These "senior officers of the Polish Army" are military professionals. The TASS reference to them as "military commissars" is wishful thinking. The Soviet news agency's statement that Jaruzelski acted as defense minister, premier, and Communist party leader may be technically correct, but does not correspond with how Jaruzelski described his own actions.[39]

The general insists that he is not establishing a military dictatorship. He has pledged to return power to civilians once order is restored. Nonetheless, martial law has meant not only a suspension of trade unions and arrest of Solidarity leaders and resisting workers but a suspension of the normal functioning of the Polish Communist party as well. According to reports from Warsaw, none of the other members of the Polish Politburo knew of Jaruzelski's intention. The charge that Moscow called the shots; that the Polish general is a Soviet puppet, largely revolve around the fact that Soviet Marshal Viktor Kulikov, Commander of the Warsaw Pact Forces was in Warsaw the Friday before martial law was proclaimed. The move to martial law was certainly a contingency plan long before it was implemented. It is something that Kulikov might well have either been informed of or even recommended. Kulikov may have given Jaruzelski an ultimatum to send in Polish troops or face an alliance sponsored Soviet intervention. There may have been a secret conference call to Moscow. We don't know.

We do know that Jaruzelski moved without high level meetings with Soviet political leaders and without the kind of public pressure that had been put on the Dubček government in Czechoslovakia in 1968. We know that during the period of breaking domestic resistance, the Party as well as the Sejm, the Polish Parliament, ceased to function. And while Jaruzelski spoke January 9 of parliament being allowed to meet to consider martial law, he did not mention when such a meeting might be possible nor when normal party activity might resume. There is an increasing likelihood of a major purge of the Polish party before it again is allowed to assume political power; a purge that has begun with arrests of those leaders blamed for the current mess, former party chief Edvard Gierek and some five other members of his Politburo.

The idea of the army purging the Party in a Communist society stands

Lenin on his head. Once it would have been unthinkable. But such a purge may be underway. If it occurs, then we can say that both Solidarity and the Polish Communist party will have undergone major surgery before returning to Poland's political stage.

The image of soldiers in politics operating as 'iron surgeons' is a familiar one in literature on civil-military relations in developing countries. And, it may well be that this literature has greater explanatory value vis-à-vis the current Polish situation than more traditional analyses of Communist political systems. The form of Jaruzelski's takeover fits the classic pattern of military coups around the world. Councils of national salvation, redemption, and renewal, are a typical response to civilian legitimacy deflation, public disorder, economic decline, and escalating political chaos.[40]

Existence of Soviet pressure as an additional precipitant is undeniable. Yet, in my view, it is one of three causes for the collapse of Poland into martial law but the other two must be considered seriously as well.

First, Solidarity itself had begun to weaken. Unable to absorb the huge growth in membership or to politically socialize its rapidly expanding leadership, the organization was prey to personality conflicts. Its charismatic founder Lech Wałęsa exercised a control more symbolic than real. Martial law followed on the heels of an ultimatum by Solidarity's National Committee that unless its seven point demands for free local elections, union-state management of the economy and new pro-trade union laws were passed by the end of the year, the union would call for a national referendum on the question of whether the Communist government should be replaced by a provisional one. In short, Jaruzelski was squeezed by pressures within as well as outside of Poland.

Secondly, whether or not the Solidarity ultimatum was the last straw, the inability of the Western governments to come up with an aid package to match their verbal support for Polish democratization played its share in the current Polish tragedy. The implications of the BBC report of a Western banker's comment that "if a few people are shot getting the economy moving again, it would be a small price to pay," are shocking.[41] The vise Solidarity found itself in was one created not only by the East but by the West. Without a really massive amount of aid for Poland in which the Party, the Church, and Solidarity could have limited public suffering while joining in charting needed reforms, the only successes possible for the trade union movement vis-à-vis its swollen constituency were those that led to political polarization with the party.

Attempting to punish Poland and the Soviet Union for martial law only makes Jaruzelski more dependent on Moscow economically. Although this may severely strain the already over-extended Soviet economy, it is simply dysfunctional with respect to influencing internal Polish developments in the desired direction. To whatever degree the Soviets control the transfer back to civilian government in Poland, it will be to the most hardline elements of a purged Polish Communist party, elements that we know Jaruzelski has resisted in the past.

Just as the unintended consequence of insufficient aid for Poland while there was still a chance for genuine democratization was to push Solidarity into an extremism that ensured its demise, the result of Western policies based on the assumption that the Polish general is only a Soviet puppet can be a self-fulfilling prophecy.

With respect to Soviet-East European relations, the bottom line is that hopes and fears in Washington and Moscow aside, there was little basis in other East European countries for a trade union movement like Solidarity. Nor was there much willingness to pay the price so graphically being paid by the Poles. On the other hand, all East European countries and the USSR itself have armies with potential political roles and aspirations. Even if General Jaruzelski manages to gracefully take Polish military uniforms off TV; to take army officers out of the ministries and industries, these days will not be forgotten. A return to the barracks will not wipe out the memory of his success and the party's failure.

Moreover, the decision to support internal Polish repression rather than send in Soviet troops means that should Moscow decide to put an unacceptable level of pressure on Jaruzelski in the future, the risk of resorting to a military solution becomes much higher than in December 1981. Soviet soldiers could find themselves facing the Polish professional armed forces instead of unarmed Polish workers. No matter how events unfold in Poland, it is easier for Moscow to support Jaruzelski than it would be to stop supporting him. Whatever short term gains, in the long run Poland will prove an increasingly expensive "client" and the dynamics of Soviet-East European relations in the 1980s have become a whole new ballgame.

NOTES

1. Harry S. Truman, *1945, Year of Decisions: Memoirs* (New York: Doubleday, 1955), pp. 404-5.

2. E. H. Carr. *Conditions of Peace* (London: Macmillan, 1943), especially Ch. 3.

3. Z. K. Brzezinski, *The Soviet Bloc: Unity and Conflict*, 4th rev. ed. (Cambridge, Mass.: Harvard University Press, 1971).

4. Among the most useful sources is Thomas Paterson, ed., *The Origins of the Cold War*, 2d ed. (Lexington, Mass.: D. C. Heath, 1974). Paterson includes key statements of both revisionist and establishment historians.

5. See Paul Marer, "Has Eastern Europe Become a Liability to the Soviet Union? (III) Economic Aspect," in *The International Politics of Eastern Europe*, ed. Charles Gati (New York: Praeger, 1976), pp. 56-80.

6. "Secret Speech of Khrushchev Concerning the 'Cult of the Individual' Delivered at the Twentieth Congress of the Communist Party of the Soviet Union," February 25, 1956, in *The Anti-Stalin Campaign and International Communism: A Selection of Documents* (New York: Columbia University Press, 1956), pp. 1-90.

7. *Rudé Pravo*, May 1, 1956. Quoted from Wolfgang Leonhard, *The Kremlin Since Stalin* (New York: Praeger, 1962), p. 203.

8. For detailed analyses see Ferenc Vali, *Rift and Revolt in Hungary* (Cambridge, Columbia University Press, 1961).

9. Useful standard references dealing with the Polish October include Flora Lewis, *A Case History of Hope* (New York: Doubleday, 1959); M. K. Dziewanowski, *The Communist Party of Poland: An Outline of History* (Cambridge, Mass.: Harvard University Press, 1959); and Adam Bromke, *Poland's Politics: Idealism vs Realism* (Cambridge, Mass.: Harvard University Press, 1967).

10. Molotov speech to the 1954 Moscow Conference, *New Times*, no. 49 (December 4, 1954), supplement, p. 11.

11. Robin Alison Remington, "China's Emerging Role in East Central Europe," in *The International Politics of Eastern Europe*, ed. Charles Gati (New York: Praeger, 1976), pp. 82–99; also Andrew Gyorgy, "The Chinese Presence in Eastern Europe: A New Perspective of the Sino-Soviet Dispute," *Towson State Journal of International Affairs* 14, no. 1 (Fall 1979).

12. BBC Summary of Hoxha's Speech to the November 1960 Moscow Conference of Communist Parties; for analysis, see W. E. Griffith, "The November 1960 Meeting: A Preliminary Reconstruction," *China Quarterly* 11 (July–September 1962): 48.

13. See Stephen Fischer-Galati, *The New Rumania: From A People's Democracy to a Socialist Republic* (Cambridge, Mass.: M.I.T. Press, 1967).

14. There is an increasingly voluminous literature on the development of Eurocommunism, among the most recent of which is *Eurocommunism Between East and West* ed. V. V. Aspaturian et al., (Bloomington: Indiana University Press, 1980).

15. Elaborated in Remington, "Yugoslavia and Eurocommunism," in ibid. pp. 202–22. See also Jiri Valenta, "Eurocommunism and Eastern Europe," *Problems of Communism* 27, no. 2 (March-April 1978): 41–56.

16. See Kevin Devlin, "The Interparty Drama," *Problems of Communism* 24, no. 3 (July-August 1975): 18–35.

17. Text of Berlin Conference final document, *New Times*, no. 28 (July 1976), p. 27.

18. Adam Bromke, "The Communist States in an Interdependent World," in *The Communist States in the Era of Détente, 1971-1977*, ed. Adam Bromke and Derry Novak (Oakville, Ont.: Mosaic Press, 1978), p. 296.

19. Among the more sophisticated of these analyses is that of Viktor Zorza, "Unmasking the Message in Moscow's Response," *The Guardian* (U.K.), September 2, 1980.

20. *The Statesman* (Delhi), February 9, 1981.

21. William E. Griffith, *1980: A Year of Crisis* (Cambridge, Mass.: M.I.T. Center for International Studies Monograph, November 1980), pp. 49–60; Robin Alison Remington, "Worker Power and Party Politics: Political Mobilization of the Polish Working Class," *Punjab Journal of Politics* 4, no. 2 (July-December 1980): 167–83.

22. Brzezinski, *The Soviet Bloc*, p. 218 ff.

23. Edward Ochab (*Nowe drogi* 10, 1956), cited by Brzezinski, ibid., p. 257.

24. *Zycie Warszawy*, April 16, 1971.

25. Originally formulated by S. Kovalev, *Pravda*, September 26, 1968; formally rejected by Brezhnev as a "Western fabrication" during his visit to Yugoslavia in the autumn of 1971. *Borba*, September 26, 1971.

26. For a comprehensive analysis of the events surrounding the Gdańsk agreement, see *August 1980: The Strikes in Poland*, ed. William F. Robinson (Munich, West Germany: Radio Free Europe Research, October 1980).

27. By summer 1980 a variety of Polish dissident groups were publishing more than 30 uncensored newspapers and magazines; Griffith, *1980: A Year of Crisis*, p. 53. For the story of their development, see *Dissent in Poland: Reports and Documents* (London: Asso-

ciation of Polish Students and Exiles, 1977); and Peter Raina, *Political Opposition in Poland 1954-1977* (London: Poets' and Painters' Press, 1978).

28. TASS, February 7, 1981, referred to Polish counterrevolutionaries launching a frontal attack on Communist power in Poland. AP report, *Times of India*, February 8, 1981. This was not an isolated statement.

29. TASS, February 1, quoted in the *Tribune* (Chandigarh), February 3, 1981.

30. *International Herald Tribune*, January 3-4, 1981.

31. *Times of India*, February 28, 1981.

32. Seweryn Bialer, "The Politics of Stringency in the USSR," *Problems of Communism* 29, no. 3 (May-June 1980): 19-33.

33. TASS economic service, quoted by the *Statesman* (Delhi), April 13, 1981.

34. A long-standing ideologue, Suslov was one whom the two Soviet troubleshooters sent to assess the situation in Hungary in October 1956 and is thought to have urged the military move into Czechoslovakia in 1968. The rising level of Soviet concern can be seen in TASS charges following his visit to Warsaw that "revisionist elements" within the Polish Communist party are attempting to paralyze the party's role by demands for reform. *Statesman* (Delhi), April 25, 1981.

35. Brezhnev's speech in Prague, quoted by the *Statesman* (Delhi), April 8, 1981.

36. *Patriot* (New Delhi), February 22, 1981.

37. Brezhnev to the CPSU 26th Congress, *Patriot* (Delhi), February 24, 1981.

38. Text of Gromyko letter, *Patriot* (Delhi), February 13, 1981. Haig's letter has not been made public, nor has a personal message sent by President Reagan during the height of the April 1981 crisis.

39. *International Herald Tribune*, December 14, 1981.

40. See Eric A. Nordlinger, *Soldiers in Politics: Military Coups and Governments* (Englewood Cliffs, N.J.: Prentice-Hall, 1977).

41. The *Sunday Times* (London) December 20, 1981.

7

CHINA AND
THE SOVIET UNION IN ASIA:
THE DYNAMICS
OF UNEQUAL COMPETITION

Rajan Menon

Both China and the Soviet Union claim to be the true representatives of a revolutionary ideology and the polemics of the Sino-Soviet dispute possess the intensity of a vast theological schism. Nevertheless, ideological issues are no longer as important as they were when Moscow and Peking publicized their split in the early 1960s. Marx has been displaced by Machiavelli; the cold and calculating pragmatism of *realpolitik* has now superseded the passion of revolutionary ideals as the motor of Sino-Soviet competition.

Nowhere is this change more clearly manifested than in Asia. Here, shrill debates over international revolutionary obligations or the correct path to socialism no longer account for the rabidity of the dispute. Instead, the rivalry manifests itself in more familiar and traditional ways: the backing of the regional rivalries in South Asia and Indochina; China's efforts to urge Japan and ASEAN (the Association of Southeast Asian Nations) to increase their military power; the massing of troops along the 4,000-mile Sino-Soviet border; China's campaign to insure that a diminished Western defense effort does not permit the Soviets to devote added resources and attention eastward; and Moscow's attempt to compound the threat Peking perceives from the north by building up Indian and Vietnamese power on China's southern perimeter.

The author wishes to express his appreciation to the Vanderbilt University Research Council for research support and to Ms. Vidya Roy for her able research assistance. This chapter appeared as an article in *Current History* (October 1981), pp. 329–33; 340–2, and is reprinted with permission of the publisher.

THE CONTEXT OF COMPETITION

In terms of tangible power, Sino-Soviet rivalry in Asia is unbalanced. Quite simply, the Chinese sorely lack the means the Soviets have to establish the economic and military presence in the region. If economic difficulties and past disappointments have led the Soviets to become more frugal with foreign aid, China's limitations are even more severe. Thus, while Soviet economic aid to South Asia between 1954 and 1979 amounted to $4,980 million (with Eastern Europe supplementing the commitment with $1,245 million), Chinese pledges totaled $1,185 million. In East Asia, given the hesitance that states in this area have shown about establishing contacts with the Communist states, both parties played a much smaller role, with the USSR providing $260 million (an amount once again added to by a $550 million East European contribution) and the Chinese $335 million.[1]

The same picture emerges if one looks at arms sales to Asia. Moscow has been able to supply over $3 billion to India, Afghanistan, and Vietnam—states it sees as pivotal for its Asian policy—while even for Pakistan, the largest recipient of its arms, China was able to provide only $230 million in weapons.[2] China does not have the ability to mount large shipments of arms to back its friends in times of need, as the Soviets did during such crises as the 1971 Bangladesh war, Vietnam's invasion of Kampuchea in December 1978, and the Sino-Vietnamese conflict of February 1979. Further, given the worldwide trend toward transferring recently developed, technologically sophisticated weaponry, Asian states cannot look to China's outdated defense plants to balance the modern weapons that their rivals acquire from the Soviet Union. While it may want to build up Pakistan to counter Soviet-supplied India and Soviet-controlled Afghanistan, and bolster the military capabilities of ASEAN against what it sees as a Soviet-directed Vietnamese quest for hegemony in Southeast Asia, China's ability to do so is constrained by both the capacity and quality of its armament industries.

The same asymmetry is apparent in the Sino-Soviet military balance. Since the 1969 clash in the Ussuri river region of the Sino-Soviet border, the Soviets have built up their military power in the Far East. Between 1967 and 1972 the number of divisions deployed along the Chinese border doubled to a present level of 46. A quarter of the Soviet Union's ground forces and tactical aviation, 500,000 of its troops, and 11 percent of its military spending are now directed at China.[3] In addition, the Trans-Siberian Railway, which runs perilously close to the Chinese border, is being supplemented as a supply line to the Far East by the Baikal-Amur line, situated more safely to the north and due for completion by 1985. Aside from increases in manpower and weapons, the military districts in the Sino-Soviet border area have been allotted competent commanders, a degree of operational autonomy sufficient to function if hostilities broke out simultaneously against China and NATO, and a modern communications net-work. These conventional military assets are supplemented by the deployment of ICBMs, together with the new SS-20 mobile IRBMs and TU-22 Backfire bombers, capable of striking China with nuclear weapons.[4]

Against this sizable military machine the Chinese have only two advantages: the superiority in manpower conferred by their 1.2 million troops (this deployment against the Soviets accounts for roughly 40 percent of the People's Liberation Army),[5] and the sheer size of a country that could draw a would-be conqueror into a protracted battle. But while these two qualities mean that China cannot be absorbed like an Afghanistan, there are drawbacks that severely limit Beijing's ability to compete with, and contain, Soviet power in Asia.

In firepower and mobility, China's infantry-dominated conventional strength badly trails the Soviet Union's; Chinese weapons are basically replicas of the weapons provided by the Soviets about 20 years ago.[6] While the Soviet ability to project power by air and sea ranks markedly behind that of the United States, it far exceeds China's. In naval strength, the Soviet Pacific fleet—headquartered at Vladivostok and second in size to the Northern fleet—must cope with some major problems. It has an adverse fleet-size-to-littoral ratio, and choke points could be used by an enemy to confine a good portion of it in the Sea of Japan. The fleet is also hampered by the Soviet navy's lack of access to reliable overseas bases such as Yokasuka, Subic Bay, and Diego Garcia, which are available to the U.S. Navy. But it faces no real competition from China's navy which, because of the limited range and capability of its ships, is, despite its size, unable to approximate the Soviet Pacific fleet in such tasks as sea-lane control, amphibious operations, and distant deployments in areas like the Indian Ocean. Nor, unlike the Soviet Pacific fleet, can it mount sea-based nuclear strikes against the adversary's homeland.[7]

While a presence does not automatically beget influence—in fact, the Soviet experience in Egypt and Somalia in the 1970s suggests that the reverse is often possible—and though limited economic and military resources do not prevent a state from mounting a successful regionwide diplomatic effort in support of its goals, Sino-Soviet competition in Asia is characterized by a fundamental inequality of power. China is a developing nation and a regional power with definite global ambitions, but it faces in the USSR a superpower with a much greater capacity for making its presence felt in the region at critical times and with economic and military assets that give it a global reach.

If the nature of the Sino-Soviet balance of power has been belabored somewhat, it is because an exaggerated notion of China's present capabilities is not uncommon. Since the 1971–72 Nixon-Kissinger breakthrough to China, there has been steady progress in Sino-American relations. The process has been marked by several major events: the establishment of full diplomatic ties in January 1979; the granting of most-favored-nation status to China in early 1980; the decision in that year to sell "dual-use" technology to Beijing; and the June 1981 announcement that the Reagan administration would sell offensive arms to China.[8] Because of the increasing attention currently devoted to the aims of Soviet foreign policy and a revival of the traditional romanticism about China's potential, it has become commonplace to speak of the establishment of a triangular global balance of power. Given the widening of the Sino-Soviet split, the diminished U.S. role in the Pacific following the unification of Vietnam in 1975, the increase in Soviet military power, the invasion of Afghanistan, and Vietnam's take-over of Kampuchea, enthusiasm for playing "the China card" to thwart Soviet activities in Asia has increased. But in terms of raw power, there really is no trilateral balance; China lacks the prowess to bring such an arrangement into being and, in the short run, the contribution that an infusion of Western arms can make to Chinese strength will be limited by the absorptive limits of China's aged defense industry and its reluctance—exhibited recently[9]—to incur large debts by making unrestrained purchases from abroad.

The Chinese are acutely aware of the superiority of Soviet power and the militancy of their pronouncements on Soviet activities in Asia do not stem from delusions. Rather, the assertive tone and the aura of boldness are designed to project an image of toughness and resolve in order to deter Soviet expansion.[10] Peking also realizes that a China that is seen as cowed and weak will not be regarded by America as an attractive partner.

China's weakness precludes the containment of Soviet power in Asia by regional diplomacy alone. To be sure, Beijing's call for a greater military buildup by Japan and the ASEAN states does show an intent to marshal local centers of power. Nonetheless, neither the Japanese nor ASEAN—for different reasons—will soon be able to provide the necessary supplement to Chinese capabilities. Beijing's ambivalance about U.S.-Soviet arms-control negotiations, its efforts to urge greater unity and expenditure within NATO, and the favorable attitude it has come to have about the American military presence in the Pacific are due to three considerations. The first is the need to ensure that a lessening of Western strength in the European theater does not permit Moscow to pursue its aims in Asia with greater strength and confidence. The second is a desire to forge closer ties with the United States and Western Europe and thereby create a constant uncertainty in the minds of the Soviet leadership about how the West would react to a Soviet attack against China. Finally, the Chinese want to see an increase in the contribution that the American military presence makes to the balance of power in Asia.

The Soviet naval presence in Asia, which so worries the Chinese, is not likely to diminish. The size of the Pacific fleet—which presently amounts to 80 submarines and 80 warships—has grown in the last few years[11] and its capabilities have been enhanced by the transfer to its command of two recently built ships: the aircraft carrier *Minsk*, and the amphibious assault vessel, *Ivan Rogov*. The access recently won to Vietnamese airfields and ports at Cam Ranh Bay and Da Nang has increased the Pacific fleet's sustainability, reach, and reconnaissance capabilities. As a show of support to the Vietnamese, the Soviets have periodically maintained a naval presence in the South China Sea since the Sino-Vietnamese war, and in February 1980, two missile cruiser task forces drawn from the Pacific fleet appeared in the Arabian Sea to monitor the two American carrier task forces that were sent there following the seizure of the U.S. embassy in Teheran.

The USSR has had a permanent naval deployment in the Indian Ocean since 1968 and there is little likelihood of a diminished presence in the region. The loss of access to the Somalian port of Berbera in 1977 has been offset by relying on Aden, and the facilities in Vietnam will reduce the logistical difficulties for the Indian Ocean task force, which is drawn from the Pacific fleet headquartered at distant Vladivostok. Between June 1977 and February 1978, ultimately fruitless negotiations were held between the United States and the Soviet Union to limit naval rivalry in the Indian Ocean. There is little likelihood of any imminent resumption; since the Soviet invasion of Afghanistan, a chill has enveloped the superpower relationship and, as part of its "get tough" foreign policy, the Reagan administration has decided to expand American naval power and retain the access to facilities at Kenya, Oman, and Somalia that was negotiated under Jimmy Carter.[12]

Chinese assessments of the naval rivalry in the Indian and Pacific Oceans do contain terse and somewhat ritualistic criticism of the Western presence. But Beijing, anxious about what it sees as an increasingly powerful Soviet navy and aware that its navy cannot serve as an effective counter, views Western naval strength as an essential balancer and deterrent to what is seen as a premeditated Soviet effort to control the "dumbbell" area formed by the Straits of Malacca and the two great bodies of water to its east and west.[13]

SOUTH ASIA: THE INTERVENTION AND ITS AFTERMATH

Having sent its troops into Afghanistan in December 1979 to rescue the wobbly Marxist regime that had come to power there 20 months earlier,[14] the Soviet Union has reaped a bitter and plentiful harvest of international criticism. The two condemnatory General Assembly resolutions of January and November 1980 were supported by a large majority. Likewise, at the conferences of Islamic foreign ministers that convened in Islamabad, Pakistan in January and May 1980, only Syria and South Yemen were in the Soviet corner. A more painful display of anger came when some 80 states boycotted the Olympic games that Moscow had organized with great anticipation and pride. More specifically, the image that even sympathetic developing countries have of the USSR has been markedly affected by the events in Afghanistan; unlike Hungary and Czechoslovakia, Afghanistan simply hit closer to home. In two important and overlapping constituencies, the nonaligned movement and the Muslim world,[15] the Soviets have been isolated and left with but few defenders.

Admittedly, arithmetical majorities in international forums and spirited defenses of the principle of nonintervention have not made Soviet troops leave

Afghanistan. But while the publicity given to the invasion has spotlighted the display of Soviet power, the Afghan situation really illustrates the limitations of military force. If Generals Pavlovsky and Yepishev (respectively, the commander of the Soviet ground forces and the head of the main political administration), who were sent to assess the situation prior to the intervention, predicted a quick campaign, this has not come to pass. Only the major Afghan cities and highways are under Soviet control. Even here, reports of ambushed convoys, and strikes and rioting in the cities of Herat, Kandahar, Jalalabad, and even Kabul, suggest less than total mastery. Nor are military installations fully secure. In June 1981, guerrillas attacked and set fire to the Bagram airbase—second in importance only to the one in Kabul—causing Soviet aircraft to be evacuated amidst explosions that continued for a day. Only one area, the Wakhan corridor, a narrow salient running between Pakistan and the USSR to the Chinese border, has been completely secured.[16]

The vast rural area is utilized by the ill-equipped but dogged guerrillas—the *mujahedeen*—who attack and, as Soviet troops arrive, retreat into the forbidding terrain, with which they are thoroughly familiar. Despite predictions that the Soviets would seal the border to prevent the guerrillas from moving to and from neighboring countries, principally Pakistan, this has not been accomplished. At a time when urban security and pacification campaigns in the countryside call for a large number of troops, any effective closing of Afghanistan's 3,000-mile frontier would unduly tax available military manpower.

The Afghan army, which had about 100,000 men before the invasion, has been decimated by defections and now has only between 35,000 and 25,000 men. To fill the void, Soviet forces, which numbered some 85,000 in January 1980, have been increased to 100,000 and bear the brunt of the war. The reliability of Afghan troops is suspect also; antitank and antiaircraft weapons apparently are no longer provided to Afghan soldiers for fear that they will be turned over to the mujahedeen by deserters.[17]

If the awesome use of Soviet military power has been a failure, it is because the problem is political. The government of Babrak Karmal is viewed by most Afghans as the creation of an imperial neighbor, and the continued presence of Soviet troops, their destruction of villages and croplands, and the periodic drives to recruit men for military service only harden this image.[18] On the other hand, any significant reduction of Soviet forces in order to allow Karmal to gain legitimacy might quickly lead to his overthrow. The Soviets are entrapped in a vicious circle.

While Moscow has learned why the old adage about its being easier to march into Afghanistan than to march out has survived through the years, the future of the resistance is uncertain. The disorganization of the past is less of a problem. The six Afghan political groups in Pakistan have cooperated to draw up a charter and establish what can loosely be called a government in exile.[19] Inside the country, the resistance is shaping up along tribal lines and reports indicate that traditional tribal rivalries are being shelved to solidify the war effort.[20] Nevertheless, the mujahedeen do not have sufficient quantities of the antitank weapons and surface-to-air missiles needed to counter Soviet armor and the deadly Mi24 helicopter gunships. Morale may not be a problem, but given the toll that the war has taken on farmland and because of the exodus of 2.1 million people to neighboring states (1.5 million to Pakistan and 600,000 or so to Iran), the shortage of food is.[21] What is likely in the foreseeable future, then, is not a victory by either side, but a stalemate. In October 1980 Karmal visited Moscow and there were indications that the Soviets privately complained about the state of the Afghan army, the problems of the economy, and the often violent disputes between the Khalq and Parcham wings of the ruling People's Democratic party. But despite mounting casualties and high costs, the Soviets publicly have given no indication of a flagging commitment.[22]

The primary Chinese response to the Soviet invasion of Afghanistan has been to launch a diplomatic campaign—through bilateral visits, their news media, and by keeping the issue alive in the United Nations—to portray it as part of a deliberate effort to control the Persian Gulf and bolster the Soviet naval presence in the Indian Ocean through an ultimate southward push aimed at wresting control of facilities on the coastline of the Arabian Sea. In short, the Chinese have tried to drive home the point that the crisis directly affects the United States, Western Europe, Japan, and the Muslim world, and is not a local problem. In keeping with this overall strategy, they have called for greater unity in South Asia, pointing out that the propinquity of Soviet power poses a threat not only to Pakistan but to India as well. Beijing has welcomed the 1979-80 consultations on the Afghan issue between Indian and Pakistani officials and has called simultaneously, and with some naiveté, for increasing Pakistan's military strength and a rapprochement between India and Pakistan.[23]

To provide a propitious setting for a mending of fences between India and Pakistan, China has, since the Afghan invasion, taken a more evenhanded position on the long-standing disputes between these two South Asian states and made an effort to improve Sino-Indian relations as well. While taking care to maintain their frequent contacts with, and support for, Pakistan, the Chinese have realized that an India that continues to view China as hostile and a partisan of Pakistan is unlikely, Afghanistan notwithstanding, to reassess its close ties with the USSR.

Since the mid-1970s, there has been a limited movement toward better Sino-Indian relations. Ambassadorial ties were reestablished in 1976 after a 14-year hiatus, and cultural and economic agreements have been signed in subsequent years. During the tenure of the Janata government (March 1977–July 1979), Prime Minister Morarji Desai once indicated that India might make some compromises to settle the border dispute. But he soon retreated to the established Indian position that none of the land lost in the 1962 war could be conceded and, as the strength of his government began to wane, he was both too preoccupied and too lacking in political confidence to launch a major foreign policy move that an Indira Gandhi on the comeback trial might have seized upon to hasten the ultimate collapse of his government. In February 1979, Desai's foreign minister, Atal Bihari Vajpayee, visited Beijing. Although this was the first ministerial contact between India and China since 1960, no major bilateral problem was resolved. In fact, since Beijing displayed a curious sense of timing and launched its attack on Vietnam while Vajpayee was still in China, he returned to India ahead of schedule.

After the Soviet entry into Afghanistan and the impressive January 1980 electoral victory of Indira Gandhi's Congress party, the Chinese began to signal their interest in a Sino-Indian dialogue. India's contacts with the Soviet Union and Vietnam were reported in the Chinese press without any stridency, and Peking seemed unusually reluctant to echo fully the Pakistani position on Kashmir.[24] In June, India's external affairs secretary visited China and was instructed to invite Chinese Foreign Minister Huang Hua to visit India. In the following month, Vice Premier Deng Xiaoping proposed that the Sino-Indian border dispute be settled through a quid pro quo whereby India would recognize the line of control in the western sector and China would accept the status quo in the east. The promising trend was stymied by India's decision to follow Deng's proposal with a recognition of the Heng Samrin government established by the Vietnamese after their invasion of Kampuchea. Although the Congress party had, in its election manifesto, committed itself to recognizing the new Kampuchean regime, in terms of its contribution to Sino-Indian relations the gesture was as ill timed as was Peking's decision to attack Vietnam during the Vajpayee mission, and it led to the postponement of Huang Hua's plans to visit India.

Coming as it did after the $1.9 billion Indo-Soviet arms deal of May 1980, the Indian recognition of the Heng Samrin regime has been widely interpreted as an instance of Soviet influence in action. But the timing of the action was not fortuitous and was designed to make plain to the Chinese that India could not negotiate the border problem on the basis of a proposal that was essentially similar to the one made by Zhou Enlai during his visit to India in April 1960. Gandhi, who was aware that the political opposition was in disarray after its electoral fiasco and in need of an issue around which to organize, wanted something more substantial. As one Indian political commentator put it, "Deng cannot expect that what Nehru rejected in 1960 can be accepted by his daughter as a reasonable proposal. Things do not quite happen that way."[25]

Despite the solid stake that India has in maintaining its close ties with the Soviet Union, it also has an interest in normalizing relations with China, at least to avoid being taken for granted in Moscow and to acquire some flexibility in foreign policy. For their part, the Chinese would welcome normalization, both for its own sake and because it holds out to them the possibility of a future loosening of Indo-Soviet relations. It is this mutual desire for movement in Sino-Indian relations that made possible the June 1981 visit, of Huang Hua to New

Delhi, which had been delayed by Indian recognition of the Kampuchean regime. During Huang's stay in India it was revealed that Prime Minister Gandhi had been invited to China and that an agreement had been reached for future negotiations on the border problem.

Some Indians have argued that the Soviet invasion of Afghanistan, coupled with the restiveness of Pakistan's ethnic minorities—primarily the Baluchis—poses a threat to the integrity of that country that augurs ill for India as well. They have suggested that India take the initiative to fashion a regional center of power by reaching an understanding with China and Pakistan.[26] If this plan has not been pursued with any great vigor, there are two explanations. The first is that the complex disagreements that India has with China and Pakistan cannot be quickly settled; the suspicions, entrenched perceptions, and domestic complications in all three countries pose formidable obstacles to speedy diplomacy. In addition, India's primary concern is that the Soviet move into Afghanistan will lead the United States to arm China and Pakistan. To cope with this eventuality, India will not impair, let alone jettison, what it regards as a tried and trusted friendship with the Soviets, who have provided arms and political support—on the Kashmir issue and during the Bangladesh crisis, for instance—at crucial junctures.

These considerations explain India's gingerly response to the Afghan crisis. This has ranged from Gandhi's initial suggestion that "other interventions" in Afghanistan explained the Soviet action and Indian abstentions from the two condemnatory General Assembly resolutions, to innocuously worded calls for the withdrawal of "foreign troops" from Afghanistan. Nevertheless, India has not, unlike Cuba, Vietnam, and Ethiopia, supported the Soviet invasion and, during the many recent visits exchanged by Indian and Soviet officials, has privately but persistently expressed its unhappiness with the Soviet presence in Afghanistan. During the visits to New Delhi of Gromyko and Brezhnev (February and December 1980) the two sides simply agreed to disagree and the communiques omitted any direct reference to the matter.[27]

India will not, however, drastically reevaluate its ties to the Soviet Union in the near future. It is true that, in addition to distancing itself from the Soviet position on Afghanistan, India has also been diversifying its arms purchases and trying to reduce its heavy dependence on the USSR. (Between 1967 and 1977 the Soviets provided 81.2 percent of the value of all arms purchased by India.) A $2 billion accord was signed in October 1978 for the purchase and local manufacture of the Anglo-French Jaguar fighter-bomber, and in October 1980 an Indian delegation visited Canada and the United States to examine antitank weapons, howitzers, and antiaircraft systems. While this does denote a decision to eschew total dependence on the Soviets, it does not necessarily portend any major reduction in the important role that the USSR has played in selling arms to India for the past 15 years. Thus, despite the trend toward diversifying procurement, a $1.7 billion deal involving the most favorable terms that the Soviets have ever given to India was concluded between the two countries in May 1980.[28] The favorable credit terms that the Soviets have been willing to extend, plus their abiding interest in building up India as a counterweight to China, will insure the continued prominence of the Soviet Union as a supplier. The announcement, in June 1981, that the United States has agreed "in principle" to sell arms to China and to propose a $3.2 billion package in economic and military aid to Pakistan will be viewed by India not as a part of American strategy vis-à-vis the USSR, but in relation to the effect that an increment in Chinese and Pakistani military power will have on its own security. The Indian response will certainly not be to distance itself from the Soviet Union.

In Pakistan a siege mentality has emerged, with the sudden destruction of the Afghan buffer that separated it from the Soviet Union. The old fear of a hostile Soviet-Indian entente has been aggravated by a belief that, in an effort to expand further south, the Soviets will ultimately support Baluchi irredentism or seek to Finlandize Pakistan on the strength of their ability to do so. Although they are joined by the Chinese in this assessment, the Pakistanis are aware that China can do little to prevent any such eventuality. While maintaining its close ties with the Chinese, Pakistan has increasingly identified with the Muslim countries, principally Saudi Arabia.[29] While this is, in part, a foreign policy strategy complementing President Zia ul-Haq's plans to establish an Islamic polity in Pakistan, it is also an attempt to acquire political support and financial aid from an important center of power. Further, some constituents of the Islamic world, such as Algeria, Iraq, Libya, and Syria, hold great importance in the Soviet scheme of things, and Zia may well believe that an anticipating of adverse reactions from these states may moderate whatever malevolent aims the Soviet Union may have against his country.

An unstable situation exists in Pakistan because of the dissatisfaction of ethnic minorities and the sizable opposition to Zia's cancellation—on two occasions since taking power in 1977—of promised elections, the incarceration of political opponents, and the hobbling of an independent judiciary. Conscious of this, aware of the proximity of Soviet power, and exposed to frequent allegations from Moscow and Kabul that U.S. and Chinese agents are training Afghan rebels in Pakistani camps, the Zia regime has displayed a mixture of resolve and caution. Pakistan has played a key role in organizing the criticism that the Soviets encountered during the two U.N. debates on Afghanistan in 1980 and at the February 1981 nonaligned meeting at New Delhi. It also hosted the two 1980 meetings of Islamic foreign ministers, during which the Soviet invasion of Afghanistan was condemned. At the same time, Pakistan reportedly toned down the resolution it introduced in the General Assembly in November 1980 after a stormy meeting between Gromyko and Zia's foreign minister, Agha Shahi, and in January 1981, indicated that it no longer insisted on a total withdrawal of Soviet troops as a precondition for negotiations with Afghanistan.[30]

EAST ASIA: OF ACTUAL AND POTENTIAL POWER

The Vietnam war gave the Sino-Vietnamese common front a resilience that enabled it to withstand the increasing strains to which it was subject after 1965. That tenuous unity, however, has now been shattered and replaced by active hostility. Following the establishment of Communist states in Indochina in 1975, the ancient rivalry between Kampuchea and Vietnam was revived by a border dispute, ideological quarrels, and Vietnam's fear of the growing closeness between the Khmer Rouge and the Chinese. As border clashes increased, Vietnam reacted by tilting toward the Soviets. Hanoi joined the Council for Mutual Economic Assistance (CMEA) in June 1978 as a full member—China responded to this by terminating its economic aid to Vietnam—and signed a security treaty with the USSR in November. Calculating that this would deter the Chinese from intervening, Hanoi responded to increasing Khmer Rouge attacks along the border by invading Kampuchea, quickly toppling the regime of Pol Pot and replacing it with a pliant one headed by a Kampuchean defector, Heng Samrin.

The Chinese were aware that their regional prestige and credibility would be hurt if they failed to respond to the toppling of a friendly government. They were also aware, however, of the danger of exposing themselves to some sort of Soviet military move from the north. In a masterly effort to deter the Soviets, China launched its carefully limited punitive attack on the Vietnamese in February 1979, just after Deng Xiaoping's visit to the United States. The timing of the attack and Deng's repeated warnings in the United States about Soviet-Vietnamese expansion were clearly designed to create suspicion in Moscow about Sino-American collusion.[31] Thus, Sino-Soviet rivalry had spilled over into Indochina and Peking had offset its weakness against the USSR by tapping American power. If the United States could play the China card, China could, in turn, play the American card.

The Chinese have adopted a dual strategy in dealing with what they view as a Soviet-supported Vietnamese drive for hegemony in Southeast Asia. They have tried to keep Vietnam off balance and increase the cost that the Kampuchean war imposes on Hanoi. To this end, China has maintained sizable forces along its border with Vietnam and supplied arms through Thailand to the 30,000 Khmer Rouge guerrillas who are battling the 200,000 Vietnamese troops in Kampuchea. It has also armed and stirred up the tribes that straddle its borders with Laos—where 50,000 Vietnamese troops underscore Hanoi's influence—and Vietnam. On the diplomatic front, China has tried to organize regional opposition to the Soviet-Vietnamese partnership, has encouraged both ASEAN and Japan to increase their military capabilities, and discreetly supports a continued American presence in East Asia.[32]

In the case of ASEAN, the Chinese effort has yielded mixed results. Jolted by the events of the past three years, the ASEAN states have increased significantly their defense spending. Member states have held joint military exercises and support has been growing for the standardization of weapons. Nevertheless, the combined armed forces of ASEAN are still smaller than Vietnam's, and given the guerrilla movements that have long existed in most of these states, their military training and operations have focused on counterinsurgency. In contrast, Vietnam's forces are battle tested and equipped to wage cross-border conventional war.[33] On the diplomatic front, ASEAN and Beijing have cooperated extensively in the United Nations. They organized support for the November 1979 and October 1980 General Assembly resolutions that called upon Vietnam to withdraw its troops from Kampuchea, and thwarted the efforts of Moscow and Hanoi to have Kampuchea's U.N. seat, now held by the Khmer Rouge, transferred to the Heng Samrin government.

Nevertheless, while there are indeed differences between individual ASEAN states on the Kampuchean issue, these are less significant than the ones existing between China and ASEAN.[34] ASEAN is keenly aware that, due to the Khmer Rouge's brutal rule in Kampuchea from 1975 to November 1978, many countries are reluctant to support enthusiastically the Pol Pot forces as the alternative to Heng Samrin. Consequently, ASEAN has supported the idea of a coalition headed by non-Communists such as Prince Sihanouk or his former prime minister, Son Sann, and a reduction in the importance within the Khmer Rouge of such top leaders as Khieu Samphan, Pol Pot, and Ieng Sary.

These proposals were put to the Chinese during visits to Beijing by Thailand's prime minister, Prem Tinsulonond, and Singapore's prime minister, Lee Kwan Yew. China's lack of great enthusiasm for the idea stems from two considerations. First, given Beijing's strong and established ties to the Khmer Rouge, it would prefer to have them govern Kampuchea in the event that the Heng Samrin regime is unseated. This would fit in better with China's strategy of balancing Soviet and Vietnamese power in Southeast Asia. Second, and this calculation is publicly stated, China is convinced that only effective and continued military pressure will, by increasing Vietnam's burdens, cause it to withdraw from Kampuchea. The Chinese believe that only the experienced and battle-hardened Khmer Rouge are capable of mounting an effective military operation against Vietnam. While the Chinese have subsequently moderated their position on a non-Communist-led united front, progress toward the goal has been limited. Son Sann has indicated a willingness to join, but Sihanouk, who strongly opposes the Khmer Rouge, has continued to waver. He decided to lead the coalition in February 1981, but subsequently indicated a lack of real commitment and an intent only to pursue protracted negotiations with the Khmer Rouge.[35]

In view of the support that China has long given to Communist insurgencies in Malaysia and Thailand, and the break in Sino-Indonesian relations after the attempted coup by the Indonesian Communist party (PKI) in 1965, the ASEAN states are wary of overly close ties with Beijing. In return for Thailand's willingness to allow China to supply the Khmer Rouge guerrillas through Thai territory, Beijing has reportedly ended its support for the Communist party of Thailand.

Deng Xiaoping is also said to have told the prime ministers of Singapore and Thailand during their visits to China that support for regional insurgencies was a past policy that would be phased out. In ASEAN, however, there are fears that this may be a temporary ploy and that the return to power of the Khmer Rouge would bring about an extension of Chinese influence in Southeast Asia fraught with dangerous consequences.[36]

There is also some concern within ASEAN that the Chinese strategy of maintaining steady and multifaceted pressure on Vietnam will, instead of forcing Hanoi to withdraw from Kampuchea, cement its ties with the Soviets even further. Indonesia, for example, has felt that a greater sensitivity both to Vietnam's security concerns in Kampuchea and its fear of China will increase its confidence and gradually encourage it to seek greater autonomy from the USSR. This willingness to be responsive to Vietnamese concerns was evident at the June 1981 ASEAN foreign ministers' meeting in Manila, where an effort was made to obtain Vietnamese participation at the international conference on Kampuchea, scheduled for July in New York, by assuring Hanoi that the purpose of the conference was not to put Vietnam in the dock. ASEAN's proposal at the Manila meeting for a withdrawal of all forces in Kampuchea, the disarming of all sides, the introduction of U.N. peace-keeping forces, and the holding of elections in which the Heng Samrin regime could participate, is indicative of this desire to propose a settlement acceptable to Vietnam.

For Moscow, supporting Vietnam has come to be a costly affair, involving the direct and indirect transfer of resources amounting to $2 million a day.[37] While the Soviets have benefited strategically from the access gained to Vietnam's airfields and ports, they have also increased the persuasiveness of China's warnings to ASEAN and Japan about Soviet-Vietnamese expansionism. Furthermore, the growing cooperation between Washington and Peking has been fueled in good measure by a common intent to halt what is viewed as a predatory alliance between Hanoi and Moscow.

For Hanoi, because of the fear of China and the U.S. effort to deny Vietnam Western sources of aid,[38] there are few incentives to reassess its relationship with the USSR, and several reasons not to do so. To cope with Chinese pressure, the deterrent value of the Moscow connection continues to be important, as does the supply of Soviet arms. Because of severe food shortages, a sluggish economy, and a shortage of convertible currency with which to trade with the West, the Soviets also remain the key source of aid. Nevertheless, the Soviet-Vietnamese relationship is less than blissful. Moscow has been impatient with Vietnam's slow progress in snuffing out the Khmer Rouge guerrillas. Soviet unwillingness to continue providing subsidized oil and the gap that has emerged between Vietnamese expectations concerning Soviet aid, especially for the 1981–85 Third Five-Year Plan, and the inability of the Soviets to meet them are also issues that have created some discord.[39] Aware of their heavy dependence on the Soviets, the Vietnamese remain sensitive to encroachments on their independence. The activities of Soviet personnel are closely monitored and Hanoi has insisted on restricting Soviet access to its air and naval facilities.

As part of their strategy of coalescing regional power against Vietnam and the Soviet Union, the Chinese have steadily increased their ties with Japan. Diplomatic relations between the two countries were established in 1972 and trade with Japan has grown much more rapidly than Soviet-Japanese trade in recent years. On the security front, a treaty of peace and friendship was signed in August 1978, which contained an antihegemony clause that the Soviets view as a reference to them. China has also abandoned its past policy of warning against the revival of Japanese militarism; instead, it supports an expanded Japanese defense effort and regularly points out how the growth in Soviet power bodes ill for Japan's security.

In Japan there has developed a defense debate that, in terms of its openness, is unprecedented in the postwar history of the country. Although its origins and the effect it will have on Japan's military capabilities cannot be gone into here,[40] it is clear that apprehension about the growth of Soviet power and the adequacy of the American security guarantee are central to it. The debate has had the effect both of causing the Soviets to perceive a Sino-American campaign to stimulate a growth in Japanese military might and of ending the period in which Japanese advocates of stepped-up defense spending were consigned to the fringe of politics.

Despite their concern over the future of Japan's military policy, the Soviets have not gone to great lengths to be flexible on major Soviet-Japanese differences. While repeatedly calling for a bilateral friendship treaty and exhibiting much interest in harnessing Japanese credits and technology to the development of Siberia's resources,[41] Moscow has been intractable on certain issues that limit the progress of Soviet-Japanese relations. For example, the Japanese claim to the Northern Islands, occupied by the USSR following World War II, has been curtly rejected with the statement that "[t]he Soviet Union has long since given the Japanese government a thorough explanation of why Japan's claims on the Kurile islands chain, which is USSR territory, are groundless. There is no territorial question between our countries."[42] Instead, in the last two years, military deployments have been increased both on the Soviet mainland adjacent to Japan and on the Kuriles. Moscow's intransigence over the Kuriles derives from a fear that, in view of other territorial gains made following World War II, it might open a Pandora's box by making concessions to the Japanese. The islands also guard the Sea of Okhotsk, which could be a sheltered launching zone for the most recent Soviet submarines.[43] Whatever the Soviet Union's motives, the Northern Islands issue, together with the greater concern over Soviet power, gives Japanese advocates of greater military power and closer ties with Peking an issue,[44] and inhibits the formation in Japan of a consensus favoring closer ties with the USSR.

CONCLUSION

In Asia, China competes with the Soviet Union from a position of weakness and her diplomatic efforts to summon the potential power of ASEAN and Japan will not rectify the imbalance in the short term. China's awareness of this is what makes the emerging partnership with the United States so vital. The prospects for the durability of this partnership are good. The Chinese are conscious of their military disparity along the Sino-Soviet border and, given the importance of Siberia for the Soviet economy, have to anticipate that Soviet activity east of the Urals will increase. For the United States, China has come to signify a vast and luring market, a center of great potential power toward which sizable Soviet resources might be diverted, and an Asian state willing to play a key role in the region's balance of power.

For the Soviets, competition in Asia has involved great costs. The uncertain Afghan campaign and deployments along the Sino-Soviet border together tie down roughly 600,000 Soviet troops, while support for the embattled Afghan regime and for Vietnam's suzerainty over Indochina are becoming costly commitments. Although it is difficult to identify many immediate benefits that the Soviets have acquired by their efforts, they have set in motion a number of trends that they have come to find worrisome. ASEAN is nervously groping toward greater unity and military strength, and looking to the United States and China for support. In Japan, apprehension about Soviet power has provided one of the major stimuli for a defense debate, which is watched with anxiety by the Kremlin. A similar concern about Soviet power has created a Sino-American partnership that threatens to actualize China's vast potential. As they contemplate the implications of this development, the Soviet leaders must worry about Deng Xiaoping's remark: "It's common sense that if China dares to stand up to the Soviet Union even if it's poor, . . . why should China seek reconciliation with the Soviet Union after it gets rich [?]"[45]

NOTES

1. Calculated from U.S. Central Intelligence Agency, National Foreign Assessment Center, *Communist Aid Activities in Non-Communist Less Developed Countries, 1979 and 1954-79*, ER 80-10318 U (October 1980), Table A-6, pp. 19-20. Aid to Vietnam and North Korea are not included.

2. U.S. Arms Control and Disarmament Agency, *World Military Expenditures and Arms Transfer 1969-1978* (Washington, D.C.: U.S. Government Printing Office 1980), Table IV, p. 160.

3. U.S. Central Intelligence Agency, National Foreign Assessment Center, *Estimated Soviet Defense Spending: Trends and Prospects* (June 1978), reprinted in U.S. Congress, Joint Economic Committee, Subcommittee on Priorities and Economy in Government, *Allocation of Resources in the Soviet Union and China—1978*, 95th Cong., 2d sess. (Wash-

ington, D.C.: U.S. Government Printing Office, 1978), p. 22; Blechman testimony in idem, *Allocation of Resources in the Soviet Union and China—1977*, 95th Cong., 1st sess. (Washington, D.C.: U.S. Government Printing Office, 1977), p. 147; George E. Hudson, "Current Soviet Security Policy and the Sino-Soviet Split," Mershon Center, Ohio State University, *Quarterly Report* 6, no. 2 (Winter 1981): 5.

4. See John Erickson, "The Soviet Strategic Emplacement in Asia," *Asian Affairs* 12 (February 1981): 10-13.

5. Hudson, "Current Soviet Security Policy," p. 5.

6. See International Institute for Strategic Studies, "China's Defense Industries," in *Strategic Survey 1979* (London: I.I.S.S., 1980), pp. 67-72, for a fuller discussion.

7. See Donald C. Daniel, "Sino-Soviet Relations in Naval Perspective," *Orbis* 24 (Winter 1981): 787-803.

8. Chinese defense needs were an item for discussion between Haig and the Chinese during the secretary of state's visit to Peking in June 1981.

9. In April 1981, Peking cancelled $2 billion in European, Japanese, and American projects planned for China. *Christian Science Monitor*, April 15, 1981, p. 4.

10. See Michael Pillsbury, "Strategic Acupuncture," *Foreign Policy* no. 41 (Winter 1980-81); pp. 44-61.

11. Cf. I.I.S.S., *The Military Balance, 1979-1980*, p. 11; ibid., *1980-1981*, p. 12.

12. The United States is also helping to expand port and airfield facilities at Ras Banas in Egypt. Sadat, on more than one occasion, volunteered access to Egyptian facilities in the event of a crisis.

13. See, for example, Ji Yanfeng, "Soviet Expansionist Strategy in the 'Dumbbell' Area," *Renmin Ribao*, June 22, 1979, p. 6 HK, tr. *Foreign Broadcast Information Service* (FBIS) 1, no. 127 (June 29, 1979), pp. C2-C4; Dan Lin, "Contention Between Superpowers in the Indian Ocean," *Renmin Ribao*, May 25, 1979, tr. ibid., 1, no. 113 (June 11, 1979), pp. C1-C2.

14. The background to the intervention has been treated extensively and will not be discussed here. For details see, inter alia, Selig Harrison, "Dateline Afghanistan: Exit Through Finland?" *Foreign Policy*, no. 41 (Winter, 1980-81), pp. 163-87; and Ronald R. Rader, "The Russian Military and Afghanistan: An Historical Perspective," *Soviet Armed Forces Review Annual* 4 (1980): 308-27.

15. Since the invasion, the Soviets have sought to stress their friendship toward the Islamic states. See Gromyko's speech to Soviet voters in *Pravda*, February 19, 1980, p. 2, tr. *Current Digest of the Soviet Press* (CDSP) 32, no. 7 (March 19, 1980): 1-3.

16. *Far Eastern Economic Review* (FEER) (Hong Kong), November 14, 1980, p. 23; and *Christian Science Monitor*, April 3, 1981, p. 3. The passes leading to China and Pakistan have been sealed, about 4,000 Soviet troops are stationed in the Wakhan panhandle, and the bulk of the area's Kirghiz tribesmen have fled to Pakistan.

17. Eliza Van Hollen, "Afghanistan: A Year of Occupation," U.S. Department of State, Bureau of Public Affairs, *Special Report*, No. 79 (February, 1981), p. 4, states that such weapons were removed from the Afghan army units in August 1980.

18. Ibid., pp. 3, 5; *FEER*, December 5, 1980, pp. 36-37; *Christian Science Monitor*, December 22, 1980, p. 13.

19. W. Eric Gustafson and William L. Richter, "Pakistan in 1980: Weathering the Storm," *Asian Survey* 21, no. 2 (February 1981): 163-64.

20. Van Hollen, "Afghanistan," p. 4.

21. See *New York Times*, May 12, 1980, p. A10 on the food and weapon shortages. On the moral issue, see *Christian Science Monitor*, April 29, 1981, p. 7.

22. *Christian Science Monitor*, December 3, 1980, p. 6. Estimates suggest about 15,000 Soviets killed and wounded. The reliability of such figures is not verifiable. If cor-

rect, these low casualty figures suggest that the Soviets have relied on armor and helicopter attacks against the resistance, rather than counterguerrilla tactics.

23. Xinhua Commentary, "Threat to Peace and Security in South Asia," *Renmin Ribao*, February 12, 1980, p. 7HK, tr. *FBIS* 1, no. 035 (February 20, 1980): C1–C2.

24. *Economic and Political Weekly* (Bombay), June 28, 1980, pp. 1082–83.

25. GPD, "Making a Point," ibid., July 19, 1980, p. 1209.

26. See, for examples, the writings of Romesh Thapar' in ibid., January 26, 1980, p. 131; Annual Number, February 1980, p. 197; March 22, 1981, p. 581. See also the editorial criticizing India's recognition of Kampuchea in *Eastern Economist* (New Delhi), July 18, 1980.

27. Texts in *Pravda*, February 15, 1980, p. 6, tr. *CDSP* 32, no. 7 (March 1980): 14, 24; *Pravda*, December 12, 1980, pp. 1–2, tr. *CDSP* 32, no. 50 (January 14, 1981): 7, 23.

28. On Indian arms purchases, see Rajan Menon, "The Military and Security Dimensions of Soviet-Indian Relations," in *The Soviet Union in the Third World: Successes and Failures*, ed. Robert H. Donaldson (Boulder, Col.: Westview Press, 1981), pp. 232–50; Mohan Ram, "Indo-Soviet Arms Deal," *Economic and Political Weekly*, May 31, 1980, pp. 953–54; Idem, "A Dog Fight Over Defense," *FEER*, November 21, 1980, pp. 23–24; and "Arms Purchases: Limited Options," *Economic and Political Weekly*, November 1, 1980, pp. 1870–71.

29. Five million Baluchis are divided between Afghanistan, Pakistan, Iran, and the Persian Gulf, and the Baluch area commands 900 miles of the Arabian seacoast. See Selig Harrison, "Baluch Nationalism and Superpower Rivalry," *International Security* 5, no. 3 (Winter 1980-81): 152–63. On Pakistani foreign policy in the wake of the Afghan invasion, see Lord Saint Brides, "New Perspectives South of the Hindu Kush," ibid., pp. 164–70; and *Christian Science Monitor*, January 12, 1981, p. 3 and February 20, 1981, pp. 1, 14.

30. *FEER*, November 7, 1980, pp. 11–12; *Christian Science Monitor*, January 12, 1981, p. 3.

31. For Soviet assessments of Deng's visit, see V. Kuzmin, "China in Washington's Aggressive Policy," *International Affairs* (Moscow), 1980, no. 4 (April), pp. 34–35; *Pravda*, February 18, 1979, p. 4; tr. in *CDSP* 31, no. 6 (March 7, 1979): 3.

32. *Renmin Ribao*, June 3, 1979, tr. in *FBIS* 1, no. 112 (June 8, 1979): C1; *Xinhua* in English June 26, 1979, in ibid., 1, no. 126 (June 28, 1979): D5; *Xinhua* Domestic Service in Chinese, August 4, 1979, tr. in ibid., 1, no. 152 (August 6, 1979: C1–C2.

33. *FEER*, October 24, 1980, pp. 32–35.

34. See ibid., November 7, 1980, pp. 13–14; December 19, 1980, pp. 29–37.

35. *Christian Science Monitor*, February 17, 1981, p. 7; March 2, 1981, p. 9; *FEER*, March 6, 1981, pp. 26–28.

36. *FEER*, December 19, 1980, pp. 30, 32; March 6, 1981, pp. 26–28.

37. I.I.S.S., *Strategic Survey 1979*, p. 60.

38. *Christian Science Monitor*, May 13, 1981, p. 3; May 14, 1981, pp. 1, 7.

39. *FEER*, February 27, 1981, pp. 32–24.

40. Details in Wolf Mendl, "The Security Debate in Japan," *International Affairs* (London) 56 (Autumn 1980): 607–21; and Gerald L. Curtis, "Japanese Security Policies," *Foreign Affairs* 59 (Spring 1981): 852–74.

41. *Radio Moscow* in Japanese, January 9, 1980, tr. in *FBIS* 111, no. 007 (January 10, 1980): C1.

42. *Pravda*, February 13, 1979, p. 5, tr. in *CDSP* 31, no. 7 (March 14, 1979): 17.

43. *Time*, March 23, 1981, p. 53.

44. For China's support of Japan on the Kurile question, see *Xinhua* in Chinese, tr. in *FBIS* 1, no. 182 (September 17, 1979): D1.

45. *Christian Science Monitor*, November 17, 1980, p. 13.

8

THE SOVIET-CUBAN RELATIONSHIP

Merritt Robbins

For more than 20 years the USSR has been Cuba's indispensable protector and benefactor; accordingly, it has been able to set the tolerable boundaries for Cuban domestic and foreign policies. The mix of dependence and interdependence, cooperation and conflict, which characterizes these relations, is the focus of this chapter. Contrasting viewpoints of Cuba's global activism illustrate the debate: it has been viewed as a compliant, Soviet-directed proxy, an ideologically motivated internationalist, a stabilizing influence, an international terrorist, and a Soviet partner, ally, or even "paladin."[1] Moreover, Cuba must function in several environments simultaneously. It has full membership in the system of Communist party states but also plays a leading role in the nonaligned movement. Cuba exports civilian and military advisers to over a dozen Third World countries, and its combat forces have intervened decisively in Angola and Ethiopia. Recently, Cuba has diversified its ties in Latin America and the Caribbean and has influenced and capitalized on the revolutionary turmoil in Central America. The size and scope of its overseas activities seems beyond the reach of an island nation with limited resources, a troubled economy, and fewer than ten million people, particularly since Cuba is strategically vulnerable in its location—6,000 miles from the USSR and in the immediate vicinity of a superpower adversary that regards the region as vital to its security.

The author wishes to thank Professors Edward Gonzalez of UCLA and the Rand Corporation, Jorge Dominguez of Harvard University's Center for International Affairs, and John Diggins of the University of California, Irvine, for providing valuable suggestions on an earlier draft of this chapter.

This analysis begins by reviewing the evolution of the Soviet-Cuban relationship and their respective ideological and geopolitical interests. Next, it examines Cuba's economic dependency, institutional processes, and military links, which require Castro to adhere to the terms of what must be described as Soviet hegemony. It then assesses the successes and failures of Cuba's efforts to establish itself and the Soviet bloc as "natural allies" of nonaligned nations, of its civilian and military assistance activities, and of Cuba's combat role in Southern Africa and the Horn. This part of the analysis will evaluate the compatibility of their aims and the various advantages, constraints, and imperatives that Cuba presents to the Soviet Union. Finally, it examines the prospects for future bilateral ties and the domestic and foreign limits to further overseas ventures.

BACKGROUND

Soviet-Cuban relations can be roughly divided into seven major phases, each marked by key turning points.

The first phase (January 1959 to February 1960) was characterized by Soviet ambivalence toward the new Castro regime. Although Castro's revolution aroused Soviet interest and coincided with an increase in long-distance support capability and resources that rendered Soviet leaders willing and able to extend a lifeline to an outpost in the Caribbean, it was still necessary for Castro and his new domestic ally and intermediary, the Cuban Communist party, to persuade the would-be backers of Cuba's Socialist (and the hemisphere's revolutionary) potential.

The second phase (February 1960 to October 1962) witnessed a growing Soviet commitment to the support of the new Cuban government, stemming from the Soviet pledge to purchase Cuban sugar and to extend credits to the year-old regime. Additional Soviet assurances of aid became essential, as Washington-Havana relations disintegrated amid threats, provocations, and retaliations.[2] Cuba's leaders perceived almost limitless opportunities for maneuverability, both between and within systems. The Bay of Pigs episode certainly encouraged their already extravagant confidence in their ability to become involved simultaneously in regional and even global struggles, defy the United States, and coax the Soviets into increasing their investment.

Retrospective treatment of the October 1962 near-catastrophe tends to stress that Khrushchev's primary motive was to redress the strategic imbalance with the United States, that Cuba's security interests were secondary, and that Castro was totally eclipsed during the critical negotiations. Nevertheless, Castro did attempt his own strategy: placing Cuba on a wartime footing on October 22, he declared the sovereign right to any arms necessary for defense; he rejected U.N. offers of mediation and the call for a cessation of work on launching pads; and he refused U.S. assurances of military nonintervention in exchange for a denuclearized Cuba. Finally, Castro blocked neutral on-site inspection arrangements to guarantee that offensive weapons would not be reintroduced; thus, the United States insisted that its no-invasion pledge be contingent on reconnaissance overflights.[3] Still dismayed five years later, Castro stated that Soviet conduct during the missile crisis "was to us a serious affront ... [and] the subsequent climate of distrust [between Castro and Khrushchev] could never be completely overcome."[4]

The third phase (November 1962 to mid-1963) was marked by public disagreements and the adoption of defiant postures designed to maneuver Moscow into a recommitment. The Chinese sought to capitalize on Soviet-Cuban discord, accusing the Soviets of both "adventurism and capitulationism" and acknowledging that Cuba had established the first "socialist state in Latin America." (The Soviets continued to segregate Cuba from the "genuine" Socialist republics.) Initially, prospects for Sino-Cuban solidarity seemed promising. Nevertheless, continued dependence on Soviet aid, with which China clearly could not compete, ultimately led to the weakening of the Peking-Havana connection. Also, Cuba refused to budge from professing strict neutrality in the Sino-Soviet rift.[5]

Cuba's exports to the USSR declined in value (to promote diversification, Cuba cut back sugar production), and Castro became unable to balance growing shipments of high-priced capital goods and imported raw materials.[6] Pre-missile-crisis amity resumed, following trade agreements signed in early 1963 and with Castro's sensational welcome to the USSR, where his statements reflected the Soviet line on the major disputed issues.[7] Thus, Cuba could finally be included in the Socialist camp—though Castro had declared his Marxism-Leninism in December 1961.

The fourth phase (mid-1963 to late 1965) was characterized by an uneasy accommodation between Moscow and Havana. In January 1964, in the midst of a severe economic crisis, Castro made a second Moscow visit and returned with additional trade concessions and promises—but no firm security guarantees. At the Havana Latin American Communist party conference in November 1964, the new mood was reflected in a compromise reached between Castro and the pro-Soviet leaders over the vexing question of armed struggle. It conceded to Cuba "active support to freedom fighters" in six countries; the conference refused, however, to endorse "the violent road" as the only means to power. In exchange, Cuba recognized the right of each Party to decide its own tactics and strategy and accepted a Soviet-sponsored condemnation of "all factional activity." Hence, a major Soviet objective was attained—driving a wedge between Castro and the Chinese; subsequent political and economic disagreements were to lead to the near-rupture of ties in early 1966.

Meanwhile, Castro acted to prevent Moscow-line orthodoxy from also threatening the guerrilla mystique of his domestic leadership. Thus, in October 1965, when he converted the PURS (United Party of the Socialist Revolution, formed in 1963) into the new Communist party (PCC), most of the old pro-

Soviet loyalists were pointedly excluded from top positions.[8] Clearly, allegiance to Fidel rather than doctrinal adherence to Soviet-style Marxism was to be the criterion for selection to leadership.

The fifth phase (January 1966 to October 1967) was characterized by escalated acts of defiance designed to embarrass and challenge Moscow into living up to its commitment to Cuba as a revolutionary base. Castro sponsored the Havana Tricontinental Conference in an effort to become a supranational anti-imperialist spokesman and take his rightful place alongside previous Third World leaders (for example, Nasser, Touré, Nyerere, and Nkrumah). In addition to providing training to students and guerrilla recruits from Africa, he also sought to revitalize his regional mission through insurrection in Bolivia. The ill-fated venture included Che Guevara and seven former members of the PCC Central Committee. In July 1967, the Havana-based OLAS was established to support and coordinate regional guerrilla activities.

Regis Debray's polemic, *Revolution in the Revolution?*, became the theoretical justification for these efforts and for the scuttling of the 1964 Havana agreements, and reflected Castro's ambition of bypassing the region's "pseudo-revolutionaries" to become the arbiter of hemispheric Marxism. It attacked the Soviets' united-front policy, rejected the Chinese notion that "the Party should direct the gun," and asserted that "proletarian internationalism" develops spontaneously in the purified minds of the guerrillas as they struggle. Thus, the rural-based *foco* (center) becomes itself the "party in embryo," which is the true "vanguard" entitled to Moscow's full support.[9] The Castro-Debray formulations were condemned by the hemisphere's orthodox and Chinese-line elements, and recognized by Soviet theoreticians as threatening the hard-won (albeit minimal) gains achieved by means that fall below the U.S. response threshold.[10]

The sixth phase (October 1967 to August 1968) was a period of intensified crisis that developed against the backdrop of threatened cutbacks in Soviet aid. The death of Guevara and the failure of the Bolivian foco symbolized the inability to export the Cuban revolution to the Americas. Thus, Castro intended to regenerate revolutionary spirits and restore credibility to his weakened image by turning the promise of producing ten million tons of sugar by 1970 into a national crusade. Meanwhile, in early 1968, a pro-Soviet dissident "microfaction" was arrested, tried, and sentenced to terms of up to 15 years for allegedly opposing Castro's foreign and domestic policies and urging his downfall. The anti-Soviet thrust of the affair was confirmed by the official report, charging "the old sectarians" with distributing propaganda "from Tass and Novosti agencies," ascribing to themselves "the role of defender of the policies of the USSR . . . and considering the departure of Guevara a healthy development." Also, in concert with Czech, GDR, and Soviet officials and citizens, they allegedly "sought political and economic pressure by the Soviet Union to force the Revolution to draw nearer to that country."[11] Shortly thereafter a messianic revolutionary offensive was launched to construct a real Communist society by expropriating the remaining private trading concerns and eradicating the residual capitalist social evils.

The Soviets had long since ceased their willingness to underwrite the experiment in import substitution, industrialization, and diversification. Cuba's rapidly increasing cumulative trade deficit ($1.7 billion) and reliance on Moscow for critical supplies of raw materials—especially petroleum—gave the Soviets ample economic leverage, which they proved willing to turn to political advantage. In addition to heightened discontent, shortages, and protest, rationing of gasoline became necessary because of Soviet supply cutbacks—though Soviet oil sales to other Latin American countries actually increased.[12]

On August 23, 1968, Castro issued his qualified endorsement of the invasion of Czechoslovakia—a major turning point that ended Cuba's crisis with the USSR and initiated the seventh phase in Soviet-Cuban relations. First, he used the speech to express displeasure with Dubček's "bourgeois liberal reforms" and those in other countries of the Socialist camp. He castigated the European Socialist states that dealt with Latin American oligarchies and took the opportunity to criticize the Czechs for the harsh trade terms with Cuba and the quality of goods, which contradicted the spirit of internationalism. He declared that, although "not the slightest trace of legality exists" for the invasion, "the flagrant violation" of Czech sovereignty was ideologically and politically *justifiable.*[13] He then implied that the Soviet bloc was obligated to commit itself to Cuba ("Will they send the divisions of the Warsaw Pact if Yankee imperialists attack our country?") and to other bona fide socialist states, for example, North Vietnam. In the words of one observer, "for some of the socialist states of Europe, the Brezhnev Doctrine was a threat, for Castro it was a promise."[14]

Gestures of solidarity followed one another in rapid succession. Castro paid tribute and expressed "deep gratitude" in January 1969 when new trade agreements were signed without undue delay. That same year, Soviet Vice Premier Novikov visited Cuba; a Soviet seven-ship flotilla (demonstrating its ability to operate in distant waters and "graphically illustrating the combat unity between the Soviet and Cuban armed forces") made a highly publicized visit to Havana harbor; and in the spring of 1970, Revolutionary Armed Forces (FAR) Minister Raul Castro made a six-week stay in the USSR, which led to agreements to modernize Cuban arsenals.[15]

The search for economic utopia and egalitarian wage distribution policies was deemphasized in the wake of the 10-million-ton harvest debacle of 1970 and replaced by Soviet-style correctives, including the doctrine that building socialism requires a high investment rate tied to low consumption and maximum technical and scientific knowledge. This reorientation led to a heightened role for Soviet advisers and to Cuba's admission in 1972 as a full-fledged member of the Council for Mutual Economic Assistance (CMEA). Within the terms of the new reconciliation, Cuba also restructured its Party and government along Soviet lines, thus helping to ensure the "irreversibility" of the revolution and providing potential access points for Soviet influence. The foreign policy shift was evident as Castro assailed leftist critics of the USSR, lauded Soviet aid in resisting "imperialism" in the Middle East and Vietnam, sided with Moscow against Peking, and retreated selectively from support of Latin American guerrillas, while seeking to expand "correct ties" on the model of relations with Mexico. By the time of Brezhnev's 1974 visit, Castro was prepared to explore opportunities for rapprochement with the United States and also undertake a greatly expanded Soviet-subsidized role in foreign affairs.

ECONOMIC DEPENDENCY

The USSR was able to take advantage of Cuba's vulnerability in 1967-68 to extract a broad range of domestic and foreign policy concessions. As a result, increased levels of military and political cooperation, ideological solidarity, and coordination of economic decision making characterize the present seventh phase in their relationship.

Economic relations are governed by 1972 agreements that deferred debts until 1986—to be followed by repayment over a 25-year period. New credits covering Cuba's 1973-75 trade deficits were granted free of interest. In 1976 Moscow concluded a five-year economic and technical agreement providing for a substantial increase in trade. By 1979, total cumulative grants from the USSR to Cuba amounted to $10.9 billion, and Soviet support had risen to more than $3 billion a year (a two-fold increase in two years), compared to an average annual rate of about $550 million in the early 1970s. The USSR also bought 3-4 million tons of sugar on a sliding scale at the equivalent of 44 cents a pound (substantially above the 10-cent world market price) and sold Cuba petroleum at about half the soaring OPEC price.[16]

In 1959 over two-thirds of Cuban trade was conducted with the United States: its value equaled 39 percent of the Cuban GNP, with the United States supplying over 70 percent of Cuba's imports and taking 66 percent of the island's exports. Currently, CMEA countries taken as a unit account for over 60 percent of Cuba's trade, and credits for capital goods from the USSR match the pre-Castro inflows of U.S. interest capital.[17] In 1959 Cuba's foreign debt stood at $45.5 million; in 1976 Cuba's external debt was nearly $6 billion, 77.6 percent of which is owed to the USSR—the world's highest per capita foreign debt. In addition, Cuba's current $1.3 billion hard-currency debt makes it the most indebted nation in Latin America on a per capita basis.[18] Clearly, Cuba is tied to foreign commodities and sources of capital formation and relies on sugar for more of its foreign earnings than it did before the revolution. Moreover, Cuba is critically dependent on a wide range of imported capital goods, including vehicles, machinery, spare parts, mineral fertilizers, cotton, and petroleum products. The USSR provides Cuba with a guaranteed market and price for much of the sugar crop (subsidizing Cuba for a total of $1 billion during the

1960s), which insulates the Cuban economy from fluctuations in the world price. Nonetheless, Cuba is vulnerable each time the annual bilateral trade agreements are negotiated.

Since Cuba's indebtedness is contrary to the aspect of Third World nationalism that is opposed to foreign domination, Castro points up the difference from the prerevolutionary period by insisting that "there is not one single Cuban working for a Soviet-owned enterprise" and denying that the relationship implies "an imperialist tie": "Where are its monopoly corporations? . . . What oil-fields does it own in the underdeveloped world? What worker is exploited . . . by Soviet capital?"[19]

Dissatisfaction with the erratic style of management and inability to meet production targets led to Soviet insistence on greater supervision of Cuba's economy in the wake of the 1968–71 collapse. During his 1974 visit to Cuba, Brezhnev noted with satisfaction that profitability had been adopted as the criterion of performance and Soviet-style cost accounting.[20] Besides exercising tighter control, Moscow's concerns about expenses have created a long-term interest in Cuba's reincorporation into the hemisphere in order to provide Cuba with access to its natural markets and primary sources of supplies. For instance, since the USSR maintains a costly, vulnerable "oil bridge," it has a triangular arrangement with Venezuela (and seeks one with Mexico) to provide for the shipment of oil to Cuba in return for Soviet deliveries of equivalent amounts to those countries' European customers.[21] Until the Angola operation interrupted and the Ethiopian intervention virtually halted normalization, the USSR welcomed the thaw in U.S.–Cuban relations.

Despite the political costs and benefits, Cuba's Soviet-subsidized overseas programs constitute a drain on scarce resources. Troops, equipment, and weapons have been transported, using part of the merchant marine and even the fishing fleet; also, the export of technicians and skilled workers has aggravated the shortage of some qualified personnel and created bottlenecks in production.[22] Though the Soviets make references to the 1979–80 economic crisis and massive refugee exodus (blaming "subjective shortcomings"), they are careful to cite *Granma* as the source.[23] Despite the unequal economic partnership that has mortgaged Cuba's future to the USSR, there are constant reminders of the accomplishments of the revolution and the need to withstand U.S. torments— still enough to persuade many students, workers, and soldiers that Cuba is freer and more independent today than at any time in its history.

INSTITUTIONALIZATION OF THE REVOLUTION

The institutions that link Cuba and the Socialist bloc provide for the stationing of an estimated 8,000 Soviet civilian advisers, the transferring of technology, and the routinization of support that symbolizes the credibility of the

Soviet commitment. Also, the establishment of a Soviet-style political order that ended 16 years of provisional revolutionary government increases the potential for cleavages to develop, based on different elite policy orientations and institutions. Thus, the USSR may have added means to guarantee cooperation, mold favorable policy dispositions, or create new opportunities for influence.

After coming to power in 1959, Castro exercised authority as commander-in-chief, prime minister, and (after 1965) first secretary of the PCC. It was not a ruling party but the mythology of maximum efforts toward apparently unattainable ends that provided the basis for Castro's charismatic authority, which, in turn, served as the indigenous source of the regime's legitimacy. Following the dislocations associated with the 1970 harvest, Castro's improvised decision making in day-to-day economic matters was curtailed. The transformation of the PCC into a genuine ruling party in the Soviet tradition culminated with the first party congress in December 1975, which elected the Castro brothers first and second secretaries; governing institutions with regularized procedures for policy formation and implementation were embodied in a new Socialist constitution, which was adopted by a national referendum in February 1976.

Though the "revolutionary family" continues to dominate party and government leadership posts, some of the guerrilla coterie have been replaced by appointees—many from the professional military—with specialized technical competence and administrative skills. Moreover, the increased importance of civilian technocratic-managerial elements has been reflected in the promotion of Carlos Rafael Rodriguez (who enjoys Moscow's endorsement and was relatively untouched by the 1960s purges) to the powerful Executive Committee of the Council of Ministers in the early 1970s and later to the Politburo. Indirect Soviet influence was also reflected in the appointment of former PSP Secretary-General Blas Roca to assignments in drafting the new constitution and as president of the National Assembly.

The close professional relationship of the armed forces with the USSR has offered Moscow the potential to exercise a more direct influence. A major channel is the General Directorate of Intelligence (DGI), which is accountable for Cuba's foreign intelligence activities and is headed by a *raulista* officer within the Ministry of Interior. In contrast to the PCC (which was not elevated to "supremacy" until 1975), the FAR (Revolutionary Armed Forces) was formed shortly after the take-over as the successor to the rebel army and, accordingly, claims revolutionary legitimacy. Its loyalty assured under Raul's leadership, it has developed into a coherent, professional, modern institution, as a result of Soviet aid and the high-threat expectations of the regime. In the mid-1970s the FAR developed the ability to assume its external operations and increased the linkages with the USSR, and Cuba's "civic soldiers" enhanced their domestic political position.[24] Armed and security forces supplied 19 percent of the delegates to the first party congress; active-duty FAR and MINFAR (Ministry of Revolutionary Armed Forces) officers, those assigned to civilian ministries and agencies, and veterans who became civilians, supplied 63 percent of the members to the 124-member Central Committee (from which technocratic ministers are often excluded); moreover, no less than nine officers were appointed to the Council of Ministers. The military continued to represent the single largest bloc in the 1980 Central Committee—27.6 percent.[25] Clearly, FAR-MINFAR officers constitute the most important elite group within the leadership and are the integral component in Castro's successful coalition building.

The professional military also represents an important foreign policy approach within the ruling circle—a role it must share with civilian elites and with veteran *fidelistas.* Tensions that may have existed in foreign policy were apparently resolved in favor of military and fidelista elements after the successful outcome of the Angola operation.[26] One observer, however, believes that some resentments may have developed among officers themselves: the Soviet Frunze Military Academy graduates (who hold important posts and control missile and radar bases), the graduates of Cuban schools, and older guerrilla veterans in less strategic positions.[27] In any event, the preeminent elite groups—civilian and military—which advocate high levels of joint overseas involvement, continue to enjoy access to the Soviet leadership and appear to remain responsive to Soviet guidance.[28]

MILITARY RELATIONSHIP

The USSR has maintained a marginal strategic interest in the Caribbean and, as part of its infrastructure for developing a global military presence, uses Cuba for the positioning and/or support of missile-bearing nuclear submarines, resident military personnel, long-range reconnaissance and transport aircraft, ships for electronic intelligence gathering, and communications facilities.[29] Cuba's armed forces also furnish the USSR a sizable rapid deployment force with ample Third World respectability. Nevertheless, despite prodigious amounts of military aid and repeated verbal assurances, Moscow refrains from signing any formal defense or alliance treaty, and Cuba has not become a Warsaw Pact member.

The USSR has increased the rate of weapons deliveries with the introduction of a costly new generation of hardware, including missile-carrying launches (which doubled Cuba's antiaircraft capacity), MIG 23s, and hundreds of experts to train Cuban personnel.[30] Nearly 1,000 Cubans were being trained in the USSR at the time of the Angola operation—more than twice the annual rate that prevailed in the 1960s—and the number of Soviet specialists (half of them military) increased from 1,000 in the early 1970s to 6,000 by 1975; moreover, the value of Soviet military aid had doubled that of the 1960s.[31] The Soviets have replaced equipment since Cuba's Africa operations, supplying newer model T-62 tanks, ZSU-23-4 self-propelled antiaircraft guns, and sophisticated MIG-

23 fighter-interceptors, which were flown by Cuban pilots in missions over Ethiopia.[32]

Soviet naval use of Cuba, particularly the Cienfuegos facility, has stretched the limits of the 1962 understanding with the United States "to keep all weapons systems capable of offensive use" out of Cuba and the hemisphere. Responding to U.S. warnings in October 1970 against construction of bases in Cuba, the USSR claimed that the allegations were groundless, declared their intention to adhere to the 1962 accords, but stressed that Cuba could permit Soviet vessels to enter its ports for "official visits and business calls."[33] U.S. and Soviet officials then apparently reached a tacit understanding that may have expanded the meaning of the original prohibitions; the United States continued to insist, however, that the servicing of atomic submarines anywhere at sea by tenders operating from Cuba be prohibited.

The frequent visits to Cuba by surface ships with antiair, antisurface, and antisubmarine capabilities are intended to test U.S. reactions and familiarize the United States with a Soviet naval presence in a sensitive area.[34] In addition, naval use of Cuba lengthens on-station time for Soviet vessels and, in conjunction with air reconnaissance, eases the task of surveillance of shipping. Also, Moscow has acquired a potential bargaining counter in future negotiations with the United States on restricting naval forces in areas considered vital to Soviet security.

The absence of a tripartite agreement formalizing the 1962 accords (and their subsequent modifications) contributed to a crisis in August-October 1979 when the United States announced that it regarded an alleged 2,000–3,000-man combat brigade on the island as a very serious matter. The Soviet brigade (discovered openly staging maneuvers in mid-August), was composed of motorized rifle, tank, and artillery battalions, and combat and service support elements. Significantly, it was not considered to be an assault force and had no airlift capability; it provided security, however, for a major Soviet-operated electronic information-gathering station. At the time there were 2,000 Soviet military advisers on the island and 50 pilots flying defense patrols for the Cuban air force.[35] In addition to training Cubans in weapons use and battlefield tactics, the brigade as a "trip wire" symbolizes Moscow's commitment to Cuba, and perhaps was part of a quid pro quo for Cuban participation in Africa. In any case, the Soviets denied that the force was a combat brigade (claiming it had been stationed there for 17 years), accused the United States of returning to "gunboat diplomacy" in staging maneuvers in the Caribbean, and declared that the existence of the Guantánamo naval training base ("the oldest U.S. base abroad") constituted a breach of Cuba's sovereignty.[36] Soviet and U.S. negotiators finally seemed to agree, however, that no Soviet combat forces would be introduced in the future.[37]

Other collaborative efforts involve the Cuban-Soviet oceanographic research and fishing fleets—both of which have naval auxiliary and intelligence-gathering functions,[38] and the development of nuclear energy,[39] and space exploration.[40] Cuba's espionage network is also coordinated with that of the USSR. Cuban DGI officials have been assigned KGB undercover tasks in Britain. Cuba maintains links to and shares information with opposition groups in countries considered to be reactionary (for example, Chile, Guatemala, Honduras, Uruguay, and El Salvador). Ties to the infamous Venezuelan terrorist "Carlos" resulted in the expulsion from Paris in July 1975 of three Cuban officials, and, in late 1976, Canada expelled five Cuban envoys from Ottawa on charges of engaging in military espionage.[41] More importantly, Cuba demonstrates its worth to the USSR through overt accomplishments: civilian and military aid programs, combat troops, and a leadership role in international forums.

TERCERMUNDISMO

Following a string of setbacks in Africa and Latin America, and in the wake of the economic collapse of 1968-71, Castro turned his attentions "with more realism and less idealism" to domestic problems and abandoned active support for insurgency abroad. During the halcyon days of détente, however, with the delegation of economic decision making to others and new assurances of Soviet backing, he regained the confidence to undertake an ambitious range of new international activities. In the process, Cuba has served as the bridge between the Soviet bloc and the Third World and implicitly repays the massive debt to the USSR with military diplomacy as the medium of exchange. By the mid-1970s Castro had recovered his somewhat eroded revolutionary credibility and bolstered the claim that Cuban and Soviet-bloc "anti-imperialism" coincides with Third World aspirations.

In the wake of Castro's 63-day trip to Africa and East Europe in May 1972 (lasting longer than all of his prior overseas visits combined) Cuban military and civilian missions appeared in Sierra Leone (1972), Equatorial Guinea (1973), Somalia (1974), and Algeria (1975). Prior to Angola, the largest number of advisers had been sent to South Yemen (600-700 military personnel in late 1973 when Iran sent troops to help Oman in the Dhofari rebellion) and to Syria (500-750 tank troops and a smaller number of air force instructors airlifted shortly after the October 1973 Arab-Israeli War). In the 1960s Cuba's military aid was limited for the most part to training liberation cadres and security forces: a guerrilla training base was established in Ghana (1961-66); arms and medical personnel were supplied to the Algerian independence movement; antiaircraft and construction crews were sent to Vietnam; and Che Guevara (in an abortive attempt to end the brief premiership of Tshombe) led a group of 200 Cubans into strife-torn Zaire (1965), and the following year helped establish a 1,000-man Cuban mission in Congo-Brazzaville. The latter became headquarters of Cuba's Africa operations, perhaps in part because of C.I.A. clandestine activities using anti-Castro Cuban exiles in support of Mobutu in neighboring Zaire. Cubans also played a direct role: regular combat troops were deployed in the Algerian border conflict with Morocco (1963-65), Cuban forces helped Congolese President Massamba-Debat defeat an army revolt (1966), and troops staffing Sékou Touré's Presidential Guard in Guinea helped repel a Portuguese assault on Conakry (1970).[42] Besides Cuba's decisive combat role in Angola and Ethiopia (see below), Castro has developed personal relations with the continent's leaders. In the year following his 1977 tour, the number of distinguished visitors to Cuba included Angola's Neto, Machel of Mozambique, Mengistu of Ethiopia, head of SWAPO (South West African People's Organization) Sam Nujama, and both Zimbabwe Patriotic Front leaders, Nkomo and Mugabe.[43]

The compatibility of Cuban and Soviet global views and the desire for Arab support determined Cuba's basic position in the Middle East. Though Cuba maintained diplomatic relations with Israel (in contrast to most Socialist-bloc countries) up to October 1973, the Tricontinental and OLAS (Organization of Latin American Solidarity) Conferences had been scenes of anti-Israeli invective; Cuban attacks developed fully after the Algiers nonaligned conference in September 1973 when diplomatic relations were finally severed. Cuban tank troops in Syria played a logistical role in the 1973 conflict and then entered into sporadic fighting with Israeli units in the Golan Heights through the spring of 1974.[44] Cuba has earned additional dividends from the Arab confrontation states by according high honors and extensive press coverage to the visits of PLO leader Arafat, by stationing medics and military advisers in Iraq, and by cosponsoring a U.N. resolution labeling Zionism a form of racism.[45]

Meanwhile, Cuba diversified its ties and reduced its isolation in the mid- and late 1970s in Latin America. Concurrently, the USSR expanded its ties in the hemisphere, beyond the usual sympathetic parties, to reform movements and even rightist juntas. Soviet trade (excluding Cuba) grew tenfold between 1970 and 1977, and Latin America accounted for more than one-third of CMEA's Third World imports.[46] Cuban and Soviet interests were further stimulated by the pressures for radicalization building in the troubled Caribbean basin. The 1979 Sandinista victory in Nicaragua that ended more than four decades of Somoza family rule, and the Bishop coup in tiny Grenada, brought to power two new regimes that display Marxist concepts for development, look to Cuba as a societal role model, and have joined the list of nonaligned nations. Also, possibilities for duplicating the Sandinista success and expanding Cuban influence emerged in strife-torn El Salvador.

Castro has not, however, been entirely successful in obscuring the reality of Cuba's dependence or the seeming dichotomy of "pro-Soviet nonalignment." At the June 1978 meetings of the OAU (Organization of African Unity), Nigeria admonished the USSR and Cuba against becoming "a new imperialist presence"; and, at the Belgrade summit that year, charges were raised that the continued Cuban and Soviet military presence in Africa posed a threat to the region's independence and autonomy.[47] Castro took the chair as the new three-year president at the sixth Conference of Nonaligned Nations in September 1979. While the Havana summit certainly enlarged Cuba's role, resolutions seemed to endorse Cuba's Africa operations, and the final declaration was vehemently anti-Western, the conference did not endorse the Cuban position that the Communist bloc is the "natural ally" of nonaligned nations. Moreover, Tito urged "resistance to bloc interests and foreign interference," and, as an antidote to Castro's opening address, Tanzania's Nyerere reminded the gathering of "the permanent interests" of "true" nonalignment. Also, in controversies over the seating of rival Cambodian delegations and the expulsion of Egypt from the movement, Cuba's pro-Soviet positions were defeated in favor of compromises. The Soviet invasion of Afghanistan was a setback to Castro's bid for permanent nonaligned leadership—as he discovered when he failed to obtain the prized rotating Latin American seat on the U.N. Security Council.[48]

Cuba's quality exports of doctors, construction workers, engineers, technicians, and teachers—who have appeared in 28 countries and are now active in 10 African countries—have greatly improved Cuba's international standing and complemented the roles of the USSR and especially East Germany. Cuba operates both military and civilian programs in the following African countries: Angola, Ethiopia, Algeria, Libya, Guinea, Guinea-Bissau, and Mozambique. Cuban civilian personnel are currently stationed in São Tomé-Principe, Tanzania, and Zambia.[49] Also, Cuban military advisers have trained SWAPO guerrillas and (prior to the Zimbabwe cease-fire) the ZAPU forces of Joshua Nkomo.[50] Some civilian programs have an important military content and are occasionally staffed by demobilized FAR personnel or those under military command (as in Angola). While the nature of Soviet involvement in these programs varies, programs in Somalia, Ethiopia, Syria, and Indochina were all joint Cuban-Soviet operations in which Cubans usually supplied support services and personnel to instruct recipients in the use of Soviet equipment and weapons.[51]

Unlike most Africa and Middle East operations, the Latin American foreign aid programs have been exclusively Cuban and have generally shown considerable flexibility. Cuba has sent disaster relief and has even responded to countries with which it has no diplomatic relations. Jamaica, experimenting with "democratic socialism" from 1975 to 1980, received various forms of Cuban aid. In Nicaragua, Cuba's principal contribution to the rebels began with training, help in unifying the Sandinista factions, asylum, and money. As the Sandinista position improved in 1979, Cuba stepped up support with clandestine arms shipments.[52] To the "revolutionary regime" (Castro's words) of Grenada, Cuba has sent military advisers to train the new army, and several hundred construction workers, a few civilian technicians, and much of the material to build a new jet airport, as an example of Cuban-backed development.[53]

Cuba's military, economic, and technical assistance activities have received a more favorable reception than those of the USSR. This seems true of Cuba's overseas missions (in Castro's words, "a new field of exports" and evidence that the revolution has succeeded at home) and on the Isle of Youth, where more than 10,000 12- to 17-year-old Third World students are attending school.[54] Observers have noted that attitudes of racial and cultural superiority often held by the Soviets contrast sharply with those of the racially mixed Cubans, who stress their people rather than materials or equipment.[55] Perhaps most important, Cuba still retains Third World admiration for many of its early revolutionary accomplishments—particularly for resisting imperialist (that is, U.S.) harassment.

INTERVENTION IN AFRICA

The commitment of troops for the explicit purpose of front-line combat duty in Angola and Ethiopia represented a qualitative and quantitative departure from Cuba's previous overseas "duties." Throughout the 1960s Castro believed that Soviet security guarantees alone could not insure his survival. Cuba's internationalist ideology and African aid programs evolved, therefore, as part of a strategy designed to acquire anti-imperialist allies, reduce Cuba's isolation, and enhance its leverage with the USSR. Thus, Cuba promoted national liberation movements with arms and advisers, helped defend friendly regimes from external and internal threat with military missions, and at least symbolically compensated for its increasingly embarrassing one-way dependence on the USSR. As noted, Cuba's major commitments of regular combat troops in the 1970s prior to Angola were in the Middle East—one of the high priority areas of intrinsic significance to the USSR. The Soviets then began to reassess the prospects for promoting their strategic interests in Africa. In agriculture and resource-rich Angola, the USSR reacted to opportunities created by the hasty liquidation of Portugal's empire after the April 1974 Lisbon coup. Following the successful operations in Angola, Mozambique (whose major non-African supporter had been China) turned to Havana and Moscow for help in securing its borders from Rhodesian and South African raids aimed at guerrilla sanctuaries. Also, the USSR succeeded in undercutting Chinese influence with Zimbabwe liberation forces operating from Zambia during the Rhodesian civil war.[56] The movement to the Left of the Ethiopian Revolution in 1976–77 provided another opening to deny the West a strategically important area and then to expand the Soviet-bloc role in Ethiopian affairs.

The USSR could not have undertaken a direct, "imperialist" combat role in Africa on its own without threat of Western sanctions, shattering détente, and crippling relations with African states, whereas Cuba could not extend large-scale military aid to Angola or Ethiopia without Soviet arms shipments and logistical support. Though Cuban aims were not always compatible with those of the USSR, the sharing of virtually identical views on global matters made coordinated military operations—particularly in the Horn—possible. Thus, Cuba could consolidate its ties with the USSR and thereby improve its economic and security position without the risk of confrontation with the United States; and the Soviets could depend on Cuba to help advance their geostrategic objectives. In short, Cuba's Afro-Spanish heritage and Third World credentials could combine with Soviet military and economic resources to obtain objectives that would be beyond their reach if they acted separately.

Angola

Cuban and Soviet operations developed independently in Angola, but became more coordinated as the civil war deepened and external threats increased. Cuban contacts with the MPLA (Popular Movement for the Liberation of Angola) of Agostinho Neto stemmed from an early affinity for the pro-Marxist, multiracial movement, which relied on support from the OAU's progressive Casablanca Group. Cuba provided guerrilla training both in Cuba and in Congo-Brazzaville (MPLA's headquarters-in-exile) from 1966. On the other hand, the USSR ceased meaningful aid to Neto in early 1974 after military setbacks and political defections, despite a relationship that dated from the early 1960s. Soviet aid did not resume until Neto consolidated control over the MPLA, the Chinese began to supply arms and training for the FNLA (National Front for the Liberation of Angola),[57] and the United States began to ship arms to the anti-MPLA forces through Zaire.[58] Thus, having overcome their initial reluctance (perhaps at Cuba's urging), the USSR responded to MPLA entreaties by shipping arms; however, the Soviets refused MPLA requests in August 1975 for advisers. Instead, 200 to 300 Cubans had been dispatched in June to staff several training camps; by mid-October, more than 1,000 Cuban troops were committed to helping the beleaguered MPLA.[59]

Each increase in aid came at MPLA request and could be justified as a response to escalations by its domestic and foreign enemies: South Africa opened training bases for FNLA and UNITA (National Union for the Total Liberation of Angola) in Namibia and Southern Angola and, in late October, about 5,000 South African troops launched a full-scale armored assault, while Zaire forces attacked in the north. Cuba's subsequent decision in favor of massive intervention was evidently made to help repel attacks on Luanda and to prevent the entrapment of its first contingent. Between November, when independence was granted, and March 1976, Cuban troop strength peaked at 36,000.[60] The South African advance was eventually halted; MPLA-Cuban forces gained the upper hand over FNLA-Zaire units in the north; and, following congressional rejection of administration appeals for financial aid to the anti-Soviet forces, South African troops finally withdrew (March 1976), and the survival of the new Marxist government seemed assured.[61]

While Cuban-MPLA commanders planned the engagements, they had at their disposal $200 million in weapons flown in by Soviet transports or shipped by East European vessels, including tanks, MIG aircraft (some assembled in Luanda), helicopters, and multibarreled rocket launchers. Soviet advisers appeared after independence, and by January 1976 the USSR provided Aeroflot Il-62 transport aircraft for Cuba's troops. The first Cuban contingents, however, arrived in freighters, old Cuban Bristol-Britannia turbo-jets, and even in chartered 727s.[62] Castro claimed that the decision to commit troops in combat units was an exclusively Cuban one.[63] Nevertheless, Cuba could not have implemented its decision without the infusion of Soviet weaponry, logistical and training support, and economic and security assurances in the event of possible U.S. punitive actions against Cuba.

The South African invasion and subsequent cross-border strikes certainly undercut the credibility of the pro-Western groups and made the large Cuban buildup and continued troop presence respectable. Some Cuban troops were also used by the Neto government to defeat an abortive, bloody coup by a pro-Soviet faction in May 1977. The Alves group (which favored black nationalist stands on issues and closer alignment with the USSR) appeared to have tacit Soviet endorsement. In sharp contrast to the Soviets in Luanda, who had foreknowledge of the coup but did not warn Neto, many Cubans joined the regime to crush the attempt. Shortly thereafter, Raul Castro visited Angola, and Cuban troop levels (which had been reduced to perhaps 12,000) increased to about 19,000.[64]

Since 1978, Cuba has helped the Angolan regime consolidate its internal position and avoid problems—such as those an enlarged war over Namibia might bring—that could increase its vulnerability. Angola actively pursues a negotiated Namibia settlement; also, Cuba urged SWAPO to accept a U.N. independence plan that called for a peace-keeping force to monitor a cease-fire and supervised elections for a national assembly. Cuba also disarmed Katangan forces after the Shaba II invasion of 1978, thus facilitating an Angola-Zaire border agreement.[65] Castro was even supportive of the decision not to expropriate Gulf Oil properties and stationed troops in the oil-rich Cabinda enclave (which Zaire wanted to annex) to guard Gulf's facilities.[66] To convert Angola into a showcase of Socialist-bloc-aided development and to help cope with the exodus of 300,000 Portuguese who supplied the technical and managerial expertise, Cuba will soon increase its economic technicians, specialists, political advisers, and medical personnel and teachers to as many as 13,000. Cuba's civilian contribution to Angola has had mixed results. A number of Cuban advisers have been removed from government ministries, and Cuban personnel in oil and sugar enterprises have been criticized for their lack of expertise and reliability.[67]

Cuba's intervention in Angola risked impairment of the normalization process with the United States, diverted manpower and resources from the economy, and perhaps strained relations in Castro's ruling coalition. Nevertheless, the overall success of the operation—especially Cuba's combat role—maximized Cuban influence with the USSR (though they were briefly at odds over the Alves coup attempt), added to Soviet prestige in Africa, helped with USSR rights to use naval maintenance facilities in Luanda, and provided a precedent for a more closely coordinated military intervention in Ethiopia.

The Horn of Africa

In contrast to the essentially reactive, incremental Angolan involvement, the rapid buildup in Ethiopia was coordinated by the USSR and Cuba from the outset; in addition, after March 1977 policy was jointly formulated and implemented. In Angola the enemy had been different: South African invaders, "neo-colonial" Zaire, and domestic adversaries who received direct Western aid. In Ethiopia, on the other hand, the invading forces were from a Third World country and the internal separatists received no direct "imperialist" support. Furthermore, Cuba lacked long-standing contacts with Ethiopia's military rulers and the ethnic/linguistic affinity it had with the MPLA. The USSR, which played a secondary role in Angola, had a more pronounced one in the Horn (indeed, the central role in planning and commanding the Ogaden campaign of 1978), where the potential naval-strategic costs and gains were greater. In the process of gaining a foothold in Ethiopia, the Soviets were required to shore up an arbitrary and brutal dictatorship, and their gains were partially offset by political and diplomatic losses. They lost the friendship of Somalia and its deep-water naval facilities at Berbera. Cuba forfeited an investment in Somalia of doctors and technicians (first dispatched in 1972) and a military program (initiated in 1974). Cuba also sacrificed influence with Eritrean guerrillas whom it had been training since 1967 for a liberation war against "Ethiopian colonialism." The intervention also ended hopes of continuing the U.S.-Cuban normalization process, imperiled East-West détente, and fueled Third World suspicions about Cuba's role in an "imperial" Soviet foreign policy.

A fast-moving chain of events were set in motion that led to a dramatic shift in the Horn's geopolitical alignments. In December 1976 the ruling Ethiopian military junta, the Dergue, which more than two years earlier had ended the 44-year reign of Haile Selassie, concluded a secret agreement with the USSR for military aid. In February 1977 a radical faction staged a coup and within hours after the take-over, the new junta, led by Lieutenant Colonel Mengistu Haile-Mariam, received its first congratulatory message from Fidel Castro. In April the U.S. military mission was expelled from Ethiopia; and in December, after months of bitter fighting in the Ogaden, the Somalis finally expelled all Soviet and Cuban personnel.[68]

In the drought-stricken Ogaden region Ethiopia faced a stepped-up war of secession from the irredentist WSLF (West Somali Liberation Front), which received invaluable aid from nominally Marxist and avid pan-Somali nationalist Siad Barre. With an efficient, formidable 22,000-man army (which had been well equipped by the USSR and trained by Cuba), Somalia became alarmed when its erstwhile allies began to develop close ties to its archenemy in Addis Ababa.

Thus, the USSR and Cuba were in the unenviable position of aiding two countries that were on the verge of war with each other. To complicate matters further, Ethiopia faced armed opposition from several guerrilla groups in its northernmost province of Eritrea, including the Marxist-oriented EPLF (Eritrean People's Liberation Front), which had placed high hopes in Cuba and risked being deprived of its entire 540-mile coastline adjacent to vital petroleum resources and strategic maritime routes.

Ethiopia claimed that Somali forces crossed into the Ogaden in late February 1977. During Castro's Africa and Middle East sojourn (overlapping then-Soviet President Podgorny's Africa tour and concluding with an unplanned stop in Moscow), he attempted to intercede with Somalia and Ethiopia (even presiding over a secret meeting in Aden between Mengistu and Barre) by proposing "an anti-imperialist, socialist federation" for the Horn region, which would include Ethiopia, Somalia, Yemen, Djibouti, and an autonomous Eritrea.[69] Such a solution failed to deter either Ethiopia or Somalia from proceeding on their collision course.

Approximately 50 Cuban military advisers were instructing Ethiopians in the use of Soviet equipment in the spring of 1977, when several thousand heavily armed guerrillas crossed into the Ogaden from Somalia. In mid-July Somali regulars invaded the Ogaden and in 12 days captured Jigiga, 85 percent of the province, and threatened Harar. By early December, after the second Somali offensive toward Harar, Cuban advisory personnel increased to 400. Clearly, the Somali invasion obliged the Soviets and Cubans to escalate their commitment to Ethiopia to a degree that narrowed their options for response in the Horn and completed the reversal of alliances. In January 1978, Raul Castro arrived in Ethiopia to plan the Ogaden counteroffensive; the following month he went to Moscow to meet with Brezhnev and the Soviet defense minister to coordinate the massive buildup. By March about 12,000 Cuban troops were fighting in Ethiopia—airlifted from Cuba, Angola, and the Congo—along with perhaps 2,000 Yemenis and 1,400 Soviet advisers.[70] The Cubans spearheaded the drive, which reconquered about 200,000 square miles, forced the Somali troops back across the border, and destroyed over 75 percent of Somalia's tanks, 50 percent of its combat air force, and many of its elite troops. Nearly $1 billion worth of material was provided by the USSR to arm the Cuban and Ethiopian forces.[71] Cuba's armored and mechanized infantry, missile units, and pilots employed classic Soviet tactics in the Ogaden campaign. Although they were led by General Ochoa, the Cubans were under the overall command of Soviet four-star General Petrov.[72]

Western neutrality and the acceptance of the intervention by most African states stemmed from several factors: Ethiopia's borders were clearly violated by Somalia; both the Cubans and Soviets initially sought a negotiated settlement and issued repeated assurances that their forces would not cross into Somalia; they had responded to requests by an incumbent regime to protect its sovereignty and preserve the status quo, and thus were keeping within majority African (OAU) principles on the inviolability of postcolonial borders.

In Eritrea, Cuba and the USSR faced another difficult policy dilemma: whether to lose influence and leverage over a "people's rebellion" or risk friction with an incumbent allied government committed to crushing it. Eritrea had been a colony of Italy, under a British colonial trusteeship, federated to Ethiopia by the United Nations, and finally annexed as a province (1962). Cuba supported Eritrean independence for 16 years and, while Castro's federated concept later included Eritrea, Cuba had adopted the Mengistu government's view that defined the rebels as "secessionists." When Ethiopian and Cuban forces were concentrating in the Ogaden, most of the northeast was lost to the insurgents. Though Cuban combat troops have avoided entering the struggle directly, Cuba's willingness to guard the Ogaden, train militia for combat duty, provide logistical support, and deliver and maintain sophisticated Soviet weapons have released the Dergue forces for offensives that have reconquered most of the rebel-held territory. The USSR has also wanted the area under government control, but for naval-strategic reasons: because of their extensive support, the Soviets have been able to obtain the use of Dahlak Island and key port facilities along the Eritrean Red Sea coast overlooking Saudi Arabia. Nevertheless, Havana and Addis Ababa have been at odds over Eritrea: Mengistu refuses to seek a negotiated political settlement and Castro refuses to offer combat troops in the struggle. Thus, with Cuban support limited to an advisory and logistical role, Ethiopian troops eventually recaptured 30 towns and broke the three-year siege of Asmara.[73]

Despite their differences, Ethiopia has accelerated its Cuban-style campaigns to combat illiteracy, build a "popular militia," and develop mass organizations, and has promised to form a "vanguard party" that may eventually become a genuine ruling Communist party. Eritrea, however, remains an obstacle, as does the mounting cost of aid: in a speech honoring Cuba's war dead, Raul Castro hinted at a linkage between future Cuban civilian aid programs and a nonmilitary solution (though without explicitly referring to Eritrea) to Ethiopia's problems of nation building.[74] In order to manage the costly joint assistance in Ethiopia and elsewhere in Africa, a division of labor has emerged among the USSR, Cuba, and other Socialist countries, which includes roles for Bulgaria, East Germany (developing communications and intelligence networks and training government and party cadres), and other recipients of Soviet-bloc aid.[75]

While they gained influence in a strategic area, Cuba and the USSR may have made greater sacrifices than either one intended or desired. Obliged to escalate their commitment to the internationally unpopular Ethiopian dictatorship, the USSR and Cuba abandoned Eritrea (and risked alienating its Islamic backers in North Africa and the Middle East) and in Somalia lost a valuable ally. Elsewhere, Cuba's cooperation with Algeria on behalf of the Polisario Liberation front in the former Spanish Sahara antagonizes Mauritania and prevents improvement of ties with France; and Castro's links to the outlaw state of Libya and support for Qaddafi's dream of an Islamic federation in Western Africa forfeits much international goodwill. How much further pressure Third World receptiveness to Cuba can withstand is difficult to calculate. If Cuba continues to defend internationally unpopular Soviet actions—for example, the invasion of Afghanistan and threats to Poland—Cuba can expect to be deprived of the earlier gains of its foreign policy. In the past, Cuba's overseas activities have generally coincided with majority African and Arab opinion and with Soviet geostrategic objectives, and enabled the USSR to channel support with increased options for response and with minimum concern about charges of big-power imperialism. In the 1980s Cuba may be required to adjust to new constraints, dictated by evolving foreign and domestic developments, that directly impinge on its ability to continue—singly and in concert with the USSR—its ambitious overseas ventures.

PROSPECTS

Historically, Cuba and the USSR have experienced political fluctuations; an undisrupted relationship, however—with both sides being aware of mutual benefits and costs—can be expected to continue in the 1980s. The poor prognosis for the health of the Cuban economy and its monumental debt suggests deepening dependence; and the minus-average annual per capita growth rate in GNP since the revolution fuels doubt about the transferability of Cuba's developmental model to Third World countries and Latin America. Owing to its staunchly pro-Soviet stands, Cuba has already begun to experience difficulty in international forums in securing support from the nonaligned for its positions. Nevertheless, if Cuba continues to prove its loyalty, it will exercise leverage and secure higher levels of support from the Soviet Union. Moreover, its Soviet-style institutions appear firm, despite recent difficulties.

Cuba's vulnerability to the capricious forces of disease, weather, and economic fluctuations led to a serious socioeconomic crisis in 1979-80. To cope with the consequences, an unsentimental advocate of tighter controls, Ramiro Valdes, was reinstalled as minister of the interior; also, identity checks were introduced, a mass roundup of suspects was begun, and antiregime leaflets and posters were reportedly appearing in Havana.[76] Out of such conditions erupted an effort begun in April-May 1980 by over 125,000 Cubans to escape in a disorderly "boatlift" to join nearly 800,000 refugees who have fled to the United States since 1959. Under such circumstances it is unlikely that Cuba can relieve its dependence on the $8-million-a-day Soviet subsidy—especially if preferential pricing for Cuban sugar and nickel and Soviet crude oil continues to make it disadvantageous for Cuba to shift its trade to other countries. Its dependent links will be reinforced, if Cuban prospects for earning hard currency deteriorate when current financial agreements expire in 1986.[77]

After years of preoccupation with Africa, Cuba and the USSR have begun to pay increasing attention to the insurrectionary currents in Central America. In late 1979 Castro took a personal role in bringing together the ideologically diverse guerrilla factions and the Communist party in El Salvador to forge them into the United Revolutionary Directorate. According to captured leftist documents, the USSR funneled weapons to Cuba, where they were stockpiled for delivery in late summer 1980 to guerrillas via Nicaragua.[78] Although the potential of the insurgents to launch another offensive against the government remains strong, the USSR can be expected to constrain Castro from high-risk behavior that could either jeopardize their present degree of influence with Managua or provoke a direct U.S. confrontation with Cuba.

A trend may be emerging in Latin America that is distinctly unfavorable to a further extension of Cuban influence: the shaky regime of Grenada is in political and economic trouble; Cuba's supporters in Surinam, who seized power in February 1980, have been ousted; and pro-Cuban parties in Antigua, St. Vincent, Dominica, St. Kitts, and Nevis, and, most important, Jamaica, have been defeated in elections. Also, Colombia and Costa Rica have broken their relations with Cuba; all diplomatic personnel have been removed from Venezuela; relations are extremely poor with Ecuador; and with Peru, Argentina, and Guyana, relations are not as favorable as they were in the mid-1970s.[79]

Though the March 1980 Zimbabwe election defeat of Joshua Nkomo by Robert Mugabe was a setback for Cuban aims, the potential for conflict and for a magnified Cuban presence in southern Africa still remains high. The 19,000 Cuban troops remaining in Angola continue to play a deterrent role against a repeat of the 1975 South African invasion or coup attempts against the Luanda regime of dos Santos. The Cuban combat function is evolving into providing garrison, logistical, artillery, and air support for the Angolan armed forces; thus, it appears that Angola will assume a steadily larger share of the defense burden and that it intends to lessen Cuba's military role. Though Cuba no longer has a significant combat role against UNITA guerrillas, the case for a prolonged Cuban presence remains strong as long as UNITA forces control much of the highlands of south-central Angola, an internal settlement is not reached, and South African troops continue cross-border strikes at SWAPO installations and Angolan infrastructure. Since a solution for Namibia along the lines that created an independent Zimbabwe is unlikely, Cuba will probably continue to strengthen the armed potential of SWAPO with training and advice as long as South Africa retains ultimate powers over Namibia. Another direct Cuban combat role cannot be ruled out in Angola (or if it is requested by Mozambique and Zambia), should an enlarged struggle over Namibia provide outright South African interventions.[80]

Cuba's Ethiopian ally continues to be torn by serious ethnic and religious differences and requires an indefinite Soviet-bloc rescue effort and Cuban troop presence. Though nearly one million Somalis have been forced out of the Ogaden, government troops and support detachments of Cuba's 16,500 expeditionary forces must cope with the determined resistance of 20,000 Somali-backed WSLF guerrillas who have regained control of the countryside and with the possibility of renewed invasion. Fundamental differences remain between Cuba and Ethiopia over the Eritrean problem, where the last of the Islamic-based insurgents conduct a "people's war" in mountainous terrain. As before, Cuba wants to avoid alienating the militant Islamic states that support the liberation movements and will probably not deploy combat troops except in the event of direct foreign intervention.[81]

Cuba's current domestic difficulties are not necessarily signs of its incapacity to embark on future overseas combat ventures.[82] One hundred thousand troops and replacements have acquired valuable combat experience in Africa; and Cuba's "civic soldiers" have enhanced their domestic status and institutional influence. New commitments would probably be accomplished by transferring a portion of the existing troops abroad rather than sending new expeditionary forces, although surplus manpower should be available for "export" to augment current FAR levels and to provide a safety valve to relieve the accumulated tensions in Cuban society.

It is unclear what role a post-Brezhnev leadership will assign to Cuba. The need to restrain Castro's own ambitions may be offset by the urge to use Cuba to influence events decisively in favor of the Socialist bloc. In the past decade, this has meant attempting to fill the vacuum left by a diminishing Western presence, particularly in target areas where U.S. commitments were poorly defined. Much depends on Soviet ability to manage economic and satellite troubles and domestic dissent and to adjust to a strategic framework dictated by the evolving relationship with the United States. Whether the USSR deescalates competition in Third World areas or launches new adventures out of frustration, Cuba may still distract the United States in the Americas, seek openings elsewhere to acquire influence for itself, and lend added flexibility to Soviet foreign policy.

NOTES

1. For an interpretation of contending views, see Edward Gonzalez, "Cuba, the Soviet Union, and Africa," in *Communism in Africa*, ed. David Albright (Bloomington: Indiana University Press, 1980), pp. 146-52. For the surrogate thesis, see Brian Crozier, "The Surrogate Forces of the Soviet Union," *Conflict Studies* no. 92 (February 1978): 1-20. See also, David Ronfeldt, *Superclients and Superpowers* (Santa Monica, Cal.: Rand Corporation, 1978).

2. This phase of U.S.-Castro relations is typified by the dispute involving Texaco, Esso, and Shell. As National Bank president, in November 1959 Guevara stopped payments to U.S. oil companies that supplied Cuba; in May 1960, the companies refused to refine substituted Soviet crude, and the Cubans seized the refineries without offering indemnity; in July 1960 the United States retaliated by cutting the sugar quota, and Socialist-bloc countries purchased the remainder; Cuba then nationalized U.S.-owned banks and industries, and

the United States set the sugar quota at zero; finally, diplomatic relations were officially severed in January 1961. See Erik Baklanoff, *Expropriations of U.S. Investments in Cuba, Mexico and Chile* (New York: Praeger, 1975), p. 28; and Andres Suarez, *Cuba: Castroism and Communism, 1959-66* (Cambridge, Mass.: M.I.T. Press, 1967), pp. 78-120.

3. Irving Horowitz, "Deterrence, Détente, and the Cuban Missile Crisis," in *Cuban Communism*, ed. I. Horowitz (New Brunswick, N.J.: Transaction, 1977), pp. 112-13. Intelligence overflights continued without harassment, even after Soviet SAMs were placed under Cuban command in 1964; they were halted temporarily, however, during the U.S.-Cuban "thaw" in 1977. See Lynn Bender, *The Politics of Hostility* (Hato Rey, P. R.: Inter-American University Press, 1975), p. 67.

4. Fidel Castro to Lee Lockwood in 1967, cited in Horowitz, "Deterrence," p. 35.

5. Andres Suarez, "Castro Between Moscow and Peking," *Problems of Communism* (September-October 1963). See also, Cecil Johnson, *Communist China and Latin America* (New York: Columbia University Press, 1970).

6. L. Gouré and J. Weinkle, "Cuba's New Dependency," *Problems of Communism* (March-April 1972): 71. See also, V. Volskii, *Kuba: 10 let revolutsii* (Moscow: Nauka, 1968), pp. 226-27.

7. See Maurice Halperin, *The Rise and Decline of Fidel Castro* (Los Angeles: University of California Press, 1972), Ch. 20.

8. There were two notable exceptions, Carlos Rafael Rodriquez and Blas Roca in the PCC secretariat; see Theodore Draper, *Castroism: Theory and Practice* (New York: Praeger, 1965), pp. 199-204.

9. Regis Debray, *Revolution in the Revolution?* (New York: Grove Press, 1967), *passim*; and D. B. Jackson, *Castro, the Kremlin and Communism in Latin America* (Baltimore, Md.: Johns Hopkins University Press, 1967), p. 131.

10. *Pravda*, July 30, 1967, reprinted attacks on "petty bourgeois adventurism, terrorism . . . and anti-Soviet attitudes." As for the Chinese, Debray declared that it was fortunate that Castro had been ignorant of Mao's works, so he could "invent, on the spot and out of his own experience." *Revolution*, p. 20. At the Tricontinental Conference Castro astonished the nearly 600 delegates from 82 countries by denouncing the Chinese for reneging on promises of rice shipments and for allegedly interfering "for the purposes of proselytism or intelligence" with Cuban armed forces and government officials. The USSR also tried to embarrass the Chinese, charging them with obstructing the transit of Soviet material for Vietnam. See Johnson, *Communist China*, p. 163.

11. Soviet envoy Rudolf Shliapnikov was linked to the group, which included (once again) Anibal Esclante. See *Bohemia* (Havana), February 2, 1968, p. 44.

12. Because of like-minded efforts at resisting Soviet pressure, Romania lent Cuba $30 million for oil-drilling equipment; see Kevin Devlin, "Rumania Intervenes in Cuban-Soviet Confrontation," (Munich: RFE Research Paper, April 26, 1968).

13. *Granma*, August 25, 1968.

14. H. Dinerstein, "Soviet and Cuban Conceptions of Revolution," *Studies in Comparative Communism* 4, no. 14 (January 1971): 15.

15. K. S. Karol, "The Reckoning: Cuba and the USSR," in *Cuban Communism*, ed. Irving Horowitz, pp. 509-11; and Edward Gonzalez, "Relationship with the Soviet Union," in *Revolutionary Change in Cuba*, ed. C. Mesa-Lago (Pittsburgh: University of Pittsburgh Press, 1971), pp. 94-95.

16. See Lawrence Theriot, *Cuban Foreign Trade: A Current Assessment* (Washington, D.C.: Department of Commerce Staff Paper, 1978); and *State Department Bulletin* 80, no. 2040 (July 1980): 77-82.

17. William LeoGrande, "Cuban Dependency," *Cuban Studies* 9 (July 1979): 13-18.

18. The rest of Cuba's debt is hard currency, owed principally to West European trade partners. Ibid., pp. 18-20; and *Los Angeles Times*, March 8, 1981, Part VI, p. 1.

19. Remarks made to the Algiers nonaligned summit where Castro defended his association with the USSR and sought to refute "the theory of two imperialisms." *Granma*, September 16, 1973.

20. *Granma*, February 10, 1974.

21. I. Petushkov and E. Sheenin, *Economika Kubi v sisteme mezhdunarodnogo sotsialisticheskogo razdeleniia trada* (Moscow: Nauka, 1976), p. 134. C. Mesa-Lago notes that Cuban refineries need remodification to process Western crude again. "The Economy and International Economic Relations," in *Cuba in the World*, ed. C. Blasier and C. Mesa-Lago (Pittsburgh: University of Pittsburgh Press, 1979), p. 205. Mexico has recently agreed to help Cuba expand oil refining and exploration. See *Los Angeles Times*, March 8, 1981, Part VI, p. 1.

22. Mesa-Lago, "The Economy," p. 174.

23. TASS, December 6, 1979. Castro revealed the depth of the 1979–80 crisis in a speech to the National Assembly on December 27, 1979 and to the 2nd Party Congress the following year. *Los Angeles Times*, May 7, 1981.

24. Jorge Dominguez, "Institutional and Civil-Military Relations," *Cuban Studies* 6 (January 1976): 39–65.

25. The 1975 Central Committee calculation (which includes ex-military to show the preferred career path and social ties that may persist) was revised from Edward Gonzalez, "Complexities of Cuban Foreign Policy," *Problems of Communism* 26 (November-December, 1977): 6. 1980 figures are from Jorge Dominguez, "The Demands for Orderliness in the Cuban Revolution in the 1980's," (Cambridge, Mass.: Center for International Affairs, Harvard University, April 1981). Unpublished manuscript.

26. Two generals who played key roles in the Angolan intervention were later appointed to the Council of State (a body where civilian "technocratic" elites remain underrepresented). Gonzalez, "Complexities of Cuban Foreign Policy," pp. 21–25.

27. Irving Horowitz, "Military Outcomes of the Cuban Revolution," in *Cuban Communism*, ed. Horowitz, p. 78.

28. Between January 1975 and December 1978, Rodriguez visited Moscow twelve times, Raul four (meeting with Brezhnev on three occasions), and Fidel made two trips (twice meeting with Brezhnev). C.I.A., *Cuban Chronology—A Reference Aid* (Washington, D.C.: National Foreign Assessments Center, 1979), pp. 79–87; and Gonzalez, "Cuba, the Soviet Union and Africa," pp. 158, 266.

29. Ronfeldt, *Superclients*, p. 3, and James Theberge, *Russia in the Caribbean* (Washington, D.C.: Georgetown University, SAIS Special Report Series, 1973), pp. 99–120.

30. Horowitz, "Military Outcomes," p. 96.

31. Dominguez maintains that the U.S. Arms Control and Disarmament Agency underestimated the receipts of weaponry by cost in the early 1970s and Cuba's actual military expenditures in the 1960s. "Armed Forces and Foreign Relations," in *Cuba in the World*, ed. Blasier and Mesa-Lago pp. 54–55.

32. Gonzalez, "Cuba, the Soviet Union and Africa," p. 159.

33. *Izvestiia*, October 9, 1970 and TASS, October 13, 1970.

34. See U.S. Congress, House Subcommittee on Inter-American Affairs, Committee on Foreign Affairs, *Soviet Activities in Cuba: Hearings, 93rd Congress* (Washington, D.C.: U.S. Government Printing Office, 1974), pp. 30–33; and B. Blechman and S. Levinson, "Soviet Submarine Visits to Cuba," in *Soviet Naval Influence: Domestic and Foreign Dimensions*, ed. M. MccGwire and J. McDonnell (New York: Praeger, 1977), pp. 428–41.

35. *Time*, October 1, 1979, pp. 12–21.

36. "A Policy of Gross Blackmail," TASS, October 2, 1979 and *Pravda* November 9, 1970. (Both parties must agree to any modification of the Guantánamo lease.)

37. Shortly thereafter, General Epishev visited Cuba for talks with Castro and FAR officials. TASS, November 16, 1979.

38. Dominguez, "Armed Forces," p. 73.

39. Cuba refuses, however, to adhere to the Test Ban Treaty, the Nonproliferation Treaty of 1968, or the Treaty of Tlateloco prohibiting nuclear weapons in the hemisphere. Ibid., p. 74 and U.S. Congress, *Soviet Activities in Cuba*, pp. 106-7, 114. See also, Jorge Perez-Lopez, "The Cuban Nuclear Power Program," *Cuban Studies* 9 (January 1979): 22, 27.

40. They reportedly completed a series of scientific experiments and photographic work in space. *Pravda*, September 21, 1980.

41. *London Evening News*, March 26, 1973; *New York Times*, July 20, 1975 and January 13, 1977. The Cuban Foreign Ministry maintained that the diplomats were recruiting English-speaking Canadians for use in South Africa. See Dominguez, "Armed Forces," p. 72.

42. The foregoing is based largely on William Durch, *The Cuban Military in Africa and the Middle East* (Arlington, Va.: Center for Naval Analysis, 1977), pp. 25-33.

43. Edward Gonzalez, "Cuban Policy Toward Africa," in *The Communist States in Africa*, ed. David Albright and Jiri Valenta (Bloomington: Indiana University Press, forthcoming).

44. See Yoram Shapira, "Cuba and the Arab-Israeli Conflict," in *Cuba in the World*, ed. Blasier and Mesa-Lago, pp. 153-65. Cuba's pro-Palestinian declarations often go beyond Soviet positions; for example, see *Granma*, October 27, 1975.

45. *Granma*, January 18, 1976.

46. *Los Angeles Times*, March 8, 1981.

47. *New York Times*, July 20, 1978; for the response from Cuban Foreign Minister Malmierca, see *Granma*, August 13, 1978.

48. On the Havana summit see William LeoGrande, "Evolution of the Nonaligned Movement," *Problems of Communism* 29 (January-February 1980): 47. Cuba abandoned the U.N. Security Council race to Mexico. *New York Times*, January 7, 1980, p. A2.

49. C.I.A., *Communist Aid Activities in Non-Communist Less Developed Countries, 1978* (Washington, D.C.: National Foreign Assessment Center, 1979), pp. 4, 14; and Gonzalez, "Cuban Policy Towards Africa," p. 15.

50. Kenneth Maxwell, "A New Scramble for Africa?" in *The Conduct of Soviet Foreign Policy*, ed. E. Hoffmann and F. Fleron (New York: Aldine, 1980), p. 520.

51. On joint Cuban-Soviet missions, see Dominguez, "Armed Forces," p. 78.

52. *State Department Bulletin* 80, no. 2040 (July 1980): 72-82.

53. *World Affairs Report* 10 (June 1980): 408.

54. *Granma*, January 15, 1978 and *Los Angeles Times*, January 1, 1980.

55. Jorge Dominguez, "Cuban Foreign Policy," *Foreign Affairs* 67 (Fall 1978): 95; and Colin Legum, "The African Environment," *Problems of Communism* 27 (January-February 1978): 10.

56. Ibid., p. 14; see, also, Henry Bienen, "Perspectives on Soviet Intervention in Africa," *Political Science Quarterly* 95 (Spring 1980): 29-42.

57. The FNLA appealed to Bakongo separatist inclinations, stressed purely military means, and received most of its backing from pro-Western Zaire. (The Cubans accused Mobutu of using anti-Castro exiles to train FNLA personnel.) Savimbi's UNITA is based on a variety of Ovimbundu populism and continues to receive aid from South Africa. See John Marcum, *The Angolan Revolution* (Cambridge, Mass.: M.I.T. Press, 1978), pp. 10, 162-67, 240.

58. See Maxwell, "A New Scramble," p. 518.

59. William LeoGrande, "Cuban-Soviet Relations and Cuban Policy in Africa," *Cuban Studies* 10 (January 1980): 14.

60. In Castro's December 27, 1979 speech to the National Assembly it was announced that 36,000 troops had been stationed in Angola and 12,000 in Ethiopia (at the

peak of the fighting in early 1976 and 1978, respectively). Earlier calculations overestimated troop levels in Angola (by as much as 50 percent) and underestimated (by about 25 percent) in Ethiopia. See Gonzalez, "Cuban Policy Toward Africa," pp. 14, 30.

61. Durch, *The Cuban Military*, pp. 48-49.

62. Nelson Valdes, "Revolutionary Solidarity in Angola," in *Cuba in the World*, ed. Blasier and Mesa-Lago, pp. 89, 91; and Jiri Valenta, "Soviet Decision-Making on the Intervention in Angola," in *Communist States in Africa*, ed. Albright and Valenta, pp. 112-15.

63. *Granma*, April 16, 1976.

64. LeoGrande, "Cuban Policy," p. 17. As many as 19,000 Cuban troops were estimated to be in Angola in 1978 and 1979. See C.I.A., *Communist Aid Activities*, p. 4.

65. On Shaba I, see *Washington Post*, March 22, 1977. Castro informed the U.S. envoy in Havana that he had tried unsuccessfully to stop the 1978 invasion; the White House later tempered its accusation, charging that Cuba could have done more to forestall the invasion. *New York Times*, May 26, 1978 and June 5, 1978.

66. Dominguez, "Cuban Foreign Policy," p. 100.

67. C.I.A., *Communist Aid Activities*, p. 14. Following Neto's death in September 1979, President dos Santos, a Soviet-educated petroleum engineer, affirmed support for his predecessor's programs.

68. *Granma*, February 7, 1977. See David Steven, "Realignment in the Horn: The Soviet Advantage," *International Security* 4 (Fall 1979): 69-90.

69. See David Ottaway's treatment in *Washington Post*, May 17, 1977.

70. *Washington Post*, February 2, 1978 and ff. 80.

71. International Institute for Strategic Studies, *Strategic Survey, 1977* (London: International Institute for Strategic Studies, 1978), pp. 16-26; International Institute for Strategic Studies, *Strategic Survey, 1978* (London: International Institute for Strategic Studies, 1979), pp. 94-99.

72. U.S. Congress, House Subcommittee on Inter-American Affairs, Committee on International Relations, *Hearings*, 95th Cong. (Washington, D.C.: U.S. Government Printing Office, March-April 1978), p. 11.

73. Cuba barely avoided official condemnation at the OAU in Khartoum by insisting that they were not involved in the Eritrean fighting. Dominguez, "Cuban Foreign Policy," p. 103. For the Cuban view, which stresses "Cooperation between Eritrean secessionists and Arab reactionaries," see Raul Valdes Vivo, *Ethiopia's Revolution* (New York: International Publishers, 1978). The Soviets refer to "foreign interests and imperialist designs"; see *Pravda*, March 15, 1978.

74. *Verde Olivo* (Havana), September 9, 1979, pp. 54-55.

75. See *World Affairs Report* 10 (September 1980): 455.

76. On Cuba's recent economic and social troubles, see *Granma*, December 28, 1980.

77. A. Borovikov, "Soviet-Cuban Economic Relations," *Foreign Trade* (Moscow) no. 2 (1978): 12.

78. While arms are perhaps also being smuggled to Salvadoran guerrillas from Costa Rica, the State Department report, "Communist Influence in El Salvador," claimed that weapons have come from Nicaragua, Vietnam, and Ethiopia (where leftover stocks of U.S.- and even Israeli-made weapons still remain) and have been supplied by the USSR and Cuba (and some even flown by Aeroflot from Havana to Managua). See *Los Angeles Times*, February 24, 1981 and *New York Times*, May 21, 1981.

79. The author is indebted to Jorge Dominguez for his observations on Cuba's hemispheric diplomatic relations.

80. *State Department Bulletin* 80, no. 2045 (December 1980): 29; and *New York Times*, January 23, 1981.

81. Somali battalions withdrew from the Ogaden in May 1978; guerrillas, however, can limit Cuban and Ethiopian forces to larger towns and main arteries. *Los Angeles Times*, February 10, 1980.

82. Gonzalez, "Cuba, the Soviet Union, and Africa," p. 116. There are unconfirmed reports that perhaps as many as one million people have registered to leave the island. See *Los Angeles Times*, May 7, 1981.

9

THE WEST EUROPEAN COMMUNIST CHALLENGE TO SOVIET FOREIGN POLICY

Joan Barth Urban

Soviet foreign policy has been challenged during the past decade from an unexpected direction: the Communist parties of Italy, France, and Spain. Long ready spokesmen for Soviet interests, by the 1970s the big three (as well as other smaller) European Communist parties had begun—at varying tempos and on diverse issues—to break with their tradition of pro-Soviet loyalism on some of the most sensitive issues of Soviet foreign policy, including the USSR's domination of Eastern Europe, Soviet hostility toward China, and even certain aspects of détente. The independence of the larger Western CPs on international issues developed in tandem with their growing political visibility and influence at home. But while non-Communist analysts closely monitored their surge in domestic clout, they often minimized or discounted the foreign policy disagreements between the West European Communists and the Soviet Union. This uneven perception resulted in part from the preoccupation of many American and European observers with the military dimension of East-West relations, especially with factors affecting the balance of power between NATO and the Warsaw Treaty Organization (WTO). On concrete military issues such as the neutron bomb and the NATO call for increased defense expenditures in the late 1970s, even the European Communist parties most critical of the CPSU tended to be ambivalent or supportive of Soviet positions.

To measure a Communist party's challenge to Soviet foreign policy according to the single criterion of its position on the intricate and controversial subject of the military balance in the European theater may be appropriate for Western policy makers concerned with the Atlantic Alliance's interests. A more balanced assessment of the extent of Western European Communist divergence from Soviet foreign policy can be arrived at, however, by evaluating this question in the light of Soviet interests as perceived from Moscow on a global scale.

This chapter therefore focuses on Western CP differences with the CPSU across the global spectrum of Soviet foreign policy. The point of departure is a classification of Soviet foreign policy goals—to be elaborated below—according to which Soviet objectives with respect to the Atlantic Alliance rank only fourth in priority after the preservation of Eastern Europe as a security and ideological buffer, the containment of China, and the projection of the USSR's influence in the Third World. Viewed from this broader perspective, the Western Communist challenge to Soviet foreign policy appears real indeed. This conclusion is corroborated by Moscow's recent shift to open attacks on the Western parties precisely because of their nonalignment or criticism of the USSR on specific foreign policy issues, a topic that was hitherto not included in public international Communist polemics. But before addressing the substance of these Soviet-European CP differences and their impact on interparty relations, a brief review of the origins and decline of the Western Communist tradition of loyalty to Soviet foreign policy may be useful.

THE WESTERN COMMUNIST TRADITION OF LOYALTY
TO SOVIET FOREIGN POLICY: ITS ORIGIN AND DECLINE

The European Communist parties became notorious for their conformity to the Soviet foreign policy line during the Comintern and cold-war eras. Indeed, by 1937 a party's loyalty to the Soviet Union had become the very "touchstone of proletarian internationalism," as the Soviet and Comintern media repeatedly intoned. From 1935 through mid-1941 the Western parties thus backed any policy that the Soviet leaders thought would protect the USSR from involvement in a war with Germany. The Comintern's popular front strategy, just as the Nazi-Soviet Nonaggression Pact of 1939, was designed to serve this end rather than the sociopolitical transformation of France or Spain, let alone the interests of their Communist parties. Once Germany invaded the USSR, moreover, pro-Soviet loyalism required that the West European CPs help to alleviate pressure on the Russian front through all-out resistance to German occupation forces on the pattern of the Yugoslav partisans[1] —notwithstanding the fact that in Western Europe such guerrilla activity was rendered particularly risky by population density and the absence of suitable geographic conditions. Even after the dissolution of the Comintern in May 1943, the Western CPs continued to function as instruments of Soviet national interests. During the middle 1940s the French and Italian parties were little more than poker chips in Stalin's drive to secure control over Eastern Europe. In early April 1944 they all but simultaneously agreed to accept secondary portfolios in provisional coalition governments, undergoing a 180-degree *volte-face* from their previous policy of intransigent opposition to cooperation on such terms, and thereby helping to signal Stalin's readiness to concede U.S.-British hegemony in the West in return for a free hand in the East.[2] This pattern of compliance with Soviet foreign policy needs continued well into the third postwar decade, with all available evidence pointing to the warm endorsement of such submissiveness by the rank-and-file members of the French and Italian parties.

The West European CPs' traditional conformity to the dictates of Soviet foreign policy is rarely disputed, even by Communist spokesmen. Less often explored are the reasons for this behavior. Far from the reach of Stalin's secret police or—as in the case of their postwar East European comrades—the Red Army, they had the ever-present option of rejecting Soviet *diktat.* Their failure to do so is often attributed to the strength of the ideological ties that bound them to the party of the Great October Revolution. But this explanation appears too facile in the face of the enduring power of nationalism within the international Communist movement. Rather, it would seem that the West European CPs' past alignment with Soviet foreign policy was motivated by considerations not unlike those that caused some of them to begin distancing themselves from the USSR's international orientation in the 1970s: namely, calculations of what was in the best interest of their own parties in terms of political effectiveness and ideological rectitude.

In the 1930s psychological and material dependence on the USSR compounded such considerations. As ineffectual electoral parties or small clandestine groups dependent on Soviet support, they perceived the future of their own cause as unavoidably linked to the fate of the USSR. Precisely because of their domestic weakness, moreover, they had little basis for questioning the wisdom of their Soviet comrades who had battled their way to victory and socialism against far greater odds than those confronted by many Western Communists. But more immediate political and ideological calculations also pointed in the direction of compliance with CPSU directives. Whatever the blemishes of Stalinism, in the eyes of Western Communist militants they paled in comparison to those of Hitler, Mussolini, and Franco, or were at least counterbalanced by the Soviet Union's championing of the anti-Fascist struggle. The Great Depression, furthermore, had seemingly validated not only the Marxist prediction of the inevitable collapse of capitalism but also the Stalinist pronouncements regarding the imminence of that collapse and hence the need for Communists everywhere to rally around the Soviet vanguard of the coming world revolution.

By the second half of the 1940s, however, the French and Italian Communist parties had begun to enjoy the domestic legitimacy and electoral influence that would have enabled them to become independent of Moscow. They had acquired mass memberships numbering in the hundreds of thousands and commanded between one-fifth and one-quarter of the popular vote in national elections. Yet just as that juncture in their organizational development, East-West polarization had the effect of relegating them to the political ghetto. Not only did the United States support centrist and conservative forces in Western Europe; it also used its political and economic leverage to promote the ostracism of the Communists on the Left.

The American animus against the West European CPs during this period is graphically illustrated by the following excerpt from a top secret telegram sent by the then director of the policy planning staff, George F. Kennan, to Secretary of State Marshall on the eve of the April 1948 Italian general elections, in which the Communists and left-wing Socialists *together* won only 31 percent of the total vote. "I question," cabled Kennan, "whether it would not be preferable for Italian Government to outlaw communist party and take strong action against it before elections. Communists would presumably reply with civil war, which would give us grounds for reoccupation Foggia fields or any other facilities we might wish. This would admittedly result in much violence and probably a military division of Italy; but we are getting close to the deadline and I think it might well be preferable to a bloodless election victory, unopposed by ourselves."[3] The point here is not to disparage Kennan but to convey some sense of how cold-war hysteria caused even the "best and the brightest" American statesmen to overreact to the Communist threat in Western Europe. While Kennan's recommendation was rejected, the American government went to great lengths, including the instigation of an Italian-American letter-writing campaign to relatives in Italy and the threat to withhold economic aid from a left-wing government,[4] to fan anti-Communist sentiment. Such U.S. attitudes and conduct had a critical impact on the West European CPs themselves. In a nutshell, they began to equate the advance of their own political fortunes with the reduction of American influence on the Continent.

The West European CPs' anti-Americanism during the cold-war years was thus as much the dictate of domestic political calculation as of allegiance to the Soviet foreign policy line. Opposition to the Marshall Plan, NATO, and all other U.S. initiatives was designed to enhance the Western parties' own political power and not merely the military position of the USSR. As for the latter, in view of the overwhelming American strategic superiority during the first two postwar decades, Western Communists could view the Soviet push for strategic parity with the West as only as advantageous to themselves, as a possible check on "imperialist" maneuvers to impede the growth of West European CP influence. Even in the 1960s the staunchly anti-Communist Charles DeGaulle discounted the threat of Soviet expansionism in Western Europe, therefore withdrawing France from NATO's integrated military command. Why, then, should Communist militants have contemplated such an eventuality during the late 1940s and 1950s when the USSR was so much weaker?

The Western Communist adulation of all things Soviet during the worst excesses of Stalinism in Eastern Europe is more difficult to explain. What can be said is that this period was brief and coincided with the peak of East-West vituperation and Soviet seclusion behind the Iron Curtain. The rank-and-file members of the West European CPs—though surely not their leaders—may have been unaware of the realities of Stalinist rule, dismissing reports of terror and deprivation as sheer anti-Communist propaganda. On the other hand, the post-Stalin increase in East-West contacts and information was accompanied by the domestic reformism of the Khrushchev regime. The dismantling of Gulag, the promise of consumerism, the shift to a more egalitarian wage structure all compared favorably, again if viewed through the rose-tinted glasses of Western Communist militants, to the socioeconomic inequalities that continued to pervade Latin Europe, despite the surge in the economic growth rates and middle-class well-being of France, Italy, and eventually Franco's Spain.

During the late 1960s, however, the West European CPs' assessment of their own best interests began to conflict with Soviet foreign policy objectives. On the one hand, a grass-roots urge for sociopolitical change, dramatized by the May 1968 student-worker upheaval in France and subsequent labor disturbances in Italy, but also reflected in an increase in antiregime activity in Spain, led to a perceptible decline in the political isolation of the West European Communists. After a temporary conservative groundswell in reaction to both the popular ferment in Latin Europe and the Soviet invasion of Czechoslovakia, the greater domestic acceptability of the Western Communists was evidenced by the creation of the French Socialist-Communist *union de la gauche* alliance in 1972, the surge in Italian Communist electoral support in the mid-1970s, and the growing strength of the Communist-dominated, semiclandestine workers' commissions in Spain. The onset of East-West détente contributed to this trend toward Western Communist domestic legitimacy.

On the other hand, there was a parallel decline in the appeals of the Soviet model of socialism, both because of the suppression of the Dubček reform movement and because of the intensification of political repression within the USSR itself. The Western CP media thus became ever more critical of the CPSU. First the Spanish and Italian Communists, and later the French, went beyond denouncing Soviet conduct in Czechoslovakia to criticizing the USSR's methods of dictatorial rule in general. This was the result not simply of electoral tactics but of ideological considerations as well. Many a Western militant had joined the Communist movement out of a commitment to social justice, not personal careerism, as was so often the case in Eastern Europe. Now that the prospect of sociopolitical change had become more likely, there was an urgent need to define the content of that change. To do so in terms of existing Soviet reality would not only be self-defeating at the polls; it would also be unacceptable to those Western Communists whose notions of socialist transformation had been shaped by the reformism of Khrushchev and Dubček.

Above all, the Soviet invasion of Czechoslovakia, combined with the surge in the USSR's overall military strength, led at least some Western Communists to perceive the vulnerability of their own parties and/or countries to Soviet military might. Geopolitical reasons made this especially true for the Italians.

They were all, however, loath to admit that the USSR might represent a threat, probably for fear of alienating those among the older party stalwarts for whom pro-Sovietism was still the measure of ideological probity. When pressed to say which side they would support in the event of an American-Soviet war in Europe, West European CP spokesmen would usually deny the very possibility of such a conflict,[5] all the while affirming their determination to defend their country against *any* external attack. The closest they would come to acknowledging their uncertainty regarding Soviet intentions was to support the principle of East-West parity in the sense of not doing anything that would tilt the military balance in favor of the Soviet Union. The Italian party was rather elliptical on this score, justifying its shift from opposition to acquiescence in Italy's membership in NATO with reference to the argument that a unilateral change in either NATO or the WTO would upset the European balance of power.[6] Spanish Communist leader Santiago Carrillo was more explicit, writing in 1977 that "the role of the Communists in the West is not to strengthen the military bloc of the East."[7]

An exception to this general reserve regarding a potential Soviet threat was Italian Communist leader Enrico Berlinguer's statement in June 1976 that he would feel "more secure" building socialism within the framework of the Atlantic Alliance.[8] Voiced on the eve of the 1976 Italian parliamentary elections, Berlinguer's allusion to a possible Soviet danger to socialism Italian-style was discounted by many Western analysts as an electoral ploy. Only years later was it revealed that this remark had in fact elicited a harsh, albeit secret, rebuttal from the Central Committee of the CPSU.[9] In the summer of 1980, moreover, the Soviets publicly reproached their Italian comrades on this account. In late August of that year, after the Italian Communist party had unequivocally sided with the Polish Solidarity unionists and Communist reformers, *Pravda* chided its Italian Communist "friends" for suggesting "the possibility of Soviet aggression against Italy."[10] Whatever the perceptions among Western observers, the Soviet leaders themselves had evidently begun to doubt the loyalty of the Italian Communist party.

In short, by the 1970s some of the major European Communist parties had arrived at a more circumspect assessment of their respective party interests in relation to the United States and the Soviet Union. While they still considered the United States as a bulwark of state monopoly capitalism and a prime socio-political opponent, they no longer saw their countries' American connection as an insurmountable obstacle to Socialist transformation. More to the point, they no longer viewed Soviet foreign policy positions as necessarily compatible with their own political objectives and values. They were thus primed for a more differentiated analysis of specific Soviet initiatives both in Europe and world-wide.

THE WEST EUROPEAN COMMUNIST CHALLENGE
IN GLOBAL PERSPECTIVE

The West European CPs differed from one another in both the nature and timing of their challenge to Soviet foreign policy. Indeed, just about the only feature all three major parties shared was the decision to break with the tradition of pro-Soviet loyalism. Otherwise, their divergence from the Soviet line reflected the variations in their respective political profiles and national settings. These variations will be briefly noted by way of introduction to a discussion of the Western parties' specific foreign policy disagreements with Moscow.

The Italian Communist party (PCI) and the Spanish Communist party (PCE) had both, by the end of the 1960s, become identified with an innovative and pluralist approach to questions of revolutionary strategy and Socialist construction. Yet the PCI had enjoyed legal status since 1945, while the PCE was a clandestine sect with its leadership in exile from 1939 until 1977; the PCI increased its share of the Italian national vote from under 20 percent in 1946 to over 30 percent in the 1970s, while the PCE was able to muster only 10 percent of the Spanish popular vote after its legalization in the post-Franco era; the PCI had to contend with a population that was largely pro-American and pro-NATO, while Spanish public opinion was rather evenly divided over whether or not Spain should join the Atlantic Alliance. On the other hand, in contrast to both the PCI and PCE, the French Communist party (PCF) was renowned for its doctrinal orthodoxy and organizational rigidity, right up through the 1970s. Its sectarian tendencies were, however, mitigated by the fact that it operated in a domestic environment not unlike that of Italy—except for the pervasive influence of French nationalism; and it was obliged by the electoral procedures of the Fifth French Republic to make concessions to the Socialists if it hoped to further its political ambitions.

The significance of the international issues upon which the Western Communists challenged Moscow also varied in the eyes of the Soviet leadership. For analytical purposes, Soviet foreign policy objectives during the past decade or so have been classified on a scale of one to five. Most important from the Soviet viewpoint was the retention of political and military dominance in Eastern Europe, as evidenced by the USSR's behavior in this area since the closing phases of World War II. The containment of China ranked second in importance after control over Eastern Europe. Since 1960 or earlier, the Soviet leaders have feared the expansion of Chinese Communist influence, first mainly within the international Communist movement but more recently within the world arena at large. One could argue that Soviet penetration of the Third World and détente with the West at times took precedence over policy toward the PRC and were even partly responsible for the initial deterioration in Sino-Soviet relations. Still, by the 1970s the specter of China's eventual emergence as a superpower, combined with Peking's anti-Soviet intransigence, compelled Moscow to assign greater priority to the Chinese question.

In recent years the promotion of Soviet interests in the Third World thus ranked third in importance, after the containment of China. The specific weight of economic, strategic, and ideological considerations varied over time, but the basic goal of seeking Soviet advantages and influence in that region at the expense of China and/or the West remained unchanged. Détente with the Western powers accordingly occupied fourth place in the scale of Soviet foreign policy priorities. For many years Soviet relations with the West and the Third World seemed to develop on parallel courses, with mutual trade-offs as warranted by circumstances (the Cuban missile crisis, the Vietnamese war, developments in the Middle East). By the second half of the 1970s, however, Soviet conduct in black Africa, Afghanistan, and elsewhere left little doubt regarding the primacy of the USSR's Third World goals over East-West détente. Fifth and last in importance was the maintenance of CPSU ideological hegemony over the world Communist movement. Moscow had always ascribed higher priority to its state interests than to international Communist harmony, as attested by the history of Sino-Soviet relations. The CPSU's altercations with the West European Communist parties in the 1970s conformed to this pattern.

Soviet Dominance in Eastern Europe

The Soviet invasion of Czechoslovakia in August 1968 represented a watershed in the attitudes of the West European CPs toward Soviet policy. Thenceforth they denounced with increasing specificity both Soviet-style methods of rule and the USSR's use of military power to enforce such rule within Eastern Europe. During the summer of 1968 the Italian, French, and Spanish Communist leaders brought behind-the-scenes pressure to bear upon the Soviets in an effort to prevent the military suppression of the Dubček reform movement.[11] When invasion nonetheless occurred, they were unanimous in their condemnation of the Soviet move. The PCI and PCE subsequently denounced the repressive character of the post-1968 Czechoslovak regime of Gustav Husak. Gradually, moreover, they broadened the target of their criticism to include violations of civil liberties and the absence of democratic norms throughout the Soviet bloc. The PCF was more cautious than the PCI and the PCE in its disapproval of the "normalization" process in Prague and the areawide repression of antiregime dissidents in the mid-1970s, defending its reserve on the grounds that these were internal party matters.[12] The PCI, on the other hand, was more active in encouraging East European Communist moderates than was the PCE, then involved in a campaign for legalization and electoral support. The Italian party, in contrast to the freeze in its relations with the sectarian Czechoslovak leaders, maintained warm and frequent contacts with the relatively liberal Hungarian party hierarchy. With regard to Poland, moreover, the PCI refrained from direct criticism of the internally divided Polish regime after Warsaw's summer 1976 crackdown on striking workers, choosing instead to express public support for leniency and reform, coupled with private backing for Polish Communist moderates in semiannual bilateral consultations with the Polish leadership.[13]

The PCI's reaction to the Polish crisis of 1980–81 illustrates the depth of the chasm that had developed between some Western Communist perceptions and Soviet foreign policy interests in this region. While the PCE also voiced unqualified support for the Polish Communist reformers, its leadership was engaged in a power struggle against a hard-line orthodox faction within its own ranks and was thus unable to devote as much attention to the epochal developments unfolding in Poland.

PCI support for the Polish reform movement in 1980 was much more assertive than its stand in behalf of the Dubček group in 1968. The Italian Communists not only accentuated the negative aspects of the political structures under attack; they also threatened a rupture with the CPSU, should the Soviets resort to military intervention, eschewing the "quiet diplomacy" that had proven so ineffective in deterring the invasion of Czechoslovakia 12 years earlier. On August 19, 1980, shortly after the eruption of massive strikes in the Baltic coast shipyards, the editor of the PCI daily, *l'Unità*, blamed the Polish crisis on the "pyramidal and totalitarian" (*totalizzante*) political organization of Soviet-style socialism (*socialismo reale*) and called for the development of "democracy and participation" forthwith.[14] Thereafter the PCI press as well as official party statements consistently hailed both the victories of the independent trade-union movement and the ascendancy of reformers within the Polish Communist hierarchy. In this latter regard, *l'Unità* commentators now expressed an unabashed preference for those elements in the Polish party establishment who had during the late 1970s unsuccessfully urged (with tacit PCI backing) political innovation as the solution to the growing economic crisis.[15] Above all, the thrust of the PCI position was that the realization of broad participatory reforms—far from abetting anti Socialist forces, as the CPSU so insistently argued—was the only sure way of defeating the opponents of socialism.[16]

As fears of a Soviet invasion of Poland intensified in the fall of 1980, the Italian party made known its unqualified opposition to such a step during top-level PCI-CPSU talks in Rome on December 9 and 10. The precise contents of what was described by both sides as a "long and frank discussion" were not disclosed.[17] The substance of the Italian position can, however, be inferred from a communique issued by the PCI *Direzione* on the first day of the talks, which warned that "military intervention" in Poland would have "the gravest consequences" and confirmed that this view had been formally communicated in no uncertain terms to the Socialist countries involved.[18] The PCI's message to the CPSU, according to non-Communist sources, threatened a de facto break in relations between the two parties in the event of a Soviet invasion,[19] a report that the PCI neither affirmed nor denied. What the Italians did say publicly in a front-page *l'Unità* editorial of December 10—while the Italian-Soviet talks were still in progress—was that the very idea of intervention "already represents an unacceptable limitation of sovereignty."[20] An actual invasion, "inconceivable as a matter of principle," would be "disastrous" not only for Poland but also for "the very idea of socialism" and the fate of the European Left.[21]

Implicit in this editorial position was the PCI's denial of the USSR's right to intervene militarily under any circumstances, even if anti-Socialist forces should prevail in Poland, as well as the Italian party's concern for its own political interests, should armed intervention nevertheless occur.

Soviet Containment of China

During the 1960s Moscow tried to combat the influence of the Chinese Communist party (CCP) within the world Communist movement by giving an air of legitimacy to the rupture in CPSU-CCP relations that had occurred by mid-1963. To this end the Soviets proposed an international Communist conference whose purpose would be the collective denunciation of the Maoist leadership. It was largely due to the opposition of the Italian Communist party that this maneuver foundered by the late 1960s.[22] While the PCI championed the USSR's positions on peaceful coexistence and the possibility of a nonviolent transition to socialism, it categorically rejected the CPSU's method of handling the controversy with the Chinese. The Italian party advocated reasoned debate and tolerance of dissent in place of the ideological polemics favored by both the CPSU and the CCP, arguing that the "language of anathema"[23] would only deepen the rift.

The Spanish Communist party joined the PCI in diverging from the Soviet position on China at the beginning of the 1970s, by which time the Sino-Soviet conflict had escalated from interparty recriminations to a great-power confrontation. Both the PCI and the PCE, as a result of their unrelenting condemnation of the Soviet invasion of Czechoslovakia, had become the targets of Moscow's verbal abuse. Indeed, the CPSU tacitly encouraged factional opposition to the Carrillo leadership among the ranks of the Spanish party.[24] Hence the two Western parties, in a quest for allies and leverage vis-à-vis Moscow, sought to normalize their relations with Beijing. Their first probes in the direction of a rapprochement with the CCP came during a visit by Carrillo to China in October-November 1971. At that time, however, the Maoists accorded only a low-level welcome to Carrillo; and they turned a deaf ear to the feelers that Carrillo extended to the CCP on behalf of the PCI.[25] It was not until Deng Xiaoping's group of pro-Western moderates took over the reins of power after Mao's death that the PCI and PCE were able to proceed with the reestablishment of party ties with Beijing.

Accordingly, during the summer of 1978 the PCI resumed in earnest its overtures to the new CCP leadership, giving favorable press coverage to developments in China and publicly reaffirming its interest in normalization.[26] The

Italians evidently calculated that Beijing's 1977–78 rapprochement with the Communists of Yugoslavia—branded by Mao as archrevisionists since 1958—had enhanced the likelihood of their receiving a positive response from the CCP. And the Chinese did in fact signal a certain receptivity to these moves. Yet in mid-October 1978 Berlinguer abruptly announced, after a summit meeting with Brezhnev and other CPSU leaders, that his party was "for now" not contemplating a resumption of ties with the CCP. In retrospect it seems clear that the Soviets had invited the PCI leaders to Moscow in reaction to the talk of a PCI-CCP rapprochement, and there they were able to exert sufficient pressure upon the Italians to delay further steps toward normalization, possibly in exchange for a Soviet promise to curb its polemics against the Italian party.[27] Whatever the case, the USSR's invasion of Afghanistan put an end to this tenuous agreement.

In April 1980 Berlinguer thus launched the "full resumption" of party ties between the PCI and the CCP with a nine-day trip to China.[28] During the course of his visit, moreover, he noted the Chinese Communists' Socialist achievements and concern with the preservation of world peace, both of which were attributes denied by Moscow with respect to the Beijing leaders. True, Berlinguer also took public issue with their call for a global "united front" against Soviet aggressiveness and hegemonic ambitions.[29] But this did not alter the fact that he in actuality contradicted the premises of the CPSU's anti-Chinese polemics. The following November the Spanish Communists followed in the PCI's footsteps, with Carrillo inaugurating the "normalization" of PCE-CCP relations during a two-week trip to the People's Republic.[30] The two Western parties thus moved from disagreement with the CPSU's mode of handling its dispute with the CCP to open defiance of the USSR's state policy of containing China's power and influence.

The Projection of Soviet Influence in the Third World

The West European CPs have always welcomed the extension of Soviet economic and ideological ties to the Third World at the expense of "imperialist hegemony" in this region. Indeed, at the very time when the PCI was intensifying its overtures to China in 1978, leading Italian spokesmen were also underscoring their party's enduring affinity with the CPSU, precisely because of the Soviet contribution to Third World liberationism.[31] About that same time, however, the Italian and Spanish parties began to reproach Moscow for its reliance on military power to advance the cause of revolution, first in the Horn of Africa and Cambodia, later in Afghanistan.

In the spring of 1978 the PCI qualified its initially favorable view of revolutionary developments in Ethiopia because of the concerted efforts of the new Addis Ababa regime, now armed with Soviet weapons, to suppress the Eritrean national liberation movement. As tensions escalated in the Ethiopian borderlands in late 1977, PCI Secretariat member Gian Carlo Pajetta had visited both

Addis Ababa and Mogadishu with the apparent aim of urging Ethiopian restraint toward Eritrea and Somali restraint in the Ogaden.[32] When such efforts proved futile, *l'Unità* shifted from implicit support for the official Ethiopian position[33] to rather evenhanded coverage of the Ethiopian-Somali border war, quoting Somali sources regarding "a Russian-Cuban conspiracy against Somalia" alongside Soviet allegations of massive "imperialist" arms shipments to Mogadishu. At the same time, the PCI daily displayed open sympathy for the Eritrean cause, quoting AFP dispatches that described lightly armed Eritrean youth bravely taking on heavy artillery and Soviet MIGs.[34] During the first few months of 1978 the PCI's political weekly *Rinascita* published an extraordinary series of letters to the editor detailing the historical and juridical legitimacy of the Eritrean cause and contesting Pajetta's positive evaluation of the Dergue and of the Soviet-Cuban military intervention in its behalf[35] —unmistakable evidence of an internal PCI controversy over the issue. Then, in mid-May *l'Unità* carried a front-page commentary that flatly declared that the two-decades-long Eritrean liberation struggle was just and that the new Ethiopian regime should prove that it was really new by recognizing the right of the Eritreans to self-government, a cause to which the Socialist countries should also commit themselves by virtue of their presence in Ethiopia.[36]

By implication, therefore, the PCI reprimanded the Soviets for their complicity in the Ethiopian campaign against the Eritrean rebels, a disagreement that was to deepen the following December when Soviet and Cuban military assistance enabled Addis Ababa to regain decisive control over the disputed territory.[37] Meanwhile, in early June 1978, a second front-page *l'Unità* piece assumed a critical posture toward overall Soviet military involvement in Africa. While justifying the initial Cuban move into Angola as a response to South African intervention, the commentator expressed alarm over the extension of the "Cuban presence" to a "Soviet military presence of notable proportions," over the re-emergence in the African context of "what seems to us a temptation . . . to make the expansion of the liberation process coincide with the stipulation of political-military alliances and the *conquest of zones of influence*."[38] This decisive broadening of the scope of the PCI's challenge to Soviet foreign policy was echoed in a report by Pajetta himself to the PCI Central Committee in November 1979. On the one hand, Pajetta regretted the post-Helsinki absence of Soviet "political-diplomatic" initiatives on "the great themes of underdevelopment and of a new *world order*." On the other hand, in what was clearly an exercise in self-criticism as well as criticism, he deplored the idea that "support for forces engaged in revolutionary transformations could be entrusted to military aid more than to solidarity linked to the political prestige or economic aid of the socialist camp."[39]

The condemnation, by both the Spanish and the Italian CPs, of the Soviet occupation of Afghanistan is familiar to readers of the Western press. Less understood are the precedents arising from conflicts in Southeast Asia in the winter of

1979. The PCE criticized the Soviet-backed Vietnamese invasion of Cambodia from the outset,[40] whereas the PCI initially refrained from passing judgment on the Vietnamese role in the defeat of the Khmer Rouge and displayed barely concealed satisfaction at the overthrow of the Pol Pot regime.[41] After China's retaliatory attack against Vietnam, however, the Italian party joined the PCE in denouncing both the Vietnamese invasion of Cambodia and the Chinese incursion into Vietnam as unacceptable violations of the principles of national sovereignty and independence.[42] Evidently Beijing's justification of its border war with Vietnam as a punitive action against Hanoi for its move against Cambodia brought home to the Italian Communist policy makers the dangers involved in countenancing any aggression whatsoever for partisan reasons. The stage was thus set for the PCI's denunciation of the Soviet invasion of Afghanistan in a *Direzione* statement of January 4, 1980.[43] As Berlinguer subsequently commented with regard to the Afghan crisis, it was incumbent upon Socialist states to respect the principles of independence and sovereignty—whatever past practice may have been—not merely because "the construction of a socialist society cannot be transplanted from the outside, cannot retrace the models of others," but also because any act of force under contemporary conditions of global interdependence could lead to a chain reaction threatening world peace.[44]

On the threshold of the 1980s, therefore, the most influential Communist party in Western Europe had begun publicly to oppose Moscow's use of its growing military might to promote either the geostrategic reach of the USSR or the cause of revolution in the Third World.

East-West Détente, Soviet Style

Beginning in the 1960s the Soviet Union sought to relax political tensions with the Western powers in the hope of securing beneficial trade arrangements on the one hand, and strategic advantage on the other, by weakening the cohesion of NATO and the European Economic Community. In pursuing détente the CPSU also acquiesced in the West European sociopolitical status quo—although never admitting as much for fear of endangering its ideological credentials. The West European CPs hailed the relaxation of East-West tensions from the outset, believing that it would help to curb domestic anticommunism. Gradually, however, the Italian, Spanish, and French parties all diverged from or openly criticized Moscow on one or another aspect of its détente policy. The PCI and the PCE wished to strengthen rather than obstruct European economic unity. The PCI supported East-West military parity rather than Soviet preeminence in Europe and, by the late 1970s, carried this position to its logical conclusion of attributing equal responsibility to Moscow and Washington for the resurgence of international tensions at the close of the decade. Above all, the French and Spanish parties charged that Soviet *raison d'état* led the CPSU actually to favor, not simply tolerate, the social status quo in the West.

The PCE was the more outspoken on this last score. The Soviet leaders favored the West European status quo, Carrillo argued, because they feared the contagious influence of a West European model of socialism on Eastern Europe[45] and because they calculated that "the existence of a Europe-NATO, controlled by the United States, justifies a second Europe on the other side controlled by the Soviet Union."[46] The French Communists were more restrained than Carrillo, ascribing the USSR's status-quo orientation to its preoccupation with developing normal interstate relations with the West rather than to concern with shoring up its hold over East Europe. But the PCF's posture was probably more galling to the CPSU, precisely because the French party had hitherto evinced greater pro-Sovietism than the PCE and PCI on such issues as the containment of China[47] and the ideological rectitude of Soviet-style socialism.

Beginning in May 1974, the PCF publicly chided the Soviet Union for its show of support for Valéry Giscard d'Estaing in his closely contested presidential race with François Mitterrand. In the autumn of 1975 it intensified its criticism of Moscow for cultivating harmonious relations with the conservative incumbent of the Elysée at a time when conditions in France were propitious for radical change. On October 13, the very day President Giscard arrived in Moscow on a state visit, the PCF daily *L'Humanité* reaffirmed the party's intention to pursue its "revolutionary struggle in France ... against the Giscardian power of the monopolies," Franco-Soviet détente notwithstanding.[48] To top it off, during the preparatory sessions for the 1976 pan-European Communist conference in East Berlin, the PCF submitted a working paper that accused the CPSU of failing to exploit to the full the "general crisis of capitalism" out of "diplomatic" considerations, arguing that "proletarian internationalism" obliged Communist parties to aid one another in their national struggles for Socialist transformation.[49] In a sense the PCF, itself increasingly challenged in the domestic electoral arena by the Mitterrand Socialists, had hit upon a shrewd way to flaunt its independence of the CPSU without compromising its otherwise quite doctrinaire views on domestic and international issues.

The Soviet hope that détente would sap the unity of Western Europe and the Atlantic Alliance was shared only partially by the PCE, still less by the PCI. Both parties advocated an economically and politically strong and interdependent Western Europe, one that could stand up, as it were, to both superpowers. The PCI had become a staunch supporter of the Common Market in the early 1960s, also approving in due course direct elections and enlarged powers for the European parliament; and the PCE favored Spain's entry into the European Community.[50] The Spanish Communists continued throughout the 1970s, however, to oppose NATO, suggesting that it be replaced by a "European defensive organization" (without explaining how such an entity might deter the threat of possible Soviet intimidation).[51] In contrast, the PCI had by 1974 accepted, for the reasons noted earlier in this chapter, Italy's membership in the

Atlantic Alliance–relegating to the indefinite future its earlier call for the dissolution of both NATO and the WTO.

To be sure, the Italian Communists' position on some of the hard military-political questions relating to Italy's membership in NATO remained selectively ambiguous.[52] The PCI insisted, for example, that the territorial scope of the alliance be restricted to Europe, thereby precluding NATO involvement in any Middle Eastern or Persian Gulf hostilities. Likewise, it criticized the commitment of the NATO countries, including Italy, to increase annual defense expenditures by 3 percent in real terms. Moreover, when the issue of the neutron bomb arose in 1977, the PCI, rather than discussing its possible technological value in promoting qualitative parity in European-theater weapons, opposed it on the purely political grounds that its deployment might fuel the arms race and thus disrupt détente. In a sense there were parallels between the PCI's approach to NATO and Romania's approach to the WTO. Just as the Italian party called for the strict delimitation of NATO's purview, so Romania balked at the Soviet proposal in November 1978 to broaden the Warsaw Pact's mutual defense provisions to include a possible Soviet-Chinese conflict. Pursuing this line of reasoning, just as the Romanians limited WTO maneuvers on their territory beginning in the late 1960s, the PCI as a partner in a governing coalition might seek to circumscribe NATO base rights in Italy. Still, during the 1970s the two parties were moving in opposite directions; that is, Romania was distancing itself from the WTO, while the PCI was coming around to acceptance of NATO.

There were in fact indications in the late 1970s that the reasons responsible for the Italian party's initial shift to tolerance of NATO–balance-of-power as well as electoral considerations–were inclining it to further accommodations in this regard. The PCI thus voted for the standardization of weapons models within NATO. It also favored maintaining Italian force levels along the northeastern frontier with Yugoslavia–pending a decision to the contrary in the East-West MBFR (Mutually Balanced Force Reduction) talks–despite the definitive resolution of the Italian-Yugoslav border dispute in 1977, an indication of its concern over the impact of a potential Soviet-Yugoslav confrontation on Italy's military requirements in that area.[53] Above all, the PCI's position on theater nuclear forces (TNF) was not incompatible with the principle of East-West military parity in Europe.

The Italian party's approach to the TNF controversy was evenhanded in the sense that it called from the outset for East-West negotiations to determine the true state of the military-strategic balance in Europe rather than itself taking a stand on whether or not the Soviet replacement of older weapons with the mobile and MIRVed SS-20 intermediate-range missiles had titled that balance in the USSR's favor. To be sure, the PCI opposed the NATO plan to deploy U.S. Cruise and Pershing II medium-range missiles on the Continent and voted against Italy's support for it. But it also declined to accept at face value Brezhnev's October 1979 assertions to the effect that the USSR had in no way altered the

Eurostrategic balance. Instead the PCI formally proposed, in a *Direzione* resolution of October 16, 1979, that a NATO-WTO conference "ascertain the real state of nuclear armaments in Europe," correcting by means of arms reductions any imbalances that might come to light.[54]

In December 1979 the NATO members decided to proceed with preparations for the installation of the U.S. missiles in late 1983, while Moscow rejected the West's parallel bid for Eurostrategic arms talks and accelerated its buildup of the SS-20s. At that point the PCI persisted in its call for "negotiations between the two blocs . . . on medium-range missiles in Europe";[55] and after some vacillation it came around to the view that a moratorium on Euromissile production, as opposed to deployment, should not be a precondition for such talks—a position backed by Western officials but long rejected by the Soviet Union.[56] In April 1980 the Italian party underscored its divergence from the CPSU on this issue by boycotting, along with the Romanian, Yugoslav, and Spanish Communists, a Soviet-inspired pan-European Communist conference convened for the sole purpose of condemning the NATO TNF decision, to the exclusion of any discussion of the "military equilibrium" in general, let alone the developments in Afghanistan.[57]

Gian Carlo Pajetta boasted in his mid-November 1979 report to the PCI Central Committee that the Italian party was free of "any prejudice toward this or that great power" in taking the position it did on the TNF issue the previous October. This remark, however self-serving, was indicative of a growing tendency among the Italian Communists to treat the Soviet-American relationship as a great-power confrontation in which ideological considerations had become secondary. All the same, the PCI was still not ready to lay equal blame on Moscow and Washington for the deterioration of détente. For instance, in the same report cited above, Pajetta explained the worsening of Soviet-American relations in a manner reminiscent of revisionist interpretations of the origins of the cold war: to wit, he suggested that influential U.S. circles were seeking a confrontation with the Soviet Union in order "to impose 'American' solutions to the commercial and monetary contentiousness" and political disagreements that had arisen between Europe and the United States; this, in turn, had revived symptoms of the old Soviet "encirclement complex," leading Moscow to fortify its own "political-military and economic bloc" and to deal with Third World liberation movements "in terms of bloc or power politics."[58]

In the wake of the Soviet invasion of Afghanistan, however, PCI analyses became notably less encumbered by such ideologically conditioned arguments. Thus in January 1980 party spokesmen and documents denounced the USSR for its "act of aggression"[59] against Afghanistan and the United States for its provocative hard-line posture toward the USSR (the TNF decision and the shelving of SALT II), inveighing against the "logic of confrontation" between the two superpowers that was threatening the world with nuclear disaster.[60] Similarly, when Berlinguer was asked upon his return from China who most threatened world peace, he replied: "The greatest danger . . . arises from a growing confrontation [*contrapposizione*] between the two supreme powers."[61] If this assessment had the effect of mitigating the censure of the USSR with regard to Afghanistan, it also precluded undue emphasis on American responsibility for the worsening of international tensions. Most importantly, it permitted the PCI to take a more evenhanded approach to the transgressions of the two superpowers, while maintaining its ideological preference for the Socialist world.

THE SOVIET REACTION:
FROM DEFENSIVENESS TO CONFRONTATION

For decades CPSU policy makers had had no reason to doubt the West European CPs' readiness to back Soviet foreign policy aims, and they were clearly reluctant to concede publicly that this might no longer be the case. Hence, even as discord mounted within the pan-European Communist movement during the 1970s, the Soviets attempted to maintain a facade of unity on international issues. Accordingly, during the first half of the decade Moscow responded to the almost universal West European CP disapproval of the invasion of Czechoslovakia by championing ideological probity within the world Communist movement, while sidestepping specific differences on foreign policy. This approach was facilitated by the still limited nature of the Western CP foreign policy divergences from Moscow. Indeed, an initiative such as the PCI's switch to support for NATO, dismissed by many non-Communist observers as an electoral ploy, may have been initially viewed from Moscow as a defensible tactic or, at the very least, as harmless in terms of practical effect. In any event, the Soviet ideologues concentrated their attention on propounding the need for every Communist party to abide by the CPSU's formulations on "proletarian internationalism" and the "general laws" for building socialism, all the while engaging in veiled polemics against the PCI-PCE insistence on a pluralist model of socialism and the primacy of national CP interests over international Communist obligations.[62]

Still, the Soviet leaders were obviously on the defensive over the French and Spanish Communist allegations, made ever more openly in the mid-1970s, that Moscow would sacrifice the chance for Socialist transformation in Western Europe in order to promote détente. These charges threatened the CPSU's ideological credentials, both at home and abroad, by undermining its claim to represent the vanguard of world revolution. They coincided, moreover, with discernible pressure from within the CPSU hierarchy itself for greater militancy, just as revolutionary situations were developing in Portugal and its African dependencies. Thus, after lambasting the PCE leaders in early 1974 for presuming to question its commitment to social change, the Brezhnev leadership felt compelled to come to terms with this latest Communist challenge. On the one hand, it made numerous concessions to its West European (and Yugoslav) Communist critics during the 20-month-long preparations for the June 1976 pan-European Communist conference in East Berlin, including agreement on the very idea of preparing for such a conference in tandem with the Helsinki talks.[63] On the other hand, the USSR embarked upon a large-scale transfer to Angola of Cuban troops and Soviet military equipment to shore up its embattled client, the Popular Movement for the Liberation of Angola (MPLA), in that country's rapidly escalating civil war.

This dramatic Soviet initiative was the culmination of a gradual buildup in military aid to the MPLA as well as the result of many considerations,[64] not the least of which was the earlier setback to Communist fortunes in Chile and in Portugal itself. All the same, it seems entirely possible that Moscow's delivery of massive military assistance to Angola in October-November 1975 was prompted to some extent by the French Communist party's unparallelled public airing in mid-October of its doubts concerning the CPSU's commitment to revolutionary change. (Likewise, the USSR's shift to a more activist posture may help to explain the PCF's later return to the pro-Soviet fold on foreign policy issues, underscored by its flamboyant endorsement of the invasion of Afghanistan.)[65]

The CPSU nevertheless continued during the mid-1970s to avoid, where possible, a public confrontation over foreign policy issues, probably in part because it was reluctant to disclose to its own citizens the West European CPs' mounting criticisms in this regard. The Soviets apparently still felt that it was important for reasons of domestic legitimacy to project the public image of a West European Communist constituency firmly united behind the Soviet Union. There was, in addition, the possibility that one or more of the major Western CPs might assume some form of governmental responsibility, an eventuality that the Soviet policy makers did not want to be charged with obstructing. True, the CPSU did attack Carrillo in June 1977 for his advocacy of a united Western Europe independent of the USSR and the United States, arguing—unconvincingly—that this would be tantamount to strengthening NATO. Moscow waited, however, until after the Spanish parliamentary elections had revealed the PCE's electoral weakness to level this and other charges. And even then, it voiced them in a newsweekly destined for foreign rather than domestic distribution. Meanwhile, the Soviet leaders went to great lengths to maintain the appearance of harmony with the powerful Italian Communist party.[66]

Only in the winter of 1980-81 did the CPSU shift to the offensive against the PCI on account of its foreign policy stand. A harbinger of the criticism to come was the *Pravda* complaint in late August 1980, cited earlier in this chapter, that Italian Communists had suggested "the possibility of Soviet aggression against Italy." Then, in January 1981, the authoritative Soviet journal, *Problems of the History of the CPSU*, flatly declared on the occasion of the Italian party's sixtieth anniversary that the PCI's foreign policy positions "raised doubt regarding its traditional proletarian internationalist orientation." After deploring the

Italian Communists' "contradictory search for an 'intermediate' place for the PCI in a world divided into blocs," author G. P. Smirnov–a close associate of CPSU Secretariat member Boris Ponomarev–went on to say that the statements of "certain Italian comrades" with regard to NATO revealed an urge "to take an 'intermediate' position, to avoid a clear characterization of this aggressive organization."[67] A more visible signal of the CPSU's displeasure was its refusal to permit Pajetta, head of the PCI delegation to the 26th CPSU Congress in February 1981 (Berlinguer declined to attend), to present his party's customary greetings from the podium of the congress unless he agreed to delete some rather indirect and circumspect allusions to the Soviet intervention in Afghanistan and intimidation of Poland. As Pajetta refused to do so, he was obliged to present his remarks to an audience of 500 or so persons several blocks from the Kremlin, without national television exposure.[68] This incident came on the heels of the mysterious leak to an Italian newsweekly of a highly confidential CPSU Central Committee letter to the PCI. The letter, in whose drafting Smirnov reportedly participated, accused the Italian party of objectively taking the side of "those forces which have in Poland unleashed a veritable offensive against socialism."[69]

The CPSU oligarchs had thrown down the gauntlet, for reasons that remain unclear. Perhaps the emergence of a new ideological constituency among the Third World radical liberation movements had in their eyes lessened the urgency of cultivating pan-European Communist solidarity. Then again, the Soviets' earlier campaign against the Spanish Communist leaders was working to their advantage. Indeed, at a congress of the influential Catalonian affiliate of the PCE at the beginning of 1981, anti-Carrillo forces–among them a number of outright pro-Soviets–had won a majority on the key issue of removing the term "Eurocommunism" from the party program.[70] The possibility of a similar showdown at the next national PCE congress was not to be dismissed. Under these circumstances the CPSU policy makers may have reasoned that a similar polemical assault on the PCI might rally traditionalist members of its working-class base and intermediate cadres against the reformist strategy and international initiatives so objectionable to Moscow. In the ensuing policy struggle, the party might be weakened and hence eliminated as a contender for national power. But its challenge to Soviet foreign policy would likewise be tempered.

It may even be that the Polish crisis of 1980-81 had led the Soviet leaders to conclude that the best way to secure unchallenged control over Eastern Europe was to promote far more aggressively than hitherto the neutralization of Western Europe–that is, to encourage a situation in which the Western governments not only loosened their ties to the United States but also agreed, much on the pattern of little Finland, to refrain from publicly criticizing or otherwise undermining the USSR's *modus operandi* in Eastern Europe. If so, one promising means of achieving that goal might lie in a policy of grudging tolerance of the Polish reformers conbined with a sharpened confrontation with their troublesome Western comrades; for, whereas restraint toward Poland would assuage

Western fears of Soviet military might, criticism of the local CPs would engender confidence among establishment leaders in the West regarding Moscow's disinclination to alter the sociopolitical status quo.

Whatever the reasons for the CPSU's decision to take the offensive against the PCI over foreign policy disagreements, it marked a turning point in Soviet relations with the West European Communist parties. Barring a decisive turn toward moderation in the USSR's foreign policy during the post-Brezhnev succession, there was as of mid-1981 every reason to anticipate the further intensification of discord within the pan-European Communist movement. For one thing, contrary to the widespread assumption among non-Communist analysts that a worsening of Soviet-American relations would rally the West European CPs behind the CPSU, the PCI had instead been galvanized into more searching criticism of Soviet foreign policy. For another, the PCF's urge to share in the spoils of Mitterrand's presidential victory of May 1981 had obliged it to back off from support for Moscow on the key issues of Afghanistan, Poland, and the emplacement of U.S. missiles in Europe. Finally, both the Mitterrand victory and the PCI's continuing attachment to Eurocommunism would probably help to shore up the Carrillo wing of the PCE. In short, the cleavages that had opened up between the CPSU and the major West European Communist parties after the Soviet invasion of Czechoslovakia seemed likely to become chasms during the 1980s.

NOTES

1. "Bor'ba narodov Evropy protiv okhupantov," *Kommunisticheskii Internatsional* nos. 10-11 (1942): 70; cf. B. Voinich, "Boevoi primer Iugoslavii," *Kommunisticheskii Internatsional* nos. 2-3 (1942): 30.

2. Togliatti announced the PCI's decision at a press conference on April 1, 1944; *Times* (London), April 3, 1944, p. 4. The PCF shift took place during the first week of April 1944; Alfred J. Rieber, *Stalin and the French Communist Party, 1941-1947* (New York: Columbia University Press, 1962), pp. 55-59.

3. *Foreign Relations of the United States 1948*, vol. 3, "Western Europe" (Washington, D.C.: U.S. Government Printing Office, 1974), pp. 848-49.

4. Ibid., pp. 816-90.

5. Ciro Elliott Zoppo, "The Left and European Security: France, Italy, and Spain," *Orbis* 24, no. 2 (Summer 1980): 296.

6. Joan Barth Urban, "Moscow and the PCI in the 1970s: Kto Kovo?", *Studies in Comparative Communism* 13, nos. 2-3 (Summer/Autumn 1980): 116.

7. Santiago Carrillo, *"Eurocommunism" and the State* (London: Lawrence and Wishart, 1977), p. 169.

8. Urban, "Moscow and the PCI," pp. 116-17.

9. Carlo Rossella, "Non prendiamolo alla lettera," *Panorama* (Milan), March 2, 1981, p. 39. The same issue of *Panorama* published the "leaked" text of a 1981 CPSU letter to the PCI, the accuracy of which was not contested by either party.

10. Editorial article, "Trevozhnye dni italii," *Pravda*, August 29, 1980, p. 4.

11. Jiri Valenta, *Soviet Intervention in Czechoslovakia, 1968* (Baltimore, Md.: Johns Hopkins University Press, 1979), pp. 67–69; Eusebio Mujal-Leon, "Spanish Communism and Political Change in Spain." Ph.D. diss., Massachusetts Institute of Technology, 1980, pp. 279–80.

12. Urban, "Moscow and the PCI," pp. 138–41.

13. Joan Barth Urban, "The Impact of Eurocommunism on the Socialist Community," in *Innovation in Communist Systems*, ed. Andrew Gyorgy and James A. Kuhlman (Boulder, Col.: Westview Press, 1978), pp. 134–37.

14. Alfredo Reichlin, "Il nostro invito," *l'Unità*, August 19, 1980, p. 1; cf. unsigned editorial, "La Polonia è già diversa," *l'Unità*, August 31, 1980, p. 1.

15. See Franco Fabiani, "Le radici del malessere e il dibattito nel POUP," *l'Unità*, August 19, 1980, pp. 1, 11; Silvio Trevisani, "Come non furono capiti gli scioperi del 1976," *l'Unità*, August 23, 1980, p. 13; Giuseppe Boffa, Lì si narra anche di noi," *l'Unità*, September 2, 1980, p. 1.

16. See Paolo Bufalini's report on the Polish situation to the PCI Central Committee, *l'Unità*, December 18, 1980, pp. 1, 7.

17. *L'Unità*, December 11, 1980, p. 1; *Pravda*, December 11, 1980, p. 4. The Soviet delegation was headed by Vadim Zagladin, first deputy head of the CPSU international section. Significantly the Italian delegation included Antonio Rubbi, the official who had represented the PCI in its periodic consultations with the Polish party in the aftermath of the 1976 labor crisis and who had, to boot, just returned from three days in Warsaw where, as reported by *l'Unità* on Dec. 7, 1980, p. 1, he had a "long and *cordial* discussion" with Polish leaders; emphasis added.

18. "Passi officiali del PCI presso i PC dell'Est," *l'Unità*, December 10, 1980, pp. 1, 15.

19. *La Repubblica* (Rome), December 9, 1980.

20. "L'unico vero aiuto," *l'Unità*, December 10, 1980, p. 1.

21. Ibid.

22. Kevin Devlin, "The Challenge of the 'New Internationalism,'" in *The Sino-Soviet Conflict: A Global Perspective*, ed. Herbert J. Ellison (Seattle: University of Washington Press, 1981).

23. The phrase is Devlin's; see ibid.

24. Mujal-Leon, "Spanish Communism," pp. 271–96.

25. Devlin, "The Challenge of the 'New Internationalism.'"

26. Urban, "Moscow and the PCI," p. 155.

27. For a discussion of the PCI-CPSU October 1978 summit, see ibid., pp. 157–58.

28. See Berlinguer's declaration to *l'Unità*, April 13, 1980, p. 1.

29. See Renzo Foa's report on Berlinguer's press conference in Peking, *l'Unità*, April 23, 1980, pp. 1, 15.

30. "Hu Yaobang accoglie Carrillo a Pechino," *l'Unità*, November 11, 1980, p. 16.

31. Urban, "Moscow and the PCI," pp. 156–57.

32. See Emilio Sarzi Amadè's reports on Pajetta's trip, in *l'Unità*, November 24, 25, and 26, 1977, pp. 14, 14, and 1, respectively.

33. See, for example, Amadè's report in *l'Unità*, November 28, 1977, pp. 1, 12.

34. See the unsigned report in *l'Unità*, December 29, 1977, p. 14.

35. *Rinascita* 35, no. 1 (January 6, 1978): 46; ibid., no. 8 (February 24, 1978): 31; and ibid., no. 10 (March 10, 1978): 30–31. See also Gian Carlo Pajetta, "Scegliamo il fronte della trattativa e della pace," ibid., no. 7 (February 17, 1978): 7–8.

36. Romano Ledda, "L'Eritrea non è l'Ogaden: La prova di forza etiopica non si giustifica," *l'Unità*, May 18, 1978, pp. 1, 13.

37. "Eritrea: Il prezzo della soluzione militare," *Rinascita* 35, no. 48 (December 8, 1978): 32.

38. Romano Ledda, "Ma l'Africa non è degli africani?" *l'Unità*, June 7, 1978, pp. 1, 13; emphasis added. The quoted passages are on p. 13 of an article whose general thrust is directed against French intervention in Zaire and Western efforts in general to shore up reactionary and racist regimes in Africa.

39. Text in *l'Unità*, November 15, 1979, pp. 8–9.

40. Ronald Koven, "Western European Communists, In Turnaround, Back Soviets," *Washington Post*, February 20, 1977.

41. See the editorial, "Capire," *l'Unità*, January 8, 1979, p. 1; and the editorial commentary by Romano Ledda, "Il vero senso di questo dramma," ibid., January 9, 1979, p. 1.

42. See Berlinguer's March 30, 1979 report to the PCI's fifteenth national congress, *XV Congresso del Partito comunista italiano: Atti e risoluzioni* (Rome: Editori Riuniti, 1979), vol. I, p. 27.

43. Text in *l'Unità*, January 6, 1980, pp. 1, 15.

44. See the report of Berlinguer's speech on the PCI's fifty-ninth anniversary, *l'Unità*, January 21, 1980, pp. 1–2.

45. Mujal-Leon, "Spanish Communism," pp. 316, 306–7.

46. Quoted in "Madrid: la riposta di Carrillo in una conferenze stampa," *l'Unità*, June 28, 1977, p. 1.

47. Annette Eisenberg Stiefbold, *The French Communist Party in Transition* (New York: Praeger, 1977), p. 108.

48. For a discussion of these developments, see Joan Barth Urban, "The Ties That Bind: West European Communism and the Communist States of East Europe," in *The European Left: Italy, France, and Spain*, ed. William E. Griffith (Lexington, Mass.: Lexington Books, 1979), pp. 217–19.

49. Ronald Tiersky, "French Communism, Eurocommunism, and Soviet Power," in *Eurocommunism and Détente*, ed. Rudolf L. Tökés (New York: New York University Press, 1978), pp. 165–66. Cf. Stiefbold, *The French Communist Party*, pp. 117–19, 140–41.

50. Heinz Timmermann, "The Eurocommunists and the West," *Problems of Communism* 28, no. 3 (May-June 1979): 44–47.

51. Carrillo, *"Eurocommunism" and the State*, pp. 108–9.

52. For a discussion of this ambiguity see Timmermann, "The Eurocommunists and the West," pp. 48–50; Stefano Silvestri, "The Left and Security Problems in Italy, France, and Spain," in *The European Left*, ed. Griffith, pp. 148–53; and Ciro Elliott Zoppo, "The Military Policies of the Italian Communist Party," *Survival* 20, (March-April 1978): 63–72.

53. Silvestri, "The Left and Security Problems," pp. 152–53.

54. Text in *l'Unità*, October 18, 1979, pp. 1, 15.

55. See note 44 above.

56. Ronald Koven, "Italian Communists looking West," *Washington Post*, June 8, 1980, p. A20.

57. See editorial, "Conferenza indetta dai PC francese e polacco," *l'Unità*, April 2, 1980, p. 1.

58. Text in *l'Unità*, November 15, 1979, pp. 8–9.

59. The phrase is used editorially in a report on Berlinguer's speech to a meeting of PCI provincial secretaries, in *l'Unità*, January 27, 1980, pp. 1, 18.

60. See ibid.; also text of *Direzione* resolution, *l'Unità*, January 6, 1980, pp. 1, 15; and Berlinguer's speech on the fifty-ninth PCI anniversary, *l'Unità*, January 21, 1980, pp. 1–2.

61. Berlinguer press conference, *l'Unità*, April 28, 1980, pp. 1–2.

62. For a review of the polemics, see Urban, "Moscow and the PCI," pp. 121–35.

63. Cf. Urban, "The Ties That Bind," pp. 211–24.

64. See Jiri Valenta, "Soviet Decision-Making on the Intervention in Angola," in *Communism in Africa*, ed. David E. Albright (Bloomington: Indiana University Press, 1980), pp. 102–14.

65. PCF leader Georges Marchais defended the CPSU's action in a television broadcast from Moscow; text in *L'Humanité*, January 12, 1980, pp. 8–9.

66. Urban, "Moscow and the PCI," pp. 144–50.

67. G. P. Smirnov, "Ital'ianskaia Kommunisticheskaia Partiia," *Voprosy istorii KPSS* no. 1 (1981): 98; cf. *l'Unità*, February 7, 1981, p. 17, regarding the identity of the author.

68. See the reports of this incident in the *Washington Post*, February 27, 1981, p. A21; *la Repubblica* (Rome), March 1–2, 1981, p. 3; and *l'Unità*, February 28, 1981, p. 1. The text of Pajetta's speech appears in ibid., pp. 1, 18.

69. Text in *Panorama* (Milan), February 23, 1981, pp. 83, 85.

70. Eusebio Mujal-Leon, "Cataluña, Carrillo, and Eurocommunism," *Problems of Communism* 30, no. 2 (March-April 1981): 40–47.

PART FOUR

The Soviet Union and the Industrialized World

POLITICAL AND STRATEGIC FACTORS IN SOVIET RELATIONS WITH THE WEST: SOVIET PERCEPTIONS

Roger Hamburg

The 1980s have been ushered in with a period of renewed tension and accelerated rivalry between the United States and the Soviet Union. This has resulted in political fallout in a Western Europe that is increasingly concerned about Soviet military power and its growth, but unwilling to follow the American lead completely because of economic and other ties with the Soviet Union and doubts about the political sagacity and steadiness of American policy.

Soon after the Soviet invasion of Afghanistan, President Carter stressed to the Soviet leaders that superpowers have an obligation to "exercise restraint in the use of our great military forces." They must not threaten the integrity of small states. The implication of the Soviet move into Afghanistan, however, "could pose the most serious threat to peace since the Second World War."[1] Such a danger could mean, from an American point of view, a serious deterioration of détente in the sense of making cooperative efforts toward reducing the danger of war and implementing cooperative agreements between the superpowers in areas of mutual interest and concern. Brezhnev, in partial response, contended that it was vitally necessary to "eliminate conflict situations" in the Middle and Near East and Southeast Asia and to "use any device if it leads to a lasting peace." But those conciliatory words were blurred by his view that "détente is a common accomplishment of the peace-loving states and the reckless imperialist forces must not be allowed to destroy its fruits."[2]

This vague statement could mean many things and its ambiguities conceal Soviet pride, assertiveness, fear, heightened security anxieties, and all the accompanying concerns that comprise the alloy of Soviet foreign policy. Europeans reacted to the Soviet move and declaratory statements with their customary admixture of vigilance and prudence, fearing that unchecked hostility toward the Soviet Union could lead to a new cold war. Furthermore, it was argued that if diplomacy were totally forsaken for a new arms race, would the West be better off if all communication links to the East were severed? The long European isolation from the major crises of the post–World War II era seemed to be at an end. There was also the possibility, especially for states closer to the Warsaw Pact area, that Soviet military power might be used in areas more immediately threatening to European interests. This would clearly be the case if Soviet fears about the repercussions of internal events in Poland resulted in a perception that Communist party hegemony was threatened there. As a by-product of such developments the Soviets and East Germans might reopen the dormant Berlin and East German questions.[3]

The Soviet move, despite its geographic remoteness from the center of NATO power, was close to the economic lifeline of Europe, its oil supply through the Persian Gulf. In less apocalyptic terms, it focused concern anew on Soviet intentions, because of constant anxiety about the geographic contiguity to Western Europe of large, well-equipped Soviet and Warsaw Pact forces and the fact that Western Europe has always been central to Soviet security considerations. For historical and cultural reasons the Soviet Union has tended to evaluate itself continuously in relation to West Europeans, especially the Germans, whom the Soviets have alternately feared and admired. The Soviet Union has seen Western Europe, as well as the United States, as a major source for the investment and technological assistance that the Soviet system has increasingly sought in order to compensate for chronic weaknesses of its own in economic innovation. It has also focused on Western European states because of their alliance with the United States, the strongest Soviet rival that—with NATO—could still pose a major barrier and threat to the Soviet Union and its allies.

SOVIET POLICY IN WESTERN EUROPE

Europe, both East and West, is the linchpin of Soviet strategy and it is here, with Eastern Europe an area of imperial control and Western Europe with its high industrial potential coupled with American nuclear weapons, that the constant and continuing Soviet military buildup is most pronounced. The Soviet and Warsaw Pact conventional military advantage over NATO forces has grown in recent years, although NATO countries have increased defense expenditures in the last two or three years in an attempt to narrow the gap. The Soviet Union has not been content with parity with the West in any category of conventional military strength and has sought quantitative and qualitative improvements without visible restraint. When American defense efforts flagged, the Soviets continued their steady buildup, and their conventional advantage is pronounced in the European region. Nevertheless, the risks of war as premeditated Soviet action are not excessive because of the uncertainties of escalation, the possibility of engaging the American nuclear deterrent, or even the uncertain effects of the new precision-guided munitions.[4]

Yet as noted above, the Soviets assume that war could be *imposed* on them and its doctrine of mass and rapid advance could be put into play. There are a number of circumstances under which war could occur in Europe. Many involve leftist takeovers in which, besides nonmilitary help, the Soviet Union might respond to pro-Soviet forces requesting Soviet intervention. Alternatively, it might grant nonmilitary help in return for basing rights to increase the Soviet presence (and partial control) in these areas or threaten to intervene and make this visible by appropriate maneuvers. Italy comes most readily to mind in this connection. War between NATO powers, with the weaker side calling in Soviet forces as an act of desperation, is a possibility. Recurring Greek and Turkish war and tension over Cyprus is the most likely case in point. Yugoslavia, with the possibility of ethnic tensions exploding in civil war in the post-Tito environment, provides two possibilities. In one instance, a faction favoring the Soviet Union might call for Soviet intervention and the Soviets would respond in the interests of solidarity. In the other, the Soviets might respond defensively if a faction took power and called in the NATO camp. In this case Yugoslavia's buffer, non-aligned status between East and West would be upset and the Soviets might feel compelled to intervene.

West Germany offers similar possibilities, although they are not likely and the consequences of Soviet intervention are far more imponderable. A worker movement might gain power but be in the process of suppression by counter-revolutionary elements. Or right-wing, even neo-Nazi elements might seize power and raise possibilities that even in Germany's truncated state are only too familiar to the Soviet leadership.[5]

Warsaw Pact commentators are quite aware of the fact that in Europe "two military-political groupings confront each other as opposite class entities, and powerful armed forces and weapons systems, including nuclear weapons, are stationed on the continent." It is widely believed that an armed conflict in Europe could hardly be maintained as a local one.[6] Charles Burton Marshall's comments that the "Soviet Union's aim is to have its way without having to fight," as well as his remark citing the Soviet government's firm desire to avoid "large-scale nuclear hostilities" were approved as "objective true statements."[7]

If large-scale military action is not likely to be a preferred Soviet policy, what are Soviet aims in Europe? Basic is a "recognition (dictated by Europe's historical experience) of the European frontiers that emerged as a result of the Second World War and post-war development, and also of political realities, as a solid basis for peace on the continent." This was accomplished by the Conference on Security and Cooperation in Europe (CSCE) in which the Soviets sought to put the final gloss on a process begun in Europe during the Brandt *Ostpolitik* era in the early 1970s. These steps included a treaty between the Federal Republic of Germany (FRG) and the Soviet Union on August 12, 1970; a treaty between the FRG and Poland on December 7, 1970, concerning the basis for normalizing their mutual relations; a treaty between the FRG and GDR (German Democratic Republic) on December 21, 1972 (recognizing East Germany); a treaty on mutual relations between the FRG and Czechoslovakia on December 11, 1973; and the Quadripartite agreement in Berlin on September 3, 1971. These legalized and legitimated the territorial status quo in Eastern Europe and provided opportunities for the Soviets to enlarge their influence throughout Europe, as the risk of confrontation seemed to lessen (especially over the Berlin problem, which had appeared to constitute a potential threat to peace in central Europe from 1958 through the 1960s). This, in the Soviet view, would finally recognize the new inviolability of Europe's postwar frontiers, codify relations between states with differing systems, and also lead to greater cooperation in industry, science, and technology.

With a lessening of the perceived military danger from the East, durable political stability would undermine West European integration and stability, bring in economic changes from the West, but leave Eastern Europe free from the pressures of internal liberalization. Greater influence in Western Europe has led at times to pressure for reduced control in Eastern Europe, as the perceived need for it lessened. The final CSCE meeting also produced "Basket 3," with its calls for free movement of people and ideas that provided a legal basis for Western cultural intrusion into Eastern Europe and the Soviet Union in the human rights campaign.[8]

Soviet concern for legitimating Europe's borders, making the line of demarcation established after World War II juridically permanent, and forcefully reflected in part by her large military forces, shows that she is preeminently a European power. But these large and growing forces do not provide her security, which remains tentative and unstable largely because of Atlanticism—American partnership with the capitalist countries of Europe. This allows the United States to affect strongly, if not control, political and economic developments in Western Europe. In the Soviet view NATO and its instruments are a powerful collective and the means by which Western capitalist powers coordinate foreign and domestic policies. Since the United States is involved in NATO, Soviet ability to affect European affairs is less than optimal.

Ultimately, the Soviets would like to fragment the Atlantic Alliance and arrange the withdrawal of American forces. The abolition of NATO might, from the Soviet point of view, decouple U.S. conventional and perhaps strategic forces from Europe's defense and undermine the rationale for the American military presence there. While not regarding any such withdrawal as imminent, the Soviets have felt that they could persuade NATO countries that dependence on the United States is expensive, inhibiting, and possibly dangerous. Drawing these countries away from dependence on the United States has been a central Soviet objective, provided that as a consequence an American withdrawal would not unleash anti-Sovietism and produce a European military union. Such a force would bring about an extension of the West German armed forces. Even a continued American military presence with a stronger West German role and a common military policy would not be a desirable development. A West European nuclear consortium would also be alarming to the Soviets. They would prefer that NATO remain as it is, a "loose collection of independent states with minimal cooperation on defense-related issues."[9]

Soviet commentators seek to exploit differences between NATO countries and the United States on a variety of diplomatic, military, and economic matters. A recent article in the main theoretical journal on international politics, *World Economics and International Relations*, recalled that when NATO was established, the Soviet Foreign Ministry warned Europeans that NATO's goals were "closely connected with the plans of the establishment of world Anglo-American rule under the aegis of the United States." Membership in NATO would deprive European states of the "possibility of conducting an independent foreign and domestic policy." Bloc countries would be "directly dependent on Washington" and be converted into a "beachhead for deploying American troops, nuclear and other US military bases." The Soviet commentator cited approvingly de Gaulle's concern that Europeans might have been drawn into the Korean War and possibly into Vietnam. He also cited other instances where NATO forces might be involved outside of the European theater and noted European comments that this should be avoided.[10]

NATO is depicted as a "powerful military machine" whose forces are being developed in "immediate proximity to the boundaries of the socialist states of Europe." It has recently "sharply increased" its military efforts, raising defense expenditures up to 3 percent a year, and has called for weapons modernization, with West Germany's military expenditures second only to those of the United States. NATO is allegedly part of Washington's plan to create a "ring of military bases around the USSR."[11]

Soviet press organs have sought to appeal to public opinion in NATO countries to prevent the implementation of a NATO desire to install medium-range U.S. Pershing II and cruise missiles in Britain, West Germany, and Italy. The Netherlands, Belgium, Denmark, and Norway were particularly singled out for attention. The Soviets sought to emphasize doubts in Belgium, Norway, and Denmark, criticized West Germany and Britain for agreeing to accept new missiles on their territory, and warned West Europe as a whole that it would be vulnerable to future attack. Concern about Warsaw Pact arms increases was dismissed as "prattle."[12]

Soviet Defense Minister Ustinov stated some of these concerns in particularly striking terms. While the "whole world knows" that the Soviet Union "was not preparing an armed attack on anyone and will never make such an attack," the whole world "also knows" that Soviet armed forces are "ready to beat off an attack by any aggressor." Retribution for an attack on the Soviet Union or on other countries of the Socialist commonwealth will be inescapable. "We say this in the strongest possible terms."[13]

Nor is the threat, in the Soviet vew, confined to NATO territory itself. NATO, Ustinov notes, is considering the "possibility of delivering modern weapons to China and is encouraging Peking's military preparations aimed against neighboring states." Other Soviet analysts have expressed the warning that there would be "no place for détente" if China "became some sort of ally to the West, even an informal ally." China, as NATO's "Eastern member," in another view seeks to "influence West European countries in order to sabotage actions aimed at consolidating security in Europe." China allegedly seeks to put together a coalition of the "chief capitalist powers of Europe, Japan, and of course the US" as a part of a "common front" against the USSR. In an American view, a Soviet strategy of calming Europe to deal with China would backfire if the British or Europeans sold arms to it. A new European strategy to deal with Europe-China links would be necessary and the Soviets would be faced with the choice of furthering détente in Europe, on the condition that European assistance to China be curtailed, or a revival of pressure in Europe.[14]

Could the Soviets strike a bargain with the United States and Western Europe that might reduce Soviet advantages in Europe in return for some understanding in Western relations with China?[15] This may put new urgency in the usual Soviet calls for a dissolution of blocs in Europe or, failing that, some sort of mutual reduction and withdrawal of forces in the central theater. The Soviets have advanced the idea of the joint dissolution of NATO and the Warsaw Pact, with tranquillity assured through collective security, although no mechanisms are suggested to implement this scheme. Failing this, the Soviets have sought to reduce the danger of an outbreak in Europe by strategically timed offers of withdrawal of forces, confidence-building measures like advance notice of and limitations on military maneuvers, and further strategic-arms-control measures. They have also been involved in force-reduction talks in Europe with NATO representatives (MBFR in Western parlance). This has been done to preserve and legitimize the Soviet position relative to NATO. The latter's attempts to offset Soviet preponderance in tanks and manpower by urging greater cuts in Warsaw Pact forces than those of NATO has been met by Soviet insistence that the East-West balance must be preserved by equal cuts in all force categories and by constant Soviet concern about the West German armed forces.[16]

Brezhnev insisted in Bonn that there was not much difference in the size of the armed forces of NATO and the Warsaw Pact and their level has remained more or less equal. Therefore, the "correlation between the two opposing sides must not change"; and Soviet proposals call for an "equal reduction that does not lead to a change in the correlation of strength in Central Europe in favor of any of the two participants in the talks."[17] The Soviets were also concerned that, if U.S. forces were reduced, the proportion of West German forces in NATO would not rise but be cut proportionally. This would have the effect of strengthening centrifugal tendencies within NATO on the entire question of German participation. The Poles and the Soviet Union are politically sensitive on the German question and the entire MBFR focus is viewed as a means of curbing growing German strength.

Soviet writing on MBFR has constantly expressed the fear that NATO would seek to improve the existing correlation of forces. Soviet policy has sought to keep a manpower and tank superiority by calling for equal reduction of forces. They have also not been forthcoming in providing independently verifiable data on the size of their armed forces prior to any carrying out of cuts. But the Soviets have sought to keep the talks going, with Brezhnev's withdrawal of 20,000 troops from East Germany the latest sign of this.

Soviet negotiations reflect the notion that parity or a stabilization of a correlation of military forces on anything other than a temporary basis is unacceptable. There must be a margin of Soviet superiority except where Soviet forces are markedly inferior, and parity is a step in the correct direction.[18] Yet the existing balance may begin shifting away from the Soviets in Europe, and recent Soviet note of increased NATO military budgets and planned emplacement of missiles that could reach Soviet territory reflects this Soviet concern.

The Soviets support their position that the balance is "more or less equal" by quoting American statements, like that of then Secretary of Defense Schlesinger to the Senate Foreign Relations Committee on July 27, 1973, that the situation in Europe was "fairly stable" and a subsequent remark that NATO and the Warsaw Pact had "more or less numerical equality." They have also quoted West German Federal Minister Scheel who declared that troop reductions in Central Europe must not change the existing balance of forces. The Soviets claim that focusing on the balance in terms of ground forces alone ignores other elements of the balance such as air forces (where the Soviet Union and Warsaw Pact have also made gains) and nuclear weapons. They dismiss American concern about the difficulty of returning to Europe, in a crisis, troops that have been withdrawn as part of a disengagement agreement, because they claim that even heavy equipment can be transported rapidly across the seas.[19] They insist that alleged superior Soviet mobilization capacity is not validated and should not be a part of the negotiations. In addition, the Soviets contend that this capacity, if it exists, is counterbalanced by the fact that "the Soviet Union would have to move its forces from as far away as, say, the Urals, or even the Baikal, and that these distances would in a certain sense even exceed that between New York and London."

The Soviets argue that in the event of a military conflict in Europe, "the relationship of forces in Central Europe cannot be regarded in isolation from other regions and from the global balance as a whole, especially if we remember that the mobile forces, the air force, the missile units, the naval forces, etc., now make up a large proportion of the armed forces as a whole, and that their sphere of operation cannot be limited to any particular area."[20]

While Central Europe is the main area of confrontation between NATO and the Warsaw Pact, in the event of a military clash there, "it would not be confined to this region alone." Instead, it would develop into a "global conflagration between NATO and the Warsaw Treaty Organization, other countries possibly being involved, too." In this event, the "global balance of forces would be critical" and here NATO countries are far superior to the Warsaw Treaty countries. Therefore, "Is it not clear that not only the distance from Western Europe to the US and the USSR, but also those, say from Alaska to Okinawa to Vladivostock, are equally important?"[21] One would have to include U.S. bases and aircraft carriers. Therefore, in the Soviet view central Europe cannot be viewed in isolation, but must be considered as part of a larger whole. Even if there were a local asymmetry, in the Soviet view this would not justify disproportional Soviet force cuts. SALT I, after all, allowed an asymmetry in missile booster numbers and even SALT II balances offer advantages and disadvantages to both sides.[22]

Other comments by Soviet officials reveal the same mixture of assertiveness and defensiveness in the Soviet position, deny aggressive intent, and keep open the possibility of continued arms reduction talks. For example, reflecting sensitivity on NATO plans to deploy missiles on West German territory, Foreign Minister Gromyko reasons as follows: First, the Western view is that these missiles are necessary as a reaction to Soviet missile deployments aimed at Western Europe (what the West calls SS-20s); second, this is simply a modernization of existing systems; third, the Soviet modernization is simply a response to NATO weapons modernization; and finally, though the West contends that the latter step was taken long ago, is it "better or worse that the Western countries modernized earlier than the Soviet Union? Maybe we should have done this earlier." Gromyko urged that deployments be frozen, "with no decision made on the deployment of new types of nuclear missiles in Western Europe." But the Western response, Gromyko avers, is to produce and deploy the weapons first "and only then will we begin to talk with you." This is disingenuous, Gromyko implies, because past statements to the "effect that there is now an approximate equality of forces between East and West" are belied by "representatives of Western countries, including the US," who "suddenly claim there is no equality and it will be achieved only after the NATO plans we have been talking about are implemented." What is the true NATO and U.S. position, Gromyko asks, especially taking into account U.S. allies with nuclear weapons?[23]

Defense Minister Ustinov argues in a similar view that the West seeks to start the talks "from a position of strength" and that parity, which Western countries asserted existed in the past, "doesn't suit" NATO strategists. Therefore, they are calling for an arms buildup. Perceptually, Soviet concerns depict a NATO TNF (Theater Nuclear Forces) force that, with U.S. forces, could hit the Soviet Union itself (with great accuracy, given the relatively short distance involved), while NATO sees a larger Soviet force pointed at Western Europe rather than at NATO bases there.[24]

According to John Lehman, Soviet policy in MBFR and related questions has attempted to "maintain and if possible solidify the existing correlation of forces" in the political-military situation in Europe. The Soviets have sought to preserve advantages that they have in Europe and to take special pains to place specific limitations on the size of the West German armed forces. Recently Soviet concern about such forces has been reflected in criticism of the large FRG share of any enhanced Western military buildup in Central Europe, West German influence on the TNF decision, and a larger West German naval role in the Norwegian area and the Indian Ocean. They have also sought MBFR to "foster the policy of détente and the appearance and atmosphere of a warming of relations between East and West." But Gromyko and Ustinov's comments indicate that the key question is maintenance of the political-military status quo rather than limiting German military power or reducing U.S. influence in Western Europe.[25]

In addition MBFR, by providing a sense of reduced threat in Europe, helps to preclude the threat or use of force in international relations. From the Soviet point of view it creates a climate in which it would be more difficult for the United States to legalize the use of such force. The Soviet insistence on equality and equal security upholds Soviet status, and the insistence on preserving an equitable bargaining relationship preserves Soviet interests.[26] It reflects Soviet concern about a possible erosion of its military edge brought about by increased Western military expenditures and even the increasing closeness of Sino-Western ties. Ustinov and Gromyko's words probably reflect these same concerns. The Soviets rationalize their position by pointing to geographic and technological disparities that allegedly favor the West or at least compensate for Soviet advantages. This is particularly the case with the concerns about the West Germans and the anxiety that they might acquire nuclear weapons. They reveal the peculiar admixture of Soviet confidence and unease on the state of détente and the alleged propensity for history to be moving favorably in their direction.

An analysis of Soviet force deployments in European regional contexts, other than the central-front area where the large concentration of forces on both sides limits the scope of military pressure and the credibility of Soviet aims, reveals the mixed-motive character of Soviet policy. Soviet ambivalence in brandishing arms to influence state attitudes forcibly, without bringing on an adverse military reaction that could in the long run reduce Soviet security, is not a major problem here. Moscow's relations with the Scandinavian countries for example, are an area of such concerns. The seas adjacent to northern Europe have become more important to the Soviet Union in recent years. Oil resources have been found in the North Sea and there is a possibility that petroleum and natural gas deposits may be found in the Barents Sea off the North Cape and the Kola Peninsula. This complicates Soviet relations with Norway, already made delicate by the fishing rights issue.[27]

But the military significance of northern Europe is particularly critical for the Soviet Union. The Soviets' Northern Fleet is totally dependent on the 400-mile gap between Spitzbergen and the Scandinavian mainland for entrance to the Atlantic Ocean. NATO has increased its electronic and aerial surveillance of the area in recent years and the Soviets have expressed concern. Passage out of the Arctic waters is critical for the Soviet Union, not only for defensive purposes but also to project Soviet naval air power beyond Soviet territorial boundaries. Therefore, the Soviet Union carefully notes and criticizes Western efforts to affect the military balance in this area. Such criticism has recently taken the form of polemics against Norway's plans for creating a permanent weapons depot for outfitting an American marine brigade that could land on Norwegian soil in an emergency. The Soviets have assigned all their western-based strategic submarines and a large proportion of their overall strategic submarines to the Northern Fleet. There are also indications of greater parity in allocating surface vessels, including cruisers, to that fleet. The Soviet position toward the northern area thus reflects geopolitical realities and the Soviet perception of the strategic value of the area.[28]

A consideration of the northern area of Europe in connection with Soviet policy inevitably raises the issue of Finlandization, a term generally derived from what is said to describe the relationship between the Soviet Union and her northern neighbor, especially since the end of the 1939–40 winter war. In a general sense, Finlandization means a process or state of affairs in which a state maintains friendly relations with the Soviet Union but at the expense of its sovereignty. More specifically, it means responsiveness to Soviet policy preferences, abstention from attitudes deemed hostile by the Soviet Union, acceptance of neutrality in peace or war, noninvolvement in regional and international groupings that Moscow considers hostile, media restraint to muffle or stifle criticism of the Soviet Union to avoid provoking it, evenhanded gestures in commercial and cultural contacts with the Soviet Union to offset any perceived disparity in relations between the USSR and West European countries, and openness to penetration by Soviet ideas and media. Finlandization thus describes "the behavior of a country where foreign policy and domestic politics are strongly conditioned by a conscious desire to mollify and maintain friendly policies with Moscow, at the expense if need be of close ties with formal allies and its traditional friends or its own sovereignty."[29]

Closely related to Finlandization is neutralism, where, in one Soviet view,[30] "by dint of objective concerns of an internal and international character, the neutral state cannot yet participate in the defensive agreements of the socialist countries." Neutralism is, in this view, a compromise solution, a transitional phase with an impetus toward overt association with the Socialist bloc.[31]

Does Finlandization apply to Western Europe or, indeed, to Finland itself? The record is clearly a mixed one and raises subtle internal European issues beyond the scope of this chapter. But in West Germany greater independence from U.S. policy does not appear to have led to a transference of dependence on the USSR. Despite the delicate position of the FRG, directly confronting Soviet military power and seeking to improve relations and increase human contacts with its fellow countrymen in Eastern Europe, West Germany would not appear to meet the definition of Finlandization. Brandt's *Ostpolitik*, involving concessions on ratifying the status quo in Europe, expressed in "normalization" of Europe's post-World War II frontiers (a preferred Soviet usage), could not be called German neutrality. The Soviet response to Brandt's initiatives may have been dictated by fear of China after Soviet clashes with it, beginning in 1969. Nor is there any evidence of German media restraint in dealing with the Soviet Union, another element of Finlandization. Moreover, a more neutralized FRG would be less available as a Soviet foil to maintain discipline within the Warsaw Pact and might play a more independent political and military role, whose promotion, as noted above, is certainly not a goal of Soviet policy.[32]

In the Nordic area Norwegian politicians have evolved the theory of Nordic balance. In response to fears that it might unduly antagonize the Soviet Union, Nordic balance is said to counter Soviet pressure on Finland. Furthermore, the Norwegians claim that their freedom to lift self-imposed qualifications of their NATO association (no nuclear weapons, no foreign troop contingent, no NATO exercises near Soviet territory) deters Soviet designs on Finland. Norway has also increased its defense budget and sentiment is more pro-NATO than ten years ago. Nor are pro-Moscow Communist parties in Scandinavia, with a "minuscule and stagnant" electoral base, a significant factor domestically. Such parties regularly denounce Soviet policy and cooperate with the left wing of the pro-NATO Socialist Democratic parties. Finlandization cannot fairly be used to describe the current status of Soviet relations with Norway, Denmark, Sweden, or Iceland.[33]

Legvold, in describing the prototypical case, has observed that Finland is a special situation not likely to be replicated elsewhere in Europe. Unlike other nations not under Soviet sway, Finland has nearly been absorbed into the Russian and Soviet empire. Finland is also more dependent economically on the Soviet Union, importing 80 percent of its petroleum from her. It has a powerful Communist party and a Socialist party that defers to Soviet feelings. Finally, no other nation is "so overshadowed by Soviet military power and so defenseless before it."[34]

Finnish government spokesmen have expressed concern that the Norwegian theory of Nordic balance could spur Soviet pressure, rather than discourage it. But legitimate doubt arises when one asks whether Finland has been Finlandized or not. Article I of the Treaty of Friendship and Cooperation with the Soviet Union, concluded on April 6, 1948, states that if Finland or the Soviet Union through Finnish territory is attacked by Germany or a state allied with her, the Finns would seek to repel the attacker with the assistance of or jointly with the Soviet Union. This could furnish a pretext for Soviet intervention, depending upon the latter's interpretation of this clause. But the preamble to the treaty also states that Finland's aspiration is to "remain outside the conflicting interests of the Great Powers." Furthermore, interpretations of Article I also indicate that even if a NATO fleet began hostile operations in the Baltic Sea against the Soviet Union, the presence of a Soviet force in Finland would not automatically follow. Nor does Finland belong to the Warsaw Pact or engage in maneuvers with Warsaw Pact troops. However, Finland and neutral Sweden train troops to fight any aggressor and practice with weapons pointed east and west, but Finnish and Swedish conscripts admit that if called up they expect to aim east.[35]

Finland continues its existence as the only bourgeois state with which the Soviet Union has a security agreement, but in that anomalous state it maintains and develops relations with both East and West. But Finland entered the Nordic Council and has a special relationship with the EEC. The Finns have been inhibited in commenting on Soviet institutional life in mass media and books. Such institutions, however, are either ignored or given superficial coverage, while American ones are treated at far greater length and with more critical comments. The Communist party is a strong factor in Finnish internal life, but it has been integrated into traditional Finnish structures and most Finnish Communists accept parliamentary and presidential democracy. While Finland is heavily dependent on Soviet trade and imports, Finnish exports are competitive with Soviet ones, preventing too close an integration with the Soviet economic system, and must also be sold to Western markets.[36]

One could argue, of course, that Finland is "on a leash," that the Soviet Union has *allowed* this degree of independence for higher reasons of state as yet obscure, and that Finnish independence will always be tenuous, since it confronts contiguous Soviet military power. Yet Soviet-Finnish interaction does not conform to the more denunciatory descriptions of Finlandization. Admittedly, the Soviet presence restricts Finnish international maneuverability more than is the case with other Scandinavian states, but in other ways affords respect to Finnish sovereignty. Geopolitical strategic considerations of Soviet policy in the northern area are perhaps as important, if not more so, in describing the Soviet-Finnish relationship, as a desire for control of Finnish internal life.

The Finnish case exemplifies other means of Soviet leverage over the foreign policies of West European states—the presence of Communist parties and the economic instrument. In the former case, Soviet authorities might welcome the coming to power of Communist parties, especially in Italy and France where they would indicate a dramatic defeat for Atlanticism. "Successful" governments there, even if formally continuing NATO membership, would undermine the political cohesion and military effectiveness of the NATO alliance.[37] But countervailing considerations apply here as perhaps nowhere else in Soviet-West European policy.

Soviet analysis traces the growth of leftist popular forces in Western Europe as a consequence of the general crisis of capitalism. Inflation, recession, unemployment, higher taxes, and a lower standard of living are all said to be causing the general public to become convinced of the need for radical reforms. Soviet commentators note approvingly the electoral program of the Italian Communist party and attack attempts of West European ruling circles to weaken the position of leftist forces. In this connection Soviet writers attacked the governments of the United States, West Germany, France, and England for threatening to withdraw all financial and economic aid if Communists entered the Italian government. The Soviets have alleged that at the end of the 1960s and in the early 1970s a U.S. document existed (plan 100-1) that proposed that, in "extreme circumstances" in Western Europe, the United States reserved the unrestricted right to use any weapon on national intelligence information to "punish or reward" as it saw fit. American troops could suppress any movement "threatening US strategic interests" and "take full power in their hands."[38]

Such an alleged American reaction would be understandable in the Soviet view because the creation of a leftist government with Communist participation would reveal the futility of Washington's postwar efforts in Europe, directed at preventing those nations from moving to socialism, and weaken the American economic position in Europe. It would also discredit NATO, including its "loss of prestige among ruling circles in Western Europe." The Soviets contend that some American admirers of the "tough approach" described above, open military intervention, would halt such a leftward movement from the very beginning because they perceive that the assumption of power by leftist forces would cause a chain reaction in nearby states. Western ruling circles would not be able to control this reaction.[39]

Ginsburgs and Rubinstein note that the presence of an unstable situation in tandem with a cooperative Communist party lends itself to the creation of a crisis, or helps destabilize the ruling apparatus and provides the Soviet Union opportunities to monitor the conduct of a state at home and abroad. The Soviet Union could then sit back and observe the state's move to a neutralist and eventual pro-Soviet position without playing the more open role of bearing "the burden of either mid-wife or policeman."[40]

But the actual seizure of power by a Communist party or even sharing of power in a coalition government, at least initially the preferred public strategy of the Italian and Spanish Communists, poses other problems. Soviet reaction to this as something other than a theoretical possibility reveals corresponding ambivalence.

There are a number of opposing considerations involved. On the one hand, there were the events in Portugal from 1974 through 1975. Here a Communist party espousing a very orthodox Leninist position on the need for revolutionary violence, totally uncompromising in eschewing alliances with bourgeois elements, and making no secret of its intention to achieve a total control of Portuguese society according to the East-European model, elicited considerable Soviet caution. The Soviets took to heart the lessons of Chile, that military force must be in the hands of the insurgents to achieve power (the Communists were strong in a wing of the Portuguese armed forces); but events in Portugal increasingly accelerated Western apprehensions. West Europeans, especially West Germans, were beginning to treat the move to the Left in Portugal as prefacing a grave alteration of the political situation in Europe. The Soviets adopted a low-profile approach, denying a direct involvement in Portuguese affairs or any intention of subverting Portugal, and trying to make developments there appear as unthreatening as possible. Soviet press comments tried to reassure private capital about its future role in the Portuguese economy, and it is possible that the Soviets cautioned their Portuguese comrades about moving too recklessly or with too little regard for events outside of Portugal.[41]

A sharp turn to the Left in Portugal, for example, might bring Western military intervention, a strengthening of the Right within Portugal, or even, in the context of economic woes in Western Europe, a sharp rightward turn in France or West Germany. Short of these calamities, a more militant, pro-NATO mood in key countries like West Germany would not be welcome. Soviet comment reflects a diversity of Soviet views on these questions, with those pushing détente and especially a new SALT agreement relatively more cautious about revolutionary developments. One Soviet comment, for example, criticized the "insufficiency of the political maturity and degree of organization of the working class" and the threat of a "new era of fascist vandalism." Commentary revealed neither acceptance of the status quo nor a call for uninterrupted revolution. Instead, Communists were prudently to create an "active political majority," sooner or later "securing the leading role."[42]

The Eurocommunist parties, discussed elsewhere in this volume, present another set of considerations. The Communist parties of Spain and Italy, in particular, have sought some measure of independence from the CPSU organizational model. In foreign policy the Spanish party (PCE) has advocated a neutralist Socialist Europe tied to neither camp. Soviet authorities expressed some apprehension over this, with Suslov asking a PCI delegation in July 1977, whether a "neutralist Europe might not involve the risk of your slipping into the other camp."[43]

But the differences between the Eurocommunist and Soviet parties appear manageable from the standpoint of Soviet deviation control. One PCI ideologist, Radice, when asked what the party would do in a world crisis, said, "We would choose the Soviet Union, of course."[44] Despite the fact that Eurocommunist parties oppose the Soviet Union in modifying the Leninist model to be more viable domestically, they have, for the most part, not shown much interest in disobeying it on matters of major international concern.

The Soviets have an elaborate apparatus to discourage such independence. The International Department of the CPSU sends liason officers to a large number of parties abroad. Nonruling European party representatives also travel to the Soviet Union and Eastern Europe. The Soviets have the "stick" of utilizing prestige among the militant rank and file of such parties and financial "carrots." The latter involve funding from the USSR and Eastern Europe usually provided by preferential trade agreements with Communist-run firms.[45]

Ultimately, a Communist assumption of power might be desirable to the Soviets but hardly likely and, in current conditions, counterproductive. But in the short run such parties are useful, even if Soviet theorists do not appear to be waiting for a revolutionary situation from which they might profit. Soviet concern has rested with the politics of French, Italian, and Spanish governments and how they affect Soviet interests. If they espouse goals favorable to Soviet interests, this might be more important than what the respective Communist parties are saying or doing. But their foreign policy position, despite Soviet concern expressed about neutralism, is pro-Soviet, as Radice admitted. Even as they declare their independence and refuse to accept the idea of the need for a guiding center for the international Communist movement, this may be all the Soviets really want at this stage. The Communist parties of the West are, therefore, desirable, not so much as "revolutionary instruments but political forces within the Western countries which exert an influence in the desired direction."[46] They may be more effective in this role because their independence in party relations demonstrates their credibility.

Another lever to move Western European societies in the desired direction, as well as one responding to certain domestic considerations, is the Soviet desire to import more high technology and industrial goods from Western Europe and some sign that Western Europe wants certain Soviet materials, especially oil and natural gas. While the United States might be able to afford the loss of the Socialist market, this would be a serious blow for Western Europe, in the Soviet view. Trade with Socialist countries guarantees work for two million people in developed capitalist states—a large figure, especially when one considers that Western Europe has 6 million unemployed. While the United States is accused of seeking to utilize economic relations to influence the Soviet political system, thereby impeding the détente process, Western Europe utilizes economic ties with the East, which in the final analysis promotes the deepening of détente.[47] Improved trade and economic dealings with the Soviet Union might also affect certain Western European political figures who, in one Soviet account, meet American campaigns like that of human rights "without enthusiasm," though perhaps paying lip service to them.[48]

An increase in Soviet trade with Western Europe helps the Soviet Union facilitate an atmosphere of détente, enables the bloc to acquire high technology and manufactured items, and also confirms that the Soviet Union is an equal partner, a particularly major consideration in Soviet dealings with the industrialized countries of the West. But does it offer an important lever for influence within Western countries; that is, does export of materials, including oil and natural gas, provide political leverage? Conversely, does the availability of the Soviet Union as a *customer* for Western European products also provide leverage in a sometimes depressed world market? Would this leverage split Western Europe from the United States, particularly when West Europeans have periodic doubts about U.S. foreign policy acumen and are loath to give up or restrict economic ties with the Soviet Union in the interests of NATO solidarity?[49]

Soviet economic dependence on Western Europe has not been great. Soviet interest in imports of Western machinery and know-how, especially since the 1960s, has not been translated into a decisive increase in their importance to the Soviet economy. This is not surprising, since machinery trade in exports from the Soviet Union remains pitifully small. The pattern is one of selective importance, with imports of Western machinery important for some sections of the Soviet economy compared to imports from other sources. These key areas are computers and equipment for the motor industry. But there is little Soviet dependence on Western Europe for material in coal mining, iron and steel, electric power supply, and agriculture, or in the defense industry. There is much greater importance for technology transfer in chemicals, the motor industry, food processing, some light industry, timber, paper and pulp, as well as, of course, computers. While Western Europe remains the predominant source of machinery supplies to the USSR, it is not a qualitatively large source of Soviet growth. Soviet spokesmen often reveal a "sense of loss" that the Soviet Union has been left out of the rapid circulation of new technology in the West.[50]

Nor are EEC countries dependent on the Soviet economy as customers or as energy suppliers. In the case of oil, the Soviet Union's share of EEC imports and the world market is small and by itself has only a marginal influence on the market for oil. Some Western firms may become dependent on Soviet suppliers of parts for industrial products, but any substantial dependence of the EEC as the result of industrial cooperation with the East is a long way off. Soviet purchases may well be useful for sectors where there are surpluses or surplus capacity, such as the computer industry, and might be a factor in the sales of particular firms. The Soviets may increase trade with countries whose policies are favorably regarded or which they want to influence. Soviet technology for other than military purposes tends to be discounted, although there have been achievements in particular industries and the Soviets sell several thousand licenses each year to firms in the West.

Unless there is economic disaster in the EEC, it is doubtful that the economic relationship with the Soviet Union implies any general danger of dependence unless Soviet market power can be combined with other means of pressure. Unlike oil, natural gas may be a growth area for East-West trade, but this will not create a burdensome dependence, though it may be concentrated in certain areas rather than spread through the economy. Energy, however, does provide a possibility of an uncomfortable degree of West European dependence on the Soviet Union.[51]

Soviet economic policy toward Europe is hardly capable under present conditions of promoting major dependence, an economic Finlandization that would promote greater neutralism and fissures between the United States and NATO countries. But it may have a marginal role in providing greater economic independence from the United States, particularly if states like France see this as a subtle way of showing disagreement with U.S. policies or judgments.

This chapter has periodically stressed the Soviet desire to split the Western alliance from the United States or at least to accentuate disagreements between them. Soviet writers do not exaggerate such fissures where they occur, however. One writer, for instance, observes that on questions of military détente NATO presents a united front, "class solidarity," and "almost military discipline" on force reduction talks. Warsaw Pact participants have noted the "growing concentration" of the military efforts of the West.[52]

But there are differences in the approach of the United States and Western Europe to détente. A Soviet commentary argues that this reflects historical experience, since Europe experienced the Second World War and its consequences on its own territory. Europeans, therefore, are more prepared to undertake negotiations concerning European security. The fact that if a new world war breaks out, the worst shocks will fall on their territory creates a sense of insecurity that impels the Europeans to find a way out of this situation. They seek to cooperate with states with different social systems to respond to this need. West Europeans also reportedly value more highly than the United States the positive consequences of détente, especially in the economic area, where trade relations with the Socialist states have become a factor of economic stability.

Détente has a special meaning from the perspective of Western Europe's mutual ties with Washington. Strengthening European security reduces the significance of the military factor in international relations generally, particularly in U.S.-West German military relations. This enhances the importance of nonmilitary relations, especially the economic and scientific-technical sectors. In these areas Western Europe is more comparable with the United States and, accordingly, has greater ability to counter any U.S. attempts to use its position for the economic, technical, or political exploitation of its partners.

Leftist forces of Europe, especially Communist and worker parties, have more influence on policy formation on détente matters than in the United States. Their parliamentary and extraparliamentary activity complicates rightist maneuvers in foreign policy. The United States might seek to bring about a harder line from Western Europe, but Western Europe politicians would not, without serious opposition, allow themselves to be led from a course "which has already brought them certain dividends." U.S. attempts to do so might lead to "further mutual alienation" of their NATO partners. The U.S. "weakened international position" makes it "more compliant" in relations with its allies and their support becomes an increasingly important factor.[53]

Despite its "weakened position," the United States remains the chief Soviet enemy—the one state that can grievously affect Soviet security—but also a partner in avoidance of direct conflict. It is relations with its transoceanic adversary, which except for nuclear missiles is geographically removed from the center of Soviet power, to which Soviet commentators devote particular attention.

The Soviet Union seeks at least parity of influences on a global basis with the United States. It also seeks, as it does from Western Europe, access to technology and capital, both for pragmatic internal economic reasons and as a symbol of its acceptance into the exclusive ranks of superpower status. But Soviet analysts are confounded by many aspects of U.S. policies and the operation of the American political system and it is these that will now be considered.

SOVIET-AMERICAN RELATIONS

Adam Ulam shows the difficulties involved when two states, starting from such different premises, compete and yet strive to keep the competition within bounds and unlikely to lead to nuclear war. It is true, as he observes, that one must impress the Soviet Union with U.S. firmness and determination to protect vital interests, and yet assuage Soviet fears and counter overperceptions of threat from the United States. But this works two ways, he notes. Brezhnev tried to reassure U.S. senators that the USSR did not think it could win a nuclear war, yet at the same time the United States must be impressed by Soviet power. But how does one impress the Americans "without frightening them to the point where it becomes counterproductive?"[54]

Michael Deane documents disagreements within the Soviet military and political hierarchy on the proper course to pursue toward the Americans and détente in general. One group of Soviet leaders, he avers, concludes that a world nuclear war would destroy both superpowers and cannot be used to achieve political aims. They would contend, in terms of the priority spending question, that there are objective limits to the amount that can be diverted to military needs. The opposing group argues that imperialism is making preparations to destroy the Communist camp and is deterred from this only by fear of its destruction. Therefore, the Soviet Union must be able not only to repel an enemy but achieve victory.

Furthermore, it contends, military power is a critical instrument for use in attaining foreign policy goals, and "other factors in the struggle for peace" would not have been effective except for the presence of strong Soviet military forces. The familiar argument is made that strategic nuclear parity compelled the United States to abandon its policy of dictation to the Soviet Union "from a position of strength." It has sobered "sensible circles" in the capitalistic world. Therefore, there is the logical policy consequence—continued strengthening and augmentation of the armed forces, despite the fact that the military is making ever-increasing demands on the economy. This goes beyond a defensive orientation for Soviet forces, with insistence on a "deepening of the external function of the Soviet armed forces." Deane indicates that the leadership is undecided. Again the issue remains: what proper combination of military and nonmilitary elements will restrain the United States without frightening it into aggressive counteraction?[55]

This mixed Soviet view of the efficacy of military force in confronting its chief rival inevitably colors Soviet assessments of the United States. If Soviet commentators depict a United States that is tough, strong-willed, and ready to defend its interest, does that indicate a policy of caution or the need to be even more aggressive and forward to deter the imperialists from "adventures"? Could American moves ever be seen as partially justified in response to Soviet moves and statements? Finally, how do Soviet analysts and commentators decipher the often confusing, often contradictory nature of American politics, and what effect, if any, do they think their actions or statements have on it?

In responding to these questions it is necessary to describe in broad outline the Soviet view of détente. Dmitri Simes's views on this question are most instructive. Simes, a former researcher at the Institute of World Economy and International Relations from 1962 to 1967, contends that the Soviets are well aware of American military limitations that were self-imposed. They have not contended that American involvement in Egypt, which helped bring about a settlement with Israel from which the Soviet Union was excluded, and corresponding Soviet reverses were reasons to bury détente. Nor have the Soviets, in their view, violated détente even in the Middle East (the 1973 war). They have, however, used their growing military forces to expand their influence at the expense of U.S. interests. The United States must look after those interests and must not expect that the Soviet Union will do so. Détente, after all, involves a trade-off between competitors, not an arrangement where new friends swear to end the contest.[56]

N. I. Lebedev, in a major Soviet work on international relations, contends that there is no alternative to détente. A brink-of-war strategy will not bring advantages to the West, in his view. With the balance of world forces tipping in favor of socialism, détente is not a form of war (as critics charge) but "a way to winning more favorable conditions for the struggle for peace and social progress." Capitalism has been restricted by military power but "we cannot help thinking that our critics have lost faith in capitalism's ability to survive without resorting to aggression." Lebedev notes that Whetten, an English writer, defines détente as a "deliberate mutual decision to explore areas of accommodation during periods of persisting tension and distrust." It is a continuum on which participants seek to promote some degree of adversary cooperation in an issue-oriented, nonbellicose atmosphere that is not based on principles or values. This definition, in Lebedev's view shows "common sense and realism" in its approach to international processes.[57]

Lebedev rejects "systems theory," which naturally gravitates to a notion of stability and balance. This would emasculate the class nature of international politics. Rather than obeying the rules of a system, states operate in a context in which peaceful coexistence and the renunciation of war are brought about by a deliberate change in the balance of forces in favor of socialism, by conscious policy of the Socialist states. This is not a spontaneous, mechanical, or automatic process of self-regulation. It is not a spontaneously maintained stability or a passive adaptation to change. It must be organized, guided, and corrected.[58]

Détente, in the Soviet view, is not an equilibrium process where the rules are determined by American theoreticians in or out of government. Instead, it is a moving equilibrium, a process of adjustment that seeks to work out imperfect understandings but involves enormous rivalry, competition, cool heads, and cold blood. In the Soviet view these qualities are not often found in the American political system, and this difference in the approach and character of the system is a key, if not *the* key source of conflict between them.

V. F. Petrovsky, in a major work on American foreign policy thought,[59] presents a brief historical survey exploring the reasons for the American conversion of détente. In his view, U.S. containment of the Soviet Union and conduct of the cold war against it did not impede constant Soviet movement toward its goals and did not restrain the growth of its international authority and prestige. The "bankruptcy" of U.S. policy in Vietnam proved this. The absence of a dialogue with the Soviet Union turned against the United States itself. The United States could not preserve a world order that it saw as its own image. It could not "maintain within its orbit" states that it considered part of its common fate, such as Cuba, besides the states of Europe and Africa. Reliance on military force as the main weapon of foreign policy brought fewer and fewer results. Forceful confrontation with the Soviet Union did not bring dividends at home or abroad. American military doctrines, like flexible response as applied in Vietnam, brought neither victory nor political gains. Nor did foreign aid strengthen the "positions of force" position. The International monetary system, which the United States had created, no longer corresponded to current needs.[60]

Military-force and dollar diplomacy, the basic tools for fulfilling U.S. international obligations, led to overcommitment in international affairs and an overstrained economy. The United States was drawn into various military adventures and conflicts, but its allies declined to participate in these actions under different pretexts and did not bear their share of the financial burden, from the U.S. point of view. The United States had to adjust its interests to new realities. The "objective development of the international situation" and the necessity of changing certain methods and foreign policy means—but also changes in the form and scope of the implementation of these means—came to demand U.S. attention. Accordingly, Petrovsky observes, a certain realism developed, with the

United States acknowledging the equality of states and the necessity of peaceful coexistence as the only alternative to nuclear war. U.S. realism, however, means "a change not in the nature of American imperialism itself and its aggressive essence, but in the environment, which surrounds it." Objective processes and the "conscious, purposeful foreign policy actions of the Soviet state . . . reduced the possibilities of aggressive actions of imperialism and led to a re-examination of basic U.S. foreign policy arrangements."[61]

Petrovsky adds the usual Soviet disclaimer. Peaceful coexistence means that conflicts between states cannot be resolved by war or applying force or the threat of force, but it does not mean preservation of the status quo. The greatest social problems of modern times are decided and will be resolved not by agreements between states, important as they may be, but by processes occurring within states.

The United States has admitted, he concludes, that the Soviet Union is now a superpower, a term it previously reserved for itself. The two superpowers have a special responsibility, as permanent members of the Security Council, to preserve world peace, although this is not a scheme or condominium of the two superpowers and must not infringe upon the rights of other states and peoples.[62]

Petrovsky's comments can be read in many ways, among them satisfaction that the United States, from a position of overweening pride, has been humbled, obliged to recognize the Soviet Union as a superpower, and confounded in formulating a political-military doctrine in a nuclear age and chaotic world. It cannot be read as a statement of Soviet belief in a U.S. collapse of will or loss of capability. Indeed, the view that the United States and the USSR have a special responsibility to preserve the peace, as long as it does not affect the right of the Soviet Union to aid other states or movements, indicates a residual respect for U.S. power and capability. Finally, the stricture that the key factors in international politics are internal to states indicates Soviet emphasis on the effect that external developments have on internal processes within states, on the minds of men and social interaction, not on mechanical or legalistic abstractions.

Status is a major Soviet concern. Foreign Minister Gromyko lauds the fact that the Soviet Union has "ties of various kinds" with "more than a hundred states," as if this in itself were significant. But they are by no means certain of themselves nor their ability to influence events. Parenthetically, Zamyatin, Gromyko's press aide, indicated that, while the Soviet Union was invited into Africa, "we'll be invited out."[63] Since the Soviets are unsure of their own status and ultimate success internationally, they are under no illusions about American adaptability and capability. Georgi Arbatov, head of the Institute of the U.S.A. and Canada, observed that even though Vietnam was a defeat for the United States, which paid for a bad policy, no one believed that the United States had "stopped being a big country and lost her influence." The Soviet Union, he added, "has no wish to play chicken with America. We understand the importance of peace and détente."[64]

Soviet analysis reveals respect and even fear of U.S. scientific-technical progress. One study, for example, emphasizes the necessity for further Soviet efforts in this area because the United States in the 1970s assimilated new achievements in the scientific-technical sector, leading to a more effective utilization of American scientific-technological potential. The United States plans to increase expenditures on research and development in the future. Brezhnev takes note of its "powerful, highly organized, productive mechanism" and its "colossal scientific-technical potential."[65] Arbatov notes the obvious military implications of this capability in the U.S. MIRV and Trident systems and the momentum of U.S. science. The "military-industrial complex follows the traditional practice: first create a problem and afterwards propose a 'solution' for it in its interest." This pertains to the Trident program.[66]

Nor are Soviet writers convinced of the lessons that the United States has supposedly learned from Vietnam. While the growth of Soviet military power, the establishment of a strategic balance, and the loss of the invulnerability of U.S. territory cause U.S. "ruling circles" to become more "circumspect" in using military force, especially nuclear missiles, U.S. foreign policy makers have by no means removed such force from the agenda. They seek to find more flexible means, range, and effectiveness in using military force, recognizing that in the present world strategic situation, growing military potential "by no means increases the possibility of its practical utilization."[67]

Military force, in one Soviet view, comprises the alpha and omega of U.S. foreign policy. The United States does not accept equality and identical security with the USSR, but seeks certain advantages as a form of psychological pressure on the Soviet Union. This was accompanied by a turn to China, "which in the foreseeable future will not act in solidarity with the USSR, in any particular crisis situation that the US and its allies provoke."[68] The new U.S. strategy of one and one-half wars, the reduction of the capability to conduct a large war in Asia (which it could do under the two-and-one-half-war strategy) is an "unambiguous signal to China that the US will exert no military pressure on it." This will "untie the hands of the Maoists for its active military preparations in the north." Yet the October 1973 war in the Middle East, in the Soviet view, demonstrated to the United States that it no longer had more effective strategic weapons than the Soviet Union and could no longer restrain it any more effectively than the Soviet Union could restrain the United States. A strategic arms agreement with the United States would moderate the rivalry, establish certain limits on the forces of the opposing sides, and reduce the pressure of domestic forces in favor of military programs directed at responding to the efforts of the other side.[69]

In analyzing U.S. "crisis response" doctrine, one Soviet analyst noted the reduction of U.S. conventional forces as a consequence of the "Vietnam syndrome" in 1969-74, but he also observed that this policy began to be reversed in the 1970s.[70] The U.S. raising of the readiness of its forces at the time of the

October war in the Middle East in 1973, the Mayaguez affair, and even the small abortive intervention in Angola showed "determined efforts to break the 'post Vietnam syndrome'." The Carter administration sought to make a distinction between the U.S. intervention in Indochina (acknowledged as unacceptable) and other possibilities for U.S. interventionary actions. Massive U.S. military intervention was "irrational" in contemporary conditions, for it could lead to "new Vietnams." Soviet writers describe the post-Vietnam debate in the United States on the more "circumspect" use of force within existing treaty agreements, especially in the Middle East and Persian Gulf. The United States also increased weapons deliveries to its allies, especially in the Near and Middle East, stepped up C.I.A. "subversive activities," and established a "propaganda campaign" to exert "psychological pressure on forces opposing the US and its allies, especially in Angola and the Horn of Africa."[71]

The United States has sought to apply a certain restraint and endeavored to avoid situations like Indochina, a development closely connected with détente. It is important to search for militarily acceptable solutions in the course of the development of an international crisis. This is more difficult to do in areas where there is no direct confrontation between the Soviet Union and the United States, just as the process of lessening tensions in the area of arms control is less successful than in areas of direct confrontation. In these areas further efforts and mutual restraint are necessary. The United States, however, has also periodically tried to demonstrate its capacity to apply force, not excluding its application on a large scale for furthering its interests. The Democratic administration sought to improve the quality of U.S. conventional forces and raise their readiness, which was connected with an increase in military expenditures. It has restored the reliability of these factors for an interventionary role.[72]

Soviet analysts are equally impressed by the nonmilitary capabilities of U.S. technology. Brezhnev noted that there was no international problem in the solution of which the Soviet Union was not ready to contribute. Clearly, access to U.S. technology and economic largesse was one of those problems. Besides the USSR, not a single country has approached the American level of published scientific literature and the United States has had a large number of trade patents and licenses. It has virtually monopolized the world capitalist market for electronic computer technology and the "technological gap" between it and its capitalist rivals has been growing, not being reduced. The United States is a key source for innovation and know-how, as well as for the export of managerial techniques. Through its scientific-technological potential, it has allegedly sought to dictate to other states in the capitalist sphere of the world economy. Also allegedly, only the Soviet Union has the capacity to oppose this, to neutralize the negative consequences of the United States using its scientific-technical potential and to bring about a situation that "would truly be based on equality, constructive and advantageous for all who participated in such collaboration."[73]

Soviet comments—like those above—which catalogue, with some anxiety, the colossal economic power of the United States and present a by no means convincing argument that only the USSR can neutralize it for the benefit of all concerned, reveal the ambivalence of Soviet involvement in economic relations with the United States (and some Soviet preference for Western Europe). While American specialists assert that the USSR can successfully create a situation of economic leverage over the United States in some cases with large purchases of U.S. products and acquire militarily useful technology in several instances,[74] Soviet reaction is contradictory.

On the one hand, Soviet writers complain about the American attempt to exert leverage over Soviet foreign and domestic policies by refusing to grant most-favored-nation treatment and by seeking to exact "political tribute" through legislation like the Jackson-Vanik and, especially, the Stevenson amendments. They complain about limitations on U.S. credits to purchase American goods, always a problem in Soviet-American trade relations. Growing protectionism in the United States also concerns Soviet commentators, who describe Soviet-American trade as extremely unstable.[75]

Increased trade with the United States would create its own problems, however, as would a higher volume of technology transfer. Integration into the international economic division of labor that this would imply would constitute involvement in a system the Soviets do not like or trust and one that is not within their control. Nervousness about U.S. "trilateralism" and vain emphasis on Soviet economic strength reveal this. The idea of the United States, Western Europe, or even Japan investing in Soviet energy resources also contains much of the classical colonial relationship within it, and the often expressed need for Western technology may be a source of embarrassment and wounded professional pride, even for those Soviet elites who would appear to be most favorably inclined toward it.[76]

Soviet commentators clearly consider the United States a formidable competitor in key aspects of state-to-state interaction, but tangible factors of power are something the Soviets, as self-professed realists, can understand and react to as part of the power equation. They are either confused, however, by an American tendency to denigrate or understate U.S. advantages, or else treat it as part of cynical U.S. attempts to justify unnecessary steps the United States does not need to take in the competition.

It is in analyzing the U.S. policy process itself, particularly the domestic environment in which policy evolves, that Soviet writers have the most difficulty. The fact that there are many sources of access to power in the American system and many areas to evaluate is particularly a problem for Soviet analysis. Typically, Soviet writers argue that there are two tendencies in achieving goals within capitalist states, a military-aggressive and a more restricted realistic posture, with corresponding political forces and factions grouping around these poles. The military-aggressive path allegedly seeks confrontation and projects an uncompromising position, while the realists recommend a more objective assessment of the world situation, moderation in the conduct of foreign policy, and compromise. This struggle goes on perpetually in the United States and is most sharply revealed in relations with the Soviet Union.[77]

Clearly, internal factors are most critical in Soviet analyses of international relations. For example, in one view those who advocate détente are attacked in the United States as "capitulationists" in international conflicts and are in danger of losing the internal struggle to those who seek a more active use of force in international affairs.[78]

Which group is ultimately stronger and on which issues? Can Soviet foreign policy affect the struggle? Simes contends that many in the United States fear that the U.S. political structure by its very nature cannot compete with "shrewd and cynical Soviet [C]ommunists." Others oppose the Soviet regime on moral grounds, especially ethnic minorities and the Jewish community, which opposes official Soviet antisemitism and Soviet support of the more militant Arab positions. Others, who lost the Vietnam debate, use the Soviet threat as a foil to get even with domestic opponents. While the Soviets display "arrogance, insecurity, and cynicism," Simes notes, the Soviet military buildup is not new. There is too much oversimplification of the problem in the United States, too many swings of mood from euphoria to despair, a lack of a steady course in U.S. policy toward the Soviet Union.[79]

Foreign Minister Gromyko claimed that the Carter administration was unable to get the SALT II agreement ratified because it was "vacillating, indecisive, and inconsistent" and "negatively affected by the operation of forces trying to break up détente."[80] An editorial response to President Carter's Annapolis speech of June 1978 contended something more malevolent—the president had no answer to U.S. domestic problems, especially inflation and unemployment, and artifically sought to whip up external alarms. The president was accused of fanning an anti-Soviet campaign and trying to solve his foreign, domestic, and even personal problems with attacks on the USSR. By linking the cooperative aspects of détente with Soviet policies (though not linking SALT directly to events in Africa) the administration was "not delivering a proper rebuff to the opponents of détente," not "defending it in Congress and in front of America, and not seeking to normalize other spheres of Soviet-American relations." The administration was considered unreliable and, whatever the content of Soviet policies, Carter, in Soviet eyes, could not deliver for domestic reasons.[81]

Carter was accused of reversing an agreement previously negotiated by the Ford administration, by including new deep cuts in strategic arms in March 1977. Such actions contributed to "instability" in U.S.-Soviet relations and did not contribute to the "trust and respect for American pledges and confidence in the validity of agreements signed by the US." This and the Carter human rights campaign, with its public attacks on Soviet internal practices, were also viewed as attempts to embarrass the Soviet government and, in the latter case, rally the flagging zeal of an American public disillusioned by Vietnam and Watergate. The Soviets have expressed the cautious hope that the situation will improve under the new Reagan administration, with which the Soviet Union seeks "normal relations."[82]

Soviet analysts also closely study Congress, especially on trade questions, which certain members of Congress link with "totally unrelated matters."[83] While the president is to some extent "forced to take the realities of international life into consideration," members of Congress do not bear this kind of extensive responsibility, due to their need for reelection in districts where "businessmen or anti-Communists of the far right" play the key decision-making role. While most Americans support improved Soviet-American relations in principle, these groups are not "embodied in strong, organized action; and groups like the "military industrial complex, the Zionist lobby and anticommunists of every shape" struggle against détente. Those who advocate an arms buildup, it is charged, are always in the majority in Congress and whenever the White House advocates a "tough line," it can depend on these groups. Congress is fragmented and "monopolies and other influential groups who seek to exert pressure to slow down or obstruct any new initiative in Congress or the administration" often hold sway.[84] Congress can, thus, counteract but seldom positively influence foreign policy. Nevertheless, the Soviets are increasingly conscious of the need for senatorial support on issues like SALT and have talked to key senators, especially Senator Byrd.

Soviet writers have difficulty in evaluating mass attitudes, usually arguing that such people are the innocent victims of elite groups or else unable to make their wishes known effectively. But a recent study contends that the American public has noted the "gigantic growth of the economic, scientific-technical and defense potential of the Soviet Union; which exerts greater and greater influence on the general cause of events in the world." Public opinion polls show the "constant growth of . . . tendencies in favor of the development of Soviet-American relations, which creates favorable conditions for US officials who want to reconstruct Soviet-American relations on the principles of peaceful coexistence." Such polls also allegedly reveal that people connect the development of relations between the United States and the Soviet Union to successfully resolving their critical economic problems.[85]

Public opinion, however, reveals "certain fluctuations," according to this study, especially as when Americans felt deceived because they believed the Soviet Union had one-sided advantages from détente and the United States received less than they expected, especially in the economic area. More "sober, realistic" people believe in the inevitability of the existence of the Socialist commonwealth, and its further strengthening. But by a narrow margin (43 percent versus 40 percent) Americans rejected Carter's proposal, introduced in the 1976 election campaign, to cut defense spending $5 to $7 billion a year, and 61 percent said that arms spending should be significantly more in America than in any other country, even if this were to mean an increase in the defense budget. In 1972-74 there was reduced support for the United States as world leader, including its arms role. Recently, however, under the influence of "reactionary propaganda," many Americans say that the United States should start up the arms race again. The Soviet authors observe that these figures must hearten the supporters of increased U.S. military expenditures. Indications are contradictory, and it would be premature, in the Soviet view, to speak about a growth of confidence in military power supposedly taking place in the United States, although in principle such a tendency is possible, reflecting fluctuations among some Americans today.[86]

American public opinion, however, does not support U.S. military intervention abroad or acts that would lead to this eventuality. The U.S. public did not support assistance to antigovernment groups in Angola, for example. American public opinion, though fluctuating, was broadly realistic. Ninety-six percent of the U.S. public supported the achievement of agreement with the Soviet Union to "put an end to all war."[87]

Public opinion is said to be under the rightist influence of the official government course and mass media propaganda. The tendencies noted above are also reflected in mass outlooks. Soviet specialists on the United States consider that U.S. public opinion is more likely to react to foreign policy in terms of propagandistic stereotypes than on other issues.[88]

The policy implications gleaned from Soviet analysis of the domestic scene are not clear, but they do not suggest lack of will in the American populace. The concern about the Soviet threat is counterbalanced by an unwillingness to be drawn into Vietnam-type situations. Direct involvement of Soviet troops, such as occurred in Afghanistan and might occur in other areas, might be a different matter. Therefore, it can come as no surprise to the Soviets that the Afghan move has resulted in much greater American domestic support for increased defense spending. Even before this occurred, Soviet public opinion analysts had to conclude that the impact of greater Soviet defense spending and strengthening of their armed forces were having a negative effect on the United States. This was particularly the case when Soviet analysis itself implied the tenuous support for détente in the United States and the strong anti-Soviet feeling that existed just below the surface of public attitudes. There was also the possibility of Soviet conduct helping to shift administration, congressional, and public attitudes very sharply to the right; it was somewhat tendentious to blame this on right-wing propaganda and simple propagandistic stereotypes. In this and other areas Soviet foreign policy is, of course, affected by international concerns of its own beyond the purview of this chapter[89] and by considerations having little to do directly with American policies or perceptions. The public record, however, would seem to indicate concern, even fear, about a process that their own experience and tools of anlaysis do not always equip them to understand. It would also suggest some reasons for caution in a Soviet foreign policy "forward strategy."

CONCLUSION

The Soviet Union finds the United States a formidable antagonist, whatever its policies, simply because of its inherent strengths, and the Soviets display a strong mixture of respect and fear. U.S. "public ideology," innovations in science and technology, events of cultural life, styles, and so forth are all potential U.S. weapons. "Sociological propaganda" combines a "dose of fresh and valuable information" with "noisy claims that the US is a model for emulation."[90] Aspects of this model include multinational corporations, professional organizations of managers, and the like.

Comments like the above reveal a Soviet belief that the Soviet Union cannot match these U.S. "trumps" and would find it difficult to maintain the pace of competition under circumstances where such trumps would dominate, a commercial world where Soviet military power would be largely irrelevant. As William McCagg has observed, peace in the Western sense was not attainable after World War II under any circumstances and was unacceptable to the Soviet regime. The Western powers could "afford a *laissez faire peace.* They were economically the strongest and richest countries in the world. They had populations long accustomed to modern urban life, domestic procedures, and rule by law."[91] The Western powers had no border problems and left their frontiers open because their populations would not rise against them. Moscow had no such assurances. It was not competitive in free markets. It did have border problems and neighbors who were by tradition unfriendly. Stalin's talk of peace did not mean the "grandeur of world-wide social and economic integration" to which Americans aspired but, at most, "a continued effort at building bridges across the profound national cleavages in a divided world—institutionalization of conflicts, one might call it."[92] Stalin called his objective "peaceful cooperation," something more than "just coexistence" but decidedly less than laissez faire.

Vojtech Mastny, in his seminal *Russia's Road to the Cold War*, notes that Averell Harriman was disturbed by a country like the Soviet Union that expands under the guise of security, for it then becomes difficult to draw a line. If the Soviet Union can penetrate a neighbor for security reasons, penetration of the next immediate neighbors becomes equally logical.[93] Litvinov, Mastny records, had warned that Soviet security needs had grown because the West had not opposed them in the Balkans and Eastern Europe and, after the Soviets were in strength there, it was "too late to complain." Western complaints only "aroused suspicion."[94]

The Soviet Union said that it sent a "limited military contingent" into Afghanistan because of unlimited support supposedly given to Muslim insurgents by U.S. circles and the Peking leadership. This was described as a threat to the southern border of the Soviet Union. Even though the United States and China had not *in fact* provided such assistance on a large scale, given the beleaguered tate of the Soviet Afghan client, they might eventually have done so, and the

Soviet Union lashed out against a potential threat, resulting in the statement made by President Carter at the beginning of this chapter.[95]

To Brezhnev, U.S. policy revealed the unreliability of the United States. The partial grain embargo and the freezing of SALT negotiations meant that Washington "was again speaking in the language of the cold war." The United States showed itself an "absolutely unreliable partner" in interstate ties. A state with a leadership "prompted by some whim, caprice or emotional outbursts," or by considerations of "narrowly understood immediate advantage" is "capable at any moment of violating its international obligations, and canceling treaties and oil agreements signed by it."[96]

Miles Kahler, in comparing the current world climate to the pre-World War I situation, asks whether the Soviet Union displays that combination of "insecurity and confidence in its power" that characterized pre-1914 Germany. If so, this is doubly dangerous when Soviet-American competition is superimposed on new elements of multipolarity in the present international scene, and confused with local quarrels, as in 1914.

For the Soviet Union, Kahler notes, one combines a relative military apogee with growing economic and social difficulties, especially the nationalities issue, which might provide opportunities for meddling by China or other states. This could provide a basis for a stridently aggressive foreign policy.[97]

Kahler suggests four rules to apply to the current scene from the 1914 analogy. First, he asks for a reexamination of an adversary's intentions and the sources of its behavior. The Soviet Union does not seek war and is concerned about the playing of the China card. Misplaced notions of geopolitical drive or Hitlerian analogies should be avoided in analyzing Soviet foreign policy actions. Second, he says that an opponent's survival may save one's life. Clearly, a self-confident, expansionist state is dangerous, but so is a world of great powers that sense themselves in decline but increase their military strength. Such states may be even more prone to crises and conflict. Third, he contends that "bargaining over influence may be more advantageous than spurring competition." Instead of indiscriminate U.S. counterintervention, Kahler cautions, the United States might indicate which types of Soviet influence in which countries are objectionable. Fourth, he expresses concern about growing too comfortable with crisis management because, as the number of postwar crises surmounted rises, so does a potential for unwarranted complacency when crisis situations are likely to appear in widely separated areas.[98]

Litvinov's concern about tardy Western warnings and Harriman's apprehension about the implications of grandiose Soviet security needs are applicable to the present scene, but so are Kahler's. One must make explicit to the Soviet leaders what NATO and U.S. interests are and see to the cohesion of Western Europe and the United States, both externally and internally. The Soviets have responded to this, and indications are that they will do so again. This, however, must be done in a way that responds to the dangers inherent in the peculiar

Soviet combination of apparent confidence (with its military power at its highest point in relation to others) and a growing sense of insecurity brought on by both its internal problems and responses of others to its actions.

NOTES

1. *The President's State of the Union Address to the Second Session of the 96th Congress.* Office of the White House Press Secretary, The White House, January 23, 1980, p. 3.

2. Quoted in Joseph C. Harsch, "How the Kremlin Misread the Times," *Christian Science Monitor*, February 8, 1980; and "As Superpowers Scratch for Support," *U.S. News and World Report* 77, no. 6 (February 18, 1980).

3. Joseph Joffe, "Afghanistan Rouses West Europe out of Long Era of Peace," *Christian Science Monitor*, January 16, 1980; John Vinocur, "NATO Warns Soviet Invasion of Poland Would End Détente," *New York Times*, December 13, 1980; Tad Szulc, "Poland and Berlin," *New Republic*, 184 (January 3 and 10, 1981): 11, 12.

4. David J. Finely, *Some Aspects of Conventional Military Capability in Soviet Foreign Relations*, ACIS Working Paper, no. 20 (Los Angeles: Center for International and Strategic Affairs, University of California, Los Angeles, February 1980), pp. 14, 16, 23, 24. For a more detailed balance sheet on the military balance in Central and Southern Europe see International Institute for Strategic Studies, *The Military Balance 1979-80*, (London: International Institute for Strategic Studies, 1979), pp. 108-12.

5. Uwe Nerlich, "Soviet-American Bilateralism: Constraint on Soviet Behavior?," in *The Political Implications of Soviet Military Power*, ed. Lawrence Whetton (New York: Crane, Russak, 1977), p. 146; Peter H. Vigor, "Military Options Open to the Warsaw Pact," in *Détente and Soviet Military Strategy*, Tenth Annual Soviet Affairs Symposium, 1976-1977, U.S. Army Institute for Advanced Russian and East European Studies, (Garmisch, West Germany, 1977), p. 35; Roger Hamburg, "Low Intensity Conflict: The Soviet Responses," in *U.S. Policy and Low-Intensity Conflict*, ed. Sam C. Sarkesian and William L. Scully (New Brunswick, N.J.: Transaction Books, 1981).

6. Vaclav Regner, "For Military Detente," International Affairs (Moscow), no. 7 (July 1979), p. 85.

7. Marshall is quoted with approval in S. H. Sankoyev, "Europe After the Helsinki Conference," ibid., p. 73.

8. Walter Hanisch, "Long Term Programme of Action," ibid., p. 77; Karl Mottola, "Norms and Conflicts in Detente," paper presented at the Moscow IPSA Congress of August 12-18, 1979, p. 3; Stephen J. Flanagan, "The CSCE and the Development of Detente," in *European Security: Prospects for the 1980's*, ed. Derek Leebaert (Lexington, Mass.: Lexington Books, 1978), pp. 193, 194, 197-201.

9. Cort Dennis Blacker, "The Soviet Perception of European Security," ibid., pp. 137-43.

10. D. Vladimirsky, "NATO: real'nosti epokhi (k 30-letiiu severnoatlanticheskogo bloka)," *Mivovaia Ekonomika i Mezhdunarodnaia Otnosheniia (MEMO)*, 1979, no. 5, pp. 56, 57, 64.

11. Ibid., pp. 58-61.

12. David K. Willis, "Soviets Hope Public Opinion Is NATO's Achilles Heel. Russia Tries New Tacks to Block Nuclear Missiles in Europe," *Christian Science Monitor*, December 14, 1979.

13. Marshal of the Soviet Union D. Ustinov, "Military Detente is a Command of the Times," *Pravda*, October 25, 1979, pp. 4-5, translated in *Current Digest of the Soviet Press (CDSP)* 31, no. 42 (November 14, 1979): 2.

14. Ibid., p. 4; Jonathan Powell, "The New Voice of the Kremlin," *Observer* (London), November 12, 1978, p. 16; G. Apalin, "Peking, the West and Detente," *International Affairs* (Moscow), 1979, (February), p. 53; V. Borisov, "Vneshne politichesky kurs Pekina," *MEMO*, 1978, no. 8, p. 20; William G. Hyland, "The Sino-Soviet Conflict: A Search for a New Strategy," in *Asian Security in the 1980's: Problems and Policies for a Time of Transition*, ed. Richard H. Solomon, (Santa Monica, Cal.: RAND Corporation, 1979), p. 50.

15. Hyland, "The Sino-Soviet Conflict," p. 40.

16. Blacker, "The Soviet Perception," p. 150; Ustinov, "Military Detente," p. 42; Jane M. O. Sharp, "Is European Security Negotiable?," in *European Security*, ed. Leebaert, pp. 226-67.

17. A. L. Valentinov, "Political Detente Must Be Complemented with Military Detente," in *Europe and Detente*, ed. G. A. Ponomarev, (Moscow: Progress Publishers, 1978), pp. 69, 71.

18. Peter Vigor, "Soviet Military Negotiations" in *The Soviet Union as a Negotiator*, Ninth Annual Soviet Affairs Symposium 1974-75, U.S. Army Institute of Advanced Russian and East European Studies, (Garmisch, West Germany, 1975), p. 24.

19. O. Khlestov, "Mutual Force Reductions in Europe," (reprinted from *MEMO*, 1974, no. 6) in *Survival* 16 (November-December 1974), p. 294.

20. Yu. Kostko, *MEMO*, no. 6, 1973, quoted in C. G. Jacobsen, *SALT; MBFR: Soviet Perspectives on Security and Arms Negotiations.* (Cambridge, Mass.: Harvard University Center for International Affairs, 1973), p. 46.

21. Ibid., pp. 46-47.

22. Ibid., pp. 47-48.

23. "A. A. Gromyko's Press Conference in Bonn," *Pravda* and *Izvestiia*, November 25, 1979, translated in *CDSP*, 31, no. 47 (December 17, 1979): 2, 3.

24. Ustinov, "Military Detente,"; see also Raymond L. Garthoff, "The TNF Tangle," *Foreign Policy* no. 41 (Winter 1980-81), p. 88.

25. John Lehman, "Soviet Policy in Mutual and Balanced Force Reductions: Finlandization Denied" in *Soviet Policy Toward Western Europe*, ed. George Ginsburgs and Alvin Rubinstein, (New York: Praeger, 1978), pp. 198-99. See also Mikolai Portugalov, "The Lion's Share," *Literaturnaya Gazeta*, May 14, 1980, translated in *CDSP* 32, no. 19 (June 11, 1980): 2, 3.

26. Stanley Riveles, "Soviet Perspectives on Arms Control," paper presented at the biennial conference of the Section on Military Studies, International Studies Association, Pittsburgh, Pennsylvania, October 1979, pp. 3, 4.

27. Blacker, "The Soviet Perception," pp. 151-52.

28. Ibid.; C. G. Jacobsen, "Moscow and the Northern Rim," unpublished paper presented at the Annual Meeting of the American Association for the Advancement of Slavic Studies, Washington, D.C., October 1977, pp. 9, 10, 12, 24; A. Petrov, "Violating the Rules of Good-Neighborliness," *Pravda*, February 19, 1980, translated in *CDSP* 32, no. 7 (March 19, 1980): 6.

29. Walter Laqueur, "Europe: The Spectre of Finlandization," *Commentary*, no. 6 (December 1977): 37. See also George Ginsburgs, "Finlandization: Soviet Strategy or Geopolitical Footnote?" in *Soviet Policy Toward Western Europe*, ed. Ginsburgs and Rubinstein, p. 5.

30. G. Starushenko, "Uncommitted Countries: Allies in the Struggle for Peace," *International Affairs* (Moscow), no. 4, 1964, p. 94, cited in George Ginsburgs, "Neutralism à la Russe," in *Soviet Policy Toward Western Europe*, ed. Ginsburgs and Rubinstein, p. 21.

31. Ibid.

32. Angela Stent Yergin, "Soviet-West German Relations: Finlandization or Normalization?," in *Soviet Policy Toward Western Europe*, ed. Ginsburgs and Rubinstein, p. 103-28.

33. Jacobsen, "Moscow and the Northern Rim," pp. 4-5, appendix.

34. Legvold, "Finlandization and Franco-Soviet Relations," pp. 96-97.

35. George Maude, "Has Finland Been Finlandized?," in *Soviet Policy Toward Western Europe*, ed. Ginsburgs and Rubinstein, pp. 48, 50-51.

36. Ibid., pp. 54-62.

37. Blacker, "The Soviet Perception," pp. 153-54.

38. A. F. Gorelava and U. P. Davydov, "United States and the Left in Europe," *SShA: Ekonomika, Politika, Ideologica*, no. 2 (February 1978), pp. 3, 4; translated in *Joint Publications Research Service (JPRS)* 70747 (March 8, 1978), pp. 1-5.

39. Gorelova and Davydov, "United States and the Left," pp. 6, 8.

40. Ginsburgs and Rubinstein, *Soviet Policy Toward Western Europe*, pp. 9-10.

41. Robert H. Legvold, "Four Policy Perspectives: The Soviet Union and Western Europe," Department of State Project, Russian Research Center, Harvard University, January 30, 1976, pp. 86, 87, 88.

42. Soviet comments are cited in Joan Barth Urban, "Contemporary Soviet Perspectives on Revolution in the West," *Orbis* 19, no. 4 (1976): 1375, 1378, 1381. Urban notes that Soviet policy at the time was split on the desirability of a Communist seizure of power in Portugal versus the possible adverse consequences within Portugal and elsewhere of such a development.

43. Cited in Charles Gati, "The Europeanization of Communism," *Foreign Affairs* 55, no. 3 (1977): 541-42.

44. Cited in Leonard Schapiro, "The Soviet Union and Eurocommunism," *Conflict Studies*, no. 99 (September 1978); pp. 1, 12. See also "Contrary to the Interests of Peace and Socialism in Europe," concerning the book, *Eurocommunism and the State* by Santiago Carrillo, General Secretary of the Communist Party of Spain, *New Times*, no. 26 (June 1977), pp. 11-12; and J. W. Friend, "The Roots of Autonomy in West European Communism," *Problems of Communism* 29, no. 5 (1980): 40.

45. Ibid., p. 39.

46. John C. Campbell, "Eurocommunism: Policy Questions for the West," in *Eurocommunism and Detente*, ed. Rudolf L. Tökés, (New York: New York University Press, 1978), p. 545.

47. John P. Hardt and Ronda A. Bresnick, "Brezhnev's European Economic Policy," in *Soviet Policy Toward Western Europe*, ed. Ginsburgs and Rubinstein, p. 201. See also Yu. P. Davydov, "Razriadka, SShA i Zapadnaia Evropa," in *SShA*, (March 1979), p. 27.

48. Davydov, "Rozriadka," p. 28.

49. On European disagreement with the United States on the Carter administration's policies, the Soviet move into Afghanistan, and general doubts about American foreign policy past and present, see Louis Wiznitzer, "Paris, Bonn Worry about US 'Excesses'," *Christian Science Monitor*, February 12, 1980; and Joseph Joffe, "Germans Swing on Tight Rope Between East and West," *Christian Science Monitor*, February 6, 1980.

50. Philip Hanson and Michael Kaser, "Soviet Economic Relations with Western Europe," in *Soviet Strategy in Europe*, ed. Richard Pipes, (New York: Crane, Russak, 1976), pp. 221-53.

51. John Pinder and Pauline Pinder, "West European Economic Relations with the Soviet Union," in ibid., pp. 269-303.

52. Davydov, "Detente," p. 30.

53. Ibid., pp. 30-31. Characterizing the situation in Afghanistan, a senior U.S. official said that "in situations like these we plunge, and we plunge in public. The Europeans take it very carefully." See David Southerland, "Carter Cools Rhetoric; Europeans Back Embargo," *Christian Science Monitor*, February 11, 1980.

54. Adam Ulam, "US-Soviet Relations: Unhappy Coexistence," in "America and the World 1978," *Foreign Affairs* 57, no. 3 (1979): 556-67, esp. 566.

55. Michael J. Deane, "Political Control and Contemporary Soviet Military Development," paper delivered to the Ninth National Conference of the American Association for the Advancement of Slavic Studies, Washington, D.C., October 1977, pp. 17-31. See also major Soviet statements implying the possible use of Soviet forces abroad in Roger Hamburg, "Low Intensity Conflict."

56. Dmitri K. Simes, "Detente, Russian Style," *Foreign Policy* no. 32 (1978), pp. 48-57.

57. N. I. Lebedev, *A New State in International Relations* (New York: Pergamon Press, 1978), pp. 221, 223. Lebedev cites the Soviet-American agreement on the prevention of nuclear war (1972), a favorite détente document for Soviet writers. Ibid., p. 219.

58. Ibid., pp. 225-26.

59. V. F. Petrovsky, *Amerikanskaia Vneshne-Politicheskaia Mysl' (American Foreign Policy Thought)* (Moscow: Mezhdunorodnye Otnosheniia, 1976).

60. Ibid., pp. 177-78.

61. Ibid., pp. 178-80.

62. Ibid., pp. 218, 282, 283.

63. Quoted in Joseph Kraft, "Letter From Moscow," *New Yorker*, October 16, 1978, pp. 116-17.

64. Arbatov, quoted in interview with Jonathan Powell, "The New Voice," p. 16.

65. Cited in V. I. Gromeka, *SShA: Nauchno-Tekhnichesky Potentsial.* (Moscow: "Mysl'," 1977), p. 241.

66. A. G. Arbatov, "Traident–diskussiia strategicheskoi programmy," *SShA*, no. 3 (1977), p. 31.

67. V. F. Petrovsky, "Silovoi Faktor v global'noi strategii SShA," *SShA* no. 5, (1979), p. 27.

68. G. A. Trofimenko, "Evoliutsiia Amerikanskoi voenno-politicheskoi mysli," in *Sovremennye Vneshnepoliticheskie Kontseptsii SShA*, ed. G. A. Trofimenko, (Moscow: Nauka, 1979), pp. 85-87.

69. Ibid., pp. 99, 101-2, 132.

70. V. V. Zhurkin, "Novye tendentsii v Amerikanskoi politike 'krizisnogo reagirovaniia' (ispol'zovanie sily v konfliktakh)," in ibid., p. 175.

71. Ibid.

72. Ibid., pp. 177-79, 198; E. G. Grigor'yev, "The US Armed Forces After the Vietnam Syndrome," *SShA*, no. 7 (July 1980), translated in *JPRS* 76507 (September 26, 1980), p. 26.

73. G. S. Khozin, "Globalnie problemy nauchno-tekhnicheskoi revoliutsii i ikh rol' v vneshei politike SShA," in ibid., p. 364. See also L. I. Sheioina, "Nevoennye faktory sily v instrumentarii vneshnei politiki SShA," in ibid., pp. 205-45. Soviet writers are also concerned about U.S. "trilateral" strategy—an attempt to create a global tripartite center of power (United States, Western Europe, Japan) based on economics and technology, with the United States playing the decisive and leading role. This would be designed to "stabilize the situation within the capitalist world." N. D. Turkatenko, "Sources and Aims of 'Trilateral' Strategy," *SShA*, no. 9 (September 1977), translated in *JPRS* 69985 (October 1977), pp. 30-31.

74. Nathan Leites, *The New Economic Togetherness: American and Soviet Reactions* (Santa Monica, Cal.: RAND Corporation, 1973); Gregory Grossman, "The Economics of Détente and American Foreign Policy," in *Defending America*, ed. James Schlesinger (New York: Basic Books, 1977), p. 67.

75. Lebedev, *A New Stage*, pp. 144-45; Daniel Yergin, "Politics and Soviet-American Trade: The Three Questions," *Foreign Affairs* 55, no. 3 (1977): 517-30; B. Pichugin, "Soviet-Western Economic Relations," *International Affairs* (Moscow), no. 8 (August 1979), pp. 17-19.

76. Hamburg, "Low Intensity Conflict"; Bruce Parrott, "Soviet Technological Progress and Western Technology Transfer to the USSR: An Analysis of Soviet Attitudes," unpublished paper, July 1978, p. v.

77. V. F. Petrovsky, *American Foreign Policy Thought*, p. 189.

78. V. V. Zhurkin, "New Tendencies," p. 180.

79. Dmitri K. Simes, "The Anti-Soviet Brigade," *Foreign Policy*, no. 37 (Winter 1979-80), pp. 28-43. For a useful study discussing "twenty principles for dealing with the Soviets" by a senior U.S. foreign security officer with two tours in Moscow, see Marshall Brement, *Organizing Ourselves to Deal with the Soviets* (Santa Monica, Cal.: RAND Corporation, 1978), p. v.

80. A. A. Gromyko, "The Foreign Policy of the Soviet Union—a Powerful Tool of Communist Party in the Struggle for Peace and Social Progress," *Novaia i Noveisha Istoriia*, no. 5 (1978), pp. 3-15, translated in *Soviet Press, Selected Translations* 79, no. 4 (April 1979): 152.

81. "O nyneshnei politike pravitel'stva SShA," *Pravda*, June 17, 1978.

82. P. T. Podlesny, "US Debate Over Detente Policy Hinders Its World Cause," *SShA*, no. 9 (September 1978), translated in *JPRS* 72235 (November 15, 1979), p. 69; R. B. Tumkovsky, "The Soviet-American Strategic Arms Limitation Talks," *Problemy Istorii*, no. 3 (March 1979), pp. 70-86, translated in *CDSP* 31, no. 29, (August 15, 1979): 7-8; Roger Hamburg, "The Carter Administration, Human Rights and the Soviet Union," paper delivered at the Annual Meeting of the International Studies Association, Washington, D.C., February 22-26, 1978, p. 16.

83. V. S. Anichkina, "Struggle in Congress on Soviet-American Relations," *SShA*, no. 6 (June 1974), translated in *JPRS* 62492, (July 17, 1974), p. 84.

84. Yu. A. Ivanov, "Congress: Labyrinths of Power and Foreign Policy Making," *SShA*, no. 6, (June 1978), translated in *JPRS* 71548 (July 22, 1978), pp. 102, 109; R. G. Tumkovsky, "Soviet-American Talks," pp. 7-8; see also Roger Hamburg, "The Carter Administration," p. 16.

85. I. A. Ivanian and M. M. Petrovskaia, "Obshchestvenoe Mnenie i vneshnaia Politika SShA," in *Amerikanskoe Obschestvennoe Mnenie i Politika*, ed. Iu. A. Zamoshkin, (Moscow: Nauka, 1978), pp. 236-38.

86. Ibid., pp. 240-43.

87. Ibid., pp. 244-46.

88. Ibid., p. 247.

89. Breslauer argues that many Soviet dissidents agree that a return to confrontation with the United States, U.S. ultimatums to the USSR, or a U.S.-Chinese alliance would "almost certainly trigger an isolationist, siege mentality and a right-wing reaction." George W. Breslauer, *Five Images of the Soviet Future: A Critical Review and Synthesis, Policy Papers in International Studies* (Berkeley: Institute of International Studies, University of California, 1978), p. 5.

90. I. L. Sheidina, "Non-Military Factors," p. 242.

91. William O. McCagg, Jr., *Stalin Embattled 1943-1948* (Detroit, Mich.: Wayne State University Press, 1978), p. 258.

92. Ibid.

93. W. Averell Harriman, quoted in Vojtech Mastny, *Russia's Road to the Cold War* (New York: Columbia University Press, 1979), pp. 112-13.

94. Ibid., p. 283. Litvinov made the comments in an interview with Edgar Snow.

95. A. Petrov, "K sobytiiam v Afghanistane," *Pravda*, December 31, 1979.

96. "Excerpts from Brezhnev Statement Answering a Question on World Situation," *New York Times*, January 12, 1980.

97. Miles Kahler, "Rumors of War: The 1914 Analogy," *Foreign Affairs* 58, no. 2 (1979-80): 377-89.

98. Ibid., pp. 394-96.

11

THE SOVIET THREAT AND THE SECURITY OF JAPAN

Hiroshi Kimura

SUDDEN AWAKENING OF CONCERN
OVER THE SOVIET THREAT

A specter is haunting Japan—the Soviet threat. It is hard for anyone in present-day Japan to deny the presence, or at least the prevailing influence, of this threat. Just as the movie *Shogun* stimulated wide interest and mass media coverage of things Japanese in the United States, so has the subject of the Soviets mesmerized and monopolized the Japanese press and its audience in recent years. The author is able to trace briefly this recent awakening of Japanese concern for the maintenance of national security and peace with their northern neighbor from personal experience in publishing books on Soviet affairs.

Twenty years ago, in 1962, a Japanese translation of the late Philip M. Mosely's masterpiece, *The Kremlin and World Politics*, failed to sell the first printing of 1,000 copies and the publishing house itself went broke. A second translation of an English book, *Marxism in the Modern World* edited by Milorad M. Drachkovitch, sold 3,000 copies in 1966. At that time one publisher stated that the Japanese were not as interested in Soviet and Communist affairs as were Americans and Europeans, and that books dealing with these subjects did not find a commercial market in Japan. Around the end of the 1970s, however, a phenomenal change of outlook appeared when this author released a hastily assembled report on the Soviet incursion into Afghanistan, entitled *The U.S.S.R. and the Russians* (1980). Not only were the first 10,000 copies promptly sold but the book is currently in its sixth printing and still finds eager readers. Even more revealing is the fact that the book has been eclipsed by several other best-selling works such as Hiroomi Kurisu's *The Soviet Threat* (1980) and Naoki Komuro's *The Decline of the Soviet Empire* (1980), which have sold 50,000 and 320,000 copies, respectively! Added to this is the interest sparked by the profusion of major newspaper and magazine articles dealing with the subject of the Soviet threat.

In examining this sudden burst of interest in Russian affairs, it is important to understand that unlike the American spark of curiosity ignited by the movie *Shogun*, the Japanese interest has its roots in the people's fear that Japan can no longer afford to be indifferent and conciliatory toward the Soviet Union. Clearly, the Japanese have begun to link the subjects of national security and the threat of the Soviet Union, although views vary as to the extent to which these are related. To give only a few illustrations of the opinions being voiced, the daily *Asahi Shimbun* carried a 14-installment series entitled "Is the Soviet Union a Threat?" from November 28 to December 13, 1980, and the *Tokyo Shimbun* ran a similar series questioning "Is the Soviet Union a Frightful Country?" from January 1 to February 5, 1981. Needless to add, these two series drew an extensive readership and demonstrated that the subject of the Soviet threat is not merely a journalistic ploy.

Before examining the question of how the Japanese relate the Soviet threat to national security, it may be useful to survey some of the background incidents and issues that have brought the subject so compellingly into the spotlight. First, although the fact is commonly known, it is necessary to emphasize the impact that recent changes in the world power balance have had on this subject. In recent years the Japanese have watched with growing alarm the persistent, massive buildup of military might by the Soviets and have become all too aware of the parity with the United States that the USSR has achieved, especially in strategic nuclear warfare devices, as the Soviets themselves have claimed.[1] The following passage from Brezhnev's "secret speech" at Minsk on March 14, 1970, has been cited in the Japanese mass media: "At the present time, the world's single largest problem cannot be decided without our participation nor the consideration of our economic and military might."[2] From a careful study of Soviet strategic military periodicals and newspapers such as *Kommunist voorzhennykh sil* and *Krasnaia zvezda*, Kuniko Miyauchi, a professor at the Japanese National Defense College, reported that in the late 1960s the Soviet Union made a decision to convert its strategic-military orientation from an "introvert" system to an "extrovert" one.[3] Miyauchi's assertion coincided with what Western Soviet strategy watchers such as William F. Scott had observed.[4] Scott quoted the following words of the late Soviet Defense Minister Andrei A. Grechko in 1974: "At the present stage the historic function of the Soviet Armed Forces is not restricted merely to their function in defending our Motherland and the other socialist countries. . . . The Soviet state supports the national-liberation struggle and resolutely resists imperial aggression in whatever distant area of our planet it may appear."[5] This purpose was later demonstrated by the Soviet military ventures in Angola, Ethiopia, and Afghanistan.

Another factor that has fueled recent Japanese concern about the Soviet military buildup is the problem of the decline of American supremacy in the political, military, and economic spheres. The debacle in Vietnam, the decision—though not carried out—to reduce the number of U.S. ground forces stationed in Korea, the spectacle of Iran's 444-day holding of American citizens—all of these, and more, reinforced the image of a country no longer able to wield the big stick over its opponents. In addition to the events themselves, policies such as the one stated clearly in the Nixon Doctrine have urged American allies and friends to lower their expectations of American might in world affairs. The doctrine declares that "the United States will participate in the defense and development of all allies and friends, but America cannot—and will not—conceive *all* the plans, design *all* the decisions and undertake *all* the defense of the free nations of the world."[6] One can perceive that the Nixon Doctrine, in the sense cited above, has become a basic foreign policy orientation of subsequent U.S. administrations as well, although, of course, with some amendments and modifications. Thus the Japanese see that Washington has voluntarily withdrawn from being the sole protector of peace and security in the free world and has instead called for participation in the maintenance of these goals by NATO, Japan, other allies, and even China. The late Japanese prime minister Masayoshi Ohira was well aware of the change in both American capability and acceptance of responsibility, when he remarked on April 27, 1980: "The United States is not a superpower any longer. The days are gone when we were able to rely on America's deterrence."[7]

Along with having to face the indisputable dilemma of now being unable to rely assuredly upon American military supremacy, the Japanese have also been awakened by reports of the rapid buildup of Soviet military forces in the Far East. The 1980 Japanese *Defense White Paper* noted that "the Soviet Union has been striving to increase its military strength in this region [Northeast Asia]."[8] The Japanese have also learned that the *Minsk*, the second *Kiev*-class aircraft carrier, and the Backfire supersonic bombers have been deployed in the Far East. It has also been revealed that the Soviets have deployed SS-20 mobile IRBMs in the Far East,[9] the range of which can cover the entire Japanese archipelago. This means that Japan is no longer secured from the possibility of attack, except by the threat of a U.S. counterattack with strategic nuclear weapons. And closer to home is the threat of a military division of about 7,000 men equipped with 130 mm cannons, Mi-24 attack helicopters, and so forth, already deployed on the Kurile Islands of Kunashiri, Etorofu, and Shikotan. Apart from the real Soviet motivations, the psychological impact of these Soviet actions upon the Japanese people, who continue to regard these particular northern islands as an integral part of Japan, is great.

Furthermore, recent incidents, such as the landing in September 1976 of the Soviet MIG-25 fighter plane piloted by Lieutenant Victor Belenko at Hakodate Airport in Hokkaido, have shown the Japanese the fearful capability of Soviet planes to elude detection by the radar facilities of the Japanese Self-Defense Forces (SDF). Similarly, the crash of a Soviet TU-16 Badger reconnaissance attack plane into the Sea of Japan (June 1980) and the violation of territorial waters by the disabled Soviet nuclear submarine (August 1980) have unforgettably underscored in Japanese thinking the threatening nearness of the Soviet military machine.

In another area, two incidents in Soviet-Japanese relations that occurred in the same year of 1980 also sent shock waves through the nation. In the first, three fishermen from Hokkaido were arrested in January for having bribed Soviet coast guards with gifts and strategic documents relating to the northern territories in exchange for relaxed fishing restrictions. Shortly thereafter came the news of the arrest of Yukio Miyanaga, a retired major general in the Japanese SDF, and two incumbent members of the SDF for complicity in a spy ring involving the military attaché to the Soviet Embassy in Tokyo, Colonel Yuri Kozlov.

Third, the normalization of Sino-Japanese relations and the burgeoning of cooperation between the two nations ever since have further focused attention on the danger from the north. No longer considering the PRC as a potential enemy, Tokyo concluded the peace and friendship treaty in 1978, and in a reciprocal move, Beijing abrogated the 30-year Sino-Soviet treaty of friendship in which Japan was cited as a common enemy. In a complete reversal of prior policy, Beijing has not only avidly endorsed the U.S.-Japan Security Treaty but has begun to defend vigorously the need for a rapid military buildup in Japan against Soviet "hegemonism." Of course, the Japanese have not allowed the so-called China fever to last long enough to distort the actuality of dealing with the Chinese. Several breaches of contract and faith by the PRC have given the Japanese a more sober view of the economic and political risks of dealing with an unstable, unreliable country. It is just this instability and unreliability, however, that bolster the Japanese belief that China is no longer a military threat to Japan, although China watchers such as Mineo Nakajima, professor of Foreign Studies at Tokyo University, warn against Japan's becoming a prisoner of the "myth of Sino-Soviet conflict."[10] It is a fact that in February 1981, Leonid Gudoshnikov of the Institute of the Far East, attached to the Soviet Academy of Sciences, during an interview with the Japanese Kyodo News Service expressed the view that Soviet relations with China "will be improved without fail." He even added that some of his colleagues hold the view that relations may be normalized as early as the second half of the 1980s.[11] Taking this simply as another example of the familiar Soviet technique of political *ballon d'essai*, most Japanese are convinced that the Chinese would lose more than they obtain by realigning with Russia.

The last factor that has awakened the Japanese to the Soviet threat concerns Japan's economic position, which in turn influences the psychology of the

Japanese people. Japan has achieved second place in the world in terms of gross national product. Although in terms of per capita income Japan still does not rank among the top ten nations of the world, no one can deny Japan's position as a "have" nation. As for the country's perennial problem of having to seek new energy sources from abroad, the overall attitude is that Japan will succeed, even in the event of future hardships. Having successfully overcome several threatening crises in the past, the Japanese feel strongly that things will continue to work out. Even though Japan produces domestically only 1 percent of its oil needs, the government plans to reduce its dependence on imported oil from the current 75 percent of total energy supplies to about 50 percent by the year 2000, and the citizenry has cooperated admirably in helping to put these aims into practice. As an example, the MIIT (Ministry of Industry of International Trade) proudly announced in February 1981 that thanks to the efforts of the Japanese people, Japan had managed to conserve more oil in 1980 than the ministry had expected. Another noteworthy example of Japanese determination in this area is the recent action by the Hokkaido area to abandon a plan to import natural gas from Soviet Sakhalin, since efforts to switch energy sources to coal and other fuels have been quite successful.

Clearly, the Japanese are determined to maintain their economic status, both as a nation and as individuals. This determination springs from postwar memories of deprivation and excessive loss. Understandably, during that period when there was nothing to lose, Japanese people did not overly concern themselves with the security problem. In recent times, however, this situation has become a long-past memory. According to a survey conducted by the Institute of Commodity Science (Tokyo), the average Japanese family owns 710 consumer items, compared to 640 for British, 636 for French, and 627 for German families.[12] The accumulation of material goods and the wealth of the Japanese middle class have played a role in increasing the concern of the general public with the security issue.

THE DEBATE ON SECURITY

As mentioned earlier, the year 1980 marked a significant increase in the number of books and articles dealing with Japan's current and future defense needs. It is not the author's purpose to summarize these materials, but to examine how the Japanese have related the Soviet threat to Japan's security. To what extent has the recognition of the recent Soviet military buildup throughout the world affected public attitude in matters of security and contributed to changes in the nation's long-standing defense policy?

Though almost all Japanese readily recognize the rapid growth and superior quality of the Soviet military capability, there is no general consensus concerning the intentions behind the recent Soviet military buildup. The wide range of divergent opinions may be classified, for sake of convenience, into the following groups: the alarmist, the realist, and the pacifist.

Members of the alarmist group include Osamu Miyoshi, director of the Research Institute of National Security (the Japanese counterpart of the Stanford Research Institute in the United States), author of *The World Strategy of Soviet Imperialism* (1980) and coauthor of *The Day that the USSR Invades Japan* (1979);[13] Hiroomi Kurisu, former chairman of the Joint Staff Council of the SDF and author of *The Soviet Union as a Potential Enemy; How to Fight Back Against Invasion* (1980);[14] Ikutaro Shimizu, professor of Gakushuin University and author of *Japan Must Become a State; A Nuclear Choice* (1980);[15] and others. The professional careers and vociferous attitudes of some of these men give credence to their written works, some of which—as can be seen from the titles—tend toward exaggeration and sensationalism, in order to appeal to the commercial market. The views of the alarmist group can be summarized as follows: the USSR is an aggressive, expansionist state energized and guided by a Marxist-Leninist ideology and influenced by its geographical location; the increased military capability reflects the Soviet intention of expansion; the Soviet threat to the West and Japan is to be taken seriously and considered to be imminent; a Soviet invasion of Hokkaido, Japan's northernmost major territory, is most probable (Kurisu); and the Soviets would best be deterred by Japanese possession of a nuclear weapon capability (Shimizu).

The second group, the realists, is represented by scholars led by Masamich Inoki, president of the Institute of Peace and Security, (the Japanese equivalent of the London-based International Institute for Strategic Studies). According to Inoki's argument, it is unwise for Japan to base its defense policy solely on the fear of the yet unrealized dangers of the Soviet threat. His argument is best elaborated in his most recent book, *Illusion of Becoming A Military Big Power* (1981),[16] in which he voices the following contentions. First, the situation of Japan's present and future defense needs is too complicated to be analyzed from the standpoint of one particular country's military capability at one given moment. More concretely, Japan's defense policy must not be decided on the basis of the threat of Soviet military capability alone. If one says that Japan must increase its defense capability in accordance with that of the USSR, then it follows that it can be decreased commensurate with a decrease in Soviet military investments. Second, the recent Soviet buildup is, to a certain extent, to be interpreted as a political bluff. If unrealistically evaluated, it will achieve the Soviet purposes of exaggerating its power. Third, the most serious threat to Japan is the possibility that trade and economic relations with the Middle East and allied countries will be endangered by Soviet intervention in strategic sea lanes between these countries. Fourth, cooperation with the United States by annually raising the Japanese defense budget is essential, in order to demonstrate Japan's determination to fulfill its defense responsibility as a member of the Western liberal community. Finally, Japan must increase its "denial capability"—

defense capability in the case of small-scale, limited military aggression to make such aggression costly and to prevent invasion of Japan from easily becoming a *fait accompli*—while waiting for the U.S. forces to come to Japan's aid in the case of large-scale aggression. This capability, which should be developed in close cooperation with the United States, does not necessarily call for the revision of the Japanese constitution or the development of Japanese nuclear weapons.

Another realist, Yonosuke Nagai, professor at the Tokyo University of Technology, who agrees basically with Inoki's group on many points, offers a different slant to the realist position. Opposing the opinions of Inoki's group (including the present author, who contends that the recent deterioration of Soviet-Japanese relations must run its course), Nagai feels that, on the contrary, Japan should work actively toward closer ties with Russia.[17] His views can be summarized as follows: from the standpoint of military capability, there is no chance for Japan to win a war against the Soviet Union; consequently, it stands to reason that Japan's defense depends upon her position to influence the intentions of the USSR; in order to accomplish this, Japan must work both toward a deterrence capability through the Japan-U.S. Security Treaty and close cooperation with the West, and toward building a network of mutually beneficial relations with the USSR through trade, the joint development of Siberia, and other forms of economic cooperation. The present author questions how, in practical terms, these two apparently incompatible strategies can be realized simultaneously. It would seem that a quick look at the shifting balances of power among the nations, and incidents such as the Soviet incursion into Afghanistan and the consequent U.S. countermeasures, would provide convincing evidence of the near impossibility of effecting such measures.

Nagai also draws attention to what he calls the "asymmetries of interests" between Japan and the USSR. He explains that, as a global power, the Soviet Union must concern itself with almost all of the problems and changes taking place around the world—an effort that of course serves to prevent its sole attention to Japan. In contrast, however, as a "middle power" Japan needs to concentrate her efforts only on her own problems. Removed from active involvement in the problems of other countries, Japan has the advantage of being able to deal with powers as influential as the USSR without damaging its relations elsewhere.

The third group, the pacifists, draws its members from the Japanese Association on Peace Studies, in which professors Yoshikazu Sakamoto, Yoshiharu Seki, and Takehiko Kamo are leading spokesmen and writers for such monthly and weekly magazines as *Sekai* and the *Asahi Journal*. This group is noted for its tendency to underestimate the significant role played by military policy and power in international politics, while evaluating the changes that have been taking place in recent decades—such as the shift from the cold-war philosophy to détente, the rising trend of economic interdependence, the growth of transnational organizations, and so forth—in terms of their effect on Japanese policies.

Kamo, for instance, stresses the increasing difficulty in translating what he calls "power potential" (military, wealth, and so on) into actual spheres of influence (diplomatic concerns, negotiations, conflict solving, and the like).[18] Sakamoto points out the need for what he calls "asymmetrical defense"—namely, a policy of responding to or coping with the great powers without substantially raising Japanese military capacity. He feels that Japan should instead, pursue an "asymmetrical," different method, which should be carried out by nonmilitary means and/or guerrilla warfare. Such a defense policy, he argues, would not be interpreted by other powers as militaristic and dangerous, or place undue pressures on the country itself.[19]

Like most observers of the USSR, the author is fully aware of the expanding military capability of the Soviets on a global scale and especially in the areas surrounding Japan.[20] It is one thing, however, to recognize this increasing capability as a fact and quite another to interpret it as an aggressive and threatening intention to mount an attack. As Thomas Wolf so aptly contends, no systematic methodologies for divining Soviet military intentions have been invented.[21] Even the top Soviet decision makers themselves are probably not in a position to define their intentions concretely, particularly because Soviet policies are so often scrapped or altered according to changes in world geopolitical and domestic circumstances. Intentions are contingent upon many circumstances that no leadership can fully foresee. Thus, the answer to the question "Will the Soviet Union invade Japan?" is an indecisive yes or no or "It depends."

Very few things in this world warrant an absolute answer and this is especially true where highly fluid international politics is concerned. All nations, including the Soviet Union, are influenced by the moves of other countries and ever-changing circumstances that dictate foreign policy. The USSR, however, is frequently considered to be a nation that bases its external policies and conduct in foreign affairs methodically and systematically on Marxist-Leninist principles. Nevertheless, history and experience have demonstrated that the Soviet Union is more situation-oriented and opportunistic in deciding its external policies and behaviors than is generally supposed. The Soviet modus operandi is to advance into areas where there is little or no resistance and to withdraw from areas where there is. The term "amoebic diplomacy" has been given to this approach. Some observers have labeled the Russians "hotel thieves" for their propensity to take advantage of what is not guarded.[22]

It seems, therefore, that unless certain favorable circumstances develop, the Soviets are unlikely to move militarily into Japan. "Favorable circumstances" means such developments as the establishment of a Socialist or Communist-oriented government, the abolition of the Japan-U.S. security treaty, the concluding of a Japanese-Soviet treaty of friendship, amity, and cooperation that includes a clause ensuring mutual security consultation and cooperation in times of emergency—such a clause was in fact proposed in the Soviet draft of the Treaty of Good Neighborliness and Cooperation between the USSR and Japan—

and the loss of capable leadership in the event of national crisis. In short, what the Soviets are currently contemplating is, in this author's view, not a military invasion of Japan but rather a scheme of measures that would work to "Finlandize" Japan, or enable them to occupy the country without inflicting hardships on its industrial capacities and gradually to influence it militarily in the process.

The views briefly examined above represent, for the most part, the attitude of Japanese intellectuals and influential spokesmen. Although their presentation and support of these views exert a significant influence on the general public and in certain government sectors, they still do not constitute any specific official policy concerning Japan and the security issue.

It is necessary, then, to try to pinpoint how the present Japanese government regards the security issue. One interesting recent event comes to mind in this examination of leaders' attitudes. On January 22, 1980 late Prime Minister Ohira made an inept and potentially detrimental statement to the effect that the Soviet Union is a defensive nation, a statement that unleashed a rash of criticism both at home and abroad.[23] In amending his remarks later at a meeting of the Budget Committee in the House of Representatives on February 1, 1980, Ohira explained, "It is an objective fact that the Soviet Union has been buttressing and greatly developing its military capacity in the northern islands and in other areas. Thus I cannot help but regard the Soviet troops there as a *potential* threat to Japan"[24] (emphasis added). Once again, the flames were fanned, as this was the first time in the postwar history of Japan that a Japanese prime minister had officially in the Diet called the Soviet forces a threat to Japan. When asked by the Committee to define more explicitly what he meant by a "potential threat," Ohira replied: "It is not erroneous to interpret the Soviet military capability as a potential danger to this country. The question is whether or not the Soviet initiatives will be exercised."[25] Whereas Ohira had previously understated his views on possibly explosive or controversial issues involving Japanese security and the Soviet Union's activities in this regard, it was apparent that in the few months before his death he had experienced a change of mind. One high official, Kichizo Hosoda, then director of the Defense Agency, was particularly encouraged by this shift in Ohira's public stance, as he had personally regarded the Soviet armed forces a *"serious"* threat to Japan[26] (emphasis added), although he was later forced to revise his statement by saying that what he really meant was not so different from the view that was expressed by Prime Minister Ohira.[27] Ohira's statements were carried even further in the official *Defense White Paper* published in August 1980, very soon after Ohira's death. The paper states: "The phenomenal buildup and activities of the Soviet Far Eastern forces are now affecting the military balance between the United States and the Soviet Union in the Western Pacific, and they are regarded as an *increasing* potential threat to the security of Japan"[28] (emphasis added).

The most recent authoritative government view of the Soviet threat was expressed by the incumbent prime minister, Z. Suzuki, in a Diet session held on

January 30, 1981. Having stated the general principle that "a threat becomes actual when the capability is connected with the intention of invasion," Suzuki pointed out that he does not feel that Japan is vulnerable to an imminent Soviet threat. He went on to say, however, that "there is every need to take into consideration the capability of Soviet military power around Japan, since the situation may undergo change."[29] Two conflicting interpretations of this statement by the top Japanese decision maker have been made. Some officials feel that the prime minister dismissed the possibility of a Soviet threat,[30] while others contend that the statement introduces the need for increased awareness and appropriate measures of vigilance to be taken in the event of such a threat.[31]

CHANGED ATMOSPHERE OR POLICIES?

As is seen from the brief review of several of the major shifts in Japanese attitudes and responses toward the security issue, many persons are acutely cognizant of the need to assess correctly some of the recent demonstrations of Soviet military strength in certain strategic areas of the world. The Soviet invasion of Afghanistan was one particularly shocking event that helped to accelerate the attitude of anxiety and unabated concern among the general populace. It is important to mention here, however, that these changing perceptions represent an *atmosphere* of enlightened awareness, rather than a distinctive body of interpretations that require definite action. This hesitation to act or simply to define terms is in agreement with the Japanese art of avoiding, as much as possible, active participation in logically based debates leading to firm conclusions.

The Japanese political climate is a register of moods, which exerts its own significant pressures on decision making. This so-called *funiki-zukuri*—or creation of a mood or atmosphere—is the force behind political maneuvering and the *modus operandi* by which Japanese leaders operate to achieve their goals. One apt illustration of this unique Japanese approach to politics is the process that led to the conclusion of the Sino-Japanese peace treaty. Although almost six years went by before the document was finally signed, most Japanese had been leaning favorably toward the restoration of Sino-Japanese relations and had reached a unanimous positive decision by the time the Fukuda administration had dispatched the negotiating delegation to Beijing in 1978. All of the political parties eventually unanimously supported the treaty. It did not seem to disturb anyone that the treaty-making process had been stretched out over such a long period or that most of the deliberations had taken place quietly and, in most cases, without the favor of extended and heated debate involving public opinion. The atmosphere was right and, therefore, so was the decision.

It must also not be overlooked that, despite Japanese persistence in delaying decision making until the proper atmosphere is in place, certain concrete measures have been taken in recent years to define and fortify Japan's position among her Pacific neighbors. For one thing, the treaty of peace and friendship represented a decisive effort on Japan's part to abandon its long-standing azimuthal diplomacy by which it had hoped to keep its two powerful Communist neighbors equidistant. Although then Prime Minister Takeo Fukuda had stated that "Japan's China policy is not connected with her Soviet policy,"[32] the words of Sunao Sonoda, then foreign minister, rang closer to the truth when he said, "Japan's decision to conclude the peace treaty with the PRC reveals its acceptance of and agreement with the U.S. global policy."[33] By this statement Sonoda meant that Japan was simply in no position to resist cooperation with the United States in its global strategies concerning China.

The Japanese government has also exerted pressures on the Soviet Union, in cooperation with the United States, by participating actively in the U.S. economic sanctions against the Soviet move into Afghanistan, by joining in the boycott of the Moscow Olympic Games, and by freezing official personal and cultural exchanges between the two countries.[34] The later decision led to the rejection of the planned visit of Soviet Foreign Minister Andrei Gromyko to Tokyo, a painful decision because of the great hope on the Japanese side that the unresolved territorial question between the two countries could be negotiated and possibly settled in a peace treaty of some kind. Similarly, a planned meeting with Alexander Polyansky, Soviet ambassador to Japan, and the scheduled visit to Tokyo of members of the Supreme Soviet for the purpose of exchanging views with members of both houses of the Japanese Diet, was cancelled. In the economic area, Japan's participation in the U.S. trade embargo against the USSR caused it to drop suddenly from second to fifth position among Western countries in terms of trade activities with the USSR in 1980. To express in more concrete terms its support of President Carter's embargo of U.S. grain sales to the USSR, the Japanese Ministry of Agriculture purchased an additional 1 million tons of wheat and corn in 1980. And in one extreme burst of Japanese support for the American cause, a group of professors advocated that Japan purchase the entire 17 million tons of embargoed grain!

Needless to say, Japan is dependent on trade and economic relations with the USSR because of its dire need of resources and accessible markets for its goods. Breakdowns in economic cooperation, such as those mentioned above, upset to a tremendous degree the delicate economic machinery that keeps the nation solvent. On the one hand, however, there is the fact that Japan's relationship with the United States far outweighs in importance that with the USSR. Among the reasons for this are the following: the all-important atmosphere of friendly relations between the countries is highly prized; in terms of military capability, Japan is almost totally dependent upon U.S. defense measures and support; and Japan relies on the U.S. presence in the Middle East as a deterrent to any moves by unfriendly nations to cut off oil supplies to the East.

Another evidence of recent moves to define Japan's position in relation to the Soviet Union can be seen in the strong opinions expressed by Prime

Minister Suzuki, as compared to those of his predecessors. In his administrative policy speech made in the Diet on January 26, 1981 the prime minister unreservedly stated:

> With regard to the Soviet Union, the [Japanese] Government will continue to discourage Soviet military interference in Afghanistan and the military buildup in the northern territories. We will continue to pursue the conclusion of a peace treaty accompanied by a resolution of the northern territorial question with the Soviet Union. We hope that the Soviet Union will show its sincere intentions toward Japan by responding to this concrete sign of mutual cooperation.[35]

The important points to notice in these remarks are that, first, the military and security question has been given greater priority than the territorial question, and second, the Afghanistan problem, which is mentioned first, is accorded greater importance than Japanese problems vis-à-vis the Soviets. In short, the withdrawal of Soviet military forces from Afghanistan is regarded by Suzuki not simply as a precondition to improve Japan-Soviet bilateral relations but as the most important condition to be met—even above the territorial question. For the past 35 years Japan has been hoping to resolve the territorial issue by using it as a prerequisite for the normalization of relations between the two nations.

   In his approach to the northern territorial issue, Suzuki has clearly demonstrated a strong attitude. With Suzuki's approval, Foreign Minister Masayoshi Ito, after an eight-year interval of silence, discussed the problem officially in his speech at the United Nations on September 23, 1980. And in a public move to demonstrate his feelings, the prime minister declared February 7 Northern Territorial Day in commemoration of the day when Japan obtained Kunashiri, Etorofu, Habomai, and Shikotan islands under peaceful circumstances, as a result of friendly negotiations with the Russians and the conclusion of the Treaty of Shimoda in 1855. Suzuki has also stated his intention to make an inspection trip to the northern territories sometime in June 1981. He would thus be the first Japanese prime minister to set foot in this controversial territory. Of course, these initiatives have been bitterly criticized by the Soviets as "measures evoking artificially in the Japanese people a feeling of hostility against the U.S.S.R. and a ballyhoo around their fabrications of the Soviet threat."[36]

   In the military sphere, as well, recent Japanese administrations have demonstrated a positive attitude toward cooperating as fully as possible in Japan-U.S. defense maneuvers within the limits of domestic support. Some of the recent evidence that confirms this attitude include the following. In November 1978, the report entitled "Guideline for Japan-U.S. Defense Cooperation" was completed. Since then, meetings between high-level defense spokesmen from the United States and Japan have been held regularly to ensure mutual understanding and to exchange information. The Japanese Self-Defense Forces have participated in joint military maneuvers with U.S. forces. One especially epoch-making event was the participation for the first time of the Japanese SDF in the RIMPAC-80 Pacific Ocean naval exercises together with naval units from the United States, Canada, Australia, and New Zealand during February-March 1980. This act of cooperation, which was promoted by the late Ohira, gave the Soviets good cause to attack Ohira's "Pacific Basin Cooperation Concept"[37] as a military thrust to alienate the Soviet Union from its Pacific neighbors and, in the worst case, to form an alliance called JANZUS (alliance of Japan plus ANZUS). The Suzuki administration has already committed the SDF to participate in RIMPAC-82.[38] Japan has been moving toward sharing with the United States some of the maintenance costs of the U.S. forces stationed in Japan. In addition to bearing some of the cost of maintaining facilities and areas used by the Americans, the Japanese Government decided in 1978 to undertake the costs of reconstructing and improving the living quarters and other facilities used by these forces and to share in the labor expenses of the Japanese citizens employed on the bases.[39]

Efforts to analyze the security issue have been made in private circles as well. One such study group, headed by Masamich Inoki,[40] former president of the National Defense Academy and currently president of the Institute of Peace and Security, and authorized by Ohira, submitted an influential report in July 1980, which recommended that increased self-defense efforts be made on the Japanese side.[41] Unfortunately, the Suzuki cabinet has not—or could not—adapt the budget allocations recommended by this group. The cabinet did, however, establish the Comprehensive National Security Council,[42] a modified form of the study group's proposal to coordinate security policies through an active body of experts in the field.

Finally, it remains to consider some of the subjects related to the security issue that have long been considered taboo in postwar Japanese thinking, which are now surfacing in public discussions. The first concerns the so-called three nonnuclear principles of no possession, no manufacturing, and no introduction of nuclear weapons into Japan. These three principles have thus far been unviolated and have defined the past defense policy of Japan. The Japanese have naturally accepted these restrictions because of their first-hand experiences with the devastation caused by the use of nuclear armaments before the close of World War II. In recent years, however, some Japanese politicians and defense experts have begun to question the feasibility of continuing to abide by these rigid principles. They have focused their views particularly on the observance of the third principle—the prohibition of nuclear weapons in Japan. Many feel that it is suicidal for Japan to prohibit U.S. naval and air forces from introducing tactical nuclear arms in Japanese waters and air space when Soviet SS-20s and Backfires have already been deployed along Far Eastern coasts and are capable of destroying Japan without having to prepare for counterattack by strategic nuclear weapons.[43]

The second point of discussion concerns the dispatch of SDF forces overseas in recent months. Many have interpreted this as a violation of the principles set forth in the constitution, which discourage the overseas activities of Japanese military enterprises and manpower. Destined to remain a trade state for her survival, however, Japan more than any other state must cooperate with peace-keeping efforts around the globe within the constraints of her constitution. The question of how to interpret and possibly amend the sections in the constitution that prohibit the pursuit of military aims, in view of the changing global strategies, has forced its way into the mass media and, most significantly, into the policy deliberations and public statements of the incumbent prime minister. By declaring without reservation that his administration is "definitely not planning to revise the Constitution,"[44] Suzuki has fueled the controversy and focused on the changing attitude of Japan toward the security issue. The fact that Suzuki has reconfirmed publicly the cautious responses of his predecessors to the question is an open signal that indeed the atmosphere in Japan is changing.

The Americans and Europeans, however, remain unconvinced of Japan's changing attitudes toward self-defense and active participation in peace-keeping efforts, despite some of the recent changes in policy and the actual actions taken. Much of the misunderstanding and outright irritation is due to the painfully slow and inconsistent character of Japanese policy making, and more explicitly, to the Japanese reluctance to raise the defense budget to the 9.7 percent figure urged by the United States. It should be stressed, however, that it would only be counterproductive to push the Suzuki administration too hard to achieve the desired reforms in Japanese defense policy making.

Admittedly, the Japanese process of decision making defies comparison with that used in most other contemporary governments and any well-intentioned attempts to revise it fall on deaf ears. The indirect and zigzagging process more than likely involves waiting until the last minute—when there is no alternative but finally to make a commitment. Also, since Japanese leaders do not discuss with the general public issues under consideration, they rely instead on the development among the public of a mood or atmosphere that will eventually facilitate the acceptance of a possibly controversial policy. By taking advantage of this manipulated environment Japanese leaders are able to push through their policies without much opposition and resistance from those who are not in the know, as illustrated earlier in the discussion of the process leading to the treaty with the PRC.

In conclusion, the following points should be reiterated. The Japanese have begun to reevaluate their attitudes and actions toward the Soviet Union an and the security issue. The number of Japanese who regard increased defense sharing with the United States as an undeniable necessity is steadily growing. One proof is the increased number of citizens who replied affirmatively to the question, asked by a survey team of the *Yomiuri Shimbun*, whether Japan should increase its defense capability. Compared to the low 25 percent who answered the same question affirmatively in February 1980, the percent increased to 41.4 percent in January 1981.[45] To be sure, even though it appears from the American perspective that the Japanese are purposefully stalling in building up a firm national consensus regarding the handling of crucial defense issues, care must be taken not to use undue pressure or force the hand of Japanese leaders beyond reasonable limits. One reason for this warning is clearly seen in the fact that, along with Japan's increased awareness of the Soviet threat and the corresponding need to define its defense capability, a clear sense of pride, faith in national character, and even a sense of nationalism have steadily grown. This development must be understood, and its positive aspects respected by Japan's allies, while its negative influences are carefully controlled. In this author's opinion, mutually productive agreements between Japan and the West can be realized only when the unique and tradition-based character of the Japanese and their way of decision making are accepted for what they are and handled with a blend of sensitivity and, when necessary, carefully applied diplomatic pressures.

NOTES

1. B. Zanegin, "Aziatskaia bezopasnost': dva podkhoda," *Azia, Afrika segodnia*, March 3, 1978, p. 2. For an earlier discussion of growing Japanese concern about the Soviet Union, see Hiroshi Kimura, "Japan-Soviet Relations: From Afghanistan to Suzuki," *Slavic Studies* (Hokkaido University), no. 27 (1981), pp. 1-26.

2. Quoted from Dvian, *Voiskovye manevry provedennye na territorii belorussii v marte 1970 goda* (Moscow: USSR Ministry of Defense, 1970), p. 8.

3. Kuniko Miyauchi, "No Slowdown in Soviet Security Buildup: Why USSR Switched From Introvert, Economic National Policy to Extrovert Military One," *Japan Times*, May 13, 1979.

4. William F. Scott, "The USSR's Growing Global Mobility," *Air Force Magazine* (March 1977), p. 57.

5. A. A. Grechko, "Rukovodiashchaia rol' KPSS v stroitel'stve armii razvitogo sotsialisticheskogo obshchestva," *Voprosy istorii KPSS*, no. 5 (1974), p. 39.

6. *U.S. Foreign Policy for the 1970s: A New Strategy for Peace*. A Report to the Congress by Richard Nixon, President of the United States, February 18, 1970 (Washington, D.C.: U.S. Government Printing Office, 1970), p. 6.

7. *Asahi Shimbun*, April 28, 1980.

8. *Defense of Japan 1980* (Tokyo: Defense Agency, 1981), p. 49.

9. *Sankei Shimbun*, February 5, 1980.

10. Mineo Nakajima, *Chuso-tairitsu to Gendai* (Tokyo: Chuoloronsha, 1978), pp. 251-62.

11. *Japan Times*, February 15, 1981.

12. Quoted from Taichi Sakaiya, *Hachiju-nendai no Yomikata* (Tokyo: Kobunsha, 1979), p. 193.

13. Osamu Miyoshi, *Soren-Teikokushugi No Sekai-senryaku* (Kyoto: PHP kenkyu sho, 1980); O. Miyoshi et al., *Soren ga Nihon o Shinryaku-suru Hi* (Tokyo: Kokusai-shogyo shuppan-sha, 1979).

14. Hiroomi Kurisu, *Kasotekikkoku Soren: Warera Ko Mukae Utsu* (Tokyo: Kodansha, 1980).

15. Ikutaro Shimizu, *Nippon yo Kokka tare: Kaku-no Sentaku* (Tokyo: Bungei-shunju-sha, 1980).

16. Masamich Inoki, *Gunji-Taikoku eno Genso: Shinni Kuni o Mamoruniwa* (Tokyo Toyokeizai-shinpu-sha, 1981).

17. Yonosuke Nagai, "Noratorium Kokka No Boei-ron," *Chuo-koron* (January 1981), pp. 84-85.

18. Takehiko Kamo, "Kokusaiseiji no Henyo To Nihongaiko," *Sekai* (January 1978), pp. 53-70.

19. Yoshikazu Sakamoto, "'Boei' mondai no Otoshiana," *Asahi Shimbun*, January 13, 1981.

20. See Hiroshi Kimura, "Relax–The Russians Are Not Coming," *Japan Times*, November 16, 1980.

21. Thomas W. Wolf, "Soviet Military Capabilities and Intentions in Europe," in *Soviet Strategy in Europe*, ed. Richard Pipes (New York: Crane, Russak, 1976), p. 158.

22. Foy D. Kohler and Mose L. Harvey, eds., *The Soviet Union: Yesterday, Today, Tomorrow* (Washington, D.C.: Center for Advanced International Studies, University of Miami, 1975), p. 213.

23. *Hokkaido Shimbun, Asahi Shimbun, Japan Times*, February 1, 1980.

24. *Japan Times*, February 2, 1981.

25. Ibid.

26. *Asahi Shimbun* (evening edition), February 5, 1980.

27. Ibid.

28. *Defense of Japan 1980*, p. 49.

29. *Hokkaido Shimbun* (evening edition), January 30, 1981; *Yomiuri Shimbun, Japan Times*, January 31, 1981.

30. *Yomirui Shimbun*, January 31, 1981.

31. Ibid.

32. See *Asahi Shimbun*, April 6, 1978; August 13, 1978.

33. *Asahi Shimbun*, January 26, 1978.

34. For a more complete discussion of these policies see Hiroshi Kimura, "The Impact of the Afghanistan Invasion on Japanese-Soviet Relations," in *Soviet Foreign Policy and East-West Relations*, ed. Roger E. Kanet (New York: Pergamon, forthcoming).

35. *Asahi Shimbun*, January 27, 1981.

36. *Pravda*, January 29, 1981.

37. See Hiroshi Kimura, "Japanese Concept of 'the Pacific Basin Cooperation' from the Soviet Perspective." Unpublished paper read at the Annual Convention of the International Studies Association, Philadelphia, March 17-21, 1981.

38. *Izvestiia*, February 24, 1981.

39. *Asahi Shimbun*, January 28, 1981.

40. The author of this chapter is one of the members of this study group, called "The Comprehensive National Security Study Group."

41. *Report on Comprehensive National Security* (English translation) (Tokyo: Cabinet House, 1980), pp. 7, 9, 19-23, 45-49.

42. Ibid., pp. 12, 72.

43. Masashi Nishihara, "Japanese Defense and New Implications On the U.S.-Japan Security Treaty." Unpublished paper, read at a conference, Tokyo, December 8-9, 1980, under the auspices of the Joint Japan-U.S. Security Study Project of the Japan Center for International Exchange and the Council on Foreign Relations.

44. *Japan Times*, September 17, 1980.

45. *Yomiuri Shimbun*, February 9, 1981.

12

SOVIET EAST-WEST TRADE:
CAN THE MEANS BECOME THE END?

Marshall I. Goldman

By the time this volume appears, President Brezhnev may already have died or been replaced. If not, it should be only a question of months before such a change is made. A turnover of this sort is likely to have a significant impact on a vast range of Soviet policies. After all, depending on how the measurements are made, the Soviet Union has had only three or four different administrations since 1950 and only one since 1964. Regardless of how collective decisions of the Soviet leadership have been made in the past, it would be strange if a new leadership failed to place its own imprint on Soviet economic and political policies.

A review of events in 1979 and 1980 suggests that policies in several important areas have already been altered, reflecting a new sense of priorities. Some of these new strategies have been effected not only by decisions of the Soviet leadership but by the outside world. Foreign trade is a particularly good example of where the two forces interact. For example, Soviet foreign trade policies are dependent not only on how much Soviet planners decide to set aside for export and how much they decide to import but on the attitudes of other countries. Thus, just as the Soviet Union does when it trades with the West, so most countries trading with the USSR carefully monitor and regulate not only their imports from the USSR but also their exports. These decisions reflect political as well as economic considerations. Until recently a mutual desire for

An earlier version of this chapter appeared as an article in *Current History* (October 1980), pp. 84–87, 102–3. It is reprinted here with permission of the publisher.

détente served to increase the volume of trade. A surge of human rights violations, however, capped by the invasion of Afghanistan and uncertainty over
Soviet intentions in Poland, have led several trading partners in the non-Communist world to cancel or at least moderate some important trade initiatives.

What has been the effect of this post-Afghanistan tension and what impact
will it have on the emerging Soviet leadership? Finally, to what extent do these
changes in Soviet foreign trade foretell the future directions of other Soviet
policies?

DÉTENTE AND THE EXPANSION OF SOVIET TRADE

Because Soviet foreign trade policy has always been a closely regulated
monopoly of the state through the foreign trade organizations of the Ministry
of Foreign Trade, Soviet exports and imports reflect not only world economic
fluctuations but Soviet political trends. Thus, after World War II the increase in
Soviet trade volume, not only in comparison with trade in the mid-1930s but by
world standards, was only modest (see Table 12.1). More importantly, the
increase that took place was limited almost entirely to the newly declared Communist regimes in Eastern Europe and China (see Table 12.2). Initially the Soviet
Union was very dependent on Eastern Europe, which supplied in particular
necessary shipments of machinery, oil, and coal. As the Soviet Union began to
recover from the devastation of war, its productive capabilities increased, as did
its exports, particularly of raw materials.

In contrast, Soviet trade with the capitalist world was not much greater
than it had been in the years preceding World War II. Recently some have begun
to argue that this is due as much to American and Western as to Soviet policy.[1]
There does, however, seem to be good evidence to indicate that more than anything else the decision to limit contacts with the West was Stalin's. Reflecting
this is the fact that those countries outside American influence, such as Sweden,
had a trade volume that was only slightly higher than that of more compliant
countries such as the United Kingdom and France. The Swedes may have been
willing to sell, but the Soviets simply weren't buying. In any event, as the cold
war developed in intensity, the West, led by the United States, adopted very
strict trade controls that served to bar the export of most strategic goods. In
general the United States sought to isolate the Communist world from the West.

For many years this shunning of the USSR did not have much impact. Regardless of the West's policies, the Soviets were not really interested in disturbing
their isolationism. In 1952, however, Stalin announced what seemed to be a
change in attitude. He convened an international trade conference in Moscow
and invited a large number of Westerners to visit Moscow and talk about trade
for the first time; but this opening was apparently no more than a temporary
one and it was not followed by any substantive transactions.

TABLE 12.1

Soviet Exports and Imports
(in billions of rubles)

Year	Exports	Imports
1930	.8	.8
1931	.6	.9
1932	.5	.6
1933	.4	.3
1934	.3	.2
1935	.3	.2
1936	.2	.2
1937	.3	.2
1938	.2	.2
1939	.1	.2
1940	.2	.2
1941	.2	.3
1942	.1	.2
1943	.1	.2
1944	.1	.2
1945	.3	.3
1946	.6	.7
1947	.7	.7
1948	1.2	1.1
1949	1.3	1.3
1950	1.6	1.3
1951	2.1	1.8
1952	2.5	2.3
1953	2.7	2.5
1954	2.9	2.9
1955	3.1	2.8

Source: Ministerstvo Vneshnei Torgovli SSSR, *Vneshniaia torgovlia SSSR, 1918-1960* (Moscow: Mezhdunarodnye Otnosheniia, 1967), pp. 8-9, 62-65.

It was only with Khrushchev's rise to power that a significant opening to the West took place. In 1959 Khrushchev concluded that in order to increase agricultural yields, the Soviet Union would have to increase fertilizer production. To increase fertilizer production, however, the Soviet Union needed a substantial increase in the size and capability of its chemical industry. Accordingly, in March 1959 Khrushchev decreed that the Soviet Union must embark on a drive to build up a chemical industry, just as Lenin before him had sought to build up electricity.[2] In a manner calculated to stir memories of Lenin's assertion that

TABLE 12.2

Share of Soviet Foreign Trade by Category[a] of Country
(percent)

	Socialist Countries		Nonsocialist Countries	
				Industrially Developed
				Capitalist Countries
Year	Total	CMEA[b]	Total	official Soviet list[c]
1946	54	41	46	38
1947	61	39	39	34
1948	60	43	40	30
1949	72	52	28	21
1950	81	57	19	15
1951	81	58	19	15
1952	81	59	19	15
1953	79	55	21	17
1954	79	53	21	15
1955	79	53	21	15
1956	76	50	24	17
1957	74	54	26	17
1958	74	52	26	16
1959	75	52	25	16
1960	73	53	27	19
1961	72	55	28	19
1962	70	57	30	18
1963	70	59	30	19
1964	70	59	30	20
1965	69	58	31	19
1966	66	56	33	21
1967	68	57	32	21
1968	67	58	33	21
1969	65	57	35	22
1970	65	56	35	21
1971	65	56	35	21
1972	65	56	35	23
1973	59	50	41	27

[a]As defined by Soviet Statistical handbooks. Includes imports and exports.
[b]Bulgaria, Czechoslovakia, East Germany, Hungary, Mongolia, Poland, Romania.
[c]Includes Austria, Belgium, Canada, Finland, France, West Germany, Great Britain, Italy, Japan, The Netherlands, Sweden, United States.
Source: Various issues of *Vneshniaia Torgovlia SSSR*.

"electricity plus the Soviets" would bring communism, Khrushchev proclaimed that electricity plus chemicalization plus the Soviets would bring communism. The only difficulty was that the Soviet Union lacked the capability to build its own chemical industry. Instead, it would have to call in foreign equipment and imports.

The next few years brought a surge of Soviet contracts for Western companies, the first since the last nonwar peak of trade in the early 1930s. From 1959 to 1961 the Soviet Union ordered approximately 50 complete chemical plants from foreign suppliers.[3] In the four-year period 1960 to 1963, chemical sales to the Soviet Union totaled $132 million from the United Kingdom, $93 million from West Germany, $72 million from Italy, and $61 million from France.[4] Unfortunately the flow of orders proved to be only temporary. After the bad grain harvest of 1963, hard currency had to be set aside for grain imports. Even more important, as a result of what were called his "harebrained ideas," Khrushchev suddenly found himself purged. Not surprisingly, his successors declared a moratorium on many of Khrushchev's initiatives. One casualty was the expansion of foreign trade. Thus from 1964 to 1967 there was a noticeable fall-off in hard-currency (that is Western) orders (see Table 12.3).

After a thorough assessment of Soviet foreign trade policy, Premier Kosygin in April 1966 concluded that if Soviet industry was to be modernized, the Soviet Union would have to increase its imports of foreign technology. He criticized, however, many of the nonchemical industry imports of the pre-1966 period. Traditionally Soviet engineers had followed a policy of reverse engineering. Soviet importers would buy a single prototype of some advanced foreign product and would then attempt to determine how it was manufactured and set up a production line of their own. The theory was that although such a procedure was time-consuming and risky, it should be cheaper. After reexamination of the matter, however, Kosygin determined that, on the contrary, reverse engineering was a mistake, and that it would be not only more efficient but ultimately cheaper, to buy the turnkey manufacturing plants and technology in the usual capitalist way; that is, contract to have the suppliers furnish the complete plant.[5] That, after all, was how the Japanese were doing it, and even as early as 1966 the results looked impressive. The Soviets hoped to be able to duplicate the Japanese success. Thus, beginning in August 1966 with the signing of a contract with Fiat of Italy to build a massive automobile assembly plant at Togliatti, the Soviets moved rapidly to buy Western technology, and in 1968 trade volume with most of the Western European countries and Japan rose sharply.

The United States was one of the few industrialized countries that held back from this newly reopened market. American public opinion had not yet reconciled itself to the end of the cold war. While the American standoffishness offended some Soviets, it suited others. They were distressed by what they viewed as the callous American behavior in Vietnam. Consequently, it was a surprise for them when, of all people, Richard Nixon announced that he had

Imports and Exports of Selected Countries with the Soviet Union (in millions of dollars)

Year	United Kingdom Imports	United Kingdom Exports	France Imports	France Exports	Germany Imports	Germany Exports	Italy Imports	Italy Exports	Japan Imports	Japan Exports	United States Imports	United States Exports
1958	167	146	95	76	92	72	40	31	22	18	18	3
1959	177	98	101	90	105	91	78	44	40	23	28	7
1960	210	149	95	116	160	185	126	79	87	60	23	38
1961	238	194	97	110	198	204	150	90	145	65	23	46
1962	236	161	111	138	215	207	166	102	147	149	16	20
1963	271	179	141	64	209	154	176	114	162	158	21	23
1964	272	111	141	64	234	194	147	91	227	182	21	146
1965	333	129	146	72	275	146	181	98	240	168	43	45
1966	352	141	172	76	286	135	190	90	300	215	50	42
1967	337	179	187	155	274	198	274	132	454	158	41	60
1968	379	250	183	257	294	273	285	179	464	179	58	58
1969	473	233	205	265	335	406	247	285	462	268	52	106
1970	528	245	203	273	342	422	281	307	481	341	72	118
1971	512	216	256	260	367	460	297	295	496	378	58	162
1972	612	227	296	342	430	712	325	268	593	505	96	550
1973	880	238	434	577	762	1184	442	352	1078	487	215	1190

Source: From country-by-country data in various editions of International Monetary Fund, *Direction of Trade.*;

been invited to Moscow in May 1972—as it turned out, just after the United States decided to blockade Haiphong Harbor and resume the bombing of North Vietnam. Whatever his visit may have meant in hypocrisy, it led to a noticeable improvement in U.S.-Soviet relations and ultimately trade, and marked the beginning of détente.

In the expectation of great things to come, the United States and the Soviet Union in 1972 signed a trade agreement setting out mutual concessions. While some of the expectations about trade levels were realized, especially in grain sales, many concessions were never fully implemented. Before the Soviet Union could avail itself of most-favored-nation status, for example (tariffs for the USSR would be reduced so that they would be no higher than those paid by our most favored trading partners), the U.S. Congress insisted that the Soviet Union would have to begin allowing the emigration of as many as 60,000–70,000 people (mostly Jews) a year. This stipulation was embodied in American law as the Jackson-Vanik amendment to the United States Trade Administration Act of 1975.

Amazingly enough, whereas before 1970 the Soviets seldom allowed more than a few hundred emigrants a year, by 1973 they were allowing emigration of 30,000 a year, and there were clear signs that while the Soviets were still being nasty about how they processed those emigrants, they had become considerably more accommodating than before. Many viewed this change in Soviet emigration policy as a desire to win favor with the American business community and, in time, Congress.

In any event, Soviet purchases from the United States increased sharply. While the level and nature of these purchases were undoubtedly very much affected by political considerations, there was no doubt that Soviet planners were interested in trading with the United States for more than just the political considerations; they were hungry not only for American agricultural products but for its technology. Whereas, before, most Soviet industrial purchases were made in Western Europe and Japan, by the beginning of 1972 many American manufacturers began to sign some substantial contracts. In particular, American manufacturers played an active role in supplying the equipment for projects such as the billion-dollar Kama River truck plant, pipeline and railroad construction, and a series of ammonia and chemical plants.

In agriculture the Soviets began by purchasing American wheat to supplement periodic harvest shortfalls, but soon they were making annual purchases of feed grains in order to build up a livestock herd. By the late 1970s they were purchasing as much as 10 million tons of corn a year, even when their harvest was good.[6] The Soviet Union is located too far north for it to grow sufficient quantities of corn, and since the United States is virtually the only country in the world that can produce enough surplus corn to supply Soviet livestock needs, the decision to build up a livestock herd committed the Soviet Union to what in effect was a perpetual import dependency on the United States.

All of this was a marked departure from the traditional Russian policy of autarky. Opening the country to foreign technology meant a continuing dependence on the supply of foreign spare parts, just as increasing the livestock herd meant a continuing dependence on foreign feed grains. In the same way the Soviet Union began to turn to other suppliers for imports of almost half of its bauxite and aluminum.[7] Like other industrialized countries, the Soviet Union began to discover that it was no longer as self-sufficient as it once was. As its own deposits became depleted, it found that it needed more and more raw material imports to sustain production. As a measure of how far the Soviet Union had moved from its one time autarkic state, by the late 1970s it was importing over 11 percent of all the raw materials it used in production.[8] The Soviet Union even began to import natural gas from Iran and Afghanistan.[9] This was more for regional convenience than because of any serious material shortage. After all, the Soviet Union has 40 percent of the world's reserves of natural gas and is currently the world's second largest producer and exporter. These gas imports were small, amounting to less than 3 percent of total Soviet production, but to the local users, particularly in Armenia and Georgia, these supplies were important.

Compared to other countries, exposure of such a limited sort would hardly count as a pro-foreign-trade posture. After all, Soviet exports (both to convertible and nonconvertible countries) amounted to about 8 percent of the Soviet GNP.[10] Nevertheless, by traditional Soviet or even Russian standards, this was a marked departure from the even more autarkic policy of the past, and in the minds of some, exposed the Soviet Union to a high degree of vulnerable interdependency.

NEW LIMITATIONS ON SOVIET TRADE

Soviet fears were not all fantasy. By the late 1970s some of the great expectations for trade had become bitter disappointments. For one thing, Western technology was not always easily or efficiently absorbed into the Soviet system. There were countless instances where imported machinery was left standing in the open for months; frequently it would then be cannibalized by Soviet spare-parts seekers. Moreover, when finally installed, it was rare that the equipment ever operated at 40 percent of the efficiency of comparable machinery installed in the United States. This is not to deny that 40 percent was almost always an improvement over what existed before; the point is, however, that imported technology did not prove to be the panacea that it was expected to be for all the Soviet Union's production difficulties. Then there were instances where the equipment could not be made to function at all. Reportedly hundreds of millions of dollars worth of equipment from one U.S. manufacturer for the construction of ammonia plants bore absolutely no fruit, and the plants even now cannot be made to function. This so infuriated the late Premier Kosygin that in 1979 he personally called for a reassessment of Soviet import policy. For a time he demanded complete performance guarantees from Western manufacturers on all new purchases, a condition that few Western suppliers dared realistically to provide. In any event, one by-product is that Soviet Ministry of Trade officials have been taking a harder look at all Soviet import requirements, with the result that, despite inflation, the value of nonagricultural Soviet imports from hard-currency countries decreased or increased only moderately in 1977 and 1978.

The Soviet advocates of foreign trade were dealt another blow after the collapse of the shah of Iran and the embargo on American grain sales in 1980. The new government of Iran disrupted and ultimately cut off the flow of natural gas to the Soviet Union in late 1978. While the Soviet Union as a whole did not suffer, this proved to be a terrible inconvenience for the Soviet republics that had become dependent on these regional supplies, especially because the winter of 1978-79 was one of the coldest since World War II. Under Khomeini, the Iranians also announced the suspension of all plans for the construction of a second natural gas pipeline that would have involved a massive and expensive swap arrangement with Western Europe as well. Finally the restriction of American grain sales to the Soviet Union threatened the survival of livestock herds and this more than anything else called into question the wisdom of exposing the Soviet Union to the uncertainties of foreign trade and the political whims of the United States. Undoubtedly the advocates of autarky in the Soviet Union have gained new strength and will make themselves a serious force to contend with in any new successor government.

PETROLEUM AND THE PROSPECTS FOR SOVIET TRADE

But whether Soviet officials want to or not, some Western analysts argue that the Soviet Union will not have much choice about whether it should trade. As these observers see it, the Soviet Union needs Western technology, if it is to sustain its production of raw materials. The Soviet Union needs Western equipment to maintain its raw material output, particularly the technology needed to find, develop, and drill its petroleum deposits and transport its natural gas.

This will become even more important if, as the C.I.A. has predicted, the Soviet Union and its East European allies find themselves forced to import a maximum of 3.5 to 4.5 million barrels a day of petroleum. The C.I.A. subsequently reduced its estimate of how much the Soviet Union and East Europe will have to import; but even if the Soviet Union's import needs are reduced to 1 million barrels a day, that should still cause it enormous economic difficulty. This would mean that the Soviet Union had ceased to be self-sufficient and that it had lost its most important export product, which it needs to pay for its imports. Despite the fact that the Soviet Union is the world's second largest industrial power, virtually no one in the hard-currency world wants its machinery. Consequently, only countries without the choice provided by hard currency are normally willing to buy Soviet equipment. Instead, about 85 percent of all Soviet hard-currency exports (other than military equipment and gold) consists of raw materials. Of that, the largest share—over 56 percent in 1979—is generated by petroleum. It is not entirely inappropriate to say that petroleum is to the Soviet Union what coffee is to Colombia—that is, that the Soviet Union, despite its economic power, is a one-crop economy.

If the Soviet Union did not have petroleum to export, that would mean that in 1979 its hard-currency export earnings would have fallen by over half, from $11 billion to $6.5 billion. If at the same time it were forced to import as much as some of the extreme C.I.A. predictions indicate, the Soviet import bill would grow to about $50-58 billion, leaving an annual trade deficit of $44-52 billion. It is unlikely that an annual trade deficit of that magnitude could be sustained for long by the Soviet Union. No one would lend them the money. Therefore it is likely that the Soviet Union will move vigorously to sustain petroleum output and at the same time increase its output of alternative fuels and its emphasis on conservation. Reflecting this necessity, the Soviet Ministry of Trade has increased the share of mining and raw-material-producing equipment in its total import package. These purchases have been sustained, despite the leveling off of other industrial imports.

To the extent that it is able to sustain its production of petroleum, the Soviet Union will have little trouble in paying its import bill. For that matter, it may even be able to do this while reducing the quantity of petroleum and exports. Thus, after the OPEC price increase in 1979, during the first six months of that year the Soviet Union apparently reduced its petroleum exports by 20 percent, while at the same time increasing export earnings by 30 percent. Subsequently, petroleum exports for all of 1979 seemed to reach or exceed 1978 levels so, that ultimate earnings for the year rose by almost 40 percent.

The evolution of past Soviet foreign trade policy has not always followed a predictable course, and it is all but impossible to foretell what Brezhnev's successors will do. One group of cautious observers in this country has begun to argue that, instead of seeking to become more integrated into the world economy and offering more of its resources for sale, the USSR may move in the opposite direction and seek to hoard or control and withhold various crucial resources. They see this as part of an effort to cripple economic and military production in the non-Communist world. As part of this alleged Soviet strategy, these critics see the Soviet Union seeking to extend its political and military control over particularly crucial regions of Africa and Asia, especially those areas that are the sources of some of these diminishing supplies.

While there indeed may be some in the USSR who advocate such a tactic, the pressure to import advanced Western and Japanese technology and the need to generate the exports to pay for those imports would seem to point the USSR in the opposite direction; that is, they are more likely to export what they have than try to corner the market. As they try to expand exports, however, the Soviet Union will seek to move from the export of products with a high raw-material content to those that require more manufacturing and, thus, more value added. In other words, whenever possible they would prefer to sell items where an ever-increasing portion of the value of the goods derives from the manufacturing, not the mining, process. That, after all, is the goal of all countries. Unfortunately, the USSR has had a good deal of difficulty in trying to attain that goal.

Not surprisingly, if the Soviets produce poor-quality goods for home consumption, the likelihood is that they will also produce poor-quality goods for export. Moreover, all the problems that plague domestic industry, such as poor marketing service and lack of spare parts, will inevitably affect exports as well. These shortcomings, more than anything else, explain why the Soviet Union has difficulty selling manufactured goods in hard-currency markets. Where customers have a choice, they usually buy elsewhere. The only thing the Soviets have going for them is the low price they are generally willing to accept, which sometimes is enough to offset the poorer quality. Customers in a developing country who have no choice because they lack hard currency, will be much more receptive to Soviet goods, but that is because usually they would otherwise be unable to buy anything. This explains why the Soviet Union is the world's largest exporter of machine tools, but its markets are normally restricted to only Eastern Europe and the developing countries.

Before the Soviets are able to crack the hard-currency markets, they will have to undertake a far-reaching reorganization of their planning, marketing, and production systems. Superficially that may look easy; but like the man who finds it so easy to stop smoking that he stops every few months, so the Soviets have found it difficult to make a once-and-for-all reform. As with the smoker, they keep trying.

Their most recent reforms have focused on finding ways of encouraging managers to produce higher quality and more energy- and raw-material-efficient equipment. The Soviets are seeking to switch from a system that tends to reward manufacturers who produce goods with a high gross ruble sales value to a system that establishes norms for value added and tends to discourage excessive use of raw materials by increasing prices for those raw materials, especially hydrocarbons. The Soviets are gearing up to introduce their first wholesale price revision since 1967. They call for the reform to be implemented as of January 1982—an incredible 15 years since the last one was introduced.[11] Their planners promise that price reforms henceforth will be made every five years. If they hold to their promise, this will certainly be an improvement, but hardly enough to eliminate their pricing problems.

The Soviets are also seeking to improve their exporting and importing procedures. The foreign trade organizations (FTOs), the actual importing and exporting monopolies under the Ministry of Foreign Trade, have been restructured in hopes of making them more responsive to the end producer and end consumer needs. For the first time their boards of directors are being enlarged to include members from the ranks of the industrial ministries. Moreover, the FTOs will be expected to operate on a more businesslike basis, so that they will be able to make a profit.[12]

These reforms may be of some help, but in and of themselves they are probably not enough. What is doubtlessly needed is a change in strategy. The Soviets have mistakenly tried to expand their exports by concentrating on some of their more sophisticated products. Except for their military weapons exports, this approach has not succeeded. The usual strategy that other countries have followed is to begin at the lower spectrum—that is, try to move up the value-added chain from raw materials to processed raw materials to semifabricated goods, and finally to sophisticated goods. After many years of no progress, there are signs that the Soviets have begun to adopt this more rational but time-consuming approach. They will still have to worry about poor quality and waste, but one indication of their new strategy is the fact that they are beginning to supplement their export of hydrocarbons, such as petroleum and natural gas, with significant quantities of petrochemicals and ammonia, which are produced from that petroleum and natural gas. Much of the ammonia is even coming to the United States. This process is just beginning and will someday be a significant income earner, assuming, of course, that Western manufacturers of those same products do not try to erect trade barriers to keep out the competing Soviet imports. Such an effort has already been made against Soveit ammonia in the United States, but for the time being, at least, anti-Soviet trade restriction has been only partially successful.

It will take some time, however, for the Soviets to move successfully into the area of more value-added production. In the near future, therefore, Soviet exports are likely to continue to consist primarily of raw materials. Consequently, the Soviets will be forced to import raw-material-extraction equipment, so that they can continue to export to pay for their imports. Even if petroleum production should fall, such equipment will still be of critical importance, because the USSR's second most important export is natural gas. Hard-currency natural gas exports have, in the past, accounted for no more than one-fifth of what Soviet petroleum exports generate. The Soviets hope that the world price of natural gas will be increased so that it reflects the cost of the equivalent amount of energy contained in petroleum. The Soviets, however, have also planned a massive program that, if implemented, will more than double Soviet gas exports to Western Europe. To do all of this, the Soviets will have to import not only massive quantities of pipe but of construction and pipe-laying equipment.[13]

As for other imports, the likelihood is that the Soviet leaders will try to cut back, particularly where a purchase increases Soviet dependence on potentially hostile suppliers. As they seek to reshape the policy, they may find that they no longer have the freedom they once had and must continue to import American corn, some raw materials, and Western technology, regardless of the consequences. For those who hope that the Soviet Union will ultimately find itself part of the international family of nations on a regularized basis, this will be welcome. If, however, the Soviets find that they are able to tighten their belts and cut themselves off as they did in the 1930s and again in the 1950s, this turning away from increased interdependence, if it comes, may turn out to be a lost opportunity not only for the Soviet Union but for the world.

NOTES

1. Daniel Yergin, *Shattered Peace* (Boston: Houghton-Mifflin, 1977); Gunnar Adler-Karlsson, *Western Economic Warfare, 1949-1967: A Case Study in Foreign Economic Policy* (Stockholm: Almqvist & Wiksell, 1968).

2. R. Amann, J. M. Cooper, and R. W. Davies, *The Technological Level of Soviet Industry* (New Haven: Yale University Press, 1977), p. 229.

3. *Chemical Week*, September 3, 1960, p. 42; March 11, 1961, p. 3.

4. *Chemical Week*, March 21, 1964, p. 27.

5. *Pravda*, April 6, 1966, p. 7.

6. *Vneshniaia Torgovlia SSSR v 1976* (Moscow: Statistika, 1977), p. 304. (Hereafter *VT SSSR*).

7. Theodore Shabad, "Raw Material Problems of the Soviet Aluminum Industry," in *Soviet Economy in a New Perspective*, Joint Economic Committee (Washington, D.C.: U.S. Government Printing Office, October 14, 1976), p. 661.

8. O. Bogomolov, "Ekonomischeskie Sviazi SSSR s Zarubezhnymi Stranami," *Planovoe Khoziastvo*, no. 10 (1980), p. 82.

9. *VT SSSR*, 1976, pp. 214, 230.

10. Bogomolov, "Ekonomicheskie Sviazi SSSR," p. 82.

11. *Ekonomicheskaia Gazeta*, no. 17 (April 1980), pp. 7-8.

12. *Foreign Trade*, no. 1 (1980), p. 48; *Journal of the US-USSR Trade and Economic Council*, July-August 1979, p. 32.

13. *Soviet, Eastern Europe, China Business & Trade*, December 1, 1980, p. 2.

PART FIVE

The Soviet Union and the Developing Countries

13

MILITARY POWER, INTERVENTION, AND SOVIET POLICY IN THE THIRD WORLD

Rajan Menon

Nikita Khrushchev took the Soviet Union out of its continental confines, using economic aid and arms transfers to forge ties with the new nations that arrived on the international landscape with the collapse of colonial empires. Yet none of these newly independent countries was eager to trade one master for another and, at the time of his ouster, the range of the Soviet Union's involvement was far more striking than the depth of its influence.[1] Despite the energies and resources he devoted to the Third World, Khrushchev operated under the disadvantage of strategic inferiority and without the aid of a blue-water navy and a strong long-range airlift capability. Because of these constraints, Moscow's ability to supply and support its friends in times of trouble was limited; therefore, during such episodes as the 1956 Suez conflict and the 1960 civil war in Zaire (then Congo-Leopoldville), the Soviets backed Nasser and Lumumba with words rather than deeds. As the Brezhnev era enters the 1980s, most observers of Soviet foreign policy concur that the Soviet role in the developing world has, for a number of reasons, become more assertive and purposeful.

The attainment of strategic parity in 1969 brought with it a greater sense of confidence, a disposition reflected in Gromyko's oft-quoted statement before the 24th Party Congress in 1971 that no major international issue could be

The author wishes to express his appreciation for comments on an earlier version of this chapter by his colleague Johan Oneal and by Captain Gary Anderson, U.S.M.C. Neither, of course, is responsible for the views expressed here.

settled without Soviet participation. The development of a more versatile navy and its permanent deployment in the eastern Mediterranean and the Indian Ocean provided the Soviets with both a greater visibility—through port calls for showing the flag, as well as because of the interest and controversy that forward deployment generated in the West—and a motive to seek naval and air facilities in such strategically located countries as Egypt, Syria, and Somalia.

The Soviets were also aware that the Watergate scandal and the debacle in Vietnam that followed closely on its heels had generated in the United States a certain suspicion and cynicism about the government, as well as a quasi-isolationist mood. Particularly significant was the sensitivity that emerged within Congress on the need to eschew nonessential, extravagant entanglements in far-away lands and its determination to restrain any inclination that the executive branch might develop for such campaigns.[2] Aside from such American quietism, it was also true (for the Khrushchev period as well) that Third World instabilities pose opportunities for the establishment or extension of Soviet influence with small risk involved, since relatively few areas of the Third World are vital to Western security. Finally, the augmentation of the USSR's ability to convey men and material by air over great distances meant that there was now an enhanced ability to project power abroad.

The more favorable political context and the enhanced military underpinnings of policy in the Third World coalesced to produce a bolder pattern of Soviet behavior in the 1970s—one that embodied a new willingness to defend and pursue interests with the aid of military power. This is illustrated by several events of the past decade. During the 1973 Yom Kippur War, large deliveries of arms were made to Egypt and Syria by air and sea, with Brezhnev suggesting the possibility of Soviet intervention if the breached October 24 cease-fire were not reinstated and Israeli military advances in the Suez sector halted. In the 1975–76 Angolan civil war and the Somali-Ethiopian irredentist conflict of 1977–78, weapons, advisers, and Cuban troops were transported to back the parties that ultimately prevailed. A more awesome demonstration of this greater assertiveness came in the last days of the decade, when 85,000 Soviet troops were injected into Afghanistan in response to the recalcitrance and growing instability of the regime headed by Hafizullah Amin.[3]

The decisive role that the USSR played in the denouement of the crisis in Angola and the Horn of Africa, and a realization that the introduction of troops into Afghanistan represents a new threshold in Soviet activity, have stimulated an ongoing debate. It centers around a number of questions. How significant has the growth of Soviet military power and spending been and to what degree has it increased Moscow's capability to intervene in Third World crises? Is intervention likely to become a salient feature of Soviet policy in the developing areas? What constraints exist on the nature of Soviet behavior in the Third World? This analysis is an effort to come to grips with these queries.

THE THIRD WORLD AND SOVIET MILITARY POWER

One explanation for the more forceful Soviet policy in the Third World is that the USSR, which in contrast to the United States steadily increased its annual defense budget over the 1970s, has been emboldened by a perceived military edge. The lack of a correlation between American and Soviet defense spending has, for two reasons, led groups such as the Committee on the Present Danger to voice concern. First, the growing size of the Soviet defense budget was not arrested by the progress made toward détente; this has led some to wonder whether Moscow's professed interest in peaceful coexistence is genuine or duplicitous. Some have concluded that the Soviet commitment to *razryadka* contains more cynicism than sincerity. Second, it takes place at a time when there is a bolder pattern of Soviet involvement in the developing world, leading observers who discern a shift in the military balance in favor of the USSR to claim that an inevitable result will be a greater Soviet propensity toward expansion.

As Table 13.1 indicates, both in constant dollars and as a percentage of the gross national product (GNP), American defense expenditure has declined steadily since 1969. In large part, of course, this reduction followed the re-

TABLE 13.1

American and Soviet Military Expenditures, 1969-78
(billions of constant 1977 dollars)

Year	Soviet Defense Spending	GNP (percent)	American Defense Spending	GNP (percent)
1969	107.9	13.6	132.3	8.7
1970	111.2	13.0	120.2	7.9
1971	114.0	12.8	110.0	7.0
1972	118.1	12.9	109.6	6.6
1973	123.2	12.6	105.0	6.0
1974	128.4	12.6	105.0	6.1
1975	133.0	12.6	101.2	5.9
1976	139.0	12.7	96.2	5.3
1977	140.0	12.4	101.0	5.3
1978	143.0	12.2	101.0	5.1

Note: Figures have been rounded.
Source: U.S. Arms Control and Disarmament Agency, *World Military Expenditures and Arms Transfers 1969-1978* (Washington, D.C.: U.S. Government Printing Office, 1980), pp. 66, 71.

trenchment from Vietnam. On the one hand, despite the advent of détente and arms control negotiations during the 1970s, Soviet expenditures rose 32.5 percent, from $107.9 billion in 1968 to $143 billion in 1978. In contrast, U.S. defense spending dropped by 30.9 percent over the same period. Since, however, prognoses of greater Soviet adventurism in the developing countries tend to rest heavily on assessments of the Soviet defense effort, it should be noted that while the annual Soviet military budget grew steadily between 1969 and 1978, the table shows that it has not grown steadily as a percentage of the GNP. While Soviet defense spending has increased, it has been due to the expansion of the economy rather than any dogged drive to channel a progressively greater share of the GNP toward the acquisition of military might.[4] The gap that seems to have persisted between the defense expenditures of the two superpowers is better explained by the post-Vietnam wind-down of the United States than by Soviet budgetary decisions.

Furthermore, there are several reasons to suspect that the available estimates of Soviet military spending may be inflated.[5] For example, the Central Intelligence Agency's dollar estimates are based on a calculation—assuming American pay scales and production costs—of how much it would cost the United States to acquire the men and equipment constituting the Soviet armed forces. Since Soviet military manpower stood at 3,658,000 in 1980 in comparison to 2,050,000 for the United States, and because the C.I.A. does not apply a cost discount for the lower level of education and training possessed by Soviet personnel, this procedure yields inflated estimates.[6] More significantly, the dollar estimate often tends to be used in an unwarranted fashion, in defense appropriation requests and the national security debate, as an authoritative calculation of what the USSR spends on defense; this despite the C.I.A.'s description of it as an approximation of what it would cost the United States to purchase the Soviet armed forces. Since military hardware is relatively more costly in the USSR, a Soviet analyst using a similar procedure, but employing the ruble as the unit of accounting, would conclude that the U.S. armed forces would cost more than those of the Soviet Union. This would follow because, while U.S. military manpower is smaller, much of American weaponry is beyond the level of Soviet technological attainment.[7]

Arguments that depict the Soviet Union's willingness to use its military power—either directly or to ferry advisers, arms, and Cuban troops—as the obvious result of a relentless armament drive, should be scrutinized carefully for two reasons. First, the data fail to suggest any military buildup that is prepared to consume an ever-increasing percentage of the GNP. Second, available estimates of Soviet defense spending may tend to exaggerate the gap between Soviet and American military expenditure because of their debatable methodology.

Another issue that needs to be addressed is the extent to which the Soviets possess a strong capability to intervene in Third World crises and whether acquiring such means has been a high-priority item on the agenda of Soviet military planners. The areas of vital concern to them are the U.S.-Soviet strategic balance, the European theater, and what is viewed as a looming threat across the 4,000-mile Sino-Soviet border. Quite clearly, the three areas are interrelated in the Soviet view of security. The attainment of strategic parity by the Soviet Union in 1969 coincided with the clashes along the Sino-Soviet border and lent impetus to a Sino-Western rapprochement. Soviet assessments of the shift in Peking's relations with the West from minimal contact and hostility to growing cooperation—inspired by a common concern about Soviet power—betray a great deal of uneasiness. The apprehension centers on the fear that the political détente between China and West may gain enough momentum to bring about commercial agreements and a willingness—already exhibited by Britain and France—to supply arms to the Chinese. The result of a durable and substantive Sino-Western interaction with economic and military dimensions may be to alter the inequality that exists in the Sino-Soviet balance of power due to the Soviet Union's present ability to offset China's manpower advantage through a decisive economic, technological, and military lead. In a more tangible sense, and in the short run, collusion between Beijing and the West in areas such as the Persian Gulf and Afghanistan, aimed against the Soviet Union, is alleged and referred to in a manner that would indicate a fear that these instances may be the onset of a trend rather than specific cases where an intersection of interests has developed.[8]

It is, of course, impossible to separate the three areas just identified from Soviet activities in the Third World. For example, the move toward strategic parity with the United States has provided the Soviets with a greater measure of confidence about involvement in peripheral areas, and after 1965 Soviet military doctrine began to suggest that local conflicts involving the superpowers would not necessarily escalate to a nuclear war. This implied a belief that, with the deadlock at the strategic nuclear level, competition in the Third World could be waged with greater assurance and lower risk. In addition, the enhancement of conventional military power in the European sector and the Far East will undoubtedly have a bearing on Soviet power-projection strength. Finally, Moscow's perception of developments in the Third World and the nature and degree of Soviet involvement will continue to be influenced in part by the dynamics of Sino-Soviet competition.

Thus the areas of vital importance to the Soviet leadership form a triad, as a consequence of the interaction between the U.S.-Soviet strategic balance, the European theater, and Sino-Soviet relations. While the link between this triad and Soviet activity in the Third World is important, it is an entirely different matter to be moved by the events in Angola, the Horn of Africa, and Afghanistan to equate the two in terms of their importance for Soviet defense planners. As Malcolm Mackintosh has put it,

> The Soviet Union's main preoccupations are with its national security, its superpower status, its relationship with the United States,

its confrontation with the West in Europe and its relationship, and its problems with China. In some senses, the Middle East is near enough to one of those areas (Europe and the Mediterranean) to be partially involved in those fundamental relationships, and Japan is an essential element in the balance of power in the Far East. Activity in the rest of the world is regarded in Moscow as a vital aspect of a superpower's rights and duties. But, it is still very much a "bonus" in Soviet foreign policies, and the effect on the balance of power is not really significant.[9]

The resources and attention that the Soviets have devoted to building up their strategic nuclear capability and conventional power in the European and Sino-Soviet theaters have brought results that are clearly in evidence today. It is generally agreed that the forces assigned to these concerns are equal to their mission and competition. An examination of the pattern of Soviet defense spending between 1967 and 1977 indicates that the triad has been clearly favored in military resource allocation over forces intended for power projection.[10] In this period, the focus of air-force expenditure was on tactical aviation, the share of which increased from 60 percent of all air-force spending in 1967 to over 70 percent in 1977. The ground forces, the service branch that followed the air force in the rate of budgetary growth, devoted its resources primarily to increasing the armor, artillery, and antiaircraft defenses available to units in the European theater and to doubling the number of divisions stationed along the Sino-Soviet border. Spending for the navy increased more slowly than for the air force and ground forces, with most of it being devoted to acquire submarines and to enhance antisubmarine warfare (ASW) and antiship capabilities. Other missions, including amphibious warfare, were given lower fiscal priority.

Between 1970 and 1979, Soviet expenditure for forces relevant to power projection rose slightly, while U.S. spending declined. Nevertheless, in 1979 American outlays for power projection exceeded those of the Soviet Union both in absolute terms and as a percentage of total defense spending. Soviet outlays amounted to roughly $15 billion, or 9 percent of defense spending, while the United States alloted about $18 billion, or 17 percent of all defense outlays.[11]

In sum, while Soviet expenditure on power projection has increased somewhat over the past ten years, it has received much less attention than the capabilities relevant to the triad. As for relative emphasis, power projection receives a much greater share of U.S. military resources than it does in the USSR.

A comparison of the power projection assets of the two superpowers is presented in Table 13.2. While it is significant that the United States has an advantage in all categories except airborne troops and merchant cargo vessels, such a static numerical comparison needs to be supplemented with a more detailed scrutiny of relative capabilities in some of the individual areas listed.

In the case of long-range transport aircraft, not only is the Soviet fleet considerably smaller, but its payload is only 56 percent of that of the United States.

TABLE 13.2

American and Soviet Power Projection Assets

Category	USSR	United States
Aircraft carriers	2	13
Helicopter carriers	2	11[a]
Amphibious ships	28[b]	54
Merchant cargo ships	1,375	450
Tankers	350	562
Long-range transport aircraft[c]	135	350
Cargo and utility helicopters	2,740	5,022
Airborne troops	58,400[d]	39,000
Naval infantry/marines	12,000	198,000

[a]Usually listed along with amphibious ships.

[b]Does not include *Polnocny*, *MP4*, *SMB1*, and *Vydra* classes, which are not suited to long-range power projection.

[c]Excludes lift capability that could be contributed by the civilian aircraft of both sides.

[d]One of the eight divisions counted is used for training.

Note: Does not include units under construction.

Sources: International Institute for Strategic Studies, *Military Balance*, 1980-81, pp. 5-12; *Jane's All the World's Aircraft*, 1979-80, pp. 175-203; *Jane's Fighting Ships*, 1980-81, pp. 513-15, 534, 588, 665-71; John M. Collins and Elizabeth A. Severns, *United States/Soviet Military Balance*, Issue Brief Number IB 78029, Library of Congress, Congressional Research Service (July 1980), p. 15.

Neither the AN 22 Cock nor the IL 76 Candid, which together constitute the Soviet Union's long-distance airlift capability, can refuel in flight, and while the U.S. aircraft are jets, the AN 22 is a turboprop.[12]

The Soviets have eight airborne divisions, compared with two for the United States, and in recent years some have been used for diplomacy and power projection in the Third World; they were placed on alert when Brezhnev threatened to resort to military intervention in the Middle East on October 24, 1973, and were also utilized as a spearhead to secure vital positions and set the stage for entry of Soviet ground forces into Afghanistan in December 1979. In comparison, however, to American airborne divisions, which possess organic logistics and support, Soviet airborne troops are dependent for these functions on regular army units.[13] This is a drawback that diminishes their utility, except for operations in contiguous areas such as Europe and the Northern Tier countries stretching from Turkey to Afghanistan. By contrast, the American forces are better suited for power projection over great distances.[14]

As far as amphibious ships are concerned, the addition in the latter half of the 1970s of an *Ivan Rogov*-class amphibious transport dock and 13 *Ropucha*-class tank-landing ships has increased markedly the distant assault capability hitherto provided only by the *Alligator*-class ships. While these additions have sparked a good deal of discussion in the West, they are decidedly inferior to their American counterparts. Although the *Ivan Rogov* is newer than the *Austin* and *Raleigh* amphibious transport docks of the U.S. fleet, the *Rogov* is lighter than the *Austin* class, has a smaller lift capacity and less speed than both, and carries only one helicopter in comparison to six for its two American counterparts. Similarly, the *Newport*- and *Desoto*-class tank-landing ships of the U.S. Navy, while older than the *Ropucha*, are superior in terms of habitability as well as troop- and equipment-carrying capacity.[15]

The tonnage of the Soviet amphibious fleet—including the smaller ships not suited for power projection—is only 24 percent of that of the American fleet. It also lacks ships comparable to the U.S. Navy's *Blue Ridge*-class amphibious command ships—which provide command and control facilities for amphibious operations—and the large *Tarawa*-class amphibious assault ships, which are equipped with helicopters and extensive medical facilities, and carry almost 2,000 troops.[16]

In addition to being far less versatile, in a contested amphibious operation the Soviet fleet would be extremely vulnerable if it had to operate outside the range of shore-based aircraft. While the two newly built small aircraft carriers, the *Kiev* and the *Minsk*, have the potential to provide an air umbrella for such distant missions, they have yet to participate in amphibious exercises, and their primary role seems to be the protection of Soviet submarines against antisubmarine systems and to engage in A.S.W. (anti-submarine warfare).[17]

The writings of the commander in chief of the Soviet navy, Admiral Sergei Gorshkov, suggest that power projection is not stressed in Soviet naval doctrine. While Gorshkov's book, *The Sea Power of the State*, reveals a strong interest in the role of the American navy in "the local wars of imperialism," in this work and in an earlier collection of essays, the major missions of the Soviet navy were defined as deterrence, strategic strikes in the event of nuclear war, countering enemy aircraft carriers, and the advancement of state interests in peacetime through port visits and the maintenance of a permanent presence in various areas.[18] The lack of doctrinal emphasis on power projection, coupled with the absence of any indication that amphibious assaults outside the umbrella of shore-based aircraft are being prepared for, suggests that the Soviet naval infantry—which is considerably smaller than the U.S. Marine Corps—is not intended for use in distant operations. Its most salient purpose may be to control the foreign littorals commanding access to the four fleet areas, so as to enable Soviet naval units to move out to sea in wartime.[19]

The one area in which the Soviet Union has an advantage over the United States for power projection is sealift. The Soviets possess a larger, newer fleet of cargo ships, whose expansion since the late 1960s has increased the tonnage "directly of value to naval support or amphibious activities."[20] Further, while the Soviet merchant marine is more centralized and has naval representation in its organizational structure, U.S. cargo ships and tankers are distributed among the Maritime Sealift Command, the Merchant Marine, the ships under foreign registry (referred to as the Effective U.S. Controlled Fleet), and the National Defense Reserve Fleet.[21]

Taken as a whole, however, the Soviet Navy's utility for the projection of power is reduced by a number of constraints. Although the addition of the *Berezina* and *Boris Chilikin*-class fleet replenishment ships in the 1970s indicates an intent to make improvements, the Soviet navy's skills in underway repair, refueling, and replenishment rank below those of its American counterpart.[22] In the case of refueling, Soviet oilers have a smaller capacity than those of the U.S. Navy, and extensive reliance is therefore placed on unarmed merchant ships. Their refueling process is slower and the techniques less advanced than those of the U.S. Navy. Resupply operations are conducted at slow speeds with cranes being used instead of helicopters.[23] These lacks raise questions about the likely effectiveness of the Soviet navy as an instrument for intervening in distant crises in which an American counterintervention may have to be reckoned with.

Another disadvantage that the Soviet navy faces is the lack of access to an effective overseas basing system. Although much has been made about the existence of Soviet naval bases in various developing countries, much of the excitement that has been generated can be linked to a tendency to use the term "base" in rather imprecise ways. Since the evacuation of Porkkala in Finland and Port Arthur in China during the mid-1950s, the Soviets have been unable to obtain exclusive naval facilities to which access is guaranteed by treaty for a specific period of time. They have not acquired facilities comparable to those currently available to the U.S. Navy in Diego Garcia, Subic Bay, and Yokasuka. In Egypt and Somalia, where they were permitted to use ports and shore installations, the Soviets failed to enjoy security of tenure due to a deterioration of their relations with Sadat and Siad Barre. Recently gained access to Vietnamese air and naval facilities at Cam Ranh Bay and Da Nang has extended the southward reach of the Soviet Pacific Fleet and enhanced its ability to support the permanent Indian Ocean deployment. Vietnam, however, has insisted on controlling Soviet access to these facilities. The absence of full-fledged naval bases poses a logistical problem and complicates tasks of storage—whether of fuel or dry stores—and repairs.[24] The lack of land-based facilities is also a handicap in that, given the lack of a large number of aircraft carriers, Soviet naval vessels continue to require air cover from shore-based aircraft in the event of hostilities, which would restrict their range of operation. Thus, it is doubtful that the Soviet navy presently has the ability to intervene in protracted crises in distant areas in the face of parallel involvement by the United States.

Overall, the Soviet capacity to project power remains markedly inferior in relation to the United States. The Soviets would be at a severe disadvantage in a situation where their intervention was contested by U.S. forces and in locations far removed from the USSR.[25] While Soviet capabilities—especially those of the navy—have grown and will continue to do so with the passage of time, the steps being taken to improve the already potent U.S. intervention forces ought not to be neglected.

Fourteen roll-on/roll-off Marine prepositioning ships are to be built and used for storing the heavy equipment and supplies sufficient for three Marine brigades in crisis-prone areas. To strengthen further airlift capabilities, a new C-X transport aircraft capable of carrying outsize equipment over long distance is being developed, along with 26 KC-10 general-purpose aerial tankers, which would obviate the need for access to refueling facilities. Long-range airlift is also to be expanded by increasing the payload of the C-141 fleet by 30 percent.[26] Although these measures were adopted during the Carter administration, in view of the importance attached by Ronald Reagan to upgrading, U.S. military power and countering Soviet-Cuban activity in the Third World, they are likely to be supplemented further as an integral part of the effort to strengthen the much-favored Rapid Deployment Force.[27]

While the intervention in Afghanistan does demonstrate Moscow's willingness and ability to employ military might in proximate Third World countries, widespread assertions that Soviets are prepared to wrest control of Persian Gulf petroleum should not be accepted at face value.[28] While the power of propinquity is undeniable, the many problems and implications of such a campaign are not negligible and would presumably be weighed by the Soviet military and political leadership. That the threat to Western oil supplies would be tantamount to an act of war, which might extend hostilities to an area in which Moscow would not necessarily have an advantage, is but one issue that would have to be considered. In addition, a secure air corridor would have to be established by setting up anti-aircraft defenses along the over-600-mile route from the Soviet border to the Iranian oilfields, and the capability of local military forces, the effect of a hostile populace, and the poor road systems on which vast amounts of men and material would be conveyed would all have to be contended with. Finally, it is debatable whether the situation in Afghanistan is a dramatic illustration of the efficacy of Soviet military power or of the limits of armed might in general. If anything, the guerrilla movement in that country greatly intensified *after* the entry of Soviet troops, who continue to wage an uncertain war against ill-equipped, divided, but dogged resistance forces. Superior Soviet weaponry and firepower have been of no value in creating the belief among Afghans that the Karmal regime is a legitimate government and not the creature of an imperial neighbor; it is not clear how the much-vaunted geopolitical advantages of Afghanistan can be enjoyed while buttressing a shaky government in a turbulent environment.

INTERVENTIONISM AND THE
CORRELATION OF FORCES

Analyses that link the more assertive role that Moscow has played in the Third World over the past six years to a sense of confidence that the Kremlin has acquired from the attainment of strategic parity and enhanced power-projection resources need to be reconsidered. As was pointed out in the foregoing section, while the Soviet ability to convey men and material to distant areas has undoubtedly grown since the Khrushchev years, it remains substantially inferior to that of the United States. To speak of the growth of Soviet power-projection capability in a noncomparative context is not very useful, since power is essentially relative.

Of course, Soviet military power has been used decisively in many recent Third World crises. In the case of the Angolan Civil War of 1975-76, the Soviet Union's massive airlift of arms and 10,000 Cuban troops in support of Agosthino Neto's MPLA (Popular Movement for the Liberation of Angola) was of crucial importance in its defeat of Jonas Savimbi's UNITA (National Union for the Total Liberation of Angola) group and the FNLA, (National Front for the Liberation of Angola) led by Holden Roberto. In the Horn of Africa, the Soviets once again airlifted sizable amounts of material and 20,000 Cuban troops, enabling Mengistu Haile Miriam to overcome Somali insurgents in the Ogaden and the secessionist movement in Eritrea. In Afghanistan, in December 1979, the USSR took the unprecedented step of directly committing its own troops to rescue a radical government that had been given an ideological seal of approval.

The rapidity with which these episodes followed one another has fostered the impression that the growth in Soviet military power has tempted and enabled Moscow to push the historical process toward its predetermined (in the Soviet view) end more forcefully than in the past. The idea that these instances of Soviet intervention in Third World crises are primarily reducible to Moscow's confidence about its present military capabilities meshes nicely with two fairly widely held views concerning Soviet foreign policy. One is that the Soviet leadership continues, like its Czarist predecessor, to place primary emphasis on military power as an instrument with which to pursue external objectives. The other is that, in view of their economic and technological disadvantage *vis-à-vis* the West, the Soviets must seek to attain their foreign policy goals by utilizing means in which there is no marked disparity.[29] These interpretations cannot be dismissed out of hand, for they are valid to a degree. Nor is their appeal puzzling, since Soviet military power was vital in determining the outcome in Angola and the Horn of Africa and may prove to be in Afghanistan as well. These crises have sparked a continuing discussion about Soviet intentions in the developing areas and contending views regarding the role of the USSR's military power are a major feature of this debate.[30]

The Soviets have, to some degree at least, contributed to the prevalence of these interpretations by their penchant for asserting that the present "correlation of forces" (*sootnoshenie sil*) favors them. It is not clear, however, that the term connotes anything so narrow as the balance of power in a strictly military sense. Instead, the term refers to a whole array of factors that would determine the USSR's opportunities, possibilities, and constraints in a given period of time—decolonization and revolutionary trends in the Third World, the appeal of the Soviet socioeconomic model in various areas, the strength of the peace movement, international economic trends, the direction of the nonaligned movement, the distribution of military power, and the public mood in the West. Thus, Soviet observations to the effect that the correlation of forces favors the USSR indicate a feeling that the *general* international situation is supportive of Soviet interests. Much more is involved than a mere arithmetical enumeration of relative military power. As one prominent Soviet strategist has put it,

> Military power is not an independent factor, but a component of a complex system of interaction among various factors—economic, political, ideological, cultural, moral psychological, etc. All of them are mutually related and operate as parts of the overall complex.[31]

It is difficult to argue that the Soviet Union's intervention in Angola, the Horn of Africa, and Afghanistan is a consequence of its acquisition of a power-projection capability that overshadows that of the United States. Nor does the recurrent emphasis on the favorable correlation of forces denote that the Soviets perceive that the current military balance unambiguously favors them. Rather, Soviet activism has emerged as a consequence of other factors.

In each of the three crises noted above, Moscow's confidence was not due to a belief in the supremacy of Soviet power. Rather, it derived from a perception that the options of U.S. foreign policy decision makers were constrained, and that consequently, the USSR's intervention capability would not be put to the litmus-paper test by an American military response. This belief was shaped by a number of developments that took place in the United States in the aftermath of the Vietnam debacle, the controversy surrounding the Central Intelligence Agency's role in the fall of the Allende government in Chile, and the Watergate affair. The cumulative effect of these experiences was to engender both within Congress and in public opinion a mood characterized by a quasi-isolationist desire to rein in the power of the executive and prevent external involvements that displayed any potential to evolve into future Vietnams. While this feeling expressed itself in a fear of overextension abroad, the much-publicized détente emerging between the Soviet Union and the United States seemed to suggest that the atmosphere was permissive of a lower profile and a more limited range of foreign policy concerns. The euphoria accompanying détente inculcated a belief that there would be a corresponding restraint by Moscow and a reduced level of Soviet-American competition in the developing world.

It is not the acquisition by the USSR of an advantage in the ability to project power abroad that explains its recent assertiveness in the Third World. Rather, it is the Soviet Union's assessment of the effect that Vietnam, Chile, and Watergate had come to have on the ability of the United States to function as an effective competitor in the developing world. As Dimitri Simes has pointed out in a recent analysis of Soviet-American relations: "The Soviet Politburo may be guilty of many things, but it is hardly responsible for the lack of will, strategic purpose, and unity of the Western nations."[32]

In no sense were the civil war in Angola, the Ethiopia-Somali conflict, or the crisis in Afghanistan caused by the Soviet Union. While each resulted from complex indigenous factors, Moscow intervened because there seemed to be no compelling reason not to do so. Until Jimmy Carter resorted to an embargo on grain and high technology in response to the Soviet intervention in Afghanistan, commercial restrictions had been used to affect Soviet domestic policies such as those pertaining to emigration. It is doubtful, however, whether trade and credits can be successfully utilized to alter basic features of the Soviet political system. Certainly Moscow's reaction to such initiatives as the Jackson-Vanik amendment would seem to corroborate this conclusion. On the other hand, in areas such as activity in the Third World, where the stakes are not extremely high and where compromise is possible, the Soviets had not been provided with economic incentives of either a negative or positive sort.

Further, because of either the mode of Soviet involvement or the location of the crisis, the prospect of an American counterintervention was not a major concern for Moscow. In Angola and Ethiopia, it was the Cubans who were directly involved in combat; the USSR served only as a conveyer of troops and a supplier of equipment. Not only was there no direct participation by Soviet troops in the hostilities, but in the event of a military response by the United States, disengagement was possible without any direct harm to the prestige of the Soviet Union. In the case of Afghanistan, for sheer geographical reasons, Moscow could have been confident of its ability to respond to a counterintervention by the United States in the unlikely event that it materialized. In all three cases, the pattern of involvement did not entail undue military risks.

A LOOK AHEAD: INTERVENTION AS A FUTURE TREND

One major question that has been raised in recent discussions of Soviet policy in the Third World is whether intervention in crises is likely to be an abiding and inexorable future trend. A conclusive answer is of course impossible, since a great deal depends on the kinds of local instabilities that may arise and the degree to which Moscow views involvement as being either essential or cost-free. Nonetheless, there are constraints that will operate on the Soviet calculus as future opportunities for intervention are evaluated.

The Soviets clearly have been apprehensive about the possibility of strength-ened Chinese ties with Japan, Western Europe, and the United States. Beijing, which prior to the establishment of Sino-Japanese diplomatic relations in 1972 used to castigate what it perceived as a nascent militarist revival in Japan, has in recent years encouraged Tokyo to step up its defense effort. Few would dispute the view that this new approach is designed to complicate the Soviet security environment. As their criticism of the August 1978 Sino-Japanese treaty—in particular, its antihegemony clause—indicates, the Soviets harbor no illusions in this regard.[33]

In recent years, the defense issue has been discussed with unprecedented candor in Japan and influential individuals and groups have advocated an in-creased military effort.[34] The stimuli for this rethinking are several and the ultimate effect on the Japanese defense posture uncertain. Nonetheless, in a country whose economy depends upon far-flung markets, distant sources of energy, and long supply lines, sustained Soviet intervention in the Third World, if accompanied by doubts about the adequacy of American protection, will only enhance the persuasiveness of those calling for a military buildup. For the Soviets, this would be an unwelcome trend.

If anything worries the Soviet leadership more than a hostile China, it is the prospect of a hostile China fortified with Western technology and arms.[35] The Soviets are keenly aware that the transformation of Sino-American relations was influenced primarily by a shared concern about the USSR. To Moscow, the granting of most-favored-nation Status (MFN) to China in January 1980, the increase in Sino-American contacts in recent years, and the advocacy by some influential American analysts[36] that the so-called China card be played, can hardly be comforting. Washington has not gone beyond saying that civilian technology with "potential military application" will be sold to China,[37] and no such sales have yet been made. Moscow is not unaware, however, that the major element influencing a reassessment of this position will be the state of the U.S.-Soviet relationship which, as the direction of U.S. foreign policy under Ronald Reagan shows, can be shaped very definitely by perceptions of Soviet activity in the Third World.[38]

This suggests that the Soviets cannot ignore the link between the nature of their involvement in the Third World and their other foreign policy concerns. If the price to be paid for a policy of intervention in crises in the developing areas is likely to be the emergence of a Chinese-West European-Japanese-American coalition welded together by a shared suspicion of Soviet motives, not all opportunities for intervention in the Third World will be automatically in-viting.[39] Of course, it would be simplistic to underestimate the difficulties that stand in the way of the development of such a coalition; but it would be equally naive to expect that the nature of Soviet involvement in the Third World will have no bearing upon its prospects.

The Soviet Union's intervention in Afghanistan, and its role in the crisis in Angola and the Horn of Africa, have strengthened the tendency to view it as a revolutionary power: a competitor of the West committed to transforming an international system from which it is thoroughly alienated. While the rebellion against the status quo is indeed an aspect of Soviet behavior, it is important to realize the contradiction existing between this transformatory impulse and the stake the Soviets have in a stable setting that facilitates commerce with the West. Trade, loans, and technology transfers are all valued for their contribution to the economic dimension of Soviet power; the Soviets have surely not disguised their interest in expanding economic relations with the advanced capitalist countries and constantly reiterate the significance of "the scientific-technological revolution."

This interest in economic relations with the West derives from certain basic problems that have begun to affect the Soviet economy. The "extensive" strategy of growth, which sought to expand production by progressive increases in labor and capital investments, has ceased to be as appropriate as it once was. Low rates of population growth–less than 1 percent per year from 1970 to 1979[40]–and the utilization of the labor pool that could be drawn from the rural areas have made it impossible to count on the increasing availability of labor. Similarly, the crisis in Poland demonstrates the danger of constantly favoring priority economic sectors over the needs of consumers whose aspirations and awareness of living standards in other industrialized countries have grown. Soviet circumstances call for the adoption of an "intensive" approach, one that expands production through increased labor productivity and improvements in the technological level of the economy.[41] An important part of this new strategy, which would increase efficiency and counter declining growth rates (down from 6 percent a year in the 1950s to 3.5 percent in the mid-1970s),[42] would be expanding economic ties with Japan and the West that allow for the acquisition of modern technology[43] and assistance in prospecting and extracting petroleum in Siberia where terrain and climate create obstacles for Soviet drilling technology.[44]

It would be a mistake, however, to exaggerate the economic leverage that the West has at its disposal. While trade with the United States serves Soviet economic interests, it is essentially a process of exchange, bringing benefits to the United States as well.[45] Furthermore, as the American grain and technology embargo imposed in response to the Soviet intervention in Afghanistan indicated, the degree of economic leverage that is exercised is reduced to the extent that Argentinian and Brazilian farmers and West European entrepreneurs serve as alternative suppliers; effective economic pressure requires a sustained and coordinated effort by more than one nation, and in an international system characterized by the interplay of several sovereign states that pursue a variety of interests, such a precondition is not easily met. It is also true that although Western technology would better enable the Soviets to cope with the challenge posed by the need for an intensive growth strategy, the Soviet economic system is not going to collapse without it.

Two conclusions follow from this. First, there is no reason to suppose that the Soviet leadership is unaware that a regularized strategy of intervening in Third World crises may usher in a political climate ill suited to an unfettered growth in East-West commercial relations. On the other hand, it is unrealistic to expect Moscow to refrain from pursuing its vital interests for fear of economic blackmail. For example, in the case of Afghanistan the Soviets faced the prospect of a Marxist regime—with which they had forged extensive and visible ties—being toppled by an Islamic insurgency. Given the fact that Afghanistan adjoins Soviet Central Asia—an area inhabited by some 40 million people of Muslim origin—and the ambivalence that the Soviets have shown toward the present admixture of Islam and politics in neighboring Iran,[46] it is doubtful whether even the likelihood of coordinated Western economic sanctions could have dissuaded Moscow from intervening. Second, a policy of publicly linking progress on East-West commercial relations to Soviet activity in the Third World may strengthen that faction of the Soviet establishment that Alexander Yanov identifies as being uncomfortable with the idea of détente and interdependence for a variety of reasons.[47] Moscow may well opt to forego the economic benefits rather than lose face and set a dangerous precedent by succumbing to Western commercial leverage.

This does not mean that economic diplomacy is totally devoid of value in responding to Soviet involvement in the Third World. It does mean that a sober assessment of the extent of Western leverage is essential, as is an understanding of what the Soviets can and cannot be expected to do. Further, the strategy of linking Western economic relations and Soviet behavior in the developing areas is not likely to have the intended effect, if it is designed not only to affect Soviet policy but also to face down the USSR on center stage. It is also not clear that Soviet responsiveness to American interests in the developing world can be expected, when Washington simultaneously pursues a policy of seeking to exclude the Soviets from negotiations in areas that are vital to them.[48]

A final constraint on a frequent resort to intervention concerns the adverse effect this will have on the Soviet Union's persistent effort to cultivate the image of a friend of the Third World and a state whose foreign policy is not shot through with the imperial designs of capitalist states.[49] The intervention in Afghanistan affected the Third World in a way that the Soviet Union's invasion of Hungary in 1956 and Czechoslovakia in 1968 never did.

In January and November 1980, a vast majority of the General Assembly called for the withdrawal of Soviet troops. India, with its long-standing ties to the Soviet Union, has made restrained but persistent calls for the withdrawal of "foreign troops" from Afghanistan, and refused to support the Soviet position during Foreign Minister Gromyko's visit to New Delhi in February 1980 and Brezhnev's much-publicized trip in December of the same year. More strident criticism has come from Iraq—once labeled by many as a Soviet "client"—and Iran. Long sensitive about Eurocommunist critiques of its foreign policy,

Moscow has also complicated its relations with the Italian Communist party (PCI). Unlike French Communist party leader Georges Marchais who supported the role in Afghanistan, PCI leader Enrico Berlinguer reportedly commented that the intervention indicates that the Soviet Union's threat to peace is equivalent to that of the United States. Berlinguer also absented himself from the 26th Party Congress held in February-March 1981, and the PCI delegate in attendance called for the withdrawal of "foreign troops" from Afghanistan.[50]

The intervention into Afghanistan has also set in motion other adverse and more tangible foreign policy trends for the Soviets. Concern about a future use of Soviet military power in the Third World has led Egypt, Kenya, Oman, and Somalia to provide military facilities that would support a larger and more permanent U.S. presence near the Persian Gulf.[51] It has also given a fresh impetus to efforts by Saudi Arabia—about whose role in the Middle East the Soviets have always been suspicious—to form a coalition of states concerned with Persian Gulf security. These developments illustrate the operation of the balance of power in a way that is not to Moscow's liking.

CONCLUSION

While Soviet defense spending has steadily increased over the years as a percentage of the gross national product, there has been a slight decline in the expenditure devoted to military purposes. Within the context of overall spending, the development of a capability to intervene in Third World crises has not been a major priority. Soviet ability in this regard remains significantly inferior to that of the United States, and recent Soviet behavior in Angola, the Horn of Africa, and Afghanistan are not the consequence of either a confidence that the military balance favors the USSR or a belief that its power-projection capabilities have outstripped those at the disposal of Washington. Rather, the seeming confidence with which Moscow acted on these three occasions is attributable to a perception that the risks were low, the possible benefits worthwhile, and the prospect of an American counterintervention slight. None of the episodes supports the view that the Soviets are now prone to behave in a more risky and "daring" fashion.

When looking to the future, one should avoid the temptation of depicting the foreign policy choices facing Soviet decision makers as being simpler than they really are. Even assuming such a Soviet objective, the political, economic, and military consequences will have to be considered before a decision is taken to resort to intervention in the Third World as a regular means to generating an inexorable geopolitical current in favor of the USSR. The constraints that would operate against any such decision may not develop automatically, for they require a complex process of coordination. Nonetheless, the possibility that they will develop and the implications they pose will have to be considered in Moscow.

NOTES

1. See Roger E. Kanet and M. Rajan Menon, "Soviet Policy Toward the Third World," in *Soviet Politics in the Brezhnev Era*, ed. Donald R. Kelley (New York: Praeger, 1980), pp. 236–39.

2. A case in point was the opposition of the Congress to U.S. involvement in the 1975–76 Angolan civil war. See Richard J. Barnet, *The Giants* (New York: Simon and Schuster, 1977), pp. 44–45.

3. For a good analysis of the reasons for the Soviet intervention, see Selig S. Harrison, "Dateline Afghanistan: Exit Through Finland?" *Foreign Policy* no. 41 (Winter 1980–81), pp. 163–74.

4. U.S. Congress, Joint Economic Committee, Subcommittee on Priorities and Economy in Government, *Allocation of Resources in the Soviet Union and China—1978*, 95th Cong., 2d sess., June 26 and July 14, 1978, pp. 12–13. According to a recent C.I.A. report, in 1979 military spending as a percentage of GNP rose to 12–14 percent and outstripped the rate of economic growth. The report notes that the defense sector's share of GNP would be one percentage point less if the U.S. definition of defense spending is used instead of the broader Soviet one. See U.S. Central Intelligence Agency, National Foreign Assessment Center, *The Soviet Economy in 1978-79 and Prospects for 1980*, ER80-10328, June 1980, p. 16, fn. 22. Cf. U.S. Central Intelligence Agency, National Foreign Assessment Center, *Soviet and U.S. Defense Activities, 1970-79: A Dollar Cost Comparison*, SR 80 10005, January 1980, pp. 3, 5, which states that "the Soviet defense activities as defined in this report accounted for some 11 to 12 percent of Soviet G.N.P. *throughout* the decade of the seventies." (Emphasis added).

5. This appraisal of the C.I.A.'s estimates of Soviet defense spending is based on Les Aspin, "The Soviet Military Threat: Rhetoric Versus Fact," in *Detente or Debacle*, ed. Fred Warner Neal (New York: Norton, 1979), pp. 94–95; Franklyn D. Holzman, "Are the Soviets Really Outspending the U.S. on Defense?", *International Security* 4, no. 4 (Spring 1980): 86–104; idem, "Is There a Soviet-U.S. Military Spending Gap?" *Challenge* 23, no. 4 (September–October 1980): 4–8; U.S. Arms Control and Disarmament Agency, *World Military Expenditures and Arms Transfers 1968-1977* (Washington, D.C.: U.S. Government Printing Office, 1979), pp. 13–15.

6. See International Institute for Strategic Studies, *The Military Balance*, 1980–81, pp. 5, 9, for the data on U.S. and Soviet military manpower. According to Holzman, if the C.I.A. were to apply the 20 percent discount used in its calculations of Soviet spending in nondefense areas, the dollar difference in Soviet–U.S. defense spending would be reduced by 25 percent. See "Is There a Soviet–U.S. Military Spending Gap?", p. 6.

7. The C.I.A. did not make official ruble estimates of U.S. and Soviet defense spending until October 1979, and when it did, the calculations revealed that the Soviets outspent the United States. As Holzman points out, however, although about 30 percent of U.S. weapons are beyond the reach of Soviet technological attainment, such material was tagged at "ordinarily high Soviet ruble prices." Of course, this underprices the very goods in which the United States has the edge. See "Is There a Soviet-U.S. Military Spending Gap?", p. 7. Also, U.S. Arms Control and Disarmament Agency, *World Military Expenditures and Arms Transfers 1968-1977*, p. 6.

8. See, for example, Andrei Stepanov, "The Undeclared War Continues," *New Times* (Moscow), no. 10 (March 1980), pp. 8–9; idem, "New Fit of Pactomania," ibid., no. 42 (October 1979); p. 12.

9. Malcolm Mackintosh, "Soviet Foreign and Defense Policy: A Global View," in *The Political Implications of Soviet Military Power*, ed. Lawrence L. Whetten (New York: Crane, Russak, 1977), pp. 30–31.

10. The data given are presented in U.S. Central Intelligence Agency, National Foreign Assessment Center, *Estimated Soviet Defense Spending: Trends and Prospects*, June 1978. Reprinted in U.S. Congress, Joint Economic Committee, *Allocation of Resources in the Soviet Union and China*, pp. 21-24.

11. Approximate calculations derived from the data and categories in U.S. Central Intelligence Agency, *Soviet and U.S. Defense Activities, 1970-79*, pp. 3, 9-10. Power-projection forces are defined for the purposes of this analysis as the combination of mobility forces and general-purpose naval forces. U.S. aircraft carriers and their accompanying aircraft, which the Defense Department lists in the "tactical air" category, have been included in the calculation of U.S. spending on general-purpose naval forces. For a different estimate, see Stephen W. Van Evera and Barry R. Posen, "Overarming and Underwhelming," *Foreign Policy* no. 40 (Fall 1980), p. 105.

12. The payload of the two fleets is calculated from the information contained in I.I.S.S., *The Military Balance*, 1980-81, pp. 8, 12; *Jane's All the World's Aircraft*, 1979-80, pp. 175-77, 187-88; and John M. Collins, *Imbalance of Power: Shifting U.S.-Soviet Military Strengths* (San Rafael, Cal.: Presidio Press, 1978), Fig. 22, p. 198. Reserve and civilian aircraft are not included.

13. Van Evera and Posen, "Overarming and Underwhelming," p. 104.

14. A different assessment of the Soviet airborne divisions, see Captain Kenneth Allard, "Soviet Airborne Forces and Preemptive Power Projection," *Parameters* 10, no. 4 (December 1980): 42-51.

15. For the characteristics of these ships, see *Jane's Fighting Ships*, 1980-81, pp. 513-14, 668-70.

16. Tonnage calculated from data in ibid., pp. 513-15, 665-71. Attributes of the *Blue Ridge*-class and *Tarawa*-class vessels are discussed on pp. 665-66.

17. U.S. Defense Intelligence Agency, *The Soviet Naval Infantry*, Defense Intelligence Report, DDB-1200-146-80, April 1980, p. 81; International Institute for Strategic Studies, *Strategic Survey*, 1979, p. 22; idem, *Handbook of the Soviet Armed Forces*, DDB-2680-40-78, February 1979, pp. 9-13, which points out that the Soviets label their two helicopter carriers—the *Moskva* and the *Leningrad*—and their two *Kiev*-class aircraft carriers "antisubmarine cruisers." Also see Michael MccGwire, "Naval Power and Soviet Global Strategy," *International Security* 3, no. 4 (Spring 1979): 166-67, 172, 182.

18. Sergei G. Gorshkov, *The Seapower of the State* (Annapolis, Md.: Naval Institute Press, 1979), pp. 235-77, passim; idem, "Navies as an Instrument of Peacetime Imperialism," in *Red Star Rising at Sea*, trans. Theodore A. Neely, Jr. (Annapolis, Md.: Naval Institute Press, 1974), pp. 119-20; and Gorshkov, "Some Problems in Mastering the World Ocean," in ibid., pp. 128-31. The International Institute of Strategic Studies (London) notes: "The existing balance of the Soviet Navy's tasks . . . gives first priority to countering U.S. naval power, and puts the projection of power ashore, in the Western sense, well down the list. These priorities are likely to persist at least until a significant number of *Kiev*-class and *Ivan Rogov*-class amphibious warfare transports . . . become available." I.I.S.S., *Strategic Survey*, p. 23.

19. In 1980, then Defense Secretary Harold Brown was optimistic about the ability of the United States to contain or curtail the movements of Soviet ships and submarines beyond the Greenland-Iceland-United Kingdom (G.I.U.K.) line and to similarly restrict the exits of Soviet shipping from the Pacific and Mediterranean fleets out to open sea. One can assume that the Soviets are aware of such pronouncements. Harold Brown, Department of Defense, *Annual Report*, Fiscal Year 1981, January 29, 1980, pp. 9, 114.

20. *Jane's Fighting Ships*, p. 516.

21. Ibid., pp. 516-17. For an assessment of U.S. and Soviet strengths in sealift, see Lieutenant Colonel Marshall E. Daniel, Jr., U.S.A.F., *Defense Transportation Organization:*

Strategic Mobility in Changing Times, National Defense University Research Directorate, National Security Monograph 79-3, May 1979, pp. 10-15; and Collins, *Imbalance of Power*, pp. 203-10. The importance attached by the Soviets to the merchant marine as an element of sea power is clear from Gorshkov, *The Sea Power of the State*, pp. 29-42.

22. On the *Boris Chilikin* and the *Berezina*, see *Jane's Fighting Ships*, p. 530. Soviet awareness of these lacks can be gleaned from Gorshkov, "Some Problems," pp. 132-34.

23. See the excellent analysis of Charles C. Peterson, "Trends in Soviet Naval Operations," in *Soviet Naval Diplomacy*, ed. Bradford Dismukes and J. McConnell (New York: Pergamon Press, 1979), esp. pp. 60-64. Also see G. E. Miller, "An Evaluation of the Soviet Navy," in *The Soviet Threat: Myths and Realities*, ed. Grayson Kirk and Nils H. Wessell (New York: Academy of Political Science, 1978), pp. 50-53; Paul J. Murphy, "Trends in Soviet Naval Force Structure," in *Naval Power in Soviet Policy*, ed. Murphy, United States Air Force, *Studies in Communist Affairs*, vol. 12 (Washington, D.C.: U.S. Government Printing Office, 1978), pp. 126-27; Barry M. Blechman et al., *The Soviet Military Buildup and Soviet Defense Spending* (Washington, D.C.: Brookings Institution, 1979), p. 12; and U.S. Defense Intelligence Agency, *Handbook on the Soviet Armed Forces*, pp. 6-9, 9-12.

24. Michael T. Klare, "Superpower Rivalry at Sea," *Foreign Policy*, no. 21 (Winter 1975-76), p. 24. Also see the interview with Rear Admiral Gene La Rocque, U.S.N. (retd.) in *Challenge* 23, no. 2 (May/June 1980): 38.

25. The Joint Chiefs of Staff recently described the Soviet ability to project power as "minimal at present," but added that, as soon as "the early 1980s", they would acquire "viable means for military intervention in the Third World." Exactly what would bring about this sudden, radical change is not made clear. Gen. David C. Jones, U.S.A.F. (Chairman, Joint Chiefs of Staff), *United States Military Posture for FY 1981*, p. 30.

26. Ibid., and Harold Brown, *Annual Report*, pp. 10-11, 116, 181, 210.

27. For the genesis, growth, and future direction of the Rapid Deployment Force, see Michael T. Klare, "The Rapid Deployment Force: An Army in Search of a War," *Progressive* 45, (February 1981), pp. 18-23.

28. This rather widespread interpretation of the Soviet invasion of Afghanistan rests primarily on reports that the C.I.A. has issued since 1977, predicting that a decline in oil production would lead the USSR to become a net importer by 1985. For a convincing critique of the assumptions underlying the C.I.A.'s position, see Marshall I. Goldman, "The Role of the Communist Countries," in *Energy and Security*, ed. David Deese and Joseph S. Nye (Cambridge, Mass.: Ballinger, 1981), pp. 121-26. In weighing the argument that the move into Afghanistan was propelled by the lure of Persian Gulf petroleum, two points need to be made. First, no evidence exists that such a motive was indeed part of Moscow's calculations. Second, while it is true that such proof is unlikely to be accessible, it is not self-evident that other solutions to Moscow's assumed petroleum dilemma—conservation, increasing the use of other sources of energy, and the quest for Western drilling technology and participation in exploratory efforts—would have been dismissed in preference for a far more costly and dangerous remedy: costly in terms of East-West ties and Soviet relations with the Third World, dangerous as a possible prelude to a confrontation with the United States.

29. For an analysis influenced by these two perspectives, see Richard Pipes, "Detente: Moscow's View," in *Soviet Strategy in Europe*, ed. Pipes (New York: Crane, Russak, 1976), pp. 3-44.

30. See, for example, the excerpts from the testimony of Richard Pipes and George Kennan before the Senate Budget Committee (February 28, 1980) in *U.S. News and World Report*, March 10, 1980, p. 33.

31. From the conclusion of V. M. Kulish et al., *Military Power and International Relations*, in *Selected Soviet Military Writings 1970-1975*, ed. and trans. William F. Scott

(Washington, D.C.: U.S. Government Printing Office), p. 26. Along the same lines, two other Soviet analysts note: "The whole balance of strength does not at all boil down to parity in the military-strategic field." Yuri Zhilin and Andrei Yermonsky, "Once More on the World Balance of Strength," *New Times* (Moscow), no. 46 (November 1980), p. 19.

32. Dimitri K. Simes, "Detente and Conflict in Soviet Foreign Policy, 1972-1977," *Washington Papers* 5, no. 44 (1977): 21. The Soviets have consistently maintained that détente does not preclude their supporting the favored forces of change in the Third World. See Zhilin and Yermonsky, "Once More on the World Balance of Strength," p. 20; Kulish in *Selected Soviet Military Writings*, ed. Scott, p. 30.

33. Robert Rand, "Official Soviet Protest Against Signing of Sino-Japanese Treaty," *Radio Liberty Research*, RL 188/78, April 7, 1980, p. 10.

34. See Henry Scott Stokes, "Japanese Establish Arms Policy Panel," *New York Times*, April 7, 1980, p. A10; Isaac Shapiro, "The Risen Sun: Japanese Gaullism?", *Foreign Policy*, no. 41 (Winter 1980-81), pp. 62-81; Drew Middleton, "Japan Planning Sizable Increase in Arms Budget," *New York Times*, July 4, 1980, p. A4; Geoffrey Murray, "Gulf War Nudges Japan Toward Tougher Defense Stance," *Christian Science Monitor*, September 29, 1980, p. 3. Moscow's unyielding stance on the disputed Kuriles and recent moves to increase the Soviet military presence on these islands will also affect both Soviet-Japanese relations and Japan's security decisions. "The Soviets Stir Up the Pacific," *Time*, March 23, 1981; *Christian Science Monitor*, February 24, 1981, p. 5; ibid., March 19, 1981, p. 7.

35. In a recent interview with the correspondent of the *Christian Science Monitor*, Deng Xiaoping said with typical bluntness: "[I]f China dares to stand up to the Soviet Union even if it's poor, . . . why should China try to seek reconciliation with the Soviet Union after it gets rich[?]" *Christian Science Monitor*, November 17, 1980, p. 13.

36. Among them, Michael Pillsbury. It is hardly coincidental that the role of China in American foreign policy began to be analyzed with fresh vigor after the entry of Soviet troops into Afghanistan.

37. This was the position of the Carter administration. See Harold Brown, *Annual Report*, p. 52. Britain and France have already expressed an interest in selling arms to China. Negotiations for the supply of British Harrier jumpjets and French antitank and antiaircraft missiles have been held and the Chinese have placed an order with the French. Drew Middleton, "China's Strength: Arms Lag Still Apparent," *New York Times*, April 3, 1980, p. A10.

38. See, for example, the texts of Secretary of State Alexander Haig's opening statement of his January 9, 1981 confirmation hearings and his news conference of January 28, 1981. U.S. Department of State, Bureau of Public Affairs, *Current Policy* no. 257, (January 1981).

39. For Soviet views of such a coalition, see *Pravda*, September 28, 1979, p. 5, and the detailed discussion in V. Andreyev, "The Partnership Between Peking and Imperialism—A Threat to Peace and Independence," *International Affairs*, no. 11 (November 1980), pp. 68-78.

40. U.S. Central Intelligence Agency, *The Soviet Economy in 1978-79*, p. 10.

41. See for example, Felix Goryunov, "Top Priority," *New Times*, no. 50 (December 1980), pp. 7-8.

42. While the growth rate of the 1970s was still respectable, the steady decline since the 1950s, and predictions of a continued downward trend are not encouraging. See Harold Brown, *Annual Report*, p. 31; and U.S. Central Intelligence Agency, *The Soviet Economy in 1978-79*.

43. On the importance of trade with the West and technology transfer for the Soviet economy, see Herbert S. Levine, "Soviet Economic Development, Technology Transfer, and Foreign Policy," in *The Domestic Context of Soviet Foreign Policy*, ed. Seweryn Bailer (Boulder, Col.: Westview Press, 1981), pp. 179-80, 187-88. A comparison of Soviet and

Western levels of technology in various sectors is contained in a two-part series in the *Wall Street Journal*, March 21, 1980, pp. 1, 20; March 22, 1980, pp. 1, 16.

44. Because of a decline in oil production in the once-vital Urals-Volga area, Siberia has become increasingly important. For a comparison of Soviet and Western oil drilling technology that stresses the considerable lag of the former, see the remarks of Arthur Meyerhoff in WNET/WETA Television, "Soviet Oil Needs," *MacNeil-Lehrer Report*, Library No. 1121, Show No. 5141, January 14, 1980, pp. 4–5.

45. These are discussed in Alec Nove, "East-West Trade: Problems, Prospects, Issues," *Washington Papers* 6, no. 53 (1977): 60–61.

46. See Shahram Chubin, "Soviet Policy Toward Iran and the Gulf," *Adelphi Papers*, no. 157 (1980): 32–39; Ned Temko, "Soviet Union Murmurs 'Love Me, Or Else' to Iran," *Christian Science Monitor*, February 17, 1981, p. 4.

47. Alexander Yanov, *Detente After Brezhnev: The Domestic Roots of Soviet Foreign Policy*, Institute of International Studies, University of California (Berkeley), 1977, pp. 65–67, 77–78. A former Soviet journalist, Yanov emigrated from the USSR in 1974.

48. Aside from Soviet suspicions of the now faltering Camp David process, it is questionable whether a durable peace in the Middle East is feasible without the involvement of the major supplier of arms to Algeria, Iraq, Libya, and Syria.

49. This is clearly evident in the continual effort to rebut China's three-worlds theory, which posits a First World (the United States and the Soviet Union) attempting to dominate the Second World (Eastern Europe and the developed capitalist states, including Japan) and the Third World (the less developed countries). China sees itself as a constituent of both the Second World and the Third World and seeks to mobilize the two against First World hegemonism, particularly that of the Soviet Union. For Soviet analyses displaying a clear concern about the potential appeal of this thesis, see, for example, N. Kapchenko, "The Threat to Peace from Peking's Hegemonistic Policy," *International Affairs* (Moscow), 1980, no. 2 (February), pp. 71–72; Vladimir Leonidov, "An Alliance More Essential Than Ever," *New Times*, no. 47 (November, 1980), p. 15; and Andreyev, "The Partnership Between Peking and Imperialism," p. 76.

50. Flora Lewis, "European Communists Plan Meeting in Paris Soon," *New York Times*, April 2, 1980, p. A3; and Ned Temko, "Eurocommunists No Longer Scare the Kremlin," *Christian Science Monitor*, March 3, 1981, p. 6.

51. Geoffrey Godsell, "U.S. Builds Shield for Southwest Asia's Oil," *Christian Science Monitor*, March 13, 1981, pp. 1, 10.

14

THE MIDDLE EAST AND AFRICA IN RECENT SOVIET POLICY

David E. Albright

Since the beginning of the 1970s, there has plainly been a sharp escalation—though with ebbs and flows—of Soviet involvement in the Middle East and Africa. This escalation has had political, economic, and military dimensions.

In the political realm, the USSR during this period has expanded its diplomatic presence in these two areas and has established official relations with 15 additional countries (or more than one-fifth of the total of 69 states and territories). All these have been in Africa, and largely in sub-Saharan Africa.[1] More important, the USSR has concluded treaties of friendship and cooperation with ten Middle Eastern and African countries—Egypt, Iraq, Somalia, Angola, Mozambique, Ethiopia, Afghanistan, the People's Democratic Republic of Yemen) (PDRY), Syria and the People's Republic of the Congo—although in two cases the local signatories (Egypt and Somalia) have subsequently torn up these documents.[2] Prior to the 1970s, Moscow had entered into such treaties only with Communist states. In addition, the Communist party of the Soviet Union (CPSU) has forged links with a number of self-styled Marxist-Leninist ruling parties in the two regions. Its relations with those of Afghanistan, the PDRY, Angola, and Mozambique have become fairly intimate, although the level of intimacy varies from one party to another.[3]

In the economic sphere, the amount of aid that the USSR has extended to countries in the two areas has risen significantly. During 1975-79, it reached $6,595 million, compared with $3,210 million for the entire 1965-74 decade. Most of this increased assistance has gone to states in the Middle East and North

---

The views expressed in this chapter are those of the author and do not necessarily reflect the views of the U.S. government or the U.S. International Communication Agency.

Africa. Countries in sub-Saharan Africa received just $335 million in 1975-79, compared with $380 million in 1965-74.[4]

The number of Soviet economic technicians working in the Middle East and Africa and the number of Middle Eastern and African students at academic institutions in the USSR has gone up in a similar fashion. As of 1970, there were 7,940 Soviet economic technicians in the Middle East and Africa, but in 1979 the figure had jumped to 26,875. During the same period, the contingent of Middle Eastern and African students in the Soviet Union expanded from 9,660 to 21,435. In both cases, sub-Saharan African states accounted for a sizable portion of the increase. The total of Soviet technicians in these states rose from 1,585 in 1970 to 5,640 in 1979; the number of students from these countries at school in the USSR, from 6,260 to 12,865.[5]

In the military domain, the value of Soviet arms agreements with states in the two areas shot up to $24,440 million in 1975-79, nearly double the figure of $15,600 million for the whole 1956-74 period.[6] The number of recipients of such arms went up from 22 countries in 1964-75 to 29 in 1974-78. Perhaps more critical, the USSR constituted the primary supplier of arms for 20 states in 1974-78, compared with 7 in 1964-73.[7]

A modest growth of the corps of Soviet military technicians seconded to Middle Eastern and African countries accompanied the increase in supply of arms. The figure for both Soviet and East European technicians stood at 9,805 in 1970 and 11,605 in 1979. Sub-Saharan African states accounted for the largest share of this growth, with the total for these states rising from 965 in 1970 to 3,990 in 1979. The Soviet contingent in Middle Eastern countries actually dropped over the decade, from 7,820 to 4,780.[8]

Undoubtedly the most spectacular form of new Soviet military involvement in the Middle East and Africa has related to actual combat operations. In 1970 Moscow dispatched combat personnel to man the sophisticated military hardware that it furnished Egypt to deal with Israel's aerial challenge. Then in 1975-76, the USSR provided the weapons and logistical backup for the joint Soviet-Cuban intervention in the Angolan civil war in behalf of the *Movimento Popular para Libertaçao de Angola* (MPLA). Shortly thereafter, in 1977-78, Moscow not only supplied the arms and logistical support for the Soviet-Cuban operation to help Ethiopia push the invading forces of Somalia out of the Ogaden but even sent high-ranking Soviet military officers to direct the undertaking. Finally, the USSR in late 1979 employed its own combat units to take control of Afghanistan and try to prop up the tottering regime of the People's Democratic party there.[9]

Soviet policy toward the two areas, however, has exhibited far more continuity with that of previous years than such heightened involvement might tend to suggest. This is particularly true with regard to the places that Moscow has accorded the Middle East and Africa in its geopolitical priorities and to the objectives that it has seemed to be pursuing there.

STATUS IN GEOPOLITICAL PRIORITIES

Just as in earlier periods, the Middle East and Africa have in recent years fallen below Europe and East Asia on the ladder of Soviet geopolitical concerns. Europe has ranked first in Soviet geopolitical calculations ever since the Bolshevik Revolution in 1917. It was from Europe that the chief threats to the Soviets state originated during the interwar period, culminating in the traumatic German invasion of 1941. Moreover, Europe has been the main arena of the USSR's competition with the United States since the end of World War II. The possibility that in the 1980s NATO may deploy in Western Europe medium-range missiles that could hit Soviet territory has now served to reinforce Europe's key importance in Moscow's eyes.

East Asia's second position in Soviet geopolitical thinking dates from the 1930s and 1940s, when the USSR from time to time found itself in armed combat with Japan. The war on the Korean peninsula in the 1950s, which brought about U.S. intervention under U.N. auspices, confirmed for Soviet leaders the area's continuing significance to the USSR in the postwar context. It was, however, the Sino-Soviet split in the early 1960s that demonstrated to Moscow how vital its stakes in the region are. In the mid-1960s Mao Zedong's revival of Chinese complaints about the "unequal treaties" that had transferred vast Asian territories from the Chinese Empire to Czarist Russia, and Beijing's acquisition of nuclear weapons, convinced Soviet leaders that a potentially serious security threat existed on their eastern borders. The Sino-American and Sino-Japanese rapprochements of the 1970s have simply bolstered that judgment.

There has also been a relatively high degree of consistency between the exact rankings of the Middle East and Africa on the Soviet ladder of geopolitical priorities since 1970 and those of the last half of the 1960s. Prior to the mid-1960s the rankings had fluctuated a good deal—especially in the post–World War II era.[10] During the initial postwar years, for instance, the Middle East and Africa occupied positions somewhere below the colonies and newly emerging states of South and Southeast Asia. In the 1950s, as empires disintegrated and more and more colonies and dependent countries acquired or asserted their independence, Nikita Khrushchev lumped the countries of the Middle East and Africa with other non-Western areas and assigned the lot of them the third spot among his geopolitical priorities, behind Europe and East Asia. But soon disappointment with the behavior of many of these Third World states caused him to narrow his definition of this rung of his priorities to Third World countries that he deemed had genuine revolutionary potential. Although most of these states lay in the Middle East and Africa, they were widely scattered and devoid of any geographic pattern. The list included, for example, the United Arab Republic (Egypt), Algeria, Ghana, Mali, and, for a while, Guinea. In the mid-1960s, conviction that little possibility existed in the foreseeable future for Communist breakthroughs in the Third World finally led Khrushchev's successors to abandon his concept of the ranking and to redefine it in a way that has endured ever since.

Instead of taking ideological outlook as the primary determinant of third place on its ladder of geopolitical priorities, Moscow has in recent years employed geographic criteria. Specifically, it has assigned the ranking to all countries in a broad arc to the south of the USSR, from South Asia around to North Africa—regardless of whether it has viewed these countries as "socialist-oriented" or "capitalist-oriented". The grouping, thus, has encompassed the Middle East in total and North Africa.

As a consequence of this redefinition of third-level priorities, sub-Saharan Africa has consistently ranked below the Middle East and North Africa in Soviet geopolitical calculations since the mid-1960s. Within sub-Saharan Africa, furthermore—and still another element of continuity—Soviet leaders have tended to focus on countries of obvious significance because of such considerations as their size or strategic location. Nigeria and Ethiopia constitute two prime and diverse illustrations.

THE NATURE OF OBJECTIVES

Since the opening of the 1970s, the USSR has appeared to be pursuing the same four basic goals in the Middle East and Africa that seemed to underlie its activities there at least as far back as the early 1960s.[11] These have included the establishment of a Soviet presence, the acquisition of a say in regional affairs, and the weakening of Western and Chinese influence.

Establishing a Lasting Presence

From the early days of the Communist International, the Soviet Union has sought to demonstrate its relevance to the Middle East and Africa. During the interwar period and the initial years after World War II, for instance, it adopted a future-oriented approach to creating a presence there. It tried to identify itself with nationalism in the two regions, especially in the colonial and dependent countries, and to channel this nationalism in a radical direction. Through such a process, according to the underlying premise, Communist parties would form and take power throughout both areas, and the ideological solidarity of these parties with Moscow would guarantee a Soviet role there. In the 1950s, as independence movements gained strength and new states came into being in the two regions and as the countries there more and more evinced an inclination to act as a "third force" in international affairs, the USSR switched approaches. It now embraced all "anti-imperialist" movements, whether they were under Communist domination or not, and it endeavored to fashion an alliance with all emerging as well as existing states in the two areas on the basis of a common commitment to peace. Implicit in this new approach was an assumption that Middle Eastern and African governments would view a Soviet presence as advantageous to them. The imbroglio in the Congo-Leopoldville after that country had attained independence in 1960 shattered this illusion. Nevertheless, the USSR persisted in its efforts to ensure a permanent presence in the two regions. Specifically, Moscow opted to concentrate on building close relations with those states with which Soviet leaders felt some ideological affinity, particularly the so-called Casablanca group. Although Soviet undertakings gave the USSR a substantial role in countries such as Ghana, Mali, the United Arab Republic, and Algeria in the first half of the 1960s, events of the mid-1960s showed Moscow the danger of an ideological approach to the establishment of a meaningful presence in the two areas. The ouster of Kwame Nkrumah in Ghana in early 1966 and the rise to power of a military regime desiring only minimal relations with the USSR reversed the advances that the Soviet Union had previously made there. Consequently, Moscow abandoned attempts to create a presence in the two regions by relying largely on the receptivity of local actors. Instead, it moved to accomplish this end by projecting Soviet power, and especially naval power, into the Middle East and Africa. By 1970, the USSR had permanent naval forces operating in the southern and eastern portions of the Mediterranean Sea, in the waters of the Indian Ocean along the east coast of Africa and in the eastern Atlantic Ocean along the western shores of Africa. To help keep these forces at sizable levels, however, it has over subsequent years sought access to various types of naval facilities in littoral states in the two regions. For example, Soviet ships at one time in the 1970s enjoyed special rights at several ports in Egypt and at Berbera in Somalia, and they still do so at Latakia in Syria, at Socotra and Aden in the PDRY, and in the Dahlak Islands of Ethiopia.[12]

In recent years as well as in the past, Moscow's commitment to this objective has reflected essentially a Soviet desire to demonstrate global reach. Inspired by an ideology of a transnational character, Soviet leaders from the outset of the Bolshevik Revolution held that the parameters of their concerns extended far beyond the USSR's borders. In the 1950s, Khrushchev transformed this contention into a claim of global power status for the Soviet state. Although Khrushchev's successors realized that he had failed to sustain such a claim, they did not abandon it; rather, they searched for more effective ways of validating it. With the passing years, moreover, they have grown increasingly insistent on asserting it.[13] In April 1971, for instance, USSR Foreign Minister Andrei Gromyko averred: "Today there is no question of any significance which can be decided without the Soviet Union or in opposition to it."[14]

Since the early 1970s, to be sure, Moscow has displayed a conviction that the degree of Western dependence on oil and other minerals from the Middle East and Africa and on the shipping lanes through which these pass constitute a Western vulnerability,[15] and it presumably has an interest in denying the West access to such minerals and disrupting use of the sea lanes that carry them to the West. The USSR, however, has plainly lacked the capabilities to accomplish ends of this sort.[16] As a result, such options appear to have remained essentially in the realm of wishful thinking and have not assumed operational significance.

Gaining a Voice in the Affairs of the Two Regions

During the first years after the Bolsheviks seized power, the Kremlin actively cultivated varied local forces in the northern tier of the Middle East— along the Soviet Union's southern borders—that it felt would be friendly or at least resist the efforts of Western imperialist powers to exert sway there, but a relative lack of success in implanting Soviet influence, the limited nature of Soviet capabilities, and preoccupations elsewhere subsequently caused Moscow to downplay this area until the end of World War II. After the war, however, Soviet leaders turned their attention to it once again, and since then their wish to have a say in what happens there has not flagged. Moreover, the geographic scope of their concerns in this regard quickly expanded. In the mid-1950s, it came to embrace the southern, largely Arab, tier of the Middle East as well as the northern tier; by the close of the 1950s, it included all of Africa too.[17]

Although Moscow's desire to participate in the affairs of the Middle East and Africa has remained constant over the years, the precise manifestations of that desire have altered from time to time. In the 1940s it took the form of territorial demands, especially with respect to Turkey and Iran. During the 1950s the USSR began to woo local nationalist leaders. For a while, during the late 1950s and early 1960s, Moscow concentrated in particular on forging close ties with the leaders in the two regions who seemed to enjoy the greatest stature beyond their own borders. Gamal Abdel Nasser of the United Arab Republic, the ardent pan-Arabist, and Kwame Nkrumah of Ghana, the fervent champion of pan-Africanism, were the prime cases in point. In the latter part of the 1960s, however, the USSR turned more to courtship of rulers of states whose intrinsic importance gave them substantial weight in regional matters—for example, the United Arab Republic and Nigeria. Since the onset of the 1970s, the manifestations have diversified considerably. The cultivation of major states such as Nigeria has continued. In addition, the USSR has strengthened its military forces, and thus its own capacity to affect events, in such key areas as Afghanistan, the eastern Mediterranean, and the Horn of Africa. It has also striven mightily to project itself as the chief outside supporter of the drive to end white minority rule in Southern Africa.[18]

Since 1970, as well as previously, Moscow's commitment to this objective, as to the preceding one, has flowed from its aspirations to global status. Such status, as the leaders of the USSR have clearly understood, does not come about through divine right or the consent of the international community. It must be self-achieved and self-sustained. Thus, the more impact the Soviet Union has around the world, the more credible its claims to be a global power. And the Middle East and Africa, because of their geographic locations vis-à-vis the USSR, have represented prime milieus in which Moscow might seek to demonstrate clout.

Undermining Western Influence

Since the outset of the Bolshevik Revolution, the Kremlin has evinced a determination to eradicate the Western position in the Middle East and Africa. Up to the 1950s, Soviet attention in this regard focused primarily on the West European colonial powers, especially Great Britain and France, but thereafter it shifted largely to the United States.

One could offer voluminous evidence of the long-term Soviet commitment to this goal, but perhaps it will suffice here merely to mention some of the outstanding illustrations from the post-World War II era. In the mid-1950s Moscow agreed to supply to Nasser's Egypt arms that the United States had declined to provide, backed Nasser's take-over of the Suez Canal Company, and threatened to send "volunteers" to Egypt when Britain and France, in cooperation with Israel, invaded the Sinai to try to regain control of the Suez Canal. Later in the decade the USSR rushed to aid both the new West African state of Guinea and the revolutionary regime of Abdel Karim Kassem in Iraq. Guinea had rejected Charles de Gaulle's proposal of association with France and opted for independence, so the French had retaliated by setting the country adrift economically. The Kassem regime had come to power by overthrowing the pro-Western monarchy and had taken Iraq out of the Baghdad Pact, thus depriving the West of its only ally in the Arab world. In 1960 the Soviet Union tried to help Premier Patrice Lumumba of the Congo-Leopoldville reestablish central authority in the break-away province of Katanga when the Western powers refused to furnish military aid to him for this end. Toward the close of the decade, Moscow took over the role of sole supplier of arms to Somalia after Mogadishu had found Western sources unwilling to provide military assistance because of its claims on the territory of its neighbors. When the West would not pressure Israel to return the Golan heights to Syria in the wake of the June 1967 Arab-Israeli war unless Syria ended its state of belligerency with Israel and acknowledged Israel's sovereignty and territorial integrity, the USSR hastened to come to Damascus's assistance. It not only reequipped the defeated Syrian army but also furnished massive economic and technical aid to the Ba'th government. In the mid-1970s the USSR intervened in the Angolan civil war in behalf of an Angolan political faction that was fighting two other factions that had Western, and particularly American, backing. Not long thereafter the Soviet Union became the only source of arms for Ethiopia after the United States had declined to provide the weapons and materiel that the embattled military regime in Addis Ababa wanted. At the end of the decade Moscow endorsed the Islamic fundamentalist revolution in Iran that overthrew the pro-Western shah, and it even warned the United States not to take unilateral steps against Iran after the seizure of the American embassy by Iranian revolutionaries in November 1979.[19]

In recent years, it should be noted, there has been one modification in Soviet thinking concerning this objective. Specifically, the time frame for the elimination of Western influence from the Middle East and Africa has lengthened considerably. Prior to the 1970s Soviet commentaries tended to convey the impression that Western influence would disappear from the two areas in fairly short order or at least in a finite, if vague, period. Since about the mid-1970s, however, there has been increasing stress on the necessity for "a long-term strategy . . . for the industrialization of the former colonies and semicolonies according to fundamentally different principles of social and international economic relations than those inherent in capitalism."[20] Even orthodox Soviet observers have persistently argued that the more radical or "socialist-oriented" states in the Third World should attract Western capital and work out "a system of regulation . . . that will guarantee the interests of the radical regimes and grant sufficient advantages to foreign investors to attract them."[21]

Curbing and Reducing Chinese
Influence in the Two Regions

From the moment that Sino-Soviet relations began to deteriorate seriously, in the late 1950s, the USSR entered into competition with China for influence in the Middle East and Africa, and that competition turned into fierce rivalry in the early 1960s with the open break between the two Communist powers. This rivalry has persisted ever since.

Over the years Moscow has given many signs of a steadfast commitment to preventing Beijing from expanding its influence in the two areas and to weakening that influence wherever possible. During the early 1960s such an intention manifested itself most concretely in the USSR's efforts to form an anti-China front among the liberation movements of the Middle East and Africa and to acquire a role for itself in the abortive second "Bandung" conference of Asian, African, and Latin American states. The internal upheavals in China during the Great Proletarian Cultural Revolution greatly diminished the challenge from Beijing in the two regions in the late 1960s, but when China breathed new life into its enterprises in the Middle East and especially Africa in the 1970s, the Soviet Union gave plenty of indication that its resolve to at least contain the Chinese there had not waned. For instance, one reason for Soviet intervention in Angola appears to have been Moscow's wish to keep China, which enjoyed long-standing and close relations with most liberation movements in Southern Africa, from becoming the dominant outside power in this area in the wake of the collapse of the Portuguese empire. Similarly, a desire to deprive the Chinese of any impact in the strategically important Gulf of Aden seems to have been a factor in Soviet support of the ouster of President Salim Rubay'i Ali in the PDRY in 1978. To cite one final example, Moscow in the last half of the 1970s began to furnish some weapons to the guerrillas from Southern Africa training in Tanzania and Mozambique, thereby ending what had once been a Chinese monopoly.[22]

Other Features

One other aspect of continuity in Soviet objectives in the Middle East and Africa deserves mention. During the period since 1970, as during earlier periods, there has been no discernible hierarchy in these objectives. In some cases, of course, the USSR has managed to pursue a number of the goals simultaneously because they have proved basically complementary. But in other cases the goals have clashed, and Moscow has not resolved the resultant policy dilemmas in the same way in each instance.

A few brief examples will illustrate the continuity here. In the late 1950s and early 1960s the USSR declined to extend all-out support to the Algerian National Liberation Front on the grounds that the best way to curtail Western influence in the Third World was to split France off from its NATO allies. This posture antagonized a large body of opinion in the Middle East and Africa and allowed the Chinese to make political gains in the two regions, especially in Africa.[23] Toward the end of the 1960s, however, Moscow supplied arms to the federal government of Nigeria for use against the Ibo secessionists of Baifra in order to enhance the USSR's standing with this largest and potentially most powerful country in Africa. Such aid enabled the Soviet Union to counter Chinese activity in support of the Biafrans, yet it also put the USSR on the same side as Great Britain, Nigeria's former colonial ruler.[24] In the mid-1970s the USSR evidently endorsed the Algerian-backed Polisario Front, which was seeking independence for the Western Sahara (a former Spanish territory that Mauritania and Morocco had recently occupied and carved up) so as to ensure Algerian cooperation for the projection of Soviet power to Angola. This step antagonized Morocco and caused it to back away from the phosphate deal that it had been negotiating with the Soviet Union—a deal that would have created a substantial "division of labor" between the two countries and thereby reduced Western economic influence in Morocco. Soviet backing of the Polisario Front also complicated Moscow's attempts to assure itself a major voice in Middle Eastern and African affairs, for Algeria at that juncture failed to win support for the cause of the Front from either the Organization of African Unity or the Arab League. In the late 1970s, after the passing of the immediate Angolan crisis, the USSR apparently reversed its priorities and induced Rabat to conclude the phosphate agreement proposed earlier. As a quid pro quo, according to Moroccan sources, the Soviets promised not to furnish active assistance to the Polisario Front. In the late 1970s, too, Moscow initially decided to provide arms to Ethiopia to weaken Western influence in that country, at the risk of a loss of access to military facilities in Somalia. Then, after Somalia committed its regular army to the struggle to seize the Ogaden from Ethiopia, Soviet wishes to obtain a say in African affairs figured prominently in Moscow's refusal to stop furnishing arms to Ethiopia, for the USSR discovered that most African states opposed Somalia's effort to change borders by the use of force. This refusal, of course, cost Moscow the special rights it had acquired in Somalia.[25]

The only major element of change since 1970 with respect to Soviet objectives in the Middle East and Africa has involved the linkage among these objectives. During the 1950s and 1960s Moscow appeared to believe that decline of Western influence and curtailment of Chinese influence would bring about a significant Soviet presence in the Middle East and Africa and give the USSR an important say in the affairs of the two regions. A Soviet specialist on the Third World, writing in the late 1950s, capsulized this perspective fairly neatly. He observed that "we are witnessing a process of regeneration in the East—the collapse of colonialism under the impact of the national-liberation struggle and the disappearance of obsolescent social and economic institutions," and he contended that "two paths of development, socialist and capitalist, are open to the former colonies after their liberation." Then he went on to say that "now, as the Soviet Union enters its forty-second year, socialism is seen by the people everywhere as a powerful and invincible force to which the future belongs." Moreover, "socialist ideas are steadily gaining ground in the East, where the competition between the two systems is closely watched."[26]

During the 1970s, however, a reversal of this linkage seems to have occurred. Moscow now tends to see a decrease of both Western and Chinese influence as the outcome of an expanded Soviet presence in the Middle East and Africa and of the USSR's acquisition of a major voice in Middle Eastern and African affairs. A prominent Soviet analyst declared recently, for instance, that "after the collapse of the Portuguese colonial empire and especially after the Angolan events, the U.S. government drastically stepped up its diplomatic, political and ideological activities in Africa in an attempt to prop up its waning prestige and weaken the growing influence of the USSR and other countries of the socialist community."[27] Comparable arguments have been made with regard to China.[28] Soviet economic commentary has run in a similar vein. Growing numbers of Soviet writers have implicitly conceded that the struggle to extract Third World countries from the world capitalist system will in all likelihood prove to be a protracted one. Not only, they note, have many of these states registered a good deal of economic growth while remaining within the world capitalist system, but it is also going to be a long while before the output of most Third World countries assumes a character that will make them viable partners in an exclusive international division of labor with the socialist community.[29]

PERCEIVED OPPORTUNITIES

Despite the foregoing continuities between Soviet policy toward the Middle East and Africa during recent years and that of previous years, substantial changes in policy have, nonetheless, taken place since 1970. These have derived from alterations in Soviet perceptions of the nature of opportunities in the two regions, modifications in Moscow's strategy for exploiting the opportunities that it has discerned, and shifts in the means that Soviet leaders have deemed appropriate for implementing their strategy. As for perceived opportunities, the changes have had both qualitative and geographic dimensions. Furthermore, there have been distinct subperiods of change within the post-1970 era.

To appreciate the shifts in perceived opportunities after 1970, it is essential to have a base from which to make comparisons, so it is useful to look first at Soviet thinking in the 1960s about opportunities in the Middle East and Africa. During the initial half of the decade, a high degree of revolutionary optimism suffused Soviet assessments of the two areas. Weaned on the Leninist notion that the collapse of colonialism would trigger a profound transformation of these regions, Soviet leaders saw the decline of the British and French empires in the 1950s and 1960s as a harbinger of major revolutionary developments. From the Soviet perspective, such developments would inevitably entail advances for the USSR, the vanguard of "national liberation." Quite quickly, to be sure, Moscow realized that the immediate prospects for developments of this sort were better in some places than in others, and it sought to differentiate countries in the two regions on this basis. The radicalization of politics in a number of Middle Eastern and African states facilitated such a process. Among the countries that showed particular promise in Soviet eyes during all or at least most of the period were the United Arab Republic, Syria, Algeria, Ghana, Mali, and Guinea. Although the great majority were situated in North and West Africa, the group as a whole formed no coherent geographic unit.[30]

In the mid-1960s Moscow abandoned hopes for "genuine" revolutionary breakthroughs in the Middle East or Africa in the foreseeable future. Such hopes had been waning for a year or so prior to the setback in Ghana in early 1966, but this reversal delivered the death blow to them. As a consequence, Soviet leaders now concluded that the opportunities available to them in the two regions consisted essentially of chances for increased state-to-state relations of varying kinds—diplomatic contacts, trade, military cooperation, and so forth. Moreover, especially after the heavy losses that the Arab countries suffered in the June 1967 Arab-Israeli war, Moscow deemed that the openings of this nature that had the greatest potential lay in the Arab world.[31]

This general assessment persisted well into the 1970s, with one minor exception. As the years progressed, Soviet leaders discerned growing opportunities of significance in the northern as well as the southern tier of the Middle East. By the late 1960s Iran had moved to diversify its sources of economic aid and military equipment, and even though it remained within the Central Treaty Organization (CENTO), it showed an increasing willingness to look to the USSR for such inputs. A coup in Afghanistan in July 1973 not only toppled the essentially pro-Western monarchy there but also restored to power Mohammad Daoud Khan, who had followed a policy of balancing Western and Soviet involvement in Afghanistan during a previous stint as prime minister in 1953-63. Friction between the United States and Turkey over the recurrent Greek-Turkish crisis with respect to Cyprus, and especially the U.S. arms embargo after the Turkish invasion of Cyprus in 1974, left Ankara in a mood to at least reduce its tilt toward the West. At no time during this period, however, did Moscow perceive the opportunities in the northern tier to exceed, or even equal, those in the Arab world.[32]

The mid-1970s finally ushered in a revision of Soviet leaders' appraisals of the USSR's openings in the Middle East and Africa. This shift had two components. The first component was geographic in character. After the October 1973 Arab-Israeli war, Moscow found its position in the Arab world deteriorating. Not only was there an escalation of the tensions with Egypt that had begun to manifest themselves with Anwar al-Sadat's explusion of Soviet military advisers in July 1972, but Egypt gradually turned toward the United States for help in dealing with Israel. The United States, for its part, opted to moderate its heavy tilt toward Israel and to engage in "shuttle diplomacy" among the key states in the Arab-Israeli conflict. During the same period, new vistas emerged for the USSR in sub-Saharan Africa. The military coup in Lisbon in April 1974 led quickly to the dismantling of the Portuguese empire in Africa and to the rise of a number of new independent governments in black Africa. Furthermore, the breaching of the walls of the white redoubt in southern Africa with the departure of the Portuguese seemed to portend increased ferment in this area. In the Horn, a "creeping coup" engineered by elements of the military deposed Emperor Haile Selassie of Ethiopia in late 1974, and the revolution that ensued took an increasingly radical direction. Thus, Moscow now saw sub-Saharan Africa as the primary locus of opportunities in the Middle East and Africa.[33]

The second component of the revision in the Soviet assessment was qualitative. By the latter part of the 1970s a number of governments in the two regions—largely, but not exclusively, in sub-Saharan Africa—had proclaimed a commitment to Marxism-Leninism. These included particularly the regimes in the People's Republic of the Congo, Somalia, Benin, Angola, Mozambique, Ethiopia, and the PDRY. Some had even launched efforts to create "vanguard" parties. Perhaps more important, they were all disposed, in line with the concept of proletarian internationalism, to associate themselves with the socialist world. In interpreting the opportunities that such developments entailed, however, Moscow sought to learn from its experiences of the 1960s. While Soviet analysts welcomed the widening of the circle of countries of "socialist orientation" and especially the appearance of "revolutionary democratic parties of a new type," they carefully distinguished such parties from Communist parties. Moreover, they maintained that the governments of these states faced enormous problems in carrying out profound social and economic reforms, and they acknowledged the possibility of departure from or breaches in the noncapitalist way of development. In short, Soviet leaders regarded the profession of ideological commitment by the regimes in question as a basis for forging close links with them, even of a party-to-party type, but Moscow did not anticipate that these regimes would effect major revolutionary transformations in their countries, at least in the short or medium term.[34]

As the 1970s closed and the 1980s opened, another shift took place in Soviet evaluations of opportunities in the Middle East and Africa. This, too, had both geographic and qualitative elements. With respect to the former aspect, the Persian Gulf area replaced sub-Saharan Africa in Moscow's eyes as the most promising milieu for advances in the two regions. On the one hand, the USSR had succeeded in taking advantage of many of the new openings that had presented themselves in sub-Saharan Africa during the mid-1970s, and consolidation of the gains that it had achieved was now the order of the day. Moreover, in the one case where prospects for increased Soviet influence initially looked good—namely, Zimbabwe—Moscow wound up suffering a setback. The elections in March 1980 that marked the settlement of the internal conflict there brought to power Robert Mugabe and his Zimbabwe African People's Union. Indeed, the USSR had to wait several months before being permitted to set up an embassy in Salisbury, although Mugabe established relations with the West and China immediately. On the other hand, the situation in the Persian Gulf, the source of a large percentage of Western oil supplies, entered into great flux at the end of the 1970s. The trigger of this change was the Islamic fundamentalist revolution in Iran in early 1979 and the ensuing deterioration of that country's relations with the West in general and the United States in particular. Furthermore, the USSR found itself in an improved position to maneuver with regard to this area, as a result of its own incursion into Afghanistan. To be sure, Soviet support of the April 1978 revolution in Afghanistan and the USSR's subsequent invasion of the country to prevent the collapse of the revolutionary regime there appear to have flowed largely from Moscow's concerns about local circumstances rather than from any broader regional scheme on its part, but the presence of Soviet military forces in Afghanistan did enhance the USSR's ability to exert pressure on the states in the area.[35]

As for the qualitative element, there was a deemphasis on the use of ideological outlook as the basis for gauging opportunities. By the late 1970s, Soviet analysts were beginning to stress that the contradictions between the countries of "socialist orientation" and the "neocolonial" West were not the only ones that existed. For example, a deputy director of the International Department of the

CPSU Central Committee maintained that "the development of capitalism in the former backward countries . . . does not take away and does not even dull but only modifies the antagonism between these countries and imperialism, leading to an element of intercapitalist contradiction," and he drew a distinction between countries pursuing dependent capitalist development and those pursuing "national-capitalist" development.[36] Subsequently, even Islamic fundamentalism (at least outside places where it challenged governments to which Moscow had given strong backing) took on positive attributes from Moscow's standpoint, in light of its strongly anti-Western overtones. Leonid Brezhnev himself acknowledged that "the liberation struggle can unfold under the banner of Islam," and he endorsed the Iranian revolution as "fundamentally an anti-imperialist revolution." He also stated that "we are ready to develop good relations with Iran on the bases of equality and, of course, reciprocity."[37] Ideological affinity, it is true, did not become totally irrelevant as a test for opportunities, but it was plainly no longer as important in this regard as it had been in earlier years.

STRATEGY FOR EXPLOITING OPPORTUNITIES

Soviet strategy since 1970 for capitalizing on openings available in the Middle East and Africa has differed from that of prior years in two ways. First, Moscow has formulated its strategy so as to take greater account of the USSR's previous experiences in the two regions. Second, Soviet leaders have shifted their strategy in accordance with the sorts of opportunities that they have perceived in the two regions, and these have not been the same as they were in earlier times. Indeed, they have even altered significantly across the post-1970 period.

Because of this duality of change, it is essential to commence the analysis with a look at Soviet strategy toward the Middle East and Africa in the 1960s. During the initial half of the decade, Moscow searched for a strategy that would hasten along the revolutionary process that it deemed in train in both areas and believed would redound to its own benefit. In the early years of this period, it tried to encourage increased militancy on the part of radical elements of the two areas within a framework of cooperation with the currently dominant "national bourgeois" forces there. This approach underlay the calls for the establishment of "independent national democracies." According to the Soviet view, the struggle for the creation of such entities would have several distinct characteristics. Local left-wing elements would continue to participate in—or, in certain instances, seek to promote—broad national-front alliances composed of all anti-imperialist forces. While temporarily accepting the primary role of the "national bourgeoisie" within these alliances, the left-wing forces would seek to build up their strength and eventually take control of the alliances by championing the "progressive" economic and social measures that the masses presumably wanted. Depending upon circumstances, the alliance itself could assume two forms.

Where a Communist party already existed or where the dominant non-Communist party contained few leftist elements, the alliance would involve separate parties in classical Leninist tradition (thereby necessitating the formation of a Communist party in the latter case). But where the main non-Communist party was an umbrella organization and included visible left-wing forces, the party itself might serve as the alliance, and the struggle for hegemony might take place within its ranks.[38]

Before long, however, at least the dominant elements within the Soviet leadership began to have doubts about the strength of local left-wing forces in the two regions and about the willingness of extant "progressive" rulers there to tolerate activities that threatened to undermine their regimes. As a consequence, this group devised an alternative way of furthering the revolutionary process. From their perspective, a radicalization of the domestic situations of a number of "progressive" Middle Eastern and African states was proceeding under the auspices of the current rulers, and those rulers had verbally embraced "scientific socialism." Therefore, the USSR should accept the commitment of these "revolutionary democrats" as genuine and attempt to guide them toward a true understanding of scientific socialism. The transition to socialism would thus result from the conversion of existing rulers into traditional Marxist-Leninists, not from their replacement by others of such a persuasion.[39]

The debacle in Ghana in early 1966 prompted the Soviet leadership to revise its strategy entirely. Its new approach rested upon two fundamental premises: that the "revolutionary democrats" in the Middle East and Africa had such grave faults that they would in all likelihood never bring about transitions to "true" socialism in their countries, and that there were no prospects for real revolutionary breakthroughs in the foreseeable future in the two regions. In the light of these considerations, Moscow opted for a two-pronged course to enhance its status in both areas. It would henceforth woo countries and political groups there in accordance with their objective significance—as measured by size, geographic location, economic power, political influence, and so on—rather than on the basis of their ability to qualify as progressive by Soviet standards. At the same time, it would seek to build long-term structural relationships with states of the two regions by constructing an international division of labor with them. Instead of trying to use economic aid to gain political influence, for example, the USSR would attempt to capitalize on its political and economic strength to obtain privileged economic positions for itself. Such relationships would tend to mitigate the chances of abrupt swings in Soviet fortunes in the two areas because of shifts in governments.[40]

In broad outline, this revised strategy has remained operative over the ensuing years, but there have been modifications in it in line with Soviet perceptions of the changing scene in the Middle East and Africa. The initial one occurred about the mid-1970s, with the emergence of self-styled Marxist-Leninist regimes in a number of countries of the two regions. Moscow undertook not merely to construct an international division of labor with these regimes but also to help them implant themselves firmly in their local soils. Activities of the latter sort included supply of key military advisers, aid in training political cadres, assistance in building party organizations, and so forth.[41] Such enterprises reflected a Soviet conviction that the USSR had a stake in ensuring the survival of these regimes. In Moscow's eyes, to be sure, none of them passed muster as genuine Marxist-Leninist entities, but they still had some distinctly positive attributes. Their professions of ideological commitment made them far more willing to enter into close ties with the USSR than most other governments in the two areas; furthermore, several of them—for example, those in Somalia, Angola, Mozambique, Ethiopia, and the PDRY—ruled countries of strategic importance. (It should be noted with respect to the regimes in Somalia and Ethiopia that Soviet leaders eventually had to choose which to try to help stabilize, for the strife between the two ruled out efforts in behalf of both.)

This new wrinkle in Soviet strategy, however, did not mean that the self-proclaimed Marxist-Leninist regimes received all of Moscow's attention. To the contrary, attempts to fashion an international division of labor with the rulers of other states in both areas, particularly states of objective significance, proceeded apace. During the mid-1970s, for instance, the USSR offered to provide major assistance to Nigeria in developing an iron and steel complex at Ajaokuta, the largest such project contemplated in Africa. Although negotiations on the final contract for Soviet participation dragged on for several years because of differences over terms, they finally reached a successful conclusion in July 1979.[42]

Another adjustment in Soviet strategy dates from around the close of the decade. At least, the majority forces within the Soviet leadership opted to introduce a measure of expediency into the USSR's approach to the Middle East and Africa. Moscow by no means abandoned its attempts to strengthen its structural ties with countries of the two regions and to assist the self-styled Marxist-Leninist regimes there to solidify their rule, but it sought as well to capitalize upon other "contradictions" in both regions that held promise of payoffs of a more transient kind.[43] The most dramatic of these had to do with Islamic fundamentalism. After the revolution in Iran in February 1979, Soviet observers increasingly stressed that it was "no rarity for members of the clergy or broad masses of believers," especially in the Islamic world, "to speak out against capitalism, in defense of national and democratic freedoms, and in support of forces fighting for peace, democracy, and social progress," and these same sources called attention to "the possibility and necessity of joint activity by working people—atheists and believers—aimed at the revolutionary renovation of the old world."[44] Brezhnev gave this point of view his personal endorsement in his report to the 26th CPSU Congress in February 1981.[45]

MEANS OF IMPLEMENTING STRATEGY

In the post-1970 period, military means have replaced economic means as the primary instrumentalities whereby Moscow has sought to carry out its strategy in the Middle East and Africa. Soviet activities in the two areas, to be sure, have had a military component ever since they commenced in the 1950s. In fact, the total value of the USSR's arms transfers to states in the two regions (to say nothing of its military sales agreements with the countries there) has consistently exceeded the sum of the economic aid that it has extended to them.[46] Nevertheless, Moscow in earlier years tended to think of military means as merely supplementary to economic means.

From the late 1950s to the mid-1960s Soviet officials trumpeted the USSR's ability to provide economic aid to the states of the two regions to help them consolidate their political independence, and these spokesmen placed that ability in the context of the Soviet model of development. According to them, the USSR could furnish such aid because of the superiority of its socialist system. Although Russia had lagged behind the West in economic and technological terms at the time of the Great October Revolution in 1917, Russia's embrace of socialism had permitted it to close the gap in a relatively short time, and the Soviet Union was now on the verge of surpassing the West in these realms. One writer capsulized the perspective in the following words:

> With the seven-year plan [1959–65] completed, the Soviet Union will need another five years or so to advance to first place in the world in major economic indices and living standards. That will be final and irrefutable proof of socialism's superiority over capitalism. It will also be the final reply to the question that is agitating many minds in Asia, Africa and Latin America: What is the quickest way and surest way to economic prosperity, through capitalism or socialism?[47]

As the 1960s progressed, however, it became increasingly evident that the USSR's rate of economic growth was declining, that the country faced serious economic problems, and that the heady optimism of previous years about the speed at which it would overtake and pass the West in economic performance had been misplaced. Under such circumstances, Moscow felt it necessary to downplay the Soviet model. Nonetheless, it retained its preoccupation with economic means as the key tools for pursuing its strategy in the Middle East and Africa. It decided merely to take a different approach to economic activities. That is, it would henceforth extend economic aid to countries in the two areas not essentially to try to curry political favor with them but rather to attempt to work out an international division of labor with them. Such a division of labor would lay the foundation for long-term cooperation of a mutually beneficial sort and, not incidentally, loosen the "imperialist fetters" that bound these countries.[48]

The Soviet switch to an emphasis on military means is hard to pinpoint precisely, but the advance of the 1970s produced growing indications of the change. One telltale indicator was the USSR's increasing disposition to become directly involved in combat situations in the two regions. This culminated in its invasion of Afghanistan at the end of 1979. Far more revealing, however, was the shift in the balance between the economic and military components of Soviet efforts to construct an international division of labor with the states of the two areas. During 1965–74, for instance, the economic assistance that Moscow extended to both regions together ran about 50 percent of the value of the arms that it delivered to them; during 1975–79, the figure dropped to about 35 percent. The decline was especially sharp in the case of Africa (North Africa and sub-Saharan Africa combined), from about 96 percent to about 28 percent.[49]

A variety of factors seems to have prompted this shift in emphasis. To begin with, Moscow appears to have had mounting doubts about the possibility of bringing about an economic division of labor with the countries of the Middle East and Africa over the short or medium term. More candid Soviet commentators acknowledged that the share of the Third World states and the USSR in one another's overall trade turnover remained exceedingly small.[50] Other equally forthright observers pointed out that many Third World countries were in fact experiencing economic growth even while remaining within the "world capitalist economy." They thus implied that such countries did not have great incentives to look to the development of an international division of labor with the USSR as a way of making economic progress.[51] An eminent Soviet scholar summed up Moscow's general viewpoint in saying: "We cannot match the U.S.A. in industry or agriculture, but we can overtake you in military power."[52]

Second, the situation in the Middle East and Africa lent itself to increased reliance on military means. In the Middle East, the Arab-Israeli struggle raged on, even though with the passing years at least Egypt turned more and more toward the United States to bring pressure to bear on Israel. In Africa, conflict was on the rise in various respects. The choice of internal paths was producing growing strife, the black-white confrontation in southern Africa was heating up, and the borders inherited from colonial days were becoming a subject of controversy and battle between states.[53] Moreover, the widespread reticence that had marked African attitudes toward the USSR in the 1960s had faded, and Africans of many persuasions were now eager to have Soviet aid and support for their causes. As a Soviet writer, discussing the results of the July 1978 summit meeting of African heads of state in Khartoum, noted, "the leaders of Madagascar, Angola, Mozambique and other states rated highly the noble role of the socialist countries which are helping Africans defend their independence."[54]

Finally, the West, and especially the United States, displayed increased reluctance to become involved in Third World conflicts. "After the shameful failure of its aggression in Indochina," according to one pithy formulation of the Soviet view, "the United States has been somewhat wary and is inclined to operate through others."[55]

PROSPECTS FOR THE 1980s

If the foregoing features have characterized Soviet policy toward the Middle East and Africa in the recent past, what can then be said about the outlook for Soviet policy toward the two regions in the years ahead? While the number of variables involved renders long-range projections of dubious utility, it is possible to offer some worthwhile thoughts regarding the remainder of the 1980s.

First, there is little likelihood that either the positions that the Middle East and Africa have occupied on Moscow's ladder of geopolitical priorities or the nature of the basic goals that the USSR has seemed to be pursuing in the two regions will alter. The rankings of the Middle East/North Africa and of sub-Saharan Africa among Soviet geopolitical concerns have stayed constant since the mid-1960s, and those rankings have a geographic logic to them. That is, they tend to reflect the order of importance that any state situated on the USSR's land mass would accord these areas. Unless Moscow returns to criteria of a more ideological character to define its geopolitical priorities, therefore, shifts in rankings would be surprising.

As for objectives, they appear to have remained stable since the early 1960s and some of them even seem to have been operative since the early years of Bolshevik rule. Hence, one would not expect changes to occur in them either. If, of course, the USSR were to improve greatly its capability for projecting force abroad, Moscow might come to look upon the Middle East in general and the Persian Gulf in particular as an arena for confronting the West directly, rather than as a prime place in which to validate its claims to global power status. But such a major advance does not appear in the cards. This is especially true in view of the economic crunch that appears to be developing in the USSR in the 1980s and the burdens that just maintaining strategic parity with the United States will impose on it, if the Reagan administration implements its own plans for a big military buildup.[56] In operating in the Middle Eastern and African contexts, nonetheless, Soviet authorities will in all probability persist in seeing the growth of the USSR's presence and influence as the key to the curtailment of both Western and Chinese influence.

Second, while it is exceedingly difficult to foresee precisely what opportunities will present themselves to the USSR in the Middle East and Africa, these will very likely continue to be diversified, and Moscow, for its part, will probably continue to see them as such. Many Middle Eastern and African governments with little in common ideologically with the USSR now regard it as a legitimate actor in their regional milieus and a potential source of help to accomplish their purposes. Such attitudes seem bound to proliferate further. At the same time, the instability and high level of conflict that prevail in both areas make it conceivable that the number of self-proclaimed Marxist-Leninist regimes there will increase. Indeed, the political fragmentation endemic to the two regions renders the capture of power by even leftist forces with a meager popular support base a far from insurmountable undertaking. Finally, the varied currents of anti-Western sentiment that exist in the Middle East and Africa show no sign of disappearing and could well multiply in the future. Whatever the ultimate fate of the Islamic revolution in Iran, for example, Islamic fundamentalism appears destined to become a factor to be reckoned with in many countries of the Middle East.[57]

It is possible, however, that the primary geographic locus of openings that Moscow perceives available in the two areas could shift—at least temporarily. In view of the degree of flux in the Persian Gulf since the 1979 Iranian revolution and of the strategic importance of the Gulf's oil, it is relatively unlikely that Moscow would focus its attention elsewhere in either the Middle East or Africa for long. But a crisis in a place of substantial geopolitical importance could produce such a switch for a period of time. Southern Africa affords perhaps the best illustration, yet Zaire and the eastern Mediterranean hold potential in this regard too.

Third, if the previous speculation with respect to opportunities proves to be correct, the strategy that the USSR has been following in the Middle East and Africa since the end of the 1970s will probably remain the same. Moscow could, to be sure, encounter some problems in trying to juggle the different strands of this strategy to avoid negative reactions from some of the strategy's various targets. In such a case, Soviet leaders would in all likelihood be inclined to further deemphasize the ideological elements of the strategy. That, in turn, would represent a downgrading of the self-styled Marxist-Leninist states in the overall scheme of things.

It should be underscored, however, that the energy and resources that the USSR puts into this strategy will not depend solely upon conditions in the Middle East and Africa. Opportunities and demands elsewhere, especially in locales of greater geopolitical concern to Moscow, will play a role as well. If the situations in Afghanistan and Poland continue to be unsettled, for example, they will absorb a great deal of Soviet attention and resources.

Fourth, the USSR will almost certainly persist in stressing military means to carry out its strategy in the Middle East and Africa. Such an emphasis is the outcome of lengthy experimentation and disillusionment with other, particularly economic, means. It has netted the Soviet Union major gains since its adoption in the 1970s. And it responds to the preoccupations of many political forces in the two regions.

In sum, then, Soviet policy toward the Middle East and Africa in the 1980s will probably bear a strong resemblance to that which evolved during the 1970s. Although some alterations will no doubt be essential to take account of changing circumstances in what are two highly volatile regions, these shifts will in all likelihood be at the margins, rather than fundamental.

NOTES

1. Compiled from Soviet, Middle Eastern, and African press reports.

2. Drawn from Soviet, Middle Eastern, and African press reports.

3. For Soviet discussion of these ties, see, for example, K. N. Brutents, *Osvobodiv-shiesia strany v 70-e gody* (Moscow: Izdatel'stvo politicheskoi literatury, 1979), pp. 142-43; C. P. Nemanov, "Partii avangardnogo tipa v Afrikanskikh stranakh sotsialisticheskoi orientatsii," *Narody Azii i Afriki*, no. 2 (1979), p. 27.

4. See U.S. Central Intelligence Agency, *Communist Aid Activities in Non-Communist Less Developed Countries, 1979 and 1954-79*, ER 80-10318U (Washington, D.C., October 1980), p. 7. This publication, as well as earlier ones in the same series, is available from the Document Expediting Service of the U.S. Library of Congress.

5. Ibid., pp. 10-11.

6. Ibid., p. 14.

7. Derived from U.S. Arms Control and Disarmament Agency, *World Military Expenditures and Arms Trade, 1963-1973* (Washington, D.C.: U.S. Government Printing Office, 1975), pp. 67-70; idem, *World Military Expenditures and Arms Transfers, 1969-1978* (Washington, D.C.: U.S. Government Printing Office, 1980), pp. 160-62.

8. U.S. Central Intelligence Agency, *Communist Aid Activities . . . , 1979 and 1954-79*, p. 6.

9. For discussion of these various undertakings, see Yaacov Ro'i and Ilana Dimant-Kass, *The Soviet Military Involvement in Egypt, January 1970-July 1972*, Research Paper No. 6 (Jerusalem: Soviet and East European Research Centre, Hebrew University, February 1974), pp. 8-14; Jiri Valenta, "Soviet Decision-Making on the Intervention in Angola," in *Communism in Africa*, ed. David E. Albright (Bloomington: Indiana University Press, 1980), pp. 93-117; Richard B. Remnek, "Soviet Policy in the Horn of Africa: The Decision to Intervene," in *The Soviet Union in the Third World: Successes and Failures*, ed. Robert H. Donaldson (Boulder, Col.: Westview Press, 1981), pp. 125-49; Zalmay Khalilzad, "Soviet-Occupied Afghanistan," *Problems of Communism* 29, no. 6 (November-December 1980): 23-40.

10. For a more detailed and systematic analysis, with relevant documentation, of the evolution of Soviet thinking on this subject in the post-World War II period, see David E. Albright, "Moscow's African Policy of the 1970s," in *Communism in Africa*, pp. 37-49.

11. Rarely if ever, of course, does Moscow announce its objectives in any context. Consequently, these have to be inferred from various types of Soviet behavior. Yet Soviet behavior is sometimes ambiguous in import. For this reason, any discussion of Soviet objectives entails an element of hypothesis as well as fact.

12. For elaboration and documentation of these developments, see Edward T. Wilson, *Russia and Black Africa Before World War II* (New York: Holmes and Meier, 1974); Walter Z. Laqueur, *The Soviet Union and the Middle East* (New York: Praeger, 1959); Robert Legvold, *Soviet Policy in West Africa* (Cambridge, Mass.: Harvard University Press, 1970); George Lenczowski, *Soviet Advances in the Middle East* (Washington, D.C.: American

Enterprise Institute for Public Policy Research, February 1972); Colin Legum, "African Outlooks toward the USSR," in *Communism in Africa*, pp. 7–34; Albright, "Moscow's African Policy of the 1970s," in *Communism in Africa*, pp. 37–52; David E. Albright, *The Dilemmas of Courtship: The Soviet Union, China, and Ghana*, forthcoming, Chs. 1, 2, 4, and 6; International Institute of Strategic Studies, *Strategic Survey 1980–1981* (London, 1981), p. 21.

13. For analysis and sources related to this paragraph, see, for instance, Franz Borkenau, *World Communism* (Ann Arbor: University of Michigan Press, 1962); John C. Campbell, *Defense of the Middle East*, rev. ed. (New York: Harper, 1960); Adam B. Ulam, *Expansion and Coexistence: Soviet Foreign Policy, 1917–73*, 2d ed. (New York: Praeger, 1974); Vernon V. Aspaturian, "Soviet Global Power and the Correlation of Forces," *Problems of Communism* 29, no. 3 (May-June 1980): 1–18.

14. *Pravda*, April 4, 1971.

15. For examples of some of the early commentary, see V. Baryshnikov, "Raw Material Resources of Africa," *International Affairs*, no. 12 (December 1974), pp. 135–7; Dimitri Volsky, "Southern Version of NATO," *New Times*, no. 36 (September 1976), pp. 8–9. An authoritative treatment of more contemporary vintage may be found in Leonid Brezhnev's report to the 26th CPSU Congress in February 1981. See *Pravda*, February 24, 1981.

16. On the one hand, the USSR has not had the economic resources, even where it might theoretically have enjoyed sufficient political influence, to persuade the Middle Eastern and African suppliers of minerals to the West to cut off such shipments, for these countries must export their minerals to carry out their own development programs. As Soviet analysts have conceded, the share of the Third World states and the USSR in one another's overall trade turnover stayed exceedingly small throughout the 1970s. See, for instance, O. Bogomolov, "CMEA and the Developing World," *International Affairs*, no. 7 (July 1979), pp. 26–28.

On the other hand, the USSR has not possessed the physical wherewithal to deprive the West of these minerals at their sources or through disruption of the sea lanes whereby they reach the West. See, for example, Worth H. Bagley, "Sea Power and Western Security: The Next Decade," *Adelphi Papers*, no. 139 (1977): 1–40; James L. Moulton, "The Capability for Long-Range Intervention," in *Soviet Naval Influence: Domestic and Foreign Dimensions*, ed. Michael MccGwire and John McDonnell (New York: Praeger, 1977); Charles G. Pritchard, "Soviet Amphibious Force Projection," in ibid.; James M. McConnell and Bradford Dismukes, "Soviet Diplomacy in the Third World," *Problems of Communism* 28, no. 1 (January-February 1979): 14–27; International Institute for Strategic Studies, *Strategic Survey 1978* (London, 1979); idem, *The Military Balance 1980–1981* (London, 1980); idem, *Strategic Survey 1980–1981* (London, 1981).

17. For more detailed treatment, see, for example, Laqueur, *The Soviet Union and the Middle East*; Lenczowski, *Soviet Advances in the Middle East*; Campbell, *Defense of the Middle East*; Legvold, *Soviet Policy in West Africa*; Albright, *The Dilemmas of Courtship*; Alexander Dallin, "The Soviet Union: Political Activity," in *Africa and the Communist World*, ed. Zbigniew Brzezinski (Stanford, Cal.: Stanford University Press, 1963), pp. 7–48.

18. For elaboration, see, for instance, the works cited in n. 17 plus Albright, "Moscow's African Policy of the 1970s," pp. 35–66; David E. Albright, "The Soviet Role in Africa from Moscow's Perspective," in *The Communist States and Africa*, ed. David E. Albright and Jiri Valenta (Bloomington: Indiana University Press, forthcoming).

19. For further discussion, see, for example, Campbell, *Defense of the Middle East*; Lenczowski, *Soviet Advances in the Middle East*; Laqueur, *The Soviet Union and the Middle East*; Dallin, "The Soviet Union: Political Activity"; Legvold, *Soviet Policy in West Africa*; Colin Legum and Bill Lee, *Conflict in the Horn of Africa* (New York: Africana Publishing

Co., 1978); Valenta, "Soviet Decision-Making on the Intervention in Angola"; Remnek, "Soviet Policy in the Horn of Africa"; Albright, *The Dilemmas of Courtship*; idem, "The Horn of Africa and the Arab-Israeli Conflict," in *World Politics and the Arab-Israeli Conflict*, ed. Robert O. Freedman (Elmsford, N.Y.: Pergamon, 1979), pp. 147–91; Shahram Chubin, "Leftist Forces in Iran," *Problems of Communism* 29, no. 4 (July-August 1980): 1–25. On the Soviet warning to the United States regarding methods of dealing with the Iranian take-over of the American embassy in Teheran, see *Pravda* and *Izvestiia*, January 16, 1980.

20. The quotation is from V. Rymalov, "Newly-Free Countries: Problems of Economic Development," *International Affairs*, no. 7 (July 1978), p. 58.

21. The specific quotation comes from the discussion "Kak otsenivat' osobennosti i uroven' razvitiia kapitalizma v Latinskoi America," *Latinskaia Amerika*, no. 1 (January-February 1979), pp. 69–70.

22. For more extended analyses, see, for instance, Dallin, "The Soviet Union: Political Activity"; Legvold, *Soviet Policy in West Africa*; Albright, *The Dilemmas of Courtship*; Donald S. Zagoria, *The Sino-Soviet Conflict, 1956-1961* (Princeton, N.J.: Princeton University Press, 1962); idem, "Sino-Soviet Friction in Underdeveloped Areas," *Problems of Communism* 10, no. 2 (March-April 1961): 1–13; idem, "Russia, China, and the New States," in *Soviet and Chinese Communism: Similarities and Differences*, ed. Donald W. Treadgold (Seattle: University of Washington Press, 1967), pp. 405–25; William E. Griffith, *The Sino-Soviet Rift* (Cambridge, Mass.: M.I.T. Press, 1963); Sven Hamrell and Carl Gosta Widstrand, eds., *The Soviet Bloc, China and Africa* (Uppsala, Sweden: Alinquist and Weksell Bokforlag, 1964); John Kautsky, "Russia, China and Nationalist Movements," *Survey*, no. 43 (August 1962): 119–29; Richard Lowenthal, "China," in *Africa and the Communist World*, pp. 142–203; Robert A. Scalapino, "Sino-Soviet Competition in Africa," *Foreign Affairs* 42, no. 4 (July 1964): 640–54; George T. Yu, "Sino-Soviet Rivalry in Africa," in *Communism in Africa*, pp. 168–88; George Lenczowski, *The Middle East in World Affairs*, 4th ed. (Ithaca, N.Y.: Cornell University Press, 1980); David Lynn Price, "Moscow and the Persian Gulf," *Problems of Communism* 28, no. 2 (March-April 1979): 1–13.

23. For elaboration, see Dallin, "The Soviet Union: Political Activity"; Lowenthal, "China"; Legvold, *Soviet Policy in West Africa*, pp. 82–83; John K. Cooley, *East Wind Over Africa* (New York: Walker, 1965), Ch. 16; Mohamed Heikal, *The Sphinx and the Commissar: The Rise and Fall of Soviet Influence in the Middle East* (New York: Harper, 1978), p. 125.

24. For more detailed treatment, see Legvold, *Soviet Policy in West Africa*, pp. 311–30; W. Scott Thompson, "The African-American Nexus in Soviet Strategy," in *Communism in Africa*, p. 193.

25. Albright, "Moscow's African Policy of the 1970s," pp. 50–58 passim, offers more extended discussion of these cases from the 1970s. See also U.S. Central Intelligence Agency, *Communist Aid to the Less Developed Countries of the Free World, 1976*, ER 77-10296 (Washington, D.C., August 1977), p. 18; idem, *Communist Aid to Less Developed Countries of the Free World, 1977*, ER 78-10478U (Washington, D.C., November 1978), p. 14; idem, *Communist Aid Activities in Non-Communist Less Developed Countries, 1978*, ER 79-10412U (Washington, D.C., September 1979), p. 20; Stephen J. Solarz, "Arms for Morocco," *Foreign Affairs* 58, no. 2 (Winter 1979-80): 278–99; Remnek, "Soviet Policy in the Horn of Africa."

26. K. Brutents, "The Regenerated East," *New Times*, no. 45 (November 1958), pp. 5–7. Brutents, incidentally, is now a deputy director of the International Department of the Central Committee of the CPSU.

27. Anatoly Gromyko, "Africa in the Strategy of Neo-colonialism," *International Affairs*, no. 11 (November 1978), p. 86. Gromyko is not only the director of the African Institute of the USSR Academy of Sciences but also the son of Soviet Foreign Minister Andrei Gromyko.

28. See, for example, V. Sofinsky and A. Khazanov, "Angolan Chronicle of the Peking Betrayal," ibid., no. 7 (July 1978), pp. 60–69.

29. See, for instance, Ye. Primakov, "Nekotorye problemy razvivaiushchikhsia stran," *Kommunist*, no. 11 (July 1978): 81–91; Brutents, *Osvobodivshiesia strany v 70-e gody*; Rymalov, "Newly-Free Countries"; idem, "Capitalism and the Developing World," *International Affairs*, no. 1 (January 1980), pp. 40–51.

30. For more detailed analysis, with sources, see, for example, Legvold, *Soviet Policy in West Africa*, Chs. 3–6; Albright, *The Dilemmas of Courtship*, Chs. 2, 4, and 6; Lenczowski, *Soviet Advances in the Middle East*; Richard Lowenthal, "On 'National Democracy': I. Its Function in Communist Policy," *Survey*, no. 47 (April 1963), pp. 119–34; Uri Ra'anan, "Moscow and the Third World," *Problems of Communism* 14, no. 1 (January-February 1965): 21–31; Roger E. Kanet, ed., *The Soviet Union and the Developing Countries* (Baltimore, Md.: Johns Hopkins University Press, 1974).

31. For elaboration, as well as documentation, see, for instance, Legvold, *Soviet Policy in West Africa*, Chs. 7–8; Albright, *Dilemmas of Courtship*, Ch. 6; idem, "Moscow's African Policy of the 1970s"; Lenczowski, *Soviet Advances in the Middle East*; Kanet, *The Soviet Union and the Developing Countries*; Richard Lowenthal, "Soviet 'Counterimperialism,'" *Problems of Communism* 25, no. 6 (November 1976): 52–63; Fritz Ermarth, "The Soviet Union in the Third World: Purpose in Search of Powers," *Annals of the American Academy of Political and Social Science* 386 (November 1969): 31–40; Alvin Z. Rubinstein, *Red Star on the Nile: The Soviet-Egyptian Influence Relationship Since the June War* (Princeton, N.J.: Princeton University Press, 1977).

32. For more extended discussion, with sources, see, for instance, Albright, "Moscow's African Policy of the 1970s"; Lowenthal, "Soviet 'Counterimperialism,'"; Lenczowski, *Soviet Advances in the Middle East*; idem, *The Middle East in World Affairs*; Rubinstein, *Red Star on the Nile*; M. Confino and S. Shamir, eds., *The USSR and the Middle East* (New York: Wiley, 1973); Yaacov Ro'i, ed., *The Limits of Power: The Soviet Union in the Middle East* (London: Croom Helm, 1978); Robert O. Freedman, *Soviet Policy Toward the Middle East Since 1970*, 2d ed. (New York: Praeger, 1978); Karen Dewisha, *Soviet Foreign Policy Towards Egypt* (London: Macmillan, 1979).

33. For more detailed treatment and for documentation, see, for example, Albright, "Moscow's African Policy of the 1970s"; idem, "The Soviet Role in Africa from Moscow's Perspective"; Rubinstein, *Red Star on the Nile*; Ro'i, *The Limits of Power*; Freedman, *Soviet Policy Toward the Middle East Since 1970*; Dewisha, *Soviet Foreign Policy Towards Egypt*; Galia Golan, *Yom Kippur and After: The Soviet Union and the Middle East Crisis* (Cambridge: Cambridge University Press, 1977); idem, "Syria and the Soviet Union Since the Yom Kippur War," *Orbis* 21, 4 (Winter 1976): 777–802.

34. For representative Soviet commentary on these themes during the mid- and late 1970s, see O. Orestov, "Independent Africa in the Making," *International Affairs*, no. 11 (November 1975); V. Solodovnikov and N. Gavrilov, "Africa: Tendencies of Non-Capitalist Development," ibid., no. 3 (March 1976); K. Brutents in *Pravda*, February 10, 1978; Y. Tarabrin, "The National Liberation Movement: Problems and Prospects," *International Affairs*, no. 2 (February 1978); Radio Moscow in English to Africa, April 21, 1978, in Foreign Broadcast Information Service, *Daily Report: Soviet Union* (hereafter *FBIS-SOV*), May 4, 1978; V. Kudryavtsev, "Africa Fights for Its Future," *International Affairs*, no. 5 (May 1978); B. Pilyatskin and S. Linkov, "Mozambique in Work and Struggle," ibid., no. 7 (July 1978); *Pravda*, August 26, 1978; *Izvestiia*, December 5, 1978; E. A. Tarabrin, ed., *Neocolonialism and Africa in the 1970s* (Moscow: Progress Publishers, 1978); Nemanov, "Partii avangardnogo tipa."

For more extended analysis of the implications of such commentaries, see Albright, "Moscow's African Policy of the 1970s"; idem, "The Soviet Role in Africa from Moscow's

Perspective." On the outlook of the self-styled Marxist-Leninist regimes, see especially David Ottaway and Marina Ottaway, *Afrocommunism* (New York: Holmes and Meier, 1981).

35. For additional discussion, as well as sources, see, for instance, Albright, "The Soviet Role in Africa from Moscow's Perspective"; idem, "The Communist States and Southern Africa," in *Southern Africa: International Issues and Responses*, ed. Gwendolyn Carter and Patrick O'Meara (Bloomington: Indiana University Press, forthcoming); Barry M. Schutz, "The Communist Impact on Robert Mugabe's Zimbabwe," in Albright and Valenta, *The Communist States and Africa*; Paul B. Henze, "Communism and Ethiopia," *Problems of Communism* 30, no. 3 (May-June 1981): 55-74; Price, "Moscow and the Persian Gulf"; idem, "Oil and Soviet Policy in the Persian Gulf," in *Soviet Policy in Developing Countries*, ed. W. Raymond Duncan (Huntington, N.Y.: Robert E. Krieger, 1981), pp. 145-61; Robert G. Weinland, *An (The?) Explanation of the Soviet Invasion of Afghanistan* (Alexandria, Va.: Center for Naval Analyses, March 11, 1981).

The foreign policy section of Leonid Brezhnev's report to the 26th Congress of the CPSU in February 1981 provided a clear indication of the switch in the focus of Soviet attention. It barely mentioned sub-Saharan Africa but dwelt at length on the Middle East. Moreover, the bulk of the treatment of the Middle East dealt with Afghanistan, Iran, Islamic fundamentalism, and the safeguarding of peace in the Persian Gulf and approaches to it. See *Pravda*, February 24, 1981.

36. Brutents, *Osvobodivshiesia strany v 70-e gody*, pp. 31-50. The quotation is from p. 50.

37. Brezhnev, report to the 26th CPSU Congress.

38. For elaboration of this strategy, along with sources, see Albright, *The Dilemmas of Courtship*, Chs. 2 and 4. The seminal treatment of the "national democracy" approach is Lowenthal, "On 'National Democracy.'"

39. See Albright, *The Dilemmas of Courtship*, Ch. 4; Legvold, *Soviet Policy in West Africa*, Ch. 5; Ra'anan, "Moscow and the 'Third World.'" As these discussions point out, there was discord within the Soviet leadership over this strategy.

40. For more detailed analysis, along with documentation, see Albright, "Moscow's African Policy of the 1970s"; Lowenthal, "Soviet 'Counterimperialism.'"

41. For a sampling of Soviet references to these activities, see Brutents, *Osvobodivshiesia strany v 70-e gody*, pp. 142-43; Nemanov, "Partii avangardnogo tipa," p. 27; B. Ponomarev, "Sovmestnaia bor'ba rabochego i natsional'no-osvoboditel'nogo dvizhenii imperializma, za social'nyi progress," *Kommunist*, no. 16 (November 1980): 42-43.

42. For reporting on the offer and the subsequent negotiations, see Colin Legum, ed., *African Contemporary Record: Annual Survey and Documents 1975-76* (New York: Africana Publishing Co., 1976), pp. 799-800, 803; U.S. Central Intelligence Agency, *Communist Aid . . . , 1976*, p. 21; idem, *Communist Aid . . . , 1977*, pp. 18-19; Radio Moscow in English to Africa, November 23, 1977, in *FBIS-SOV*, November 29, 1977, p. H/3; *Pravda*, September 7, 1978; Radio Moscow in English to Africa, May 15, 1979, in *FBIS-SOV*, May 18, 1979, p. J/2; *Pravda*, May 19, 1979; Radio Moscow International Service in Russian, June 12, 1979, in *FBIS-SOV*, June 13, 1979, p. J/2; Colin Legum, "African Outlooks Toward the USSR," in *Communism in Africa*, pp. 17-18; *Pravda*, July 17, 1979.

43. There is evidence that this new modification of strategy did not enjoy total support within the Soviet hierarchy. Although the adjustment in no sense meant cessation of Soviet efforts to shore up the professedly Marxist-Leninist regimes in the Middle East and Africa, it did entail a certain dilution of Soviet concern with these regimes, and the decision to move in this direction seems to have reflected a degree of disillusionment with the regimes on the part of the dominant elements within the leadership. See, for example, Brutents, *Osvobodivshiesia strany v 70-e gody*, and Ponomarev, "Sovmestnaia bor'ba," pp. 30-44. As

mentioned earlier, Brutents is a deputy director of the International Department of the Central Committee of the CPSU. Ponomarev heads that department and serves, as well, as a candidate member of the Politburo.

Yet not all Soviet observers appeared to share this disillusionment with the self-styled Marxist-Leninist regimes in the two areas. Among those with a somewhat more positive view of them was Anatoly Gromyko, who, as noted previously, is not only the director of the African Institute of the USSR Academy of Sciences but also the son of Foreign Minister Andrei Gromyko, a member of the Politburo. See, for instance, Anatoly Gromyko's "Socialist Orientation in Africa," *International Affairs*, no. 9 (September 1979), pp. 95–104, and especially 100–4.

44. The specific quotations are from Professor M. Mchedlov in *Pravda*, November 16, 1979.

45. *Pravda*, February 24, 1981.

46. Soviet arms transfers to the Middle East and Africa amounted to $4,006 million in 1956–64, $6,444 million in 1965–74, and $18,920 million in 1975–79. Economic assistance offered to the two areas reached $2,190 million in 1955–64, $3,200 million in 1965–74, and $6,595 million in 1975–79. Even when the figures for the two regions are disaggregated, the only apparent exception to the generalization in the text has to do with Africa in the earliest period. North Africa and sub-Saharan Africa combined received arms transfers of $364 million in 1956–64, as compared with $740 million in economic credits. Calculated from data in U.S. Central Intelligence Agency, *Communist Aid Activities . . . , 1959 and 1954–79*, pp. 7 and 14; U.S. Arms Control and Disarmament Agency, *World Military Expenditures and Arms Transfers, 1965–1974* (Washington, D.C.: U.S. Government Printing Office, 1976), pp. 74–75.

47. L. Stepanov, "Helping Underdeveloped Countries," *New Times*, no. 52 (December 1958): 6. For comparable statements by Nikita Khrushchev, see his address to the graduates of Soviet military academies on November 14, 1958, and his report to the 21st Congress of the CPSU in January-February 1959, in, respectively, *Pravda*, November 15, 1958, and *Current Soviet Policies III: The Documentary Record of the Extraordinary 21st Congress of the Communist Party of the Soviet Union*, ed. Leo Gruilow (New York: Columbia University Press, 1960), p. 55.

48. For more detailed treatment of this shift in Soviet thinking, see Lowenthal, "Soviet 'Counterimperialism'"; Elizabeth Kridl Valkenier, "New Trends in Soviet Economic Relations with the Third World," *World Politics* 22, no. 3 (April 1970): 415–33; idem, "The USSR and the Third World," *Survey*, Summer 1973, pp. 41–49.

49. Calculated from data in U.S. Central Intelligence Agency, *Communist Aid Activities . . . , 1979 and 1954–79*, pp. 7 and 14; U.S. Arms Control and Disarmament Agency, *World Military Expenditures . . . , 1965–1974*, pp. 74–75.

50. See, for example, Bogomolov, "CMEA and the Developing World," pp. 26–28.

51. See, for instance, Rymalov, "Newly Free Countries," pp. 48–59; Brutents, *Osvobodivshiesia strany v 70-e gody*, passim.

52. Interview with a *Newsweek* correspondent, in *Newsweek*, June 25, 1979, p. 39. The individual was not specifically identified.

53. For evidence of Soviet recognition of all these sources of increased conflict in Africa, see the contributions of V. Kudryavtsev (p. 83), Y. Primakov (pp. 70–71), and Anatoly Gromyko (pp. 85–87) to the symposium on "Neo-Colonialism—A New System of Dependence and Enslavement" in the November 1978 issue of *International Affairs*; Brutents, *Osvobodivshiesia strany v 70-e gody*, pp. 36, 62–65, 72–73; Nemanov, "Partii avangardnogo tipa," p. 20.

54. Aleksandr Serbin in *Pravda*, July 26, 1978.

55. V. Kudryavtsev, "A Policy of Aggression, Threats and Fanning Conflicts," *International Affairs*, no. 11 (November 1978), p. 82. See also Brutents, *Osvobodivshiesia strany v 70-e gody*, p. 104.

56. On the difficult economic situation that confronts Soviet leaders in the 1980's and its possible implications for military expenditures, see, for instance, Seweryn Bialer, "The Politics of Stringency in the USSR," *Problems of Communism* 29, no. 3 (May-June 1980): 19-33; Abram Bergson, "Soviet Economic Slowdown and the 1981-85 Plan," *Problems of Communism* 30, no. 3 (May-June 1981): 24-36.

57. For elaboration of this point, see Arnold Hottinger, "Arab Communism at Low Ebb," *Problems of Communism* 29, no. 4 (July-August 1981): 17-32.

15

SOVIET POLICIES IN WEST ASIA
AND THE PERSIAN GULF

Zalmay Khalilzad

To the Soviets the countries in and near the Persian Gulf, especially those located on its borders, have been the object of sustained interest.[1] There are many reasons for this interest. They can be divided broadly into four interrelated categories: defensive, offensive, economic, and ideological. On the defense side, Moscow opposed the creation of Western pacts in the area and sought to weaken them, once they were established, because of fear of encirclement and the use of the region by hostile distant powers. Moscow has also opposed close relations tending to establish either formal or informal alliances between the countries of the area and its own adversaries, especially the United States and China. For example, Moscow opposed Turkey's membership in the Central Treaty Organization (CENTO) and North Atlantic Treaty Organization (NATO), Iranian and Pakistani membership in CENTO, and their 1959 defense agreements with the United States.[2]

In practice, defensive concerns have been combined with offensive interests, as the Soviet Union has sought to extend its power and influence southward. In fact, in many cases it was this expectation that the Soviets had such a desire for southward expansion that contributed to the readiness of countries in the region to seek a close alliance relationship with a countervailing force such as the distant United States. Any country on the Soviet border could be a buffer as well as the gateway to the rest of the region. The combination of Soviet defensive and offensive concerns and interests have in practice meant that typically Moscow has attributed limited sovereignty to its small neighbors.

Soviet economic interests in the area have included preferential access to the natural resources of the area (especially energy and markets), as well as access to the airspace of the area for potential projection of economic and military power to regions beyond. It has also encouraged the countries of the Gulf to use their resources as both political and economic weapons against Moscow's global adversaries. Already the Soviets have preferential access to resources of several countries. For example, as in the past, the Soviets are receiving Afghan natural gas at a price far below the international level. In the future the economic factor in relations with the Gulf states may become the most important. If, as expected, Moscow is likely to face increased economic problems not only in East Europe but also in the Soviet Union itself, it may seek to solve them by extending its influence to the Gulf, a region in which resources are worth several trillion dollars. This interest might intensify if the Russians' or their allies' need for imported energy increased substantially because of a decline in Soviet production or growth in demand, or both.[3]

Even if, however, the Soviets are not pushed toward the oil region because of economic or energy needs, they may be pulled toward it for other considerations. Oil is a valuable commodity on the international market. It is like money in the bank; one cannot have enough of it. Soviet control of oil would provide it with vital leverage vis-à-vis many countries, especially Japan, the United States, and Western European countries—Moscow's principal adversaries. For these countries and those dependent on Persian Gulf oil in the Third World, the Persian Gulf is as important as any area can be. More than three-fifths of the world's proven crude-oil reserves are located in this region. Given this heavy concentration of oil in the area, conflicts there have the potential to massively threaten the security and well-being of the rest of the world, especially the industrial countries. The Soviets do not have to destroy the oil fields to affect the behavior of countries dependent on oil from this area. Moscow might be able to affect the behavior of oil consumers, even without gaining direct control of the oil-producing area, by becoming an important factor in determining oil exports from the area. It could use its leverage to exact high economic and political prices from these countries. Given the importance of the area to the West, Soviet moves beyond Afghanistan will seriously affect relations between the superpowers.

Another major Soviet goal has been the spread of Soviet-style Marxist-Leninist ideology and the strengthening of groups adhering or sympathetic to this ideology, while hostile to the West and China. At times Moscow has demonstrated flexibility on this account, sacrificing the short-term interests of the local Communist parties to safeguard the more immediate Soviet interests. This has been done, not always successfully, with the hope of not permanently sacrificing the long-term goal of spreading Soviet ideology. In order to achieve their goals, the Soviets have relied on positive as well as negative incentives. At various times they have emphasized different goals and have relied more heavily on different means, depending on such factors as their comparative military capability. Western capability and policies, local and regional conditions in and near the Gulf, the ideological predispositions of the Soviet leaders, and Soviet preoccupations in other parts of the world.

Since the end of the Second World War, Soviet policy toward the Gulf states has had the following pattern: Moscow has responded to opportunities or crises that have arisen as a result of the many instabilities common to the countries of the Gulf region. To be sure, Moscow has not passively watched and waited; instead it has actively promoted and sought such opportunities to extend its influence. These opportunities have arisen in various ways: from a crisis in relations between a local state and a Western country, especially the United States (Pakistan and the United States after 1962, Iraq and the West after 1958); from a crisis in political and economic development producing conflicts between groups maintaining different ideological beliefs; from a crisis in national integration following regional conflicts (Iraq before 1958); from local nationalism when directed against the West (Yemeni nationalists before independence); and from Islam when directed against pro-Western regimes (Iran).

The Soviet level of active involvement, including military intervention, in countries close to its border increases as the ideological relations between such countries and Russia converge. *Prima facie*, this Soviet policy appears paradoxical, since the Soviets seem to invade countries friendly to them. Military intervention is a step one would usually expect only in the case of hostile relations between powers; nonetheless, the Soviets since the Second World War have invaded nations that have been moving toward them politically. This is paradoxical only at first glance. In fact, it is indicative of Moscow's policy of gradual extension of its power and influence both around and beyond its borders and its commitment to the doctrine of Communist "irreversibility" in these areas. For example, once a leftist nationalist government sympathetic to the Soviets and hostile to the West has come into power in a small neighboring country, Moscow increases its presence in order to protect local Communist parties. Subsequently, the Soviets encourage a Communist take-over, and if this effort succeeds, it leads to even greater Soviet participation in that country's political, economic, and military affairs. Threats to the survival of such a government or the government's unwillingness to remain servile to Moscow pave the way for large-scale direct Soviet invasion. This is clearly the pattern the Soviets followed in the case of Afghanistan. Prior to 1978 Moscow supported the local Afghan nationalist government; this gave way to indirect control through the local Communist party, and finally to direct invasion in December 1979.

One might argue that, given this pattern (invading their friends), the Soviets do not pose a direct threat to the Persian Gulf in the near future, since according to this scheme none of the major neighboring countries, or, for that matter, the oil-producing states of the area are immediate candidates for Soviet invasion. After all, more than 25 years elapsed between the time of Afghanistan's acceptance of large-scale Soviet military assistance in 1955 and the establishment of a Marxist-Leninist regime in 1978 and the actual invasion in December 1979. There is no certainty that the Soviets will follow the same time sequence in other countries, such as Iran. The region is experiencing an accelerated pace of internal and regional instability; major changes could take place far more rapidly. Accordingly, it should not be assumed that such an extended transition as in the case of Afghanistan is essential to their paradigm. Past Soviet policies were, among other things, a function of comparative Soviet power. The power balance has changed significantly, to Moscow's benefit and to the detriment of its adversaries.[4] The change in relative power might lead to Soviet policies different from those of the past. In addition, while it is trivially true that not all events or actions are predictable, it is a truism that should not be overlooked in dealings with Moscow. On several recent occasions Moscow has taken most unexpected courses of action; consider, for example, Russia's stationing of nuclear warhead-carrying missiles in Cuba, or her invasion of Afghanistan, a nonaligned Islamic country outside the Soviet satellite empire.

Future Soviet policy toward the Gulf states is likely to depend on many factors, especially the opportunities provided by developments in key countries, internal changes in the USSR, and international constraints imposed on Moscow. Only some of these factors are controlled by the USSR. And it is to the consideration of these factors that attention will now be given.

OPPORTUNITIES FOR SOVIET INVOLVEMENT

There are many potential conflicts in the Gulf area that could provide risks or opportunities for extension of Soviet influence southward. There are serious differences among countries of the area in size, resources, relative military capability, and history of political identity, as well as social and economic unity. All have enormous problems at the domestic, regional, and international levels and suffer from varying degrees of instability that could threaten existing regimes, boundaries, and oil production. The Iranian revolution, the civil war in Afghanistan prior to the Soviet invasion of December 1979,[5] the Mecca uprising in Saudi Arabia, and the Iran-Iraq war are instances of the types of conflicts that threaten the region, providing opportunities for external manipulation. In varying degrees and at several levels, each country in the area is politically fragmented. In Pakistan, Iran, Iraq, and Turkey, minorities seek various degrees of autonomy. In others such as the United Arab Emirates, Qatar, and Kuwait, there are more foreigners than national citizens; others such as Iraq, Iran, Saudi Arabia, Turkey, and Bahrain have sectarian conflicts. All contain structural sources of instability, not only because of modernization per se but also by virtue of the way modernization is being implemented; and each contains many political groups with conflicting ideological beliefs.[6] These conflicts are often further aggravated by the absence of a consensus on the manner of political competition. No matter which group comes to power, it is likely to be challenged, at times violently, by others.

Although there has been cooperation among states in the region on some issues, such as oil pricing, there are many intrastate conflicts and rivalries in the

region. These include border disputes,[7] ideological and ethnic conflicts, interference in each other's domestic affairs, alliances with outside powers or
dependencies upon them to varying degrees, and competition for regional
domination.

THE USSR AND IRAN

In various conflict situations in and near the Persian Gulf, some are likely
to receive greater attention than others. Russia has demonstrated sustained interest in Iran, and it is likely that this interest will only increase. Twice in this
century Moscow supported ethnic separatists close to their common border in
hope of drawing them under Soviet control. After the Second World War Moscow refused to withdraw troops from Iranian Azerbaijan, as agreed upon with
Britain and the United States. It took a combination of U.S. pressure, reflecting
a comparative advantage in global power, and some concessions from Iran to get
the Soviets out.[8] American supremacy in Iran from 1947 to the time of the
Iranian revolution was resented by the Soviets, who during this period used a
combination of techniques to attempt to draw Iran away from the United States.
These included propaganda attacks on Iran, accusing her of favoring "imperialist"—that is, capitalist—states and permitting her territory to be used as a base
for "aggression" against the Soviet Union. Other means used were military pressures, such as the violation of Iranian airspace and large maneuvers near the
border. Moscow also provided direct and indirect aid to the pro-Soviet Communist party, Tudeh. These negative measures were accompanied by some positive ones, such as economic and trade agreements beginning in 1970, when Iran
had begun to export large quantities of natural gas to the Soviet Union. While
emphasizing different measures at different times, the Soviet goals were to push
Iran to leave CENTO and to follow a policy of Soviet-tilted neutralism. Moscow
also wanted Iran to stop supporting the Kurds in Iraq, which had close ties to
Moscow, before the 1975 agreement between Iran and Iraq, and Moscow objected to Iranian policies in the Gulf (especially the presence of Iranian forces in
Oman), and the Iranian military buildup after 1973-74.

The Soviet strategy in Iran under the Shah had only limited success. Once
the Shah's internal troubles began to escalate in 1978,[9] however, the Soviets did
not stand behind him, as some have claimed.[10] There is much evidence that they
sought to deepen the crisis to the detriment of the United States and the Shah.
In their broadcasts to Iran the Soviets asserted that "imperialist puppets" in Iran
had put the country under American control.[11] In order to stir up the Iranians
against the United States, on many occasions in their Persian broadcasts to Iran
the Soviets "reminded" Iranians that the weapons that were being used against
them were American and that the Americans were their real enemies.[12] Finally,
Moscow implicitly promised that it would protect the opposition by warning

the United States that any interference in the affairs of Iran would be regarded by the USSR as a matter affecting its security. The Soviets also encouraged Tudeh to support Khomeini against the Shah, because the former advocated policies that were hostile to the West, while the latter was clearly allied with the West.

Since the Iranian revolution, the Soviets have aimed at encouraging continued hostility in relations between Iran and the United States. Radio broadcasts during the hostage crisis told Iranians that the Shah had more than $20 billion in the United States, that the hated SAVAK was a branch of the U.S. Intelligence Agency (C.I.A.), that the United States plundered Iranian resources, and that U.S. officials (including former Secretary of State Henry Kissinger) took "bribes" from the Shah.[13] The Soviets have sought to foster the anti-American tendencies of the Khomeini regime. They have encouraged Tudeh to continue to support Khomeini, while he continues to weaken those institutions and groups that might be friendly toward the West.

The Soviets, however, appear to be divided in their appraisal of the domestic implications of the Iranian revolution. Some analysts see the Islamic revolution in Iran as a "progressive" development leading to a "profound political and socio-economic shift in Iran." Others see it as containing a counterrevolutionary trend serving the interests of the big bourgeoisie and the professional middle class. This trend, it is argued, includes "Muslim figures," who "display a tendency to neutralize and to isolate left-wing forces." Some Soviet analysts have even called the Teheran regime a disaster, although they have avoided direct criticism of Khomeini himself.[14]

Continuous domestic and regional conflicts involving Iran might provide further opportunities for extension of its influence. Strategically, the successful pacification of Afghanistan and its integration into the Soviet satellite empire would enhance the Soviet capacity for intervention in Iran. If conflict among the many ethnic and ideological groups existing in Iran escalates to a civil war, Moscow might provide varying degrees of aid, including dispatching a large force in support of sympathetic groups. In such a case, in the familiar jargon, they could claim to be responding to a "call for fraternal assistance" by groups fighting against "the imperialist-backed factions," or they could assert that conflict in Iran was threatening Soviet security. That these explanations do not necessarily stand the test of logic has been demonstrated by events in Afghanistan, where the Soviet Union claims that the head of state invited in the very Soviet troops who were involved in his own execution.

A Soviet success in Iran would give Moscow direct land access to the Arabian Sea and the Persian Gulf and control of enormous oil and natural gas resources, as well as a large comparative advantage in projecting power to the rest of the Gulf. It would be very difficult, with Iran under Soviet occupation, for the West to meet the Soviet conventional threat on its own terms in the rest of the Gulf.

THE USSR AND PAKISTAN

Weakening Pakistani ties with the West and the People's Republic of China has been a persistent Soviet goal. As in the case of Iran, the Soviets in the past used a variety of means, both positive and negative, to persuade Pakistan to leave the Western alliance. Pakistan was encouraged to follow the example of Afghanistan and become nonaligned. Each time Pakistan expressed disappointment in its Western allies, as in 1962 when the United States shipped arms to India, or in 1965 when the United States remained neutral in the Indo-Pakistani conflict, the Soviets encouraged decreasing Pakistani ties with the West and China.[15] On the positive side, they have used economic assistance (between 1954 and 1976 Pakistan received more than $650 million in economic aid) and substantial military assistance. Positive incentives were tempered by negative ones, including increased aid for India and support for anti-Western groups inside Pakistan. Soviet pressure against Pakistan increased dramatically during the Bangladesh crisis. In August 1971 Moscow signed a treaty of friendship with New Delhi and later, during the war, provided direct assistance to India, including participation in manning its air defenses. The war brought further disillusionment of Pakistan with its Western allies. Islamabad left SEATO, emphasizing its relations with China and the Islamic world. While pleased with Pakistan's exit from SEATO, Moscow continued its effort to get Pakistan to leave CENTO and support the anti-Chinese Soviet plans for collective security in Asia.

Several years later, as Pakistan's relations with the United States deteriorated further, following the announcement of the purchase of a nuclear reprocessing plant from France, Moscow began praising the Pakistani government. Pakistani Prime Minister Bhutto was praised for his opposition to imperialism. His opponents in the 1977 elections were attacked as "tools of Western imperialism," at a time when Bhutto was charging the United States with aiding them in exchange for their promise to cancel the reprocessing deal.[16]

Since the 1978 coup in Afghanistan and especially since the 1979 invasion, the Soviet desire to consolidate its position there has led to a major deterioration of relations with Pakistan. The invasion has dramatically increased Pakistan's security problem. To the east it faces its traditional adversary, India, which is continuously increasing its comparative advantage in military capability, while in the west it now faces the direct threat from the Soviet Union in Afghanistan. Soviet-Indian relations have been further strengthened since the Soviet invasion of Afghanistan and the return of Indira Gandhi to power. Pakistan itself is a fragmented polity. It has many ethnic and ideological groups opposing the current regime in the country. These internal conflicts provide opportunities for manipulation by external powers, including the Soviet Union.

Currently Pakistan is caring for more than 1.5 million Afghan refugees and is harboring the headquarters of several Afghan resistance groups. Pakistan is also the transit route for some of the assistance to the Afghans from the outside world. Pakistan faces difficult choices in its policy towards Afghanistan. Islamabad plays a critical role in determining the fate of the Afghan resistance and, therefore, the success or failure of Soviet policy in Afghanistan. By continuing to provide sanctuary and limited support for groups fighting the Soviets, Pakistan can be an obstacle to the pacification strategy. Pakistan could also permit a much greater level of military assistance to the Afghans, making things even more difficult for the Soviets. On the other hand, Pakistan could help the Soviet cause, if it moved against the partisans.

Recognizing this, Moscow has applied considerable pressure on Pakistan. Soviet aircraft have frequently penetrated Pakistani airspace, and Kabul has threatened to support political groups inside Pakistan opposed to the government of President Zia-al-Haq, with an eye toward helping install a government that would be hostile toward the Afghan partisans. Several members of the opposition groups, including Morteza Bhutto, the son of the late Zulfikar Ali Bhutto, have visited Kabul and New Delhi. There is also the possibility of Soviet support for ethnic nationalists in the Pashtun (Pathan) and Baluch areas of Pakistan. The Kabul regime has already threatened open support for Pakistan's Baluch and Pashtun nationalists. The USSR could conceivably move against Pakistani territory for "defensive" reasons against the Afghan groups or, alternatively, it could encourage increased Indian pressure against Pakistan in areas such as Kashmir or Sind.

The Pakistanis are afraid that as long as they do not have a credible alliance relationship with the other superpower, they cannot allow major military assistance to the Afghans, lest that lead to direct confrontation with the Soviets. With Chinese support and encouragement, Pakistan has been seeking such a security guarantee and a major commitment to its military modernization from the United States. Despite official nonalignment, the Pakistani security elite continues to remain interested in strong security relations with the West.[17] On the other hand, Pakistan cannot remain indifferent to the Soviet occupation of Afghanistan. A successful Soviet pacification of that country will substantially increase Soviet ability to pressure Pakistan directly. After all, Afghanistan has traditionally been regarded as a gateway to the Indo-Pakistan subcontinent. Besides, even if Islamabad decided to stop all aid to the Afghans, it would be very hard for it to do so. Traditionally Pakistani control over its border area with Afghanistan has been limited. With the current level of military capability along this border, it would be extremely difficult for Pakistan to completely prevent the Afghan tribes and other groups from crossing the border, though Islamabad could make things very difficult for the partisans.

Current Pakistani policy can be characterized as allowing very limited military supplies to the partisans, while seeking ways and means for a political settlement of the Afghan issue that ensures Soviet withdrawal from the country and the return of the refugees to Afghanistan. Nevertheless, relations with the Soviets remain tense. A few months ago Islamabad expelled the Soviet ambassador to Pakistan, on charges of subversion. It also closed the Soviet press and information office in Karachi and asked the USSR to reduce the number of its embassy diplomats in Pakistan. New restrictions on travel by foreign diplomats inside Pakistan likewise seem aimed primarily at persons from Soviet-bloc countries.[18] The dynamics of the Afghan conflict might well lead to increased Soviet military pressure against Pakistan, with Moscow perhaps ordering attacks against the Afghan refugee camps, training centers, and supply lines in Pakistan. A large-scale ground invasion of Pakistan, however, appears unlikely without an enormous increase in current Soviet military capabilities in Afghanistan.

THE USSR AND IRAQ

Since the 1958 coup in Iraq, which overthrew a pro-Western monarchy, relations with Baghdad have been of considerable importance to the USSR. many years Iraq was Moscow's only point of entry to the Gulf, and through it Moscow affected the rest of the Gulf area. There have been many indicators of good relations between the two.[19]

First, Moscow provided a substantial supply of arms to Baghdad. This included the introduction of the first supersonic aircraft in the Gulf region in the mid-1960s. Other weapons supplied have included TU-22 bombers, MIG-23s, one of the largest numbers of tank transporters in the world, and Scud missiles. The arms supply worked out to mutual advantage. The Iraqis wanted to dominate the Gulf or at least to balance Iran. The Soviets favored this Iraqi policy and wanted Iraq to play an ever greater role in support of anti-American and anti-Iranian movements in the area. The two countries exchanged oil for arms, which, given the Soviet need for hard currency, was to Moscow's liking.

Second, in 1972 the two countries signed a treaty of friendship that Moscow called strategic. This treaty was similar to those signed between the Soviet Union and some East European countries in the 1940s and those with Vietnam, India, and Afghanistan in the 1970s. It called for "all-around cooperation" between the two countries. The Shah of Iran looked at the 1972 treaty as an anti-Iranian alliance.

The case of Iraq shows how shaky some of Moscow's "acquisitions" are, even in the case of small but noncontiguous countries not ruled by a pro-Soviet Communist party. While Iraq remains important in Soviet calculations, several problems have emerged in relations between the two countries. First, the 1975 agreement between Baghdad and Teheran resolved, at least temporarily, the territorial dispute between the two countries, ended Iranian support for the Iraqi Kurds, and Iraq agreed not to support the revolutionary movements in the area. This agreement decreased Iraqi need for strong ties with Moscow.

Second, because of the revolution in Iran and the isolation of Egypt as a result of peace with Israel, Iraq's relative position in the region has improved.

With this improvement has come a desire to play a more independent role consistent with long-term Iraqi ambitions in the region. This desire for more independent policy has led on occasion to conflict with the Soviet Union. For example, Iraq opposed Soviet policy on the conflict between Somalia and Ethiopia in 1977. While the Soviets supported Ethiopia, the Iraqis backed Somalia. The two also have differed on other major issues, such as Afghanistan.

Third, because of substantial increases in oil income as a result of increases in the price of oil, Iraq has gained more flexibility in its dealing with the rest of the world. Now it can purchase goods and services, including military equipment, from markets other than the Soviet. Diversifying its dependence has become an Iraqi strategy. Iraq has also moved closer to more conservative Arab governments of the area and has proposed a regional security scheme that will ensure itself a dominant role in the region. Such proposals have been aimed at excluding both superpowers from the area. The effect of the Iraqi proposal, if implemented, will, however, benefit the Soviets to the detriment of the West. This is true because the Soviets are already deployed in the region—in Afghanistan, in the Transcaucasus, and the Transcaspian—while the United States would come from much farther away.

Fourth, differences between the two countries have emerged because of conflict between the Ba'thist regime and the Iraqi Communist party (ICP). Ever since the 1978 Afghan coup against the Nationalist government of President Daud, the Iraqis have been worried about a similar development in their own country. There were reports of an attempted coup by the ICP in 1978.[20] While this cannot be confirmed, there is much more evidence of ICP efforts to infiltrate the armed forces, which led to a conflict with the government, resulting in an effort ruthlessly to suppress the ICP. Many party leaders were killed; others fled to Eastern Europe and the Soviet Union. Moscow has allowed Iraqi Communists to make statements from Soviet territory calling for the overthrow of the Ba'thist regime.[21] The Soviet invasion of Afghanistan, in order to keep a Communist regime in control, has further increased Iraqi suspicions of the Soviet Union.

Fifth, disagreement has also arisen between the two countries because of the Iran-Iraq war. The Iranian revolution, leading to the weakening of the Iranian armed forces and the emergence of many centers of power in that country, some of which are sympathetic to the Soviet Union, has provided opportunities for both Iraq and the USSR. Iraqi desires to demonstrate its supremacy in the region, to reverse what it perceived to be an unfavorable agreement signed in 1975, and to weaken and perhaps overthrow the Khomeini regime, which has been agitating among the Iraqi Shiites to overthrow the Ba'th government, led to its invasion of Iran. There is no evidence that the Soviets directly encouraged or assisted Iraq in its attack. Once the war had begun, Moscow sought ways of encouraging greater Iranian dependence on the Soviets without antagonizing Iraq. Later the Soviets took some measures to help Iran by allowing Libyan and Syrian spare parts to be shipped to Iran over Soviet airspace. There have also been persistent rumors of a Soviet offer to provide Iran with substantial quantities of arms. Clearly, even if the Soviets had to choose between potential influence in Iran versus Iraq, they would choose the former over the latter. From a global viewpoint, Iran is a far more important country than Iraq. Since Iran shares a long border with the Soviet Union, the emergence of a pro-Soviet regime there, for example, would be more difficult to reverse than in Iraq.

Despite these problems in relations between Iraq and the Soviet Union, there has not been a reversal of alliances in Iraqi international relations. The two still have major areas of common interest. It is possible that under some circumstances, such as a change in the Iranian government—especially if it sought military cooperation with the West—or if the current regime in Bagdad were replaced by a group more aligned with the Soviets, Iraqi-Soviet cooperation might intensify. Relations between the two countries might also improve if Iraq decided to move against some traditional Arab states such as Kuwait and Saudi Arabia. Other plausible developments, however, including the overthrow of the Ba'th regime by those more sympathetic to political Islam of the Khomeini style, might further weaken Soviet-Iraqi ties.

SOVIET POLICY TOWARD SAUDI ARABIA AND THE LOWER GULF STATES

Historically there have been few ties between the Soviet Union and the states of the Lower Gulf—Saudi Arabia, Bahrain, Qatar, the United Arab Emirates (Abu Dhabi, Dubai, Ajman, Sharjah, Fujairah, Umm al-Qaiwan, and Ras al Khaimmah), and Oman. Moscow still has diplomatic ties with only Kuwait. There is considerable divergence of interest between the regimes of the area and the Soviets. The Saudis and other Lower Gulf states at times have used their economic power to counter Soviet influence in this region and beyond. The Soviets, in turn, have followed a multipronged policy toward these states.

First, there has been continuous critical propaganda against the governments of the area. For example, the Saudi regime is described as a Western tool and afraid of the impact of the progressive changes taking place in the neighboring Arab countries. Second, Moscow has sent feelers for normalization of relations with Saudi Arabia and the Gulf states.

Third, Moscow has used its nearby clients, such as Iraq in the past and South Yemen (People's Democratic Republic of Yemen, PDRY) more recently, to influence developments in the area. Moscow has cultivated close relations with the PDRY ever since its establishment. The first shipments of Soviet arms arrived there in 1968. By 1978, the number of Soviet military personnel in the PDRY had risen to 2,000. Moscow has access to the country's excellent port facilities and used this country as a staging area for projecting Soviet power into Ethiopia in 1977. Moscow encouraged the PDRY's support of the Khofari rebellion in Oman and other radical movements in the Gulf area, including that in Iran.

The Soviet strategy—in which Moscow actually has invested very little—has not paid off in Saudi Arabia and the Lower Gulf states. The Dhofar rebellion was weakened considerably by a combination of regional and extraregional assistance to Oman, such as Iran's dispatch of armed forces to support Sultan Qabus, an end to Beijing's support of the rebellion, and Saudi financial aid to the PDRY government in return for ending its support of Dhofari insurgency. The improvement in Saudi-PDRY relations was short-lived, however, because of the overthrow of the Aden government by a more pro-Soviet regime in 1978. The important role played in the coup by the Soviet- and East-German-trained People's Militia has led some to speculate about a possible direct Soviet role. In any case, since the 1978 coup, Soviet, Cuban, and East German involvement in the PDRY's affairs has increased substantially.[22]

In the future Moscow might use Aden again for a more interventionist policy of pressuring the traditional regimes of the area. As in 1977 when Moscow was sending arms to Ethiopia, Soviet ability to give Aden as an interim destination would make it easier to obtain overflight permission from countries separating the USSR from the Persian Gulf. Given the PDRY's common border with Saudi Arabia and the large Yemeni migrant workers' community in Saudi Arabia, Aden is in a good position to promote and take advantage of instabilities in Saudi Arabia.

It is difficult to predict with any confidence developments in Saudi Arabia. Like many other countries in the area, Saudi Arabia contains structural sources of instability. Increased oil income has expanded Riyadh's ability to coopt potential opponents and initiate projects it could not afford before, including a substantial expansion of security forces for both internal and external use and greater international political and economic power. Increased oil income and the rapid economic and social changes resulting from government policies have, however, unleashed powerful new forces and antagonized some older influential elements. The Saudi economic development program has created social and cultural dislocations, greater inequality of wealth distribution, larger bureaucracies, an increase in the degree of magnitude of corruption, higher inflation, and greater dependence on the outside world.

Already there have been major challenges to the regime. These include the November 1979 attack on the Mecca mosque by Muslim fundamentalists accusing the regime of corruption and anti-Islamic policies. The Mecca incident was followed by a Shiite uprising in the oil-producing areas. The Shiites, who form a large part of the working force in oil production, were encouraged to rebel by the Khomeini regime in Teheran.[23]

Whether the current problems are likely to escalate to an insurgency against the regime, providing opportunities for outside manipulation, is difficult to predict. The Soviets are likely to seek and promote opportunities, either directly or indirectly. South Yemen is a major asset for such efforts. The level and character of Soviet involvement will be determined, in part, by issues such as whether members of the large royal family pull together in times of crisis or some segment joins with the opposition; whether the family controls official corruption or continues the erosion of legitimacy; whether it can continue to command the loyalty of the armed forces and the National Guard; and whether the regime can integrate the large number of Saudis who are being educated.

POWER, CONSTRAINTS, AND VULNERABILITIES

The absence of internal and regional conflicts in the Persian Gulf would clearly limit Soviet opportunities in the area. Given the instabilities of the region, however, there will be opportunities for Soviet activity. Of course, the opportunities to which Moscow responds are not determined by internal forces in the area alone but also, among other things, by Soviet power. The more capable Moscow is, the more opportunities it can create, find, and employ. And if its power dominates, an activist opportunist policy would entail fewer risks to itself than to its adversaries.

An unambiguous Soviet preponderance of military capability in that region might predispose the Soviets to use their leverage there for advantage over the Gulf and also over other areas. For example, in the Gulf Moscow might use its leverage to gain access to facilities, ports, and airfields of the region or to demand trade relations. And it might threaten action in the Gulf to deter Western actions in other parts of the world, including Europe and East Asia. The preponderance of Soviet power would increase the risk for the West in responding in kind to Soviet challenges in the region.

Whether the Soviets would attempt further aggressive actions in the Gulf also depends on the values of future Soviet leaders. It is unclear what Brezhnev's successors might do. Equally unclear is how long the succession process will take. Conceivably, if the struggle for succession takes a long time, the different factions might use foreign policy initiatives, including actions in the Gulf, as weapons in the struggle for power. To sketch scenarios of possible Soviet moves in the Gulf is not, of course, to assert that they are inevitable. A forward-looking Western strategy should explore ways and means by which such actions are made less probable.

The future of the Soviet position in the Gulf is likely to depend not only on local opportunities and Soviet power and goals but also on many other factors. Important among these are Western power and policies. In the past, Western strategic nuclear superiority and comparative advantage in power projection has been extremely important in Soviet calculations. Now, because of loss of Western supremacy in strategic weapons, local balance has acquired greater importance. In the long term, assisting in the establishment of economically stable, socially responsive political systems is an important element in a comprehensive strategy to deter Soviet expansion in the area. Along with this, especially in the short term, a sustained Western effort to station enough force in the Gulf region to seriously disrupt an initial Soviet move, followed by bringing more force to bear, including the possibility of escalation, is likely seriously to affect Soviet calculations. The more the West improves its power position in the area, the more credible Western declarations of intent to defend the area become. But for the military presence in the area not to create political opportunities for the Soviets, such efforts must be politically tolerable.

Besides potential Western military responses there are many other factors constraining Moscow's policies toward the Gulf. The Western allies can compete with the Soviet Union in providing economic, political, and military assistance to the countries of the area. Even in the case of countries such as Iraq, which has been largely dependent on Moscow for military supplies, such dependence has not led to Soviet control. Many of the states in the area, especially those in the Arabian Peninsula, remain hostile to Moscow, and even in the case of a revolutionary regime such as that in Iran, ideological hostility to Moscow is widespread. This hostility clearly limits Soviet options.

The Soviet invasion of Afghanistan has been politically costly for Moscow in the region. This action against an Islamic and nonaligned country came as a shock to the Gulf states. Many in the area regarded the Soviet action as a blow to Moscow's credibility as a supporter of national liberation movements against foreign domination. It increased Iraq's suspicions of Moscow. All Gulf states except South Yemen condemned the Soviet action in forums such as the United Nations and the various Islamic conferences, and a number boycotted the Moscow Olympics. Some provide financial assistance to the Afghan resistance forces.

Afghanistan could potentially become an area of major Soviet vulnerability and the evolution of the Afghan conflict might well affect Soviet behavior in the surrounding region. The Soviet strategy for pacification of that country has not worked. The Soviet occupation continues to be opposed by much of the population with varying degrees of activism. Should the resistance's effectiveness further increase because of better organization and a more reliable supply of arms, including antiaircraft and antitank weapons, the situation could become even more difficult for Moscow. The Soviets might be forced to make an increased commitment to the Afghan front or accept a settlement. In the first case, the Soviets might be forced to reduce their capability in other parts of the world as a result of new commitments to Afghanistan. Rising costs of the invasion could affect Soviet relations with its Eastern-bloc allies, succession problems in Moscow itself, and Moscow's relations with its own rapidly growing Muslim population. Continued and expanded military operations in Afghanistan might further increase hostility to the Soviets in the Muslim world. The Afghan conflict, however, could further affect the situation in the region and possibly beyond, were it to spread to the neighboring countries. The many conflicts in the area provide Moscow with opportunities, but they also constrain Soviet behavior and at times confront the Soviets with major risks. Supporting one group alienates rivals. This has been true not only in the case of Afghanistan but also in others. For example, the PDRY, the important Soviet satellite in the Arabian Peninsula, has the support of only a segment of the urban population and is opposed by a number of other groups. The government, which commands an armed force of 21,000 and 2,500 Soviet-bloc advisers, is vulnerable to internal, regional, and extraregional pressures. The overthrow of the Aden government would weaken Soviet capability for pressuring Saudi Arabia and the Lower Gulf states.

CONCLUSION

Soviet interest and involvement in countries in and near the Persian Gulf date back many years. Moscow's involvement is likely to increase, as it seeks to expand its role in affecting developments in the area. Given Iran's pivotal position in the region and its territorial contiguity, it will probably receive greater Soviet attention than the other states in the area.

Whether future Soviet policies in the area will reflect those of the past—that is, increasing the level of active Soviet involvement and military intervention as ideological relations with small neighboring countries move closer, and a more flexible policy with more distant ones—will probably depend on many factors, including the evolution of the Afghan conflict and the risks and gains perceived from various policy choices. It is possible that Moscow will face much greater risks then it did in the case of Afghanistan, if it seeks forcefully to extend its control southward. One relevant question is whether the Soviets will have an accurate perception of potential consequences resulting from a particular policy in this region. Another is Moscow's assessment of a break-even point between risks and benefits. In the case of a Soviet invasion of Iran, the potential risks would be higher than those in Afghanistan, but so would the benefits.

The category of "risk" is an analytically important one, and the concept has not received sufficient attention. The concept provides a useful focus for surveying the dynamics of power politics, and thus also of following the course of superpower activity in the arena of strategically important Third World countries. A major factor delineating the willingness of the Soviet Union aggressively to pursue its goals will be its estimation of the risks involved and the likelihood of the gains to be achieved. The relative capability of the Soviet Union, on the one hand, and that of its adversaries, especially the United States and its allies, on the other, will be a major factor determining the risks of Soviet actions. Over the recent past, the relative capabilities have shifted to the advantage of the USSR; therefore, some Soviet actions have become less risky than they would have been in the past. Concomitantly, meeting potential Soviet threats has become more risky for Moscow's adversaries. This shift in risk distribution has been one of the major international changes over the past 25 years.

Since World War II fluctuations have taken place in the relative power potential of the superpowers ideologically, militarily, and economically. Immediately following the war, Moscow's aggressive behavior toward Iran and Turkey failed, leading to alienation and suspicion on the part of these countries and consequently to a shift in favor of the United States as a counterbalancing power. Both countries, and a number of others in the area, sought close alliance relations with the West, bringing about a Western predominance that continued for a number of years. The perception of a Soviet threat declined in the region, dissatisfaction with the United States increased and some Western policies, such as the Nixon Doctrine, experienced spectacular failures. Once again a shift set in, with some important changes.

The application of direct Soviet power in Afghanistan in the aftermath of the Iranian revolution has increased the perception of a Soviet threat in the West and in the Gulf. A situation has emerged in which states of the area have become more reluctant to enter into an alliance with the United States, due to the cumulative effect of factors developing since the 1950s. These include the emergence of large groups hostile to both superpowers or only to the United States. The growth of nationalism and self-assertiveness on the part of the regimes and population of the area is a factor both superpowers will increasingly have to include in their calculations: a perception of Western unreliability, even on the part of some sympathetic groups and governments, and a feeling of intimidation by the states of the area, since Moscow is far more formidable now than it was after the Second World War.

The current configuration works to the military advantage of the Soviet Union because of the geographic imbalance. If the Soviets were to attack the Gulf region, they would be launching cross-border air and ground operations. Without facilities in the region, the United States would be thousands of miles away. This consideration makes an arms control agreement ensuring a balance of power between the two superpowers in the region unlikely in the coming few years.

Based on pronouncements from Washington, the United States intends to make a greater effort to increase its military capability in the area. In this, Washington will face the continuation of a dilemma with which previous U.S. governments have often failed to come to grips: the necessity of developing a coherent strategy for coping with requirements that are often contradictory. The task of increasing U.S. credibility with sympathetic groups rather than supporting only nondemocratic regimes is not easy to reconcile with the need for maintaining the regional and local security required to counter Soviet or pro-Soviet incursions. Developing the military capability to balance Soviet power in the region, however, may not be easy to accomplish without exacerbating internal and regional tensions to the benefit of local hostile groups or the Soviet Union.

Washington's success or failure vis-à-vis these tasks, and the developments in the area itself, will be the important factors affecting Moscow's prospects in the region in the coming years.

NOTES

1. For a historical background of Russian policies toward the countries south of her border, see Firuz Kazemzadeh, "Afghanistan: the Imperial Dream", *New York Review of Books*, February 21, 1980, pp. 10-14; G. Nollau and H. J. Wiehe, *Russia's South Flank: Soviet Operations in Iran, Turkey, and Afghanistan*, (New York: Praeger, 1963); John Campbell, "The Soviet Union in the Middle East," *Middle East Journal* 32, no. 1 (1978): 1-12.

2. Zalmay Khalilzad, *The Return of the Great Game: Superpower Rivalry and Domestic Turmoil in Afghanistan, Iran, Pakistan and Turkey* (Los Angeles: California Seminar on International Security and Foreign Policy, 1980). For a discussion of the role of Muslim Central Asia in Soviet policies toward Muslim countries, see Alexander Bennigsen, "Soviet Muslims and the World of Islam," *Problems of Communism* 29 (March-April, 1980): 38-51.

3. Central Intelligence Agency, *Soviet Economic Problems and Prospects* (Washington, D.C.: U.S. Government Printing Office, July 1977), CIA-10436U.

4. Albert Wohlstetter, "Meeting the Threat in the Persian Gulf," *Survey* 25, no. 2 (1980): 128-88. Zalmay Khalilzad, "The Superpowers and the Northern Tier," *International Security* 4, no. 3, (1980): 6-31.

5. For a discussion of the Afghan crisis, its background and implications, see Hannah Negaran (pseud.), "The Afghan Coup of April 1978: Revolution and International Security," *Orbis* 22 (1979): 93-113; Louis Dupress, "Afghanistan Under the Khalg," *Problems of Communism* 28 (July-August 1979): 34-50; Zalmay Khalilzad, "Afghanistan and the Crisis in American Foreign Policy," *Survival* (July-August 1980), pp. 151-60; William E. Griffith, "Superpower Relations after Afghanistan," *Survival* (July-August 1980), 146-51.

6. Henry S. Rowen, et al., *Persian Gulf Oil and Western Security* (Los Angeles: Pan Heuristics, 1980 Report of the Department of Energy, Contract No. HN-LV-79-2).

7. Border disputes have been the harbingers of many conflicts in the area. The completely undefined borders are those of Oman-South Yemen, Oman-Saudi Arabia, Oman-UAE, and South Yemen-Saudi Arabia, South Yemen and Saudi Arabia, and between the two Yemens. There are problems in maritime boundaries between Iran and the Sheikdoms of Ajman, Ras al-Khumah, Onn al-Quywan, and Fujayrah. See Evan Luard, ed., *The International Regulation of Frontier Disputes*, (New York: Praeger, 1970); J. P. Kelly, *Eastern Arabian Frontiers* (New York: Praeger, 1964); Richard Muir, *Modern Political Geography* (London: Macmillan, 1975).

8. George Lenczowski, *Russia and the West in Iran, 1918-1948: A Study in Big-Power Rivalry* (Ithaca, N.Y.: Cornell University Press, 1949); George Lenczowski, *The Middle East in World Affairs* (Ithaca, N.Y.: Cornell University Press, 1953), pp. 168-78.

9. For studies of domestic changes in Iran, see James Bill, "Iran and the Crisis of '78," *Foreign Affairs* 27 (January 1979): 323-42; Amin Saikal, *The Rise and Fall of the Shah* (Princeton, N.J.: Princeton University Press, 1980); Shahram Chubin, "Leftist Forces in Iran," *Problems of Communism* 29 (July-August, 1980): 1-25.

10. *Financial Times*, November 6, 1978. Yahya Armajani, "What the U.S. Needs to Know about Iran," *Worldview* 22 (May 1979): 13-19; Ian Greig, "Iran and the Lengthening Soviet Shadow," *Atlantic Community Quarterly* 17, no. 1 (1979): 66-72.

11. British Broadcasting Corporation (BBC), *Summary of World Broadcasts, the U.S.S.R.*, September 29, 1978, October 10, 1978.

12. Ibid., January 12, 1979.

13. For example, Radio Moscow Persian broadcast, afternoon of March 22, 1980 (heard by author).

14. Aleksandr Bovin, *Vedelya*, September 3-9, 1979.

15. William J. Barnds, "Pakistan's Foreign Policy: Shifting Opportunities and Constraints," in *Pakistan: The Long View*, ed. Lawrence Ziring et al. (Durham, N.C.: Duke University Press, 1977), pp. 369-402.

16. For a discussion of the Pakistani nuclear program, see Zalmay Khalilzad, "Pakistan and the Bomb," *Bulletin of the Atomic Scientists*, (January 1980), pp. 11-16.

17. Francis Fukuyama, The Security of Pakistan: A Trip Report (Santa Monica, Cal.: RAND Corporation, September 1980), N-1584-RC.

18. See Zalmay Khalilzad, "Soviet-Occupied Afghanistan," *Problems of Communism* 29 (November-December 1980): 23-40.

19. For a discussion of Soviet relations with Iraq, see Shahram Chubin, "Soviet Policy Towards Iran and the Gulf," *Adelphi Papers*, no. 157, (1980): 1-48; Francis Fukuyama, *The Soviet Union and Iraq since 1968* (Santa Monica, Cal.: RAND Corporation, July 1980), N-1524-AF.

20. Francis Fukyuama, "A New Soviet Strategy," *Commentary* 68 (October 1979): 52.

21. *Washington Post*, March 3, 1981, p. 10.

22. Alvin Z. Rubenstein, "The Soviet Union and the Arabian Peninsula," *The World Today* 35 (November 1979): 442-52.

23. Patrick Seale, "Iran Turns on the Saudis," *Observer*, January 13, 1980.

16

SOVIET INVOLVEMENT IN SOUTH ASIA AND THE INDIAN OCEAN REGION

Robert H. Donaldson

In the late 1970s and opening months of the 1980s, and especially in the wake of the Soviet invasion of Afghanistan, public officials and journalists in Washington developed a strong interest in the Indian Ocean and the states along its littoral, including those of the Indian subcontinent. For most of the postwar period, events in this part of the world had gone largely unnoticed in the United States unless they bore directly on America's political and economic interests in the Middle East and the Persian Gulf. The defense of the Khyber Pass, tribal politics in Baluchistan, or access to port facilities in the Maldives were seemingly exotic subjects of no real bearing on the vital issues in the main strategic arena where East and West conducted their competition.

Accordingly, many in the United States felt a sense of shock, tinged with an ample dose of resentment, when they discovered at the end of the 1970s that the Soviet Union had become so deeply involved in South Asia and adjoining states of the Indian Ocean littoral that Moscow was willing to invest military resources in order to protect its investments there. And yet, the Soviet entanglement in the conflicts from the Horn of Africa and Yemen eastward through Afghanistan to the Indian subcontinent, though viewed in Washington as the illegitimate meddling of an outsider, was considered by the Soviets themselves as a natural extension both of their status as a global superpower, with strong ties to a proximate geographical region, and of their role as the fraternal protector of national liberation movements throughout the Third World.

South Asia and environs had always been a higher priority area for Soviet foreign policy than for American; what had changed in the late 1970s and attracted U.S. attention was the level of Soviet involvement in the area and the instruments of policy that Moscow was willing to deploy in pursuit of its interests. But what has *not* been changed by the greater and more active Soviet presence is the considerable passion with which the peoples of the region undertake the task of safeguarding their autonomy and the skill with which they have thus far maneuvered to keep the Soviet position unsecured.

This chapter aims to aid in the understanding of the current Soviet involvement in South Asia by setting it in its historical, ideological, and geopolitical context and linking it to the broader aspects of the USSR's global activities. From this framework it proceeds to an explication of recent events in the area and to a projection of likely developments through the balance of the 1980s.

SOVIET–SOUTH ASIAN RELATIONS
IN HISTORICAL PERSPECTIVE

The Soviet Union has pursued an active policy in South Asia only since 1955—somewhat more than a quarter of a century. Still not a truly global actor and relatively isolated behind the Iron Curtain, the Soviet Union launched the effort to build stronger economic and diplomatic ties in India, the largest South Asian state, out of a mixture of defensive, counteroffensive, and preventive motives. U.S. efforts in 1954–55 to enlarge the ring of containment by enlisting military allies on the Soviet Union's southern periphery (Pakistan, Iraq, Iran) seriously alarmed the Soviets. The hostile reaction to the American policy on the part of several important and strongly nationalist states in the region, some officially neutralist in their orientation, encouraged Moscow to counterattack. Moreover, Zhou Enlai's success in capitalizing on the anti-imperialist mood at the Bandung Conference of African and Asian states, held in Indonesia in April 1955, demonstrated anew the Leninist thesis regarding the possibilities for a Communist-nationalist alliance against the imperialist designs. Indeed, Moscow's haste in launching its counteroffensive into the Third World resulted in part from its determination to prevent China from being the sole, or even the chief missionary for the Communist cause in the newly emerging nations.

From this mix of motives there developed in the Soviet leadership a reawakened appreciation of the importance of the Third World as the vital "strategic reserve" of imperialism and as an arena in which Moscow could wage the bipolar struggle with solid prospects of success, but at a lower level of risk than would be posed by a direct challenge in the main arena of confrontation. The year's significant events foreshadowed the Soviet priorities and techniques in this new arena: Moscow's entry into the Middle East by means of the arms deal with Cairo; the visit of India's Prime Minister Nehru to Moscow, and the return trip by Khrushchev and Bulganin to India, Burma, and Afghanistan; the dramatic announcement that the Soviets would finance and construct a giant public-sector steel mill at Bhilai in India (a project spurned by the capitalists in Washington). These early targets of Soviet activity were chosen for their strategic importance in the struggle with the West rather than for any particular features of their internal development. But the Marxist-Leninist approach to foreign policy demanded that an ideological justification be provided for the new policy, and so the Soviets soon set about—with great optimism but little sophisticated knowledge of the domestic affairs of the Third World states—revising the Stalinist doctrine concerning the class basis and orientation of the new Asian and African nations.

Four decades earlier Lenin had prepared the ideological foundations for the Communist alliance with the forces of national liberation in the context of his theory of imperialism. In Lenin's view, nationalist movements in Asia led by revolutionary-minded elements of the bourgeoisie were worthy of support by the proletariat, not only because they created the internal conditions necessary for capitalist (and then socialist) development but also because they were directed against the imperialist powers. Their success thus weakened the system of imperialism itself. This Leninist position, worked out before 1917, has continued to occupy a central place in the analyses of Soviet policy makers in the contemporary era.

Indeed, once in power, and largely preoccupied with problems of withdrawal from the world war and then with their own civil war and the Allied intervention, Lenin and Trotsky did give some consideration to the prospects for an assault on British India, through Afghanistan or Tibet. Here, in light of the ongoing debate over the degree to which Soviet policy was a continuation of Czarist aims, it may be helpful to recall briefly the nineteenth-century Russian designs on India.

In 1801 the "mad Czar" Paul hastily assembled an expedition of 23,000 Cossacks under Vasily Orlov, whose task was to march on India by way of Khiva and Bukhara. Napoleon, who was at war with Britain, had made preparations to send a French corps to link up with the Cossack expedition. This foolhardy adventure (Orlov was without maps of the area he was to conquer) was terminated in mid-course by the murder of Paul and the accession of Alexander, who recalled Orlov. Seven years later, in the wake of the Tilsit agreement, Alexander himself was cooperating with Napoleon in another scheme—also abortive—to defeat Britain through the conquest of India.

The middle years of the century were marked by British-Russian rivalry in Central Asia, as Palmerston strove to ward off the threat he perceived in Russian moves in the Caucasus and Afghanistan. Again in the 1870s British suspicion of Russian designs on India rose, as the distance separating the two states' Asian territories shrank. Alexander II ridiculed the British fears in an interview with the British ambassador in 1876, at the same time that General Skobelev was drawing up plans for the invasion of India. Skobelev believed that an expeditionary corps of 50,000 men, by its mere appearance on the Indian frontier, could spark a general uprising of the discontented Indian masses, thus leading to the ruin of the British Empire. Although Skobelev scrapped his plan as impracticable, his vision of engineering the fall of Britain itself by inspiring an Indian uprising was to be revived by his Soviet successors four decades later. And yet with the Czarist legacy then viewed from the Marxist-Leninist perspective, there was both a more "scientific" rationale for assuming the hostility of capitalist Britain and a more universalistic mission to be pursued in liberating the oppressed masses of Asia. The difference of perspective—whatever the short-run similarity of strategies—is sufficient to set off Soviet policies as of a different order from the more limited balance-of-power aims of Czarist expansionism.

Despite its larger ambitions, however, the besieged Soviet state in its early years had lacked the resources for an operational commitment in the east. Stalin had more resources at his command, especially after the post–World War Two lines in Europe had been firmly drawn and the Soviet Union had broken America's atomic monopoly. Even then, however, he had failed to move toward an anti-imperialist united front in Asia, for Lenin's perception of the possibilities of alliance with "bourgeois nationalism" in Asia had been blunted and distorted by Stalin after the humiliating defeat he suffered in China in 1927.

Thus it required the fresh perceptions of a new Soviet leadership to take full advantage in exploiting dynamic situations both of the new international situation and of the maximum flexibility allowed by Marxism-Leninism. Stalin's image of a two-camp world, denying the possibility of neutrality, had carried the "he who is not with us is against us" formulation to the extreme, and it had thus precluded effective Soviet action in those areas where Communist parties were weak or nonexistent. Khrushchev's interpretation in 1956, on the other hand, was to revive the Leninist perception by holding that as long as the brunt of the independence movement in the Third World was aimed against Western imperialism, Soviet assistance to this movement would further Soviet interests. Under the temporary alliance with national-bourgeois forces, the Soviet Union would be able to achieve its aim of expelling Western influence and substituting its own. In the meantime, it would be able to work toward ensuring that the future leadership of these new states would be held by forces more ideologically acceptable and more easily controllable.

Although the long-term perspective was thus compatible with Lenin's vision of a Socialist India, the beginning of Soviet involvement in the Indian subcontinent was not primarily motivated by changes occurring within India, though the ruling Congress party did declare its dedication to socialism in 1955. Rather, it was motivated by the spread to South Asia of Moscow's bipolar competition with Washington and its nascent rivalry with Beijing. In particular, Soviet activity in India followed upon the conclusion of the 1954 U.S.-Pakistani defense agreement and the agreement on Tibet concluded the same year between Zhou Enlai and Prime Minister Nehru, which proclaimed that Sino-Indian relations would be governed by the "five principles of peaceful coexistence."

Nehru had already demonstrated his actively neutralist foreign policy and his aversion to the sinful practice of imperialism, and this behavior had attracted the attention of the new Soviet leaders. In February 1955 they concluded a substantial aid agreement with the Indians, and in June Nehru was given an unprecedented lavish welcome on the occasion of his visit to the USSR. This trip was followed at the end of the year by the Soviet leaders' return visit, during which they offered reassurance to their hosts that strengthened relations need not be hindered by differences in the two states' social systems. Khrushchev and Bulganin also bestowed generous praise on India's struggle for independence and on her late leader, Mahatma Gandhi (who had earlier been denounced by Moscow as a benighted reactionary). India's present ambitions were flattered by the Soviet leaders' assertions that the imperialists had failed to acknowledge her deserved ranking as a great power. Finally, Khrushchev lent support to India on the issue embroiling her in conflict with Pakistan and most crucial to her national pride; he declared that the people themselves had already decided that Kashmir was part of India. On their return to Moscow, however, the Soviet leaders were careful to make a statement that left the door open for a warming of Soviet-Pakistani relations, should that state return to an "independent" policy. But at that time it appeared to serve Soviet purposes to seek to build influence by intervening in a regional quarrel on behalf of the party engaged in struggle against "imperialism and its lackeys."

Over the next few years there was a proliferation of exchanges between India and the USSR; almost 200 Indian delegations of various sorts traveled to the Soviet Union between 1954 and 1957. An ever increasing volume of books, pamphlets, and magazines made their way from the Soviet Union to India; whereas 17,000 books were sent in 1955, the figure had climbed to 4 million copies by 1958.[1]

Of equal if not greater importance in achieving for the Soviet Union a profound impact on Indian consciousness were the offers of economic assistance. The volume of economic contacts rose steadily, and by the 1960s India had become the USSR's most important non-Communist trading partner. By 1970–71 the Soviet Union had established itself as the largest market for Indian products, with sales of almost $380 million, amounting to about one-fifth of India's total exports. Apart from its sheer volume, India's trade with Moscow was important in that it was concentrated in key industries in the state-owned industrial sector of India's developing economy. Soviet trade has also been important in drastically reducing India's economic dependence on the West and in allowing the Indians to make important purchases without the expenditure of scarce foreign exchange.

As the 1950s drew to a close, Moscow had reason to be pleased with the progress of its strategy in India. The American effort to contain Soviet influence by enlisting the military and diplomatic cooperation of states on the USSR's southern periphery had been effectively blocked by Moscow's ability to "leapfrog" the encirclement. Just as the friendship with Egypt gave Moscow a powerful entree into the Middle East, the multifaceted development of Soviet relations with India, the leading power in South Asia and major architect of the growing neutral bloc, helped to enhance Soviet influence and prestige throughout the region. Posing as the champion of the "progressive" and "peace-loving" forces of the Third World in their struggle against the "neocolonial" and "militarist" policies of the United States and its conservative alliance partners, the Soviets seemed to be on the verge of both propaganda and diplomatic triumphs.

THE CHINESE CHALLENGE

But this relatively happy picture was shattered in the last year of the 1950s by the burgeoning Chinese challenge to both Moscow and New Delhi. In the spring of that year China charged "Indian expansionists" with having incited and aided a short-lived rebellion in Tibet, and in the summer and fall there were outbreaks of fighting along disputed areas of the Sino-Indian border. The timing of the Chinese attacks had wider significance, since Khrushchev was at this time about to embark on his visit to the United States, where he hoped for results that would show the Chinese that détente and peaceful competition could serve the Communist cause better than military force. But if the Chinese sought to sabotage the détente by forcing Khrushchev into a militant stand in support of Chinese claims in India, Khrushchev's reaction was far from obliging. On September 10 a TASS statement was issued from Moscow, expressing regret over the border conflict, asserting that the USSR enjoyed friendly relations with both parties, and urging prompt negotiations. The Chinese were indignant at the attitude of studied neutrality reflected in this statement, which they interpreted as siding with a bourgeois country against a Socialist ally.

Moreover, the Soviet stance apparently emboldened Nehru to adopt a "forward policy" on the Sino-Indian border, thus contributing to the heightening of Sino-Indian tensions. In August 1962 the Indian prime minister announced that he had accepted an offer made by the Soviets in May to supply MIG-21 fighter planes (which had not been supplied to China). The mounting conflict between the two Asian giants erupted on October 20 in fighting along the northeastern frontier of India, which turned in mid-November into a general Chinese offensive, thoroughly defeating India's army and causing Nehru to appeal to Britain and the United States for military aid. In this second round of the Sino-Indian border conflict, the Soviet Union at first seemed to side with China. But it must be remembered that the fighting had broken out almost simultaneously with the Cuban missile crisis, and in this delicate period Khrushchev dared not risk provoking disunity in the Communist camp. With the resolution of the Cuban crisis, however, the Soviets returned to a position of neutrality on the Sino-Indian conflict, complaining that only the imperialists could benefit from it.

Having demonstrated the ability of its army to drive as far as it wished into India, China on November 21 accepted a cease-fire and unilaterally withdrew to positions behind the August 1959 lines of control. The major objectives had been been accomplished: China had damaged Nehru's prestige and upset his ambitions to develop India as a model to the Third World, and had forced him to begin diverting a much larger share of India's resources to defense expenditures.

In the wake of the crisis the Soviets sent a note to the Chinese complaining that "years of hard striving for Indian friendship and Indian neutrality" had gone for nothing as a result of Beijing's actions.[2] As a consequence of their initial vacillations, the Soviets had certainly lost standing with Indian popular opinion, while the influence of the United States and Britain—which had rushed to provide arms aid to New Delhi—had risen. The conflict had polarized the Indian political scene, isolating the Left, and it had precipitated a conflict within the Communist party of India (CPI) that resulted in an open split in April 1964. The Sino-Indian conflict dramatized for the world the growing breach between Moscow and Beijing and itself became the cause for a further intensification of that quarrel.

With the growing Chinese challenge the Soviets were forced to give doctrinal justification for their support of the regime of Nehru (who died in May 1964) and his successors. This was not an easy task. India's leaders could not qualify as "revolutionary democrats" nor could their policies be characterized as leading to the "noncapitalist path." In the presence of a genuine proletariat and a long-suffering Communist party, direct support could not justifiably be given to the Congress party as a revolutionary alternative. That the Soviets continued nevertheless to give aid and support to the "bourgeois" Congress regime in India was testimony to the continued preeminence of the foreign policy criterion in determining Soviet policy. It was evidence, as well, both of the increased Soviet fear of Chinese hegemony in Asia and of Moscow's calculation that a less forthcoming policy might well have opened India to even greater Western influence.

As Soviet ideologists saw it, the vital task for India was to interrupt capitalist development and transfer the country onto the "rails of noncapitalist development." This was clearly impossible so long as the national bourgeoisie continued to monopolize political power. Thus, the Soviets urged progressive forces in India to work for the formation of a democratic coalition of the left wing of the Congress party and the CPI, which would then establish a "state of national democracy."

A consequence of the 1962 border war had been the warming of relations between India's two major adversaries—China and Pakistan. While Moscow was determined to retain the friendship of India, it was loath to abandon Pakistan to the exclusive blandishments of Beijing and Washington. Thus, as part of the large larger campaign to woo the states of the northern tier, the USSR began to improve its relations with Pakistan. In April 1965 President Ayub Khan visited

Moscow, and the resulting communique seemed to move the USSR toward a position of neutrality on the Kashmir question.

The Pakistanis had been emboldened by the changing situation on the subcontinent to press their claims to Kashmir, and in August 1965 a war erupted over the issue. The conflict was at first ignored in the Soviet press, but then Moscow issued an appeal for an end to the conflict, expressing its desire for Indo-Pakistani relations to be a stablizing factor in Asia. When China demonstrated its support for Pakistan and made threatening demands on New Delhi regarding the Sino-Indian frontier, the Soviets issued a stern warning to China not to stir up trouble on the subcontinent.

In mid-September Premier Kosygin volunteered to provide the good offices of the Soviet Union in helping to settle the conflict. This dramatic gesture, in stark contrast to earlier Soviet behavior in fanning Indo-Pakistani strife, showed how far Moscow had come in its desire to bring stability to South Asia. The Soviets expressed fear that the conflict would only play into the hands of extremists both in the belligerent states and abroad, and they also calculated (though not publicly) that it could eventuate in the destruction of the quite substantial investment Moscow had built up in the governments and economies of the two states. The offer posed the risk of failure, but the stakes were sufficiently high to warrant it. If a Soviet-sponsored mediation could produce the beginnings of a rapprochement between India and Pakistan, then it would have contributed enormously to Moscow's primary aim in South Asia: the containment of Chinese influence and expansionism.

Kosygin met with Prime Minister Shastri (Nehru's successor) and President Ayub in the city of Tashkent in Soviet Uzbekistan in January 1966, and though his mediation did not succeed in settling the political future of Kashmir, it did defuse the immediate conflict. Shastri's death at the conclusion of the conference helped to galvanize Indian support for the Tashkent Declaration, and his successor (Indira Gandhi, Nehru's daughter) pledged to continue to work for the peaceful resolution of Indo—Pakistani differences. The Soviets were widely praised for their efforts at mediation, and they managed to derive great propaganda advantage from the image they projected as a peace-loving great power endeavoring, while others fanned the flames of conflict, to bring security to a troubled subcontinent.

The great hopes engendered at Tashkent were not to come to fruition. Indian and Pakistani leaders were caught in a web of their own making: long years of fanning popular hatred and suspicion were not easily overcome, nor were the large amounts of prestige invested by each side in the emotional issue of Kashmir easily sacrificed by either state. The continuation of the conflict was evidenced in the spiraling arms race that entrapped the great-power patrons of the two combatants. The United States sought to extricate itself, suspending arms shipments after the 1965 war. But India called on the Soviets for more arms, and in May 1968 Moscow responded with a shipment of 100 SU-7 fighter-bombers. In the face of a vigorous protest from Pakistan (and fearing that she might move closer to Beijing) the Soviets agreed, in the summer of 1968, following Ayub's cancellation of the lease on the U.S. intelligence base in Peshawar, to sell weapons to Pakistan. The announcement of this deal produced in its turn protests and riots in New Delhi, demonstrating anew the unpopularity that can be reaped by a supplier to both sides in an arms race.

THE SOVIET-INDIAN TREATY

Improving Soviet-Pakistani diplomatic and trade relations were derailed in the spring of 1971 by the outbreak of a severe civil conflict in East Pakistan that soon developed into a near genocide. On April 2 President Podgorny requested that Pakistani President Yahya Khan (who had succeeded Ayub two years earlier) take the most urgent measures to stop the bloodshed and repressions against the population in East Pakistan. As the conflict continued, however, millions of refugees streamed across the border into India, further straining its already tight economy and stimulating demands for Indian military action to help create an independent Bangladesh. Alarmed at the prospect that the conflict might again embroil the subcontinent in an enervating war, in which Pakistan might be supported by China, the Soviets moved decisively in an attempt to extend their influence and deter a war.

It is in the context of the larger campaign for collective security against China that the Soviet-Indian treaty, signed on August 9, 1971, must be viewed. Negotiations had actually begun two years before, against a backdrop of sharp Sino-Soviet conflict and splits in Prime Minister Gandhi's Congress party. The Indians were apparently motivated by the increasing strain of the Pakistani civil war to resume the discussions in the summer of 1971. The other decisive new element in the situation was the trip of Henry Kissinger to Beijing in July, 1971—a journey facilitated by Pakistan. Thus, with the cooperation of India's sworn enemy, the American president was making overtures for a new relationship with China, India's second major antagonist in Asia. This dramatic shift raised serious doubts in New Delhi about the American role in a possible Indo-Pakistani conflict.

The Soviets, no less concerned over the prospect of a Sino-American rapprochement, saw the Indian dilemma as an opportunity both to gain influence in New Delhi and to deter another wasteful and destabilizing war on the subcontinent, from which they thought only China might gain. The formal linkage of Soviet and Indian interests by means of a treaty might succeed in deterring the Chinese from providing military backing for Pakistan, while placing additional pressure on Yahya to reach a political solution. The formal obligations the Soviets incurred from the treaty were minimal; its main purpose, from the Soviet point of view, was to formalize and extend Russian influence for the immediate purpose of stabilizing the situation in South Asia.

Article 10 of the treaty stated ambiguously that in the event of an attack or threat directed toward either party by a third state, they would "immediately start mutual consultations with a view to eliminating this threat." The first consultations under the treaty took place in September in Moscow. There, Kosygin reportedly lectured Indira Gandhi about the need for the Pakistani people to decide their own future: "It is not a question for India to decide. You agreed to this. Therefore, we appeal that this problem has to be solved by peaceful political means."[3] Although Soviet statements later in the fall grew steadily more critical of Pakistan, Moscow still urged a peaceful solution to the conflict. Nevertheless, the Soviets rushed substantial quantities of arms to India, thus ensuring that their clients would be well armed, should she find a military solution necessary. In the meantime the Soviets were putting heavy pressure on the Pakistanis to make political concessions to Sheik Mujibur Rahman's party in the East. Washington was also heavily engaged in the effort to restrain the two parties from going to war.

Nevertheless, India moved her troops into East Pakistan at the end of November. The brief war ended in mid-December with the unconditional surrender of Pakistani troops in the east and a cease-fire on the western front. But while the fighting on the subcontinent was proceeding, as well as in its aftermath, a torrent of impassioned words poured forth from Moscow, Beijing, and Washington, and acrimonious around-the-clock debates occurred at the United Nations. Soviet Ambassador Malik, arguing that Pakistan bore full responsibility for the conflict, used his vetoes in the Security Council to block cease-fire resolutions while the Indians were completing their military operations in East Pakistan. The United States, pressing for a cease-fire, claimed that India had attacked without justification while the United States was in the process of promoting a political settlement. As for the Soviets, Washington charged that by failing to restrain India they had pursued unilateral military advantage in the subcontinent. The Chinese went further—though not to the point of actual military intervention—in their attacks on Moscow and New Delhi, charging that the Soviets had stage-managed the whole plot and warning India that "he who plays with fire will be consumed by fire."[4]

In the immediate aftermath of the war the Soviets had every reason to be exultant. Though they had failed to bring about the removal of the refugee burden from India by peaceful means, they had at least played an essential role in India's victory over Pakistan, while their American and Chinese rivals—in the first test of the new anti-Soviet axis—had both lined up on the side of the loser. As American influence in India had declined dramatically, so Soviet influence had never been greater.

The Soviets moved rapidly to build their ties with the new state of Bangladesh. Sheik Mujib visited Moscow in March 1972, concluding agreements on economic assistance that were soon to lead to a substantial Soviet presence in Bangladesh. Two weeks later Pakistan's new leader, President Bhutto, was received in the Soviet capital for a "frank and useful exchange" on the prospects for rebuilding Soviet-Pakistani relations. In subsequent meetings with officials of all three states of the subcontinent, the Soviets consistently exerted their influence in an effort to foster reconciliation. The Simla Agreement of July 1972, in which India and Pakistan pledged their mutual desire for normalization of relations, the New Delhi Agreement of August 1973, which achieved a three-way repatriation of prisoners and refugees from the 1971 war, and subsequent agreements restoring relations between India and Pakistan were all welcomed by the Soviets as positive developments helping to restore stability to South Asia.

In the changed circumstances of the postwar period, however, Pakistan and Bangladesh were overshadowed on the subcontinent by a strengthened and confident India. For the Soviets, the essential point was that whereas prior to 1971 the balance of forces had dictated the well-nigh impossible task of uniting India and Pakistan in a common grouping against Chinese influence, the situation after the December war seemed far more manageable. By Moscow's reckoning, India—grateful for Soviet assistance and dependent on further aid—would be in the new circumstances an even more valuable partner in the effort to outflank China. But Soviet calculations projecting a firm and lasting partnership with an increasingly left-leaning India have been upset by subsequent events—and most notably by India's evident fierce determination to be the client of no other state.

SOVIET–SOUTH ASIAN RELATIONS IN THE 1970s

A survey of post-1971 Soviet-Indian relations reveals that Soviet calculations have been upset on more than one occasion. India's leaders have strongly reaffirmed their continuing nonalignment, and not only have they failed to echo the warm references made in Moscow to the Indo-Soviet treaty, but they have in fact made statements strongly critical of super-power hegemony. India has taken steps to improve her long-damaged relationships with both Washington and Beijing. She has resisted Soviet requests for naval cooperation and has even refused (despite Brezhnev's personal plea during his visit to New Delhi in November 1973) to give explicit endorsement to the Soviet plan for collective security in Asia.

The Indians did sign a 15-year agreement designed to put their economic relationship with the Soviets on a stable long-term basis, but they have denied rumors that they plan to seek formal association with the Soviet trading bloc (CMEA). And there are signs that further growth in Soviet-Indian trade may be limited, due both to noncomplementarity in the two economies and to Soviet unwillingness to provide certain raw materials needed by India. There are limits also to the expansion of Soviet-Indian military cooperation; through the treaty the Soviets have already extended their pledge of support, and by virtue of her victory in the December war, India now faces a much-reduced threat. In a determined fashion India has been seeking self-sufficiency in arms production, and her progress in building a nuclear capability—viewed with a notable lack of enthusiasm in Moscow—suggests that she may be capable of achieving it.

On balance, the Soviet-Indian relationship and the degree of Moscow's influence in New Delhi probably reached a peak in 1971. In the period since then, India's dependence has lessened, and the Soviets may now need India's support more than New Delhi needs Moscow's. If India were to become hostile or indifferent, Moscow would be left with no major asset in South Asia.

In fact, the events of the mid-1970s have represented a setback for Soviet interests in the subcontinent. The overthrow of the pro-Soviet government of Sheik Mujibur Rahman in Bangladesh in the summer of 1975, and its replacement by a more pro-Western (and anti-Indian) regime, was viewed with apprehension in Moscow. An article signed with the authoritative "Observer" name warned that forces inimical to the national liberation movement, including imperialism, Maoism, and internal reaction, were seeking to strengthen their influence in Bangladesh.[5] In the ensuing years the Soviets continued to display considerable reserve in their attitude toward the regime of President Ziaur Rahman, although they welcomed the steps taken in 1977 and 1978 that eased some of Bangladesh's strained relations with India.

As in the political realm, Moscow's economic relations with Dacca were less close in the post-Mujib period. Trade turnover, which had increased rapidly in the years immediately following independence (from 16.6 million rubles in 1972 to 58.1 million rubles in 1974) began to level off in 1975 and fell sharply in 1976 (to a volume of 36.6 million rubles). Similarly, the Soviet economic aid program slowed considerably from its initial high level of activity. In fact, Bangladesh's repayments on a 1973 Soviet wheat loan created a net negative aid flow in 1977.

The 1977 change of government in Pakistan was also not much to Moscow's liking. On the occasion of President Bhutto's visit to Moscow in 1974, the Soviet press had noted that though its path was not "bestrewn with roses," Pakistan was experiencing a "period of renewal" and "progressive forces" were on the offensive.[6] The Soviet interest in stability was again demonstrated in the press commentary on the growing postelection turmoil in Pakistan in 1977. And although they initially welcomed the end to civil strife that followed the military coup of General Zia, the Soviets took pains to praise the "foreign policy moves of the civilian administration which abandoned the disastrous course of confrontation" in the subcontinent and to warn that "the periods of civilian rule were most favorable and fruitful for Pakistan."[7]

These early unhappy premonitions were borne out for the Soviets by subsequent domestic and foreign actions of the Zia regime. In the former sphere, apart from their disapproval of the rightward turn in Pakistan's economy and the repeated postponement of elections, the Soviets expressed their sharpest criticism over the April 1979 execution of Zulfikar Ali Bhutto. President Zia had ignored a plea from Brezhnev for mercy on Bhutto's behalf (as well as similar pleas from scores of other world leaders), and Moscow showed its anger over the execution by labeling it an act of cruelty.

But it was in the foreign policy sphere that the Soviets were most critical of Pakistan. In a way, their disquiet was ironic, because it came at a time when Pakistani-American relations were reaching a new low. In the spring of 1979 Pakistan formally withdrew from the CENTO pact and joined the nonaligned powers. At about the same time, Islamabad announced that it had arranged to purchase 30 Mirage interceptors, after Washington had refused to sell an American plane. And in April Washington announced that it was cutting off all economic assistance to Pakistan (except food aid) in reaction to an evident step-up in Islamabad's drive to obtain a nuclear weapons capability. Although the Soviet press commented with favor on Pakistan's turn toward nonalignment and its distancing from the United States, Moscow's overall stance was critical, for the Soviets saw the sinister hand of Beijing in the background, fueling Pakistan's nuclear ambitions and encouraging it to play a destabilizing role in its relations with its eastern and western neighbors. And it was the latter situation—Pakistan's swiftly deteriorating relations with the new Marxist-Leninist government of Afghanistan—that drew the sharpest reaction from Moscow. Throughout the spring of 1979 the Soviet press commented darkly on the alleged machinations of American and Chinese "secret agents" who were stirring up and supporting the counterrevolutionary activities of the thousands of Afghan refugees based across the Pakistani border. The Pakistani government was accused of openly ignoring the country's objective national interests and cooperating with imperialist and Chinese schemes to intervene in Afghanistan's internal affairs. In April *Izvestiia* noted that Pakistan's provocations were a "risky undertaking" that could leave it "in an extremely disadvantageous and dangerous position."[8]

Even in allied India, Moscow suffered a setback in the mid-1970s. The mounting political instability that culminated in Indira Ghandi's proclamation of emergency rule in June 1975 was initially welcomed (as "opportune and expedient") by the Soviets for its seeming reversal of a mounting "reactionary" tide.[9] But the period of the emergency freed the prime minister of any parliamentary dependence on the CPI, and the harsh restrictions on political freedom limited the capabilities of the Communists, as well as other parties. Nevertheless, the election campaign in March 1977, following the lifting of the emergency, saw the Soviet press again supporting the Gandhi regime, though not without a tinge of criticism of its domestic policies and anxiety about the possible consequences.

Gandhi's surprising defeat in the elections was attributed by the Soviet press to the "mistakes and excesses" in implementation of the emergency, the halting of progress toward socioeconomic reform, and the Congress's refusal to conclude electoral agreements with the CPI.[10] But rather than linger in the thickets of electoral defeat, the Soviets hastily sought to salvage what they could by courting the victors. Labels of "reactionary" and "demagogue" were hastily dropped from Soviet media references to Prime Minister Morarji Desai and his colleagues, and the Soviet premier sent a message of congratulations that "expressed confidence that the traditional relations of friendship and all-round cooperation between the Soviet Union and India would continue to grow and develop in the interest of their peoples, peace, and international security."[11]

Only a month after the elections, Soviet Foreign Minister Gromyko was in New Delhi to assess the new Indian government at first hand. Desai's first foreign policy pronouncements—that the Indo-Soviet treaty "must not come in the way of our friendship with any other state; we won't have special relations with any other country"—had undoubtedly occasioned deep apprehensions in Moscow. Nevertheless, six months into the new government's life, the Soviet press was showing its relief that "the high hopes of the imperialist forces that Soviet-Indian relations would deteriorate were not justified."[12]

Nevertheless, the weakening of Soviet influence in the higher reaches of the Indian government was clearly accelerated by the coming to power of the Janata party, whose leaders had frequently criticized Gandhi for her one-sided stance toward the superpowers. Shortly after assuming his office, Foreign Minister Vajpayee declared, "At one time we gave the impression that we were pro-American. Then we gave the impression we were pro-Soviet. There must be a change in which we are genuinely nonaligned."[13]

Although Soviet-Indian relations during the almost three-year rule of the Janata party lacked at times some of the warmth shown by the preceding and subsequent Gandhi governments, the difference was clearly one of degree. On the whole, the Desai government's foreign policy during the closing years of the 1970s disappointed those observers who had expected that Gandhi's departure would produce a distinct reorientation of India's diplomatic, economic, and military bonds, away from the USSR. Thus, only a year after his remarks stressing the importance to India of being perceived as nonaligned, Vajpayee waxed as enthusiastic as his Congress party predecessors in declaring that through various trials and tests, "our country always found the only reliable friend in the Soviet Union alone."[14] For most of two decades—dating back to long before the conclusion of their formal treaty ties—political leaders in both countries have seen it in their interests to foster this perception of reliability, so that regional and global rivals are led to conclude that New Delhi and Moscow can count on each other's support, without fear of abandonment or betrayal.

SOVIET NAVAL ACTIVITY IN THE INDIAN OCEAN

The Soviet Union's friendly ties with India have taken on a wider significance in the years since the 1973 Middle East war and the Arab oil embargo, as global rivalries have focused increasingly in the region of the Indian Ocean.

Indeed, from the time in 1968 that two Soviet naval vessels first called at ports in the Indian Ocean, the Soviet naval presence there has slowly but steadily increased in both size and visibility. In recent years the Soviets have maintained a permanent squadron of 20 or more vessels, with occasional "surges" in times of crisis to well over 30.

There are several hypotheses advanced to account for Soviet behavior in the Indian Ocean. Some see it as an outgrowth of the Czarist "push to the warm waters," aimed in the period following British withdrawal from "east of Suez" at the acquisition of a Soviet capability to practice "gunboat diplomacy" and shape events in the region to Moscow's liking. Another explanation sees the Soviet deployment as a defensive reaction to the potential U.S. submarine warfare capability in the area. Yet another focuses on the growing economic-strategic importance of the Persian Gulf oil fields, citing probable Soviet and East European future oil requirements or an ascribed desire to acquire a capability to threaten or actually interdict the vital oil lifeline of the Western countries.

Although the original Soviet deployment probably stemmed from a combination of defensive strategic purposes and the organizational routines of an expanding Soviet navy, the scope and nature of Moscow's behavior over the longer run is best explained in the context of political events and trends in the littoral countries. From this standpoint, the demonstration of Soviet military capabilities, primarily in the form of "showing the flag" in calls at Indian ports, should be understood as the exploitation of yet another instrument for acquiring political influence, rather than as the acquisition of a capability for military intervention or interdiction. At times this influence-building activity has focused on particularly strategic countries, and on occasion the Soviets have utilized their capabilities for dramatic demonstrations of resolve to back up their own and their clients' interests in times of crisis (for example, the Bangladesh war of 1971 and the Arab-Israeli war of 1973).

Seen in this context, then, a certain level of Soviet naval activity seems to be a natural outgrowth of Moscow's acquisition of superpower status and global military capabilities. Though that level may have been heightened by the American response, it is not likely to disappear in any event; indeed, the Indian Ocean provides the most direct path for the routine transferral of Soviet naval units from the Far Eastern to the Black Sea fleets. As for naval activity beyond the level of routine navigational needs, research activity, or "business calls" at the ports of friendly nations, Moscow's own propaganda couches it strictly in terms of a defensive reaction to a growing American and Chinese threat. References in the Soviet press to an American strategic submarine threat to the USSR itself are usually veiled, clearly subordinated to the alleged challenge posed by U.S. naval activity to the "progressively" oriented regimes in the littoral states.

The logistical needs of the Soviet naval force in the Indian Ocean were at first (unsatisfactorily) met by the use of floating anchorages and by occasional calls at the port facilities of the littoral states. This arrangement necessitated long standstill periods and the presence of a large contingent of support vessels; the perceived need for more extensive and reliable repair and support facilities occasioned Soviet overtures in a number of quarters, including India and Sri Lanka in South Asia, as well as Singapore, Mauritius, Iraq, South Yemen, and Somalia. The most receptive responses (encouraged by large and timely provision of economic and military aid) came from the latter three states. In 1973 the Soviets began to develop for their use the port facilities at Berbera, and by August of the following year President Ford was led to declare that Moscow had acquired bases not only there but at Aden and Umm Qasr (Iraq) as well.

But if the concept of "base" is understood in terms of a reliable and secure (not to mention exclusive) facility, the term does not yet precisely fit these particular situations, as both Moscow and the host states have demonstratively pointed out. Moscow's experience with the loss of its Egyptian bases is instructive in this context; indeed, the lesson learned there has provoked the Soviets to seek to spread the risk of loss in the Indian Ocean precisely by the development of multiple facilities. But even spreading the risk can backfire if, as in the case of Ethiopia and Somalia, it draws Moscow into the embarrassing position of wooing its client's chief rival. The result in this case was, of course, Somalia's expulsion of the Soviets from the Berbera facility in November 1977.

In a region as unstable and volatile as the Indian Ocean littoral, there is little that can be regarded as reliable and secure. In the larger context of the Soviet effort to maintain and increase its political influence in the countries surrounding the Indian Ocean, the ease with which Moscow can accomplish this task should not be overestimated. The record of Soviet setbacks in the region is instructive; changes of government, Soviet heavy-handedness, creative diplomacy on the part of Moscow's rivals, or simply the sheer force of nationalism and nonalignment—all have helped to cause the Soviet Union to lose positions of influence in Egypt, the Sudan, Bangladesh, Somalia, and Indonesia, and to suffer a serious setback in Iraq.

Despite their long efforts to focus critical attention on American military facilities at Diego Garcia and to protest the innocent intentions of their own activity, the Soviets have found themselves at odds with India and most other Indian Ocean littoral states on the issue of superpower naval activity there. Almost without exception the littoral states voice support for the idea of limiting superpower naval rivalry and military installations and establishing a "peace zone" in the area. Both Washington and Moscow have objected to any such notion that limits their freedom of navigation on the high seas. In addition, each has been irritated at the failure of the Indian Ocean countries to distinguish between its own peaceful presence and the aggressive activity of its rival. Criticizing the Americans for breaking off their bilateral talks on possible naval limitations in 1978, the Soviets have characterized the proposed U.S. Rapid Deployment Force as an instrument designed to intimidate the littoral states and ultimately to seize the oil fields of the Persian Gulf region. Insisting that it has neither bases nor plans to acquire them, Moscow has also tried (without complete success) to neutralize the Western argument that more recent deployments are a natural response to the presence of Soviet troops in Afghanistan.[15]

AFTER AFGHANISTAN:
CHANGING REGIONAL RELATIONSHIPS

The Soviet invasion of Afghanistan in December 1979, far from being a calculated step on the road to the Persian Gulf oil fields or to the warm waters of the Indian Ocean, was a desperate move undertaken for the purpose of stabilizing the collapsing Marxist-Leninist regime in Kabul and staving off an anti-Communist guerrilla victory that would have cast great doubt on the credibility of Soviet treaty commitments. And yet the presence of the "limited military contingent" of 80,000–100,000 Soviet troops dramatically changed the military balance in South Asia and the Indian Ocean region, even though Soviet troops there were fully occupied in trying to cope with a rebellion that proved far more durable than Moscow ever expected. Moreover, in its immediate aftermath the invasion produced a severe diplomatic setback for the Soviets, who found themselves condemned by virtually the entire Islamic and Western worlds.

India's leaders were by no means pleased by the Soviet invasion, which took place in the midst of a fiercely fought election campaign. The occupation of Afghanistan effectively removed the historic buffer between the subcontinent and the Central Asian lands under Moscow's control. Though the Soviet-Indian alliance has been significant for both countries, Indian leaders have always been more comfortable keeping a discreet distance between themselves and the Soviets. And although the Soviet tanks across the Khyber Pass posed an immediate threat only to Pakistan, India's historic rival, still New Delhi could not relish the prospect of the occupation or further fragmentation of its neighbor, given the infectious chaos that was likely to follow such an event. Publicly, the Indians sought to view the Afghan events with concern but "understanding," while privately they urged the Soviets to arrange a rapid political settlement and troop withdrawal. Every Indian statement of regret was carefully balanced by polite nods toward the Soviet version of events and an adamant refusal to be drawn into international condemnations of the Soviet action. Joint declarations issued on the occasions of visits to Moscow by the Indian president and foreign minister in 1980 signaled the inability of the two countries to agree on a common position on Afghanistan by simply omitting any mention of the issue.[16] Similarly, there was no direct reference to Afghanistan in the joint declaration that was issued in December, following the visit to India of Soviet President Brezhnev. There was, however, a paragraph dealing with Southwest Asia, which said that "India and the Soviet Union reiterate their opposition to all forms of outside interference in the internal affairs of the countries of the region." Both sides, it said, "are confident that a negotiated political solution alone can guarantee a durable settlement of the existing problems of the region."[17] This formula was consistent with the public positions of both sides and yet committed neither one to endorsement of the other's views on the specific question of how the crisis was to be resolved. In any case, India's cool and reserved statements on the issue have been publicly appreciated as "sober" and "realistic" by the Soviets, who are undoubtedly pleased to have at least one large non-Communist country abstain from the noisy condemnation of their Afghan adventure.

For some years India has sought to preserve a measure of balance in her relations with the great powers, so as to maintain an appearance of nonalignment and avoid undue dependence on Moscow. Thus it was not surprising in the wake of the Soviet invasion of Afghanistan to see India in conversations with both the United States and China, aimed at soothing some of the troubling issues that divided them. An Indian diplomat traveled to Beijing in June 1980 for talks on the sensitive border issue. The Chinese angrily postponed the return visit of Foreign Minister Huang Hua in the wake of India's diplomatic recognition of the Heng Samrin regime in Kampuchea. But in June 1981 Huang's visit finally took place, much to Moscow's consternation. Although Huang publicly agreed to the opening of official talks on the border questions, the Soviet press commentaries sought to dampen any Indian hopes that Sino-Indian relations might actually improve: "In the view of local political commentators, it would be unrealistic and premature to hope and expect that Huang Hua's statements would be followed by concrete deeds on Beijing's part. China's entire current foreign policy gives precious little justification for such hopes."[18]

India's relations with the United States showed a slight improvement in the final months of the Carter administration. New Delhi was hardly saddened by Pakistani President Zia's angry rejection of the "peanuts" in military aid that President Carter had offered him in the wake of the Soviet invasion of Afghanistan. And the Indians managed to obtain Carter's grudging agreement to deliver a contracted shipment of enriched uranium fuel for the nuclear power plant at Tarapur, despite New Delhi's continuing refusal to open all her nuclear facilities to international inspection.

But if the Soviets were at all concerned over this seeming improvement in U.S.-Indian relations in 1980, they were surely relieved by the political storm that broke in the spring and summer of 1981, following the Reagan administration's decision to sell a substantial quantity of modern weapons—including the F-16 fighter-bomber—to Pakistan. Although India had herself made major arms purchases from both the Soviets and the British in the previous year, New Delhi viewed the American arms agreements with Pakistan as provocative and destabilizing. Even Western analysts were quick to admit that the new weapons would not be sufficient to allow Pakistan to deter or defeat a Soviet invasion.[19] Particularly in the light of the Reagan administration's failure to demand from Pakistan a commitment to cease its nuclear weapons development program or even a pledge not to use its new weapons against India, New Delhi refused to believe that the American arms would not be used in support of continuing Pakistani ambitions in Kashmir. For its part, India ostentatiously announced that it had acquired "a few" MIG-25 aircraft, and it began talks with a French delegation interested in selling the latest version of the Mirage.[20] A dramatic indicator of just how bad Indian-American relations had become occurred in September, when New Delhi refused to accept the appointment of a senior American diplomat who had been branded a spy by the local pro-Soviet media. On the whole, these events seemed to confirm the judgment of a seasoned American observer in labeling the growing conflict "the most dangerous crisis in relations between New Delhi and Washington since 1947."[21]

The Soviets could scarcely contain their glee at the deterioration of Indian-American relations. The American arms deal with Pakistan, together with the Reagan administration's decision to consider arms sales to China, effectively removed the Indian spotlight from the Soviet military presence in Afghanistan and again underscored for New Delhi the value of its alliance with the USSR. On the tenth anniversary of the Soviet-Indian treaty, Foreign Minister Gromyko accused the United States of trying to destabilize Asia by selling arms to Pakistan and China, and he pointedly warned that the Soviet Union would take all measures needed to defend itself and its allies.[22] At the same time, Moscow stepped up its pressure on Pakistan to agree to talks with the Afghan government, aimed at bringing about a negotiated withdrawal of Soviet troops.

The events of 1981 reconfirmed the continuing importance for the Soviet Union of enlisting Indian participation as a counterweight to China and the United States in the Asian balance-of-power game. Attainment of this objective has traditionally required the exclusion of Chinese influence from India and minimization of Beijing's influence in Pakistan and Bangladesh, together with the limitation of American presence and influence in the region. Thus Moscow's friendly posture toward the Indians has needed to be balanced by the maintenance of ties with Pakistan. Given traditional Indo-Pakistani enmity, this has required a delicate balancing act, generally guided by the calculation that efforts to stabilize the situation in the subcontinent best promote Soviet security.

For the foreseeable future there will continue to be certain parallels in Indian and Soviet interests in the security realm, but there also persist certain incompatibilities that raise doubts that the Indo-Soviet relationship will be free of tension. India will continue to desire more balance in its own relationship with the great-power triangle than the Soviets would like, while the Soviets will persist in the effort to maintain more balance in their relations in the subcontinent than New Delhi would like. Thus India will resent the Soviet Union's attempts to strengthen its influence in Pakistan and Bangladesh, and Moscow will be nervous about Indian efforts to improve relations with Beijing and Washington. India, moreover, will continue to take a different position on superpower activities in the Indian Ocean, seeking to insulate the ocean from great-power military activity.

On the whole, however, Soviet-Indian friendship will persist as long as the two states feel a sense of mutual dependence. Moscow's activities and investments in South Asia over the past quarter-century have been founded on a sense of need to seek influence in the region, stemming from a policy framework that sets a relatively high priority on this area of the world. Soviet dependence on India has produced a willingness to devote a steady flow of resources and diplomatic energy toward preserving Moscow's rather large investment in the Indo-Soviet friendship.[23] To lose its standing as the ally of the strongest regional power in South Asia would cost Moscow heavily. It would entail some risk to its security in a bordering region that has both offensive and defensive value in the Soviet conflict with its primary rival, China. Moscow's substantial stake in the existing order in South Asia thus gives it continuing interest in helping to stabilize the region by playing the role of "reliable friend" to India.

NOTES

1. For more details on this activity, see Robert H. Donaldson, *Soviet Policy in India: Ideology and Strategy* (Cambridge, Mass.: Harvard University Press, 1974), Ch. 4.

2. Quoted in David Floyd, *Mao against Khrushchev: A Short History of the Sino-Soviet Conflict* (New York: Praeger, 1963), p. 366.

3. *Hindustan Times*, September 30, 1971.

4. Donaldson, *Soviet Policy in India*, pp. 231-34.

5. *Pravda*, August 22, 1975.

6. *Pravda*, August 13, 1974.

7. P. Mazentsev, "Thirty Years of Independence," *New Times*, no. 32, (1977), p. 13.

8. *Izvestiia*, April 15, 1979.

9. V. Shurygin, "India: A Time of Important Decisions," *International Affairs*, no. 9 (September 1979), pp. 57-62.

10. *Izvestiia*, March 13, 1977, p. 3.

11. A. Usvatov, "Change of Government," *New Times*, no. 14, (1977), p. 13.

12. V. Shurygin, "India: Thirty Years of Independence," *International Affairs*, no. 9 (September 1977), p. 75.

13. *Far Eastern Economic Review*, April 15, 1977, p. 9.

14. Foreign Broadcast Information Service, *Daily Report: Soviet Union*, April 12, 1978, p. J1.

15. A. Alexeyev and A. Fialkovsky, "For a Peaceful Indian Ocean," *International Affairs*, (February), 1981, pp. 85-91.

16. *Pravda*, June 8, 1980, p. 4; *Pravda*, October 8, 1980, pp. 1, 8.

17. *Pravda*, December 12, 1980, p. 2.

18. *Pravda*, July 3, 1981, p. 5.

19. Drew Middleton, "Pak Aid: Frail Shield?" *New York Times*, July 12, 1981, p. 11.

20. Michael T. Kaufman, "Diplomacy Swirls Around Pakistan," *New York Times*, August 25, 1981, p. 2.

21. Selig S. Harrison, "India and Reagan's Tilt Toward Pakistan," *New York Times*, July 15, 1981, p. A23.

22. *New York Times*, August 9, 1981, p. 5.

23. A more detailed elaboration of this Soviet effort can be found in Robert H. Donaldson, *The Soviet-Indian Alignment: Quest for Influence.* (University of Denver, Monograph Series in World Affairs, vol. 16, books 3 and 4, 1979).

INDEX

Academy of Sciences, USSR, 86
Afghanistan: Soviet arms sales to, 128;
 Soviet invasion and occupation
 of, 70-71, 129, 130, 131-33,
 134,135,346; [Afghan resistance
 to, 131-33; Chinese response to,
 133, 141; Cuban support for,
 163; implications of for Cuban
 role in Third World, 156; and
 Italian Communist Party, 181;
 United Nations condemnation
 of, 278; United States response
 to, 186, 197; West European
 Communist Party response to,
 182-83, 186-87] and USSR,
 68, 70, 120, 136, 181, 314-15
Africa: Cuban involvement in, 157-58;
 Cuban military role in, 154-56;
 opportunities for Soviet involvement in, 296-97; Soviet geopolitical priorities and, 287-88;
 Soviet military support for, 301-
 3; Soviet policy toward, 6, 26,
 292-97
Agha Shahi, 136
Albania, 107, 110, 113
Alekseeva, Ludmilla, 80, 89, 92
Algeria: and Cuban involvement in
 Africa, 154; and Soviet invasion
 of Afghanistan, 70; Soviet support for, 293
Amalrik, Andrei, 81
Andropov, Yuri, 78
Angola, 152, 154, 156-57, 158-60,
 161; and Cuba, 152, 154, 158-
 60, 164; establishment of a

Marxist government in, 158;
 Sino-Soviet competition in, 292;
 Soviet support for, 158-59, 291;
 U.S. policy toward, 158; and the
 USSR, 159; West European
 Communist Party views of, 182
annexation, Soviet policy of, 73
antiimperialism (*see* National Libera-
 tion Movements)
Arab-Israeli War, June 1967: Soviet
 policy during, 66
Arbatov, Georgii: as Soviet propa-
 gandist, 91
Armenians, 61; claims of against Tur-
 key, 61
Asia: and the USSR, 51-52
Asia, Central: Russian-British compe-
 tition in, 332-33
Asia, East: Soviet foreign aid to, 128;
 Soviet geopolitical priorities in,
 287
Asia, South, 127, 133; Soviet foreign
 aid to, 127; Soviet policy toward,
 330-31
Asia, Southeast: and U.S.-Soviet con-
 flict, 197
Asian Collective Security: Soviet plans
 for, 338
Association of Southeast Asian Nations
 (ASEAN), 127-28, 130, 137-39,
 141
Atlantic Alliance (see North Atlantic
 Treaty Organization)
Atlantic Charter: Soviet views of,
 90
Azeri, in the USSR, 68

Baikal-Amur Railway, 42, 46, 128
Balkans, 105-6, 110
Bangladesh: Soviet arms aid to, 128;
    and USSR, 135, 339-40, 341
Barre, Siad, 160-61
basing system, Soviet overseas, 271,
    344-45
Basmachi, and the USSR, 71
Bay of Pigs, 145
Belgrade Review Conference (*see* Con-
    ference on European Security
    and Cooperation)
Belorussians, 60
Berlin Meeting of Communist and
    Workers Parties, 1976 (*see* Con-
    ferences of European Commu-
    nist Parties)
Berlinguer, Enrico, 87, 176, 181, 183,
    186, 189
Bolivia: and Cuba, 147
Bonner, Elena, 81, 85, 91, 93
Borisov, Vladimir, 93
Brest-Litovsk, Treaty of, 59
Brezhnev, Leonid I., 135, 149, 150,
    161, 197, 203, 208, 214; leader-
    ship of, 111, 112; policies of,
    43, 52-58; succession of, 37-38,
    40, 52-54; views of on Jackson
    Amendment, 67
'Brezhnev Doctrine," 148
British Commonwealth: and Soviet
    nationality policy, 62
Budapest Consultative Conference of
    Communist Parties, 1968 (*see*
    Conferences of European Com-
    munist Parties)
Bukovski, Vladimir, 81, 85, 95
Bulgaria, 113; and Ethiopia, 162
Bulgarians in the USSR, 63-64

Cambodia (*see* Kampuchea)
Canada, 135; and Cuban espionage, 154

Caribbean: Soviet interest in, 152
Carrillo, Santiago, 176, 180, 181, 184,
    188, 189, 190
Carter, Jimmy, 93, 94, 95, 197; and
    A. Sakharov, 86-87, 88
Castro, Fidel, 118, 145-50, 154-57,
    159, 161, 163, 164, 165; as
    Third World leader, 147; views
    of on revolution, 147
Castro, Raul, 151, 159, 161, 162
Central Intelligence Agency: and anti-
    Castro activities in Zaire, 154-
    55; attacks on by *Pravda*, 95
Central Treaty Organization
    (CENTO): and the Middle East,
    312
Chakovski, Aleksandr; as Soviet
    propagandist, 91
chemical industry, Soviet: develop-
    ment of, 249
Chile: Soviet views of "revolution" in,
    210
China, 107, 109-10; and Angola, 158;
    Great Proletarian Cultural Revo-
    lution of, 292; and India, 133-
    35; 335-37; and Japan, 140,
    234; and Kampuchea, 137, 138;
    and NATO, 202, 205; and Paki-
    stan, 133-35; and Third World,
    292; and USSR, 12, 46, 49, 60,
    64-65, 127-31, 202, 205, 276,
    335-37; and Vietnam, 137, 138;
    and West European Communist
    Parties, 171, 177-78, 180, 181,
    184
Chinese Communist Party, 180-81
Churchill, Winston, 105
civil defense, Soviet, 22-23
Communist Information Bureau
    (Cominform), 106
Communist parties, Western European,
    171-90; challenges to CPSU, 177-
    87; domestic position of, 175

Communist Party of the Soviet Union
(CPSU) 79, 80, 108, 110, 111,
113, 118, 119; and decision
making, 26–28; decline of
authority of, 28; leadership role
of, 26–28; and Marxist-Leninist
parties in the Third World, 285;
and the military, 29–30, 32–33,
34; succession problems of,
29–30

Conference on European Security and
Cooperation (CSCE; also ECSC),
86, 87–90, 92, 94–95, 96, 188,
199, 200; "Basket 3" of, 200;
Belgrade Review Conference of,
89, 93–94; Madrid Review Conference of, 94; and USSR,
187–88

conferences of European Communist
Parties: 1960 Moscow Con-
ference, 110; 1968 Budapest
Conference, 83; 1976 Berlin
Conference, 87, 112, 188; 1980
Pan-European Communist
Conference, 186

Constitutions of the USSR: 1936
"Stalin" Constitution, 79; 1977
Constitution, 77; and rights of
Republics, 7

Council for Mutual Economic Assistance (CMEA), 38, 45, 110, 113,
121, 137; Cuba's admission to,
148; Soviet policy in, 45–46

Cuba, 118, 135; and Africa, 273; and
China, 146; Communist Party of,
146–47, 151–52; and Congo-
Brazzaville, 154; and Czechoslovakia, 148; domestic problems
of, 165; economic relations of
with USSR, 149–50; foreign policy of, 147–48, 154; governmental reorganization of, 149, 151–
52; guerrilla training by, 147,

149, 154–55; international
position of, 156–57; military of,
148, 151–52, 165; military ties
of to USSR, 148, 151–54; overseas military activities of, 154–
55; and PLO, 155; and Sino-
Soviet split, 147, 149; and Soviet
intelligence, 153–54; and USSR,
145–49; and US, 145–46

Cuban missile crisis: and detente, 178

Czechoslovakia, 111, 113, 115, 117–
18, 120, 131; "Prague Spring"
of, 82–83; Soviet invasion of,
81, 82, 84, 148, 187; Western
Communist criticism of Soviet
invasion of, 175, 178, 180

DeGaulle, Charles, 174, 201

"democratization": of intra-communist decision making, 111–12; of
Soviet society, 81–84, 85, 87, 88

Deng Xiaoping, 134, 137, 139, 141,
180

Denmark: and USSR, 207

Desai, Morarji, 133–34, 343

detente: East-West, 178, 183–87;
Soviet definition of, 215–16;
and Soviet policy in the Third
World, 9, 274–75, 277–78; Soviet
policy of, 8–10, 265; and Soviet
trade, 248ff; and Western Communist parties, 175

developing countries (*see* Third World)

Djilas, Milovan, 28

economic aid, Soviet: and political
influence, 299–300; to the Third
World, 285–86, 301

economy, Soviet: and the Brezhnev
succession, 37–38, 40, 53; and
foreign policy, 47–52; growth of,

39; militarization of, 23; and
military defense, 23, 30-31, 42-
43, 45-48; modernization of,
40, 41-42, 48, 49-52; planning
and, 37, 40, 43, 139; policy
choices and, 37-39; problems of,
39; prospects for, 52-54; reform
of, 44, 257; technology transfer
and, 44-45
Egypt, 129; Soviet support for, 291
El Salvador: and Cuba, 155, 164
emigration: from the USSR, 83, 85,
253
energy needs, Soviet: and the Persian
Gulf, 313
Eritrea, 161; and the USSR, 162
Eritrean People's Liberation Front
(EPLF), 161
Equatorial Guinea: and Cuban military,
154
Ethiopia, 135, 153, 155, 156-57,
160-62; and Cuba, 153, 162,
165; and USSR, 161, 286; and
Western Communist Parties,
181-82
Europe: "balance of power" in, 202-5;
and USSR, 50-51; US military
presence in, 201
Europe, Eastern: Soviet dominance in,
177-80; and USSR, 4, 45,
105-13
Europe, Western: and USSR, 50-51,
198-214; and US, 200-1, 212
European Economic Community
(EEC), 183, 208; and USSR,
212-13
expansion, Soviet policy of, 8-12, 25-
26; obstacles to, 10-12

Finland: and USSR, 207-8
"Finlandization," 206-8, 212; of
Japan, 239

foreign policy, Soviet: global nature
of, 5-10, 25-26; influences on,
238; and military capabilities,
17-19; motives of, 12; objectives
of, 288-89; objectives of in
Third World, 303-4; priorities
of, 19
foreign trade, Soviet, 247, 256-58;
limits on growth of, 254-55;
with West, 248, 249-51, 253-54,
277
FNLA (National Front for the Liberation of Angola), 158
Ford, Gerald, 88
France, 106, 109, 171, 172, 173-75
French Communist Party (PCF), 172,
173-74, 175, 177, 178, 183-84,
187-88; challenge of to USSR,
171, 175; coming to power of,
208-9
Fukuda, Takeo, 241

Galanskov, Yuri, 84-85
Gandhi, Indira, 134-35
Georgians, 61
German Democratic Republic, 113,
115, 117; and Ethiopia, 162
Germans in the USSR, 65
Germany, Nazi: and USSR, 59, 172
Germany, Federal Republic of: mili-
tary role of, 205
Gierek, Edward, 115-16
Ginzburg, Aleksandr, 84-85
Gomulka, Wladyslaw, 109, 114-15
Gorbanevskaia, Natalia, 81
Gorshkov, Sergei, 270
Great Britain, 105, 109
Greek-Turkish War, 199
Grenada: and Cuba, 155, 164
Grigorenko, Petr, 83, 93-94
Gromyko, Andrei, 135, 136, 204-5,
289

Guevara, Che, 147, 154
Guinea: and USSR, 291
GULAG system, 46

Helsinki Agreement/Conference (*see*
    Conference on European
    Security and Cooperation)
Helsinki groups in USSR, 80–81, 87–
    92, 94
Heng Samrin, 137, 138
Horn of Africa, 160–62; geopolitical
    alignments in, 160–61; war in,
    160–62
Hoxha, Enver, 110
Huang Hua, 134–35
Human Rights, United Nations Uni-
    versal Declaration of, 83–84, 93
Hungary, 109, 110, 113, 131; Soviet
    invasion of, 81–82; and USSR,
    64; and Western Communist
    Parties, 178
Husak, Gustav, 178

Iceland: and USSR, 207
ideology, Soviet, 187-90, 289
India: and China, 335–36, 346–47;
    declaration of emergency in, 342;
    economic relations of with
    USSR, 340–41; and Pakistan,
    334, 336–37, 339–40; Soviet
    arms sales to, 128; Soviet eco-
    nomic aid to, 333–35; and Soviet
    invasion of Afghanistan, 135–36,
    346–47; Soviet support for ver-
    sus China, 335–36; and USSR,
    68, 133–36, 333–34, 338–39,
    342–43, 347; and U.S., 347–48
Indian Ocean: Soviet interests in, 343–
    45; Soviet naval operations in,
    343–45; U.S. interests in, 330
Indo-Pakistani wars, 336–37, 339–40

Indochina, 127, 137, 139, 141
Indonesian Communist Party, (PKI),
    138
international correlation of forces:
    Soivet view of, 274
intervention, Soviet, 314
Iran, 133; domestic divisions in, 317;
    Soviet goals in, 316–17; Soviet
    occupation of north in 1945-6,
    316; Soviet views of revolution
    in, 316–17; and USSR, 60, 68,
    133, 296, 298, 316–17; and U.S.,
    316; war of with Iraq, 321–22
Iraq: and Cuba, 155; role of in Middle
    East, 320–21; and Soviet invasion
    of Afghanistan, 278; Soviet mili-
    tary aid to, 320; and USSR,
    320–22; war of with Iran, 321-22
Iraqi Communist Party, 321
Israel, 109; and Cuba, 155
Italy, 106, 109, 199
Italian Communist Party (PCI), 172,
    173–74, 175–77, 178–86, 187–
    90, 210; challenge of to the
    USSR, 171, 176; Soviet view of,
    210, 211

Jackson Amendment, 67
Jamaica: and Cuba, 156
Japan, 127, 130, 139–40; and China,
    140, 234; economic position of,
    234–35; economic sanctions of
    versus USSR, 241; foreign policy
    decision making of, 240–41, 244;
    increased interest of USSR in,
    231–32; military policy of, 233,
    235–38, 243–44; security views
    of, 235–38, 241–42, 276; and
    Sino-Soviet split, 234, 240–41;
    Soviet threat to, 233–34, 239–
    40; trade dependence of, 235;
    and trade with USSR, 241; and

USSR, 140, 233, 242–42; and
U.S., 233, 242–43, 244–45
Jaroszewicz, Piotr, 115
Jaruzelski, Wojciech, 117, 119
Jews, Soviet, 65–67; and Soviet for-
eign policy, 67
Jordan: and the Soviet invasion of
Afghanistan, 70

Kama River Truck Plant, 43, 45
Kampuchea, 128, 130, 134, 137–39;
and Vietnam, 137
Kania, Stanislaw, 116–18, 120
Karmal, Babrak, 132–33
Kazakhs, Soviet, 68
Kennan, George, 174
Kenya: and USSR, 70
KGB (Committee for State Security),
78, 79, 80, 84, 89, 91
Khmer Rouge, 137–40
Khrushchev, Nikita S., 110–11, 145–
46; conflict with military by,
31–32; economic polices of,
249–51; military support for,
30, 31; policy failure of, 6; policy
revisions of, 4, 263; policy to-
ward Third World, 287, 331–32;
succession problems of, 29–30
Kirghiz, Soviet, 68
Koreans in the USSR, 63

Laos, 137
Latin America: and Cuba, 155, 163–
64; Soviet trade with, 155
Libya: and Cuba, 163
Litvinov, Pavel, 81, 83–85

Madrid Review Conference (*see* Conference on European Security
and Cooperation)

Malaysia: and USSR, 138
Mao Zedong: 107, 180–81
Marshall Plan, 174
Marxism-Leninism: in Africa, 296–97;
in Third World, 300
Mengistu, Haile-Mariam, 155, 160–62
Mexico: and Cuba, 148–49
Middle East: and Cuba, 155; and
Soviet geopolitical priorities,
287–88; Soviet military support
in, 301–3; Soviet policy toward,
5, 26–27, 290, 293–97; Soviet
views of, 295–96; and USSR,
11; and U.S.-USSR conflict,
197
military, Soviet: buildup of in Asia,
239; buildup of in Europe, 198–
99, 202–3; capabilities of, 266–
67; conventional capabilities of,
7–8; and CPSU, 24–25, 32–34;
discipline of, 22–25; domestic
roles of, 20–22; and economy,
42–44, 48–49; education of,
23–24; expenditures on, 266,
279; as foreign policy instrument, 273–74; future role of, 34;
growth of, 6–7; nuclear capabilities of, 7; parity of with U.S.,
267; role of in Third World,
264ff, 285–86, 301–2, 304–5;
political demands of, 30–31; and
political modernization, 21;
training of, 22–23; weakness of,
6 (*see* navy, Soviet)
Mitterrand, Francois, 184, 190
Morocco: and Soviet support for
Polisario Liberation Front, 293
MPLA (Popular Movement for the Liberation of Angola), 11, 158–59,
160, 286; and Cuba, 188
Mugabe, Robert, 155, 164
Muslims, Soviet; and Soviet foreign
policy, 68–71

Nagy, Imre, 109
Namibia: settlement in, 159
Nasser, Gamal Abdel, 290
national liberation movement: and USSR, 232-33, 332; Lenin's views on, 288-89
nationality: effect of on Soviet foreign policy, 59-73; effect of on Soviet territorial annexation, 60-62; Soviet policy on, 58-59, 60-62
navy, Soviet, 26; capabilities of, 268-70; development of, 263-64, 343-46; presence of in Mediterranean Sea and Indian Ocean, 289; use of Cuba by, 153-54
Neto, Agostinho, 155, 158-59
neutralism, 206, 207, 209, 210-11
New International Economic Order, 41
Nicaragua: and Cuba, 155, 156, 164; and USSR, 155
Nigeria: Soviet Military aid to, 293
Nixon, Richard, 129
Nixon Doctrine, 233
Nkomo, Joshua, 155, 156, 164
Nkrumah, Kwame, 290
Nonaligned Nations, Conference of, 156
Nordic Council, 208
North Atlantic Treaty Organization (NATO), 171-72, 174, 176, 177, 183-87, 188, 198-99, 200-4, 207-9, 212-13; China and, 202, 205; Italian Communist Party views of, 184-85, 187; and the Middle East, 312; Military bases of, 201; Soviet views of, 201-2; and the USSR, 200-1
Norway: and USSR, 205, 207

Oman, 131
Organization of African Unity (OAU), 155, 158, 162

Organization of Latin American Solidarity (OLAS), 147, 155
Orlov, Yuri, 78, 80, 87, 89, 90-91, 95-96

"Pacific Basin Cooperation," 242-43
Pajetta, Gian Carlo, 181-82, 186, 189
Pakistan, 131-33, 135-36; Afghan refugees in, 318-19; and China, 342; and India, 336-37, 339; and Muslim world, 136; Soviet goals in, 318; Soviet pressures on, 319; support of for Afghan rebels, 319-20; and USSR, 68-69, 318-20, 341-42; and U.S., 318; U.S. military aid to, 348; views of on Soviet invasion of Afghanistan, 136, 319; and West, 318
peaceful coexistence, 5
Persian Gulf: opportunities for Soviet involvement in, 315ff, 324; raw materials in, 313; Soviet goals in, 312-13; Soviet interest in, 272, 297, 304, 312-13; Soviet policy toward, 324-25
Persian Gulf states: domestic problems of, 315-16; Soviet criticism of, 322; and USSR, 322-24; Western military pacts with, 312
petroleum production, Soviet, 255-56; role of in Soviet foreign policy, 255-56
Pol Pot, 137-38
Poland, 105, 107, 108-9, 113-24; Catholic Church in, 116; Gdansk Charter in, 116; political "renewal" of, 41, 46; and Soviet annexation, 60; Soviet reaction to developments in, 114-15, 117-19, 189-90; upheavals in, 11, 47; and USSR, 72-73, 109,

163, 198; and Western Communist Parties, 179–80
Poles in the USSR, 63
Polisario Liberation Front, 293
political control, Soviet, 38–39, 49–52
political dissent, Soviet: and the Helsinki Agreements, 87–88, 89, 92–93
political participation, Soviet, 81–82
political succession, Soviet, 29–30, 32–33, 34, 41, 52–53, 247
Portugal: Soviet views of revolution in, 210
power projection: comparison of Soviet and U.S., 268–72, 274; Soviet theory of, 270–71
Poznan: strikes in, 109, 114
proletarian internationalism, 147

Reagan, Ronald, 120–21, 129–31
Republics, Soviet: and Soviet foreign policy, 59–62, 71
revolutionary democrats in the Third World, 299
risk-taking in Soviet foreign policy, 326–27
Romania, 110, 112–13; and Soviet annexation, 60, 63

Sakharov, Andrei, 79, 80–81, 82, 84–88, 90, 93, 96; and Jimmy Carter, 86–88; international conference in honor of, 87, 91
Saudi Arabia: and USSR, 136, 322–24; view of Soviet invasion of Afghanistan by, 70
security interests, Soviet, 267–68
Shcharanski, Anatoli, 78, 91, 95
Sierra Leone: and Cuba, 154
Singapore, 138
"Solidarity", 114, 116–24

Solzhenitsyn, Aleksandr, 85, 95
Somalia, 129, 131, 154, 156, 160–63; and Cuba, 154; Soviet policy toward, 293–94; and Western Communist Parties, 181–82
Southwest African People's Organization (SWAPO), 159, 164
Spanish Communist Party (PCE), 171, 175–76, 177, 178–79, 180–81, 182–84, 187–89; challenge of to USSR, 171, 176; Soviet view of, 210–11
Strategic Arms Limitation Talks (SALT), 225
Sweden: and USSR, 207
Syria: and Cuba, 154–55; Soviet support for, 291

Tadziks, Soviet, 68
Tashkent Peace Conference (1965), 337
technology transfer, 44–45, 251, 253; problems of, 254–55
Thailand, 138–39
Third World: criticism of Soviet invasion of Afghanistan by, 70; and Cuba, 154; limitations on Soviet capabilities in, 277–79, 289; radicalization of, 7, 298–99; Soviet arms transfers to, 301; Soviet intervention capabilities in, 266–68, 275, 278; Soviet objectives in, 288–89; Soviet policy toward, 26, 177–78, 181–83, 285–86, 288–89, 298, 303–5; Soviet support for, 290–91, 298–99; Soviet-U.S. competition in, 275; Soviet views of, 333; and USSR, 5, 7, 9, 41, 72, 263, 276; and the West, 7, 9–10
Tito (Josip Broz), 107
Toure, Sekou, 155

treaties of friendship and cooperation, Soviet, 285
Tricontinental Conference (Havana), 147, 155
Truman, Harry S., 105
Turchin, Valentin, 87, 93
Turkey: and USSR, 60, 69
Turkmen, Soviet, 68-69

Uighurs, Soviet, 64
Ukraine, 60, 65, 72-73
Union of Soviet Socialist Republics (USSR): as aggressive power, 236; expansion of, 4; as global power, 4ff., 217-18, 237; as regional power, 3-5; as revolutionary state, 276; as superpower, 233
UNITA (National Union for the Total Liberation of Angola), 158, 164
United States: Congressional Commission on Security and Cooperation in: Europe, 77, 78, 80-81, 98, 95; containment policy of, 331; and Cuba, 153, 160; decline of supremacy of, 233; as global power, 3; in the Middle East and Persian Gulf, 327; military facilities of in the Indian Ocean, 279; military superiority of, 3; National Academy of Sciences, 86; naval operations in Indian Ocean, 345-46; public opinion in, 222-23; and Soviet balance of power, 6, 7, 204, 205; Soviet grain embargo of, 255, 277; Soviet views of foreign policy of, 218, 220-22; Soviet views of military policy of, 219; Soviet views of technology of, 219; strategic superiority of, 6; as superpower, 217; trade of

with USSR, 220, 251-54; and USSR, 40-41, 49, 52, 153, 197, 214-23; views of on West European Communist Parties, 176; and Western Europe, 174, 197, 200
Uzbeks, Soviet, 68

Vaculik, Ludwik, 82
Vail, Boris, 82
Venezuela: and USSR, 150
Vietnam, 118, 121, 130-31, 134-35, 137-40; and China, 139-40; and detente, 178; and Kampuchea, 137; Soviet arms transfers to, 128; Soviet support for, 139-40

Walesa, Lech, 116, 199, 120
Warsaw Treaty Organization (Warsaw Pact), 81-82, 110, 112-13, 119-20, 171, 176, 185-86, 198, 199, 201-3, 208, 213; and Cuba, 148, 152; and NATO, 198-99, 204-5
Watergate and U.S. foreign policy, 264
West: dependence of on Middle East oil, 289; and the Third World, 294, 303; and USSR in Third World, 290-92
West Somali Liberation Front (WSLF), 160, 165

Yalta Declaration: Soviet interpretation of, 90
Yemen, People's Democratic Republic of (PDRY): and Cuba, 154; and USSR, 322
Yugoslavia, 107, 109, 110-11, 112, 199; and China, 181; and USSR, 109

Zaire: and Angola, 159; and USSR, 158   Zia ul-Haq, 136
Zhou Enlai, 109–10, 134   Zimbabwe, 164

ABOUT THE EDITOR
AND CONTRIBUTORS

DAVID E. ALBRIGHT is Senior Text Editor of the journal *Problems of Communism*. Previously, he worked as research associate and editor at the project on "The United States and China in World Affairs" at the Council on Foreign Relations in New York. He is the editor of *Communism and Political Systems in Western Europe* and *Communism in Africa*, as well as coeditor of the forthcoming *The Communist States and Africca*. In addition, he has contributed articles to a number of journals and symposia on the policies of the Communist states toward the Middle East and Africa and on the international politics of these two areas.

FREDERICK C. BARGHOORN is Emeritus Professor of Political Science, Yale University. After the completion of his graduate studies at Harvard University, he served for more than four years in the American Embassy in Moscow (1942-47) and also served in State Department positions in Washington and West Germany. He has been a consultant to various U.S. government agencies, has taught or lectured at numerous universities, and has held fellowships from the Guggenheim and Ford Foundations, the American Council of Learned Societies, the American Philosophical Society, and the Hoover Institution. Professor Barghoorn's long and distinguished list of publications includes numerous articles in many scholarly journals and symposia and collected works. His published books include *Detente and the Democratic Movement in the Soviet Union*, *Soviet Russian Nationalism*, *Politics in the USSR*, *Soviet Foreign Propaganda*, and *The Soviet Cultural Offensive*. He is continuing his research on dissent in the USSR, a subject to which he has devoted considerable attention in recent years.

ROBERT H. DONALDSON is Provost and Dean of the Faculties and Professor of Political Science at Herbert H. Lehman College of The City University of New York. He formerly taught at Vanderbilt University and was Visiting Research Professor, Strategic Studies Institute, U.S. Army War College. He is the author of numerous articles on Soviet foreign policy; he is also the author of *Soviet Policy Toward India: Ideology and Strategy*, and *The Soviet-Indian Alignment: Quest for Influence*; coauthor (with Joseph Nogee) of *Soviet Foreign Policy Since World War II*; and editor of *The Soviet Union in the Third World: Successes and Failures*.

MARSHALL I. GOLDMAN is the Class of 1919 Professor of Economics at Wellesley College and the Associate Director of the Russian Research Center, Harvard University. He was the first Fulbright-Hayes Professor of American Economics at Moscow State University in 1977. The most recent of his distinguished list of publications are *Detente and Dollars: Doing Business in the USSR* and *The Enigma of Soviet Petroleum: Half Full or Half Empty?* Among his earlier publications is *Soviet Foreign Aid.*

ROGER HAMBURG is Professor of Political Science at Indiana University at South Bend. His publications include a number of articles on Soviet foreign policy, Soviet-American security relations, and related topics, which have been published in scholarly journals and collected works. His most recent publications are "Soviet Policy in West Europe," *Current History* (May 1981), and "Low-Intensity Conflict: The Soviet Response," in *U.S. Policy and Low-Intensity Conflict* (edited by Sam C. Sarkesian and William L. Scully).

JOHN P. HARDT is Associate Director of Senior Specialists and Senior Specialist in Soviet Economics at the Congressional Research Service and a member of the faculty of Economics and of the Institute of Sino-Soviet Studies at George Washington University. He has edited, coordinated, and contributed to numerous congressional studies, including the Joint Economic Committee's tri-annual series on the economies of the Soviet Union, Eastern Europe, and the People's Republic of China, and *Energy in Soviet Policy.* He is the coauthor of *An Assessment of the Afghanistan Sanctions: Implications for Trade and Diplomacy in the 1980s.*

ROGER E. KANET is Professor of Political Science and a member of the Center for Russian and East European Studies of the University of Illinois at Urbana-Champaign. During academic year 1981–82 he is a full-time Associate at the Center for Advanced Study of the University of Illinois, where he is working on a study of the policies of the Communist states in Africa. He is the author of numerous articles on Soviet and East European foreign relations and has edited, among other books, *Soviet Foreign Policy and East-West Relations* (forthcoming), *Background to Crisis: Policy and Politics in Gierek's Poland* (with Maurice D. Simon), *Soviet Economic and Political Relations with the Developing World* (with Donna Bahry), and *The Soviet Union and the Developing Nations.*

RASMA KARKLINS is currently Visiting Assistant Professor of Political Science at the University of Illinois at Chicago Circle. She received her Ph.D.

from the University of Chicago where she wrote her doctoral dissertation on the interrelationship of Soviet foreign and nationality policy. She has published articles on various aspects of ethnic politics and relations in the USSR in *Canadian Slavonic Papers*, *Soviet Studies*, *Cahiers du Monde russe et soviétique*, and, most recently, in *Studies in Comparative Communism*.

ZALMAY KHALILZAD is Assistant Professor of Political Science and a member of both the Institute of War and Peace Studies and the Institute for Middle Eastern Studies at Columbia University. His publications include *The Return of the Great Game: Superpower Rivalry and Domestic Turmoil in Afghanistan, Iran, Pakistan and Turkey*, as well as articles in such journals as *Survival*, *International Security*, *Political Science Quarterly*, and *Orbis*.

HIROSHI KIMURA is Professor of Political Science at the Slavic Research Center, Hokkaido University, in Sapporo, Japan. He received a B.A. and M.A. from Kyoto University and a Ph.D. from Columbia University. He was Director of the Slavic Research Center, 1975–77, and a Special Research Associate with the Japanese Embassy in Moscow, 1973–75. He is the author and editor of several books on Soviet politics and the author of numerous articles in Japanese, Russian, and English, including articles on Japanese-Soviet relations that have appeared in *Orbis* (1980), *Asian Survey* (1980), and *Trialogue* (1980–81). He is currently engaged in research on Soviet policy in the Northeast Pacific region.

ROMAN KOLKOWICZ is Professor of Political Science and Director of the Center for International and Strategic Affairs at the University of California, Los Angeles. His extensive writings on Soviet foreign and military policy and on strategic problems include *The Soviet Military and the Communist Party*, *The Soviet Union and Arms Control*, "Strategic Elites and Politics of Superpower" (*Journal of International Affairs*, no. 1, 1972), "Theoretical Dogmas and Strategies of Warfare," in *Non-Nuclear Conflicts in the Nuclear Age*, edited by S. Sarkesian.

RAJAN MENON is Assistant Professor of Political Science at Vanderbilt University. He has published articles on various aspects of Soviet policy in the Third World, which have appeared in *Asian Survey*, *Current History*, *Osteuropa*, *Soviet Studies*, and in several multiauthored volumes. His doctoral dissertation, completed at the University of Illinois at Urbana-Champaign, concerned Soviet-Indian relations.

ROBIN ALISON REMINGTON is Professor of Political Science at the University of Missouri, Columbia. Her publications include numerous articles on the Warsaw Pact, Eastern Europe, and Eurocommunism, which have appeared in scholarly journals and collected works. Among her book-length publications are *The Warsaw Pact: Case Studies in Communist Conflict Resolution*, *Winter in Prague: Documents on Czechoslovak Communism in Crisis* (edited), and *The International Relations of Eastern Europe: A Guide to Information Sources*. She spent academic year 1980–81 conducting research in India and fall semester 1981 carrying out research in Yugoslavia.

MERRITT ROBBINS recently completed his doctorate in political science at Harvard University. He has held appointments at the University of California, Irvine, and Cabrillo College. Portions of his research for the chapter included in the present volume were drawn from a study made possible by a grant from the National Endowment for the Humanities. He is currently completing a book-length study entitled *Misunderstanding Cuba: The View from America*.

KATE S. TOMLINSON (M.A., School of Advanced International Studies, Johns Hopkins University) is a Senior Research Assistant in Soviet Economics at the Congressional Research Service. She coauthored *An Assessment of the Afghanistan Sanctions: Implications for Trade and Diplomacy in the 1980s* for the House Foreign Affairs Committee. She has also participated in a study of public-opinion polling in the Soviet Union and Eastern Europe, the results of which were published in *Survey Research and Public Attitudes in Eastern Europe and the Soviet Union*.

JOAN BARTH URBAN is Associate Professor of Politics at The Catholic University of America. Her studies of relations between the CPSU and the West European Communist parties have appeared in *Orbis*, *Studies in Comparative Communism*, and in a number of collective volumes including *Innovation in Communist Systems* (edited by Andrew Gyorgy and James A. Kuhlman), *The European Left: Italy, France, and Spain* (edited by William E. Griffith), and *Marxism in the Contemporary West* (edited by Carl A. Linden and Charles F. Elliott).